UNSUNG HEROES

By
David Chaltas

Unsung Heroes
Silent Warriors
The Stories of American Soldiers

David Chaltas
Copyright 2014
All Rights Reserved
Library of Congress Control Number:

ISBN: ISBN-13: 978-1495402487
ISBN-10: 1495402487
Cover Picture: National Achieves

All rights reserved. No part of this book may be reproduced or transmitted in any form or by any means, electronic or mechanical, including photocopying, recording, or by any information storage, and retrieval system, without permission in writing from the copyright owner.

Proudly
Printed in Charleston, South Carolina
United States of America

DEDICATION

I do not consider this to be my book. It is OUR book of American heroes, history and heritage. It does not even scratch the surface but it is my earnest prayer that all across this land people will begin writing of those brave men and women who have served. NO service is insignificant. Any that served must be remembered, for their will be again a time when the wolf is at the door and we must upon future soldiers to defend our way of life.

We dedicate this book to all those who have served and sacrificed for this land of freedom to survive. For those in our county, region and state, we say thank you for your service. For those across our nation who truly love our American way of life, we ask that you never forget. To our Wounded Warriors, MIAs and POWs we say we love you and are proud of you. To the terrorists who wish to destroy our beloved country, we stand to let you know that the old guard is watching…

To those who shared their stories and those of their relatives, I offer my thank you and my gratitude. To Anthony L. Blair, Ben Gish, Scotty K. Caudill, Russell Blair, Mike Watts, Roger Campbell Kelley, Linda Norton, Randy Seals, and Richard G. Brown: you saw the vision and helped it become a reality…

"He which hath no stomach to this fight let him depart. But we in it shall be remembered. We few, we happy few, we <u>band of brothers</u>!! For he today, that sheds his blood with me, shall always be my brother."
W. Shakespeare

FOREWORD

There are those who remember. There are those who can't forget. There are those who are still haunted by the invisible visions of wartime. Then there are those who must fight the demons.

I was told of a man who fought in Vietnam. He came home from that war a different man. He never talked of his experiences. He tried to leave it all behind. Yet there was something unresolved.

His daughter was planning a trip with her family. When he was told that his daughter was taking her children to Washington on a vacation, he asked her for a favor. He asked her if she would go to the Vietnam Memorial Wall and get an etching for him. His daughter agreed.

After a few days his daughter, son-in-law, and grandchildren returned. The old man was waiting on the porch. The grandchildren ran to their grandfather and after hugging him, proudly gave him the etching. He slowly unfolded it and looked at the name. He fell to his knees as tears streamed down his face. He shook with emotion and buried his head in his hands. His grandchildren thought they had done something wrong and ran to the grandmother bewildered. The grandmother hugged them and told the children they had not done anything to hurt their grandfather.

She walked out while holding the hands of her grandbabies. Around the neck of the old man were his daughter's arms tightly holding him. The son-in-law looked on with tears of sadness pouring down in the eerie silence. Finally the old man spoke.

"It should have been me," he said softly with a broken voice to match his heart.

The grandmother touched her husband's head as she gently said words that should never be forgotten,

"Children, the name you etched for your grandfather is the man who gave his life so your granddad would live."

This is but one reason we must remember and write down the deeds of our heroes.

What constitutes a hero? Is it a person who has accomplished missions under fire? Is it someone willing to give all for what he or she believes? To me a hero is someone who served his/her country's calling honorably. To me it is someone who denied himself and gave to others so others could have a rich and full life. Jesus Christ is the greatest example of such a hero. We mortals pale in comparison, yet we do endeavor to follow his example when duty calls.

During times of trials and tribulations heroes emerge to lead us. They range from privates, to the likes of SGT York, and finally to Generals. In these troubled times we must remember that Washington also dealt with many issues. One of the most serious was when the officers under his command began questioning the authority of the government. What he did in essence preserved the fledgling country and demonstrates the power that one man can have in creating or destroying a nation.

In an effort to offer complete authenticity, we offer the prelude to the speech, George Washington's writing comments and the postscript in entirety. When the torch of freedom was about to be extinguished, General Washington stood up as a titan and helped preserve the efforts of those wishing a new breath of freedom.

WASHINGTON'S SPEECH

At the close of the Revolutionary War in America, a perilous moment in the life of the fledgling American republic occurred as officers of the Continental Army met in Newburgh, New York, to discuss grievances and consider a possible insurrection against the rule of Congress.

They were angry over the failure of Congress to honor its promises to the army regarding salary, bounties and life pensions. The officers had heard from Philadelphia that the American government was going broke and that they might not be compensated at all.

On March 10, 1783, an anonymous letter was circulated among the officers of General Washington's main camp at Newburgh. It addressed those complaints and called for an unauthorized meeting of officers to be held the next day to consider possible military solutions to the problems of the civilian government and its financial woes.

General Washington stopped that meeting from happening by forbidding the officers to meet at the unauthorized meeting. Instead, he suggested they meet a few days later, on March 15th, at the regular meeting of his officers.

Meanwhile, another anonymous letter was circulated, this time suggesting Washington himself was sympathetic to the claims of the malcontent officers.

And so, on March 15, 1783, Washington's officers gathered in a church building in Newburgh, effectively holding the fate of America in their hands.

Unexpectedly, General Washington himself showed up. He was not entirely welcomed by his men, but nevertheless, personally addressed them...

Gentlemen:

By an anonymous summons, an attempt has been made to convene you together; how inconsistent with the rules of propriety, how unmilitary, and how subversive of all order and discipline, let the good sense of the army decide...

Thus much, gentlemen, I have thought it incumbent on me to observe to you, to show upon what principles I opposed the irregular and hasty meeting which was proposed to have been held on Tuesday last - and not because I wanted a disposition to give you every opportunity consistent with your own honor, and the dignity of the army, to make known your grievances. If my conduct heretofore has not evinced to you that I have been a faithful friend to the army, my declaration of it at this time would be equally unavailing and improper. But as I was among the first who embarked in the cause of our common country. As I have never left your side one moment, but when called from you on public duty. As I have been the constant companion and witness of your distresses, and not among the last to feel and acknowledge your merits. As I have ever considered my own military reputation as inseparably connected with that of the army. As my heart has ever expanded with joy, when I have heard its praises, and my indignation has arisen, when the mouth of detraction has been opened against it, it can scarcely be supposed, at this late stage of the war, that I am indifferent to its interests.

But how are they to be promoted? The way is plain, says the anonymous addresser. If war continues, remove into the unsettled country, there establish yourselves, and leave an ungrateful country to defend itself. But who are they to defend? Our wives, our children, our farms, and other property which we leave behind us. Or, in this state of hostile separation, are we to take the two first (the latter cannot be removed) to perish in a wilderness, with hunger, cold, and nakedness? If peace takes place, never sheathe your swords, says he, until you have obtained full and ample justice; this dreadful alternative, of either deserting our country in the extremest hour of her distress or turning our arms against it (which is the apparent object, unless Congress can be compelled into instant compliance), has something so shocking in it that humanity revolts at the idea. My God! What can this writer have in view, by recommending such measures? Can he be a friend to the army? Can he be a friend to this country? Rather, is he not an insidious foe? Some emissary, perhaps, from New York, plotting the ruin of both, by sowing the seeds of discord and separation between the civil and military powers of the continent? And what a compliment does he pay to our understandings when he recommends measures in either alternative, impracticable in their nature?

I cannot, in justice to my own belief, and what I have great reason to conceive is the intention of Congress, conclude this address, without giving it as my decided opinion, that that honorable body entertain exalted sentiments of the services of the army; and, from a full conviction of its merits and sufferings, will do it complete justice. That their endeavors to discover and establish funds for this purpose have been unwearied, and will not cease till they have succeeded, I have not a doubt. But, like all other large bodies, where there is a variety of different interests to reconcile, their deliberations are slow. Why, then, should we distrust them? And, in consequence of that distrust, adopt measures which may cast a shade over that glory which has been so justly acquired; and tarnish the reputation of an army which is celebrated through all Europe, for its fortitude and patriotism? And for what is this done? To bring the object we seek nearer? No! most certainly, in my opinion, it will cast it at a greater distance.

For myself (and I take no merit in giving the assurance, being induced to it from principles of gratitude, veracity, and justice), a grateful sense of the confidence you have ever placed in me, a recollection of the cheerful assistance and prompt obedience I have experienced from you, under every vicissitude of fortune, and the sincere affection I feel for an army I have so long had the honor to command will oblige me to declare, in this public and solemn manner, that, in the attainment of complete justice for all your toils and dangers, and in the gratification of every wish, so far as may be done consistently with the great duty I owe my country and those powers we are bound to respect, you may freely command my services to the utmost of my abilities.

While I give you these assurances, and pledge myself in the most unequivocal manner to exert whatever ability I am possessed of in your favor, let me entreat you, gentlemen, on your part, not to take any measures which, viewed in the calm light of reason, will lessen the dignity and sully the glory you have hitherto maintained; let me request you to rely on the plighted faith of your country, and place a full confidence in the purity of the intentions of Congress; that, previous to your dissolution as an army, they will cause all your accounts to be fairly liquidated, as directed in their resolutions, which were published to you two days ago, and that they will adopt the most effectual measures in their power to render ample justice to you, for your faithful and meritorious services. And let me conjure you, in the name of our common country, as you value your own sacred honor, as you respect the rights of humanity, and as you regard the military and national character of America, to express your utmost horror and detestation of the man who wishes, under any specious pretenses, to overturn the liberties of our country, and who wickedly attempts to open the floodgates of civil discord and deluge our rising empire in blood.

By thus determining and thus acting, you will pursue the plain and direct road to the attainment of your wishes. You will defeat the insidious designs of our enemies, who are compelled to resort from open force to secret artifice. You will give one more distinguished proof of unexampled patriotism and patient virtue, rising superior to the pressure of the most complicated sufferings. And you will, by the dignity of your conduct, afford occasion for posterity to say, when speaking of the glorious example you have exhibited to mankind, "Had this day been wanting, the world had never seen the last stage of perfection to which human nature is capable of attaining." General George Washington - March 15, 1783

Post-note: His speech was not very well received by his men. Washington then took out a letter from a member of Congress explaining the financial difficulties of the government.

After reading a portion of the letter with his eyes squinting at the small writing, Washington suddenly stopped. His officers stared at him, wondering. Washington then reached into his coat pocket and took out a pair of reading glasses. Few of them knew he wore glasses, and were surprised.

"Gentlemen," said Washington, *"You will permit me to put on my spectacles, for I have not only grown gray but almost blind in the service of my country."*

In that single moment of sheer vulnerability, Washington's men were deeply moved, even shamed, and many were quickly in tears, now looking with great affection at this aging man who had led them through so much. Washington read the remainder of the letter, then left without saying another word, realizing their sentiments.

His officers then cast a unanimous vote, essentially agreeing to the rule of Congress. Thus, the civilian government was preserved and the experiment of democracy in America continued.

http://www.historyplace.com/speeches/washington.htm

During these trying times, let us look to our heroes of yesterday and today for inspiration. Let us embrace the sacred principles that so many Americans gave their all to preserve. Let us not bow to tyranny but stand for truth. America, the greatest country to have ever existed, must rise from the kneeling position and allow the eagle to soar once again.

ABOUT THE BOOK

There still remains thousands upon thousands of unsung heroes. They walk among us unpretentious and silent as to their sacrifices. They are those whose story will never be told unless we, the rising generation, take it upon our shoulders to preserve their legacy. That is my purpose and I pray it inspires others to take up the pen and write of those who were willing to wheel the sword in preservation of our way of life. Freedom is never free. Heroes and those unsung paid the price with blood, sweat, and tears. Shall we do less in honoring them?

The reason I approached Richard Brown regarding this project was I knew of his love of Veterans and his willingness to honor them. The concept of writing a book honoring unsung heroes came to me as I began writing down all those men and women who served from Perkins Branch. Perkins Branch is located off Route 7 in Letcher County, Kentucky, and consists of only twelve homes. From those homes they produced men and women who were proud to serve.

I talked to a couple and started compiling a list so I could present the names to the Letcher County Fiscal Court to get the bridge named after them. It did not take long for me to realize the list was too long for such an enterprise. Who are/were these unsung heroes? What do we know about them? Is it not up to the present generation to remember the cost of freedom? The seed was planted and we have begun researching. It is our prayer that you will do the same and recall those unsung heroes who were willing or did offer their lives measure so you can enjoy this freedom we have. Let us not forget the cost and have to pay the price of losing those sacred privileges known as liberty.

Unsung Heroes of Perkins Branch, KY

Charlie Blair-WWII
Arlie Blair-WWII
Arnold Blair-WWII
Arlin James Blair-Vietnam Era
Russell Blair-Vietnam Era
Richard Hampton-Vietnam Era
Zenith Ison-Vietnam Era
David Chaltas-Vietnam Era
Hansford Whitaker-Vietnam Era
Harvey Whitaker-Vietnam Era
Elmer Caudill-Korean Era
Steve Adams
Steve Back
Ralph Blair
Charles Blair
Bobby Harold Blair

"If you are able, save for them a place inside of you....and save one backward glance when you are leaving for the places they can no longer go.....Be not ashamed to say you loved them....Take what they have left and what they have taught you with their dying and keep it with your own....And in that time when men decide and feel safe to call the war insane, take one moment to embrace those gentle heroes you left behind...." Maj. Michael Davis O'Donnell, quote from a letter home: KIA 24 March 1970. Distinguished Flying Cross: Shot down and killed while attempting to rescue 8 fellow soldiers surrounded by attacking enemy forces.

ABOUT THE AUTHOR

David Chaltas is an educator with over thirty-five years of service to troubled youth. In The Summer of 2001, he was selected Teacher of the Year by the Kentucky Council of Children with Behavioral Disorders. He is the first recipient of the prestigious award in the state of Kentucky. His innovative Alternative Education and Day Treatment Program won the coveted 2000-2001 Program of the Year by the International Association of Directors of Pupil Personnel. The program has been a model for several other facilities within the region.

Mr. Chaltas spent over six years working on Native American reservations in Arizona, New Mexico and the four corner area. He also served at Friendship services out of Gallup, New Mexico, where he worked with alcoholism. He has also taught at the college level to keep his 'balance', and is a nationally recognized living historian.

He is one of Kentucky's most prolific authors with over forty books to his credit and over one hundred articles on his resume. Some of his articles have appeared in Kentucky Explorer, Civil War Courier, News Press, Gazette, to name a few. He has over four hundred lessons for life published on line.

He is a sought after motivational speaker who shares his experiences to educators, churches, clubs, and civil organizations across this great nation. He has traveled extensively signing books and offering presentations to several states from Texas, Colorado, to Maryland, as well as Michigan to Florida.

When asked what his greatest honor was, Mr. Chaltas stated that it was serving his country. *"Being a soldier was the catalyst to my defining who I am. I consider it to have been my time of rediscovery."*

"Soldier ... there is no class of men for whom I feel a deeper solicitude, than the noble defenders of our rights, civil, political and religious. You have bared your bosoms to the cannon's mouth; and your lives may be said to be in jeopardy every hour. I would to God that you were all prepared for living, and for dying, that you might live eternally with Christ in the upper mansions." Chaplain Andrew Broadus, *J. B. Gordon's Georgia Brigade*

(Courtesy of Mrs. Brenda Nease)

OTHER BOOKS BY THE AUTHOR

Buckwheat
I am White Frog
Appalachian Rebels
Brothers Once More
When Ravens Dance
The General's Journal
R. E. Lee: Reflections
The General's Dispatch
Poetry of the Civil War
Teddy, the Sleepy Bear
The Fading of the Gray
Shadows of Gettysburg
Four Women: One War
The Valley of the Winds
The Search for Butternut
Confederate Kin I, II, &III
As Far as the Eye Can See
My Walk Upon the Wind
Beneath the Falling Waters
Mourning in the Mountains
The Mouse and the Cadillac
In the Beginning was Words
When You Follow Your Heart
An Open Book for Closed Minds
Old Maw: The Legend of Miss Kessie
Native American Sayings, Customs and Prayers

Amazon books: David Chaltas
Barnes and Noble: David Chaltas
Books a Million: David Chaltas

THE SOLDIER AND HIS FLAG
(For my Father-December 16, 1995)
Linda Morton Norton

As the music wafted across the breeze
"OH, SAY CAN YOU SEE"
I saw the old soldier struggle to his feet
Sore, tired, with faintly beating heart
With legs unsteady and faltering step
Scarred body aching with bloody wounds of long ago
Earned on frosty battlefields across the sea.

"BY THE DAWN'S EARLY LIGHT"
The old soldier peered upward
Giving homage and honor to the flag for whose nation
Indivisible, he fought so many years ago.

"WHOSE BROAD STRIPES AND BRIGHT STARS"
Red for the bloodshed by many
White for the Purity of our Lord and Nation
And Blue for the waters which boundary our nation
from shore to shore.
Fluttering above, floating in the wind.

"WHAT SO PROUDLY WE HAIL"
No need to remind the old soldier in song of his
nation's glory,
Of our nation's greatness; of our blood-bought freedom,
of good will toward men.
The old soldier's frail, trembling body,
Dulled with medicine, racked with pain, and supported
by pride
Reminds him of the sacrifice of his youth.

"AT THE TWILIGHT'S LAST GLEAMING."
The old soldier who once shouldered a massive rifle
Clutched his hat across his chest in allegiance
The piercing, falcon eyes of the young man
Now thickened, glistening in soft, brown study.

Exhausted, he sank into his seat while the music softly played

**"AND THE ROCKETS' RED GLARE, BOMBS BURSTING IN AIR
GAVE PROOF THROUGH THE NIGHT, THAT OUR FLAG WAS STILL THERE."
"OH SAY DOES THE STAR SPANGLED BANNER YET WAVE
OVER THE LAND OF THE FREE AND THE HOME OF THE BRAVE."**

The old soldier nodded in response
His eyes moistening with pride and reflection
Remembering his comrades left behind,
Whose vibrant, virile blood still warms the mother earth of Europe.
And, the Old Soldier, being old and full of Years
Was gathered to his Fathers
Succored by Faith, wrapped in Honor
Surrounded by his Family; covered with his Flag.

TABLE OF CONTENTS

Dedication 3
Foreword 4
About The Book..12
About the Author 14
Books by the Authors...16
The Solider and his Flag 17

Heroes of America

Aaron C. Torian 23
Alfred Glenn Brown 26
Alvin M. Collins 28
Andrew Jackson Smith 31
Anthony Duty..34
Archelous Craft...36
Arlie Blair 40
Arnold Blair 43
Ben Buster Taylor...50
Bennett Jonathan Adams..78
Billy McFall..81
Billy Wayne Bridgeman 82
Bobby George Fields 85
Brent Woods 91
Brownie Hall...94
Burriss Nelson Begley 96
Carl Nelson Gorman 99
Chadwick Gilliam 106
Charles Hassel Caudill..110
Charles R. Marshall 112
Charles Young 117
Charlie Blair..120
Chester Brown 123
Chester Nez...127
Christopher Andrew Landis..................................132
Clarence Bruce Varnell...135
Clarence J. Daniels...143
Clayton Shepherd..145
Dakota Meyers..150

Dan Bullock 154
Danny Webb 158
Danny O. Webb 161
D. Stanley Hollan 163
Darrell C. Powers 164
Darrell O. Holbrook 169
Darwin K. Kyle 172
Delmer Virgil Ashbrook 177
Demmer Richmond 180
Dennie Neace 190
Desmond T. Doss 193
Doyle Jannow 197
Edmond Harjo 201
Edwin C. Jenkins 204
Eli Whitt 205
Elmon Grady Potter 207
Emmitt Colon Adams 212
Eulis Ray Adkins 214
Everett Tipton Culp 219
Fast Eddie 222
Francis G. Powers 225
Frank William Jealous of Him 228
Franklin Doug Miller 233
Franklin Runyon Sousley 239
Freddie Stowers 246
French Forrest 250
Gary Owens 253
George Dee Higgins 255
George Hobert Noe 256
George William Casey 260
G. Wix Unthank 263
G. Wurl Conners 266
Harold Moore 274
Harry Monroe Caudill 282
Harry M. Revenne 286
Henry Timothy Vakoc 290
Henry Williams 293
Hercules Mulligan 295
H.T. Nicholson 298
Hugh J. Hart 299

Hunbert 'Rocky' Versace	303
Jack V. Combs	309
Jackie Coots	310
Jacob Lee Butler	312
Jacob W. Beisel	315
James Breeding	318
James E. Chaffin III	323
James Keelan	326
James L. Lollar	329
James Monroe Combs	334
James Nelson Spangler	336
James T. Pece	342
J. Clifford Jenkins	345
Jefferson Scott Dotson	347
Jesse James Gilliam	354
Jim Sayre	357
Jimmy Duncan	359
Jimmy Ellison Tolliver	364
John Chavis	369
John Curtis Stringer	376
John Edison Hampton	379
John Patrick Parsons	381
John V. Back	383
Jonathan Owens	385
Joseph Boyd Sumpter	387
Joseph E. Gantt	390
Joshua A. Gray	393
Larry Dwight Maggard	397
Leigh Ann Hester	400
Lennie Darrell Holbrook	405
Leonard Foster Mason	407
Lewis Stovall	410
Mabel Lewis Mullins	413
Michael D. Acklin	416
Mike Gerald Gibbs	419
Narce Whitaker	424
Patrick Tillman	432
Perry Benally	437
Peyton Reynolds	442
Philip Johnston	444

P.K. 'Ken' Keen	448
Ray Harding Hogg	453
Raymond Smith	465
Ricky S. Warf	469
Robert Adrian Marks	474
Robert Q. Kelly	478
Roger Dale Campbell	479
Ronnie Jordan Campbell	482
Roy G. Seals	493
Ruben Watts	497
Rudolph Valintino Short	502
Russell Blair	507
Rusty H. Christian	512
Sergeant Driscoll	516
Shelba Jean Profitt	520
Shelby Wayne Neace	525
Stevie Ray Gibson	530
Ted Cook	532
Tom Chase McKenney	544
Victor Gayle Alexander	547
Weary Clyburn	550
Wilfred Durde Cover	555
William J. Caudill	561
William Kyle Carpenter	562
William Lloyd Brown	566
William T. Jent	578
William Horsfall	579
Willie Dean Smith	583
Willie Sandlin	584
Pictures of the Past	588
War Dog-The saga of SGT Stubby	597
The Search Continues	600
Causalities from Letcher County	602
Sayings	613
It is the Veteran	615

AARON C. TORIAN
Master Sergeant
2nd Marine Special Operations Battalion
Marine Special Operations Regiment
U.S. Marine Corps Forces Special Operations Command
June 28, 1977-February 15, 2014

The month of February 2014, has seen the death of three Kentuckians in Operation Enduring Freedom. Aaron was from Paducah, Kentucky. From reading articles about Aaron, he was well liked, athletic and was family orientated. He loved his country and wanted to serve.

Aaron attended Thomas Stone High School and graduated in 1995. Aaron went to the University of Tennessee (Martin Campus) and played football. He played at UT Martin from 1995-1999. He obtained his Bachelor Degree in Education in 2001. Sergeant Aaron Torian joined the Marine Corps in March of 2003. In 2006, he joined the elite Marine Corps Forces Special Operations Command (MARSOC).

In 2005, Sergeant Torian was named the 2005, 2nd Marine Division's Noncommissioned Officer of the Year for his actions during Operation Phantom Fury in Fallujah, Iraq in 2004. He was assigned to Camp Lejeune, North Carolina. Aaron also finished his Master's Degree while serving in the Marines. He earned and was promoted to Master Sergeant on September 1, 2013.

Master Sergeant Torian was not new to fighting. In fact he was wounded on May 29, 2008, while engaged with the insurgents. He was given a Purple Heart for his gallantry.

Aaron was Killed in Action (KIA) while on combat operations in Helmand Province, Afghanistan. His remains were brought to Dover Air Force Base and were met by his loving family and friends. Master Sergeant Torian is survived by his wife, Jurley, and their three children (Elijah, 9, Laura Bella, 4, and Avery, 2), along with his mother, Esta. He was thirty-six years of age at the time of his passing. This was his sixth combat duty tour. He served two tours in Iraq and four in Afghanistan. He will be buried with full military honors in Arlington Cemetery, Washington, D.C.

Heartland Worship Center, his hometown church recalled Aaron's visit during Christmas. When news of his death reached the family, friends and congregation, they were devastated. On Sunday Pastor Nathan Joyce told the people, *"I think there's two kinds of people, those who run into the mess and danger to try to do something about it and those who run from it. Aaron was the kind to run into it. He loved being a Marine. And he loved what he did."* One of his childhood friends remembered him as being, *"Bigger than life."* He proved it by his supreme sacrifice.

AWARDS

His awards include the Purple Heart, Navy Commendation Medal with Combat Distinguishing Device, Navy and Marine Corps Achievement Medal, Combat Action Ribbon with gold star, Sea Service Deployment Ribbon with three stars, Global War on

Terrorism Expeditionary Medal, Global War on Terrorism Service Medal, Iraq Campaign Medal, Afghanistan Campaign, and the Good Conduct Medal.

SOURCES

http://www.wwaytv3.com/2014/02/17/camp-lejeune-marine-killed-ied

http://www.somdnews.com/article/20140219/NEWS/140219141/1055/thomas-stone-graduate-killed-in-afghanistan&template=southernMaryland

http://www.kfvs12.com/story/24739505/marine-from-paducah-killed-in-afghanistan

http://surfky.com/index.php/news/local/mccracken/45008-governor-beshear-recognizes-sacrifice-of-a-kentucky-marine

http://www.witn.com/home/headlines/245911981.html

http://www.ukiahdailyjournal.com/blogs/ci_25181722/from-chief-soldiers-life-aaron-torian

http://projects.militarytimes.com/valor/marine-master-sgt-aaron-c-torian/6568551

http://digital.olivesoftware.com/Olive/ODE/LexingtonHeraldLeader/LandingPage/LandingPage.aspx?href=TEhMLzIwMTQvMDIvMjY.&pageno=MTI.&entity=QXIwMTIwMQ..&view=ZW50aXR5

ALFRED GLENN BROWN
Staff Sergeant
Medium Tank Company
169th Infantry
By Richard G. Brown
October 5, 1928-Present

Alfred Glenn Brown is the son of William Henry Brown and Florence Richmond Brown. He was born October 5, 1928, at Dry Fork near Whitesburg, Letcher County, Kentucky. Letcher County is in the southeastern portion of Kentucky and is located in the Appalachian Mountains, bordering on Virginia. He goes by his middle name, Glenn. He had three brothers, Lloyd, Earl and Roy, and also a sister, Lillian. Lloyd was in the U.S. Navy during World War II and Earl was in Korea while in the U.S. Army. Glenn was married to Mattie Fern Caudill, who is now deceased. They have four children, Freda, Richard, Wendell and David.

Glenn attended grade school at Middle Dry Fork Grade School and then went to high school at Pine Mountain Settlement School, a boarding school in Harlan County, Kentucky. He was drafted into the U.S. Army on March 1, 1951. After boot camp, he was assigned to a medium tank company in the 169th Infantry Regiment. He trained on tanks at several locations, including the Mojave Desert. Glenn shipped overseas to Germany, traveling across the Atlantic Ocean on a transport ship. While in Germany, he was promoted to corporal, and later, staff sergeant. He arrived in Germany during the Korean War conflict. Some of his fellow soldiers were sent on to Korea, but Glenn received orders to stay in Germany.

While in Germany, he was awarded expert marksman medal in both pistol and rifle. He was assigned to be tank commander, after first being a driver. Their tanks were fully armed with live ammunition as they were on alert continuously, due to the Soviet Union's aggressive occupation of East Germany. Several times the American tanks were in sight of their Soviet Union counterparts. The remainder of the time spent by Glenn and his fellow soldiers was conducting the occupation of war-torn West Germany. As they treated the German people with respect, dozens of German children followed them everywhere they went. Glenn spent almost sixteen months in Germany before boarding a transport ship for his return trip across the Atlantic Ocean back home.

Not long after returning to the United States, Glenn was discharged on February 7, 1953. He traveled back home to Kentucky to reunite with his wife, Fern. He temporarily moved to Paintsville, Kentucky, to attend electrical repair classes at Mayo Vocational School under the G.I. Plan. Upon graduation, he moved back to Whitesburg in Letcher County and got a job rebuilding electrical motors used in the underground mining business. He later became an underground mining electrician and worked part-time underground and the rest outside in a shop.

Glenn raised his family in Whitesburg, where he and his wife both were very active in scouting, Fern was a den master for twelve years while Glenn was a Scout Master for several years. He now enjoys working in his garden, keeping up his large apple orchard and entertaining his great grandchildren.

ALVIN M. COLLINS
Sergeant
Squad Leader 5th Rangers
Light weapons infantrymen (LWI)
May 25, 1926 – April 15, 2005

Our nation was bursting with patriotic fever at the beginning of World War II. Old Vets nearing retirement and underage teens were trying to join the military to defend America. If you ask my Dad his age when he joined the Army he will say he was 18. However, the oldest he could have been was 17 and more likely 16 soon to be 17. I asked him once and he got mad and said, *"I told you 18 now drop it."* No matter he became Airborne qualified and trained as an Army Ranger. After landing on Normandy on D-Day he walked, crawled & I'm sure ran across France & Germany. Near the end of the war he was wounded by shrapnel in his leg which took a chunk of muscle & leaving a nasty scar.

Many combat veterans won't speak of their war time experience while others like my Dad would only relate the funny stories. My favorite occurred on a pitch black night on a hill in Germanys' Black Forrest. The Black Forrest is an old growth forest with a canopy so thick that even on the brightest day the sun light had to struggle to pierce the thick forest canopy. On an Overcast night the moon, stars and canopy created night so dark that the Rangers couldn't see the person next to them.

His unit set up their night defensive position on a hill overlooking a trail that snaked its way through the forest. As soldiers do, they prepared their NDP by digging foxholes and clearing the field of fire in front of their positions. As the darkness of night hid their position they settled in for a long night. At the darkest point of the night those on watch quietly wake the rest of the unit because there was movement at the base of their hill. As the movement appeared to be starting up the hill the Rangers had to decide how to act without giving away their position. They decided to toss hand grenades at the sound. The next morning they faced the task of searching for what caused movement. They cautiously moved down the hill fearing they might walk into a counter ambush by the wounded German soldiers. Much to their relief and amusement they discovered a deer shredded by their grenades. The Rangers saw a golden opportunity to supplement the meager K-Rations by butchering the deer and taking some the meat with them for a banquet that night.

Another story he told (which I also found in a book on Rangers) happened near the end of the war. They were holding a key crossroad well in advance of advancing American Army ("Rangers Lead the Way") and 2 American jeeps came roaring up the road from the German line. It was curious; the jeeps were coming from that direction since there weren't suppose to be any American troops in front of them. The Rangers positioned themselves to blast the jeeps and their occupants if they weren't Americans. The jeeps pulled into the crossroad and stopped. An officer started shouting orders. The officer suddenly became aware the soldiers weren't listening to him and they were pointed their weapons at them. They captured a German General and his staff.

My Dad wanted to be a lifer. But given a choice between staying in the Army and go to Germany in 1946, or getting out to be there when his first child was born he decided it more important to be there with his family.

The closest he ever came to revealing what his war was like was when he told about how he got an SS Officer's Dagger that he brought home from the war. After ambushing a German patrol they were checking the German dead for any military intelligence when he turned the SS Officer over, the German lunged at him with the knife. All he would say about that struggle was *"I won."*

SOURCE

Written and submitted by David Collins, his son.

ANDREW JACKSON SMITH
Color Sergent
41st Illinois/55th Massachusetts
September 3, 1843–March 4, 1932

He was born in Kentucky as a slave. He died as a free man. His master was Elijah Smith. Not much is known about his younger years but when the War Between the States began, his master had plans for Andrew to go with him and be in the Confederate Army. Andrew and another slave sneaked away and walked twenty-five miles to Smithland, Kentucky. Smithland is a small town in Livingston County, Kentucky, located at the confluence of the Ohio and Cumberland Rivers. There he was assigned duty with the 41st Illinois and became a servant to Major John Warner. The military post was located in Paducah, Kentucky. He was entrusted with the duty of returning all of the Major's belongings to his family in the event of his death.

In the early part of 1862, the regiment was ordered to Tennessee. He was at Fort Donelson and within a month, the nineteen year old found him entwined in the Battle of Shiloh. Major Warner was in the heat of the battle and had two horses shot out from under him. Andrew J. Smith brought him fresh horses each time. On the last occasion Smith was hit by, "A spent Minnie ball that entered his left temple, rolled just under the skin, and stopped in the middle of his forehead." The bullet was successfully removed by a surgeon. The only damage was a scar reminding him of his close encounter with death. He went with the major to Clinton, Illinois, to give Smith time to recover from his wound.

In late fall of 1864, Smith was in South Carolina, at the Battle of Honey Hill. He was a corporal with the 55th Massachusetts. The 55th and the famed 54th found themselves under heavy fire from the Confederate stronghold position. As they advanced through the swamp the color bearer was struck. With total disregard for his personal safety, Smith grabbed the flag and carried it throughout the battle. Because of his action he was given the honor of being the color sergeant. He maintained that honor until he was discharged.

After the war was over, Corporal Smith returned to Kentucky and bought some land. In 1916, he was nominated for the Medal of Honor but due to the times, it was denied this brave man. He died at age eighty-eight. He is buried in Mount Pleasant Cemetery, Grand Rivers, Kentucky, without receiving his justified honor. In 2001, Andrew Jackson Smith was awarded the Medal of Honor.

CITATION

"Corporal Andrew Jackson Smith, of Clinton, Illinois, a member of the 55th Massachusetts Voluntary Infantry, distinguished himself on 30 November 1864 by saving his regimental colors, after the color bearer was killed during a bloody charge called the Battle of Honey Hill, South Carolina. In the late afternoon, as the 55th

Regiment pursued enemy skirmishers and conducted a running fight, they ran into a swampy area backed by a rise where the Confederate Army awaited. The surrounding woods and thick underbrush impeded infantry movement and artillery support. The 55th and 54th regiments formed columns to advance on the enemy position in a flanking movement. As the Confederates repelled other units, the 55th and 54th regiments continued to move into flanking positions. Forced into a narrow gorge crossing a swamp in the face of the enemy position, the 55th's Color-Sergeant was killed by an exploding shell, and Corporal Smith took the Regimental Colors from his hand and carried them through heavy grape and canister fire. Although half of the officers and a third of the enlisted men engaged in the fight were killed or wounded, Corporal Smith continued to expose himself to enemy fire by carrying the colors throughout the battle. Through his actions, the Regimental Colors of the 55th Infantry Regiment were not lost to the enemy. Corporal Andrew Jackson Smith's extraordinary valor in the face of deadly enemy fire is in keeping with the highest traditions of military service and reflect great credit upon him, the 55th Regiment, and the United States Army."

SOURCES

http://en.wikipedia.org/wiki/Andrew_Jackson_Smith_ (Medal_ohttp://usctchronicle.blogspot.com/2011/11/remembering-andrew-jackson-smith-medal.html

Eyewitness to Shiloh earned Medal of Honor; Civil War Courier, October 2013, Volume 26, Issue 6

ANTHONY DUTY
Specialist 4th Class
MOS-ll Bravo
Recon Platoon, Company E
1st Battalion
52nd Regiment
198th Light Infantry Brigade
America Division, USARV
March 10, 1949-June 7, 1969

At the writing of this book I do not have much information but know this unsung hero must be rediscovered. I offer his story in hopes that someone will come forward and add to it. He and his family needs to be recognized for his sacrifice.

Anthony Duty was a Letcher County native. He lived in Neon, Kentucky. He was drafted and his tour began on December 18, 1968. He was twenty years of age. His ID number was 51647717.

Specialist 4th Class Duty was killed in action in Quang Ngai on June 7, 1969. Noting that on the Vietnam Memorial Wall (Panel 23w, row 99) several are listed as falling in battle. From official military records we know that on June 7, 1969, that a night offensive was launched by the North Vietnamese Army around Quang Nam Province. The fighting was intense and several lost their lives. Also there was other action and noting that Specialist Duty was in Recon, his demise could have happened while on a mission. At the writing of this book there is limited information.

This we know: he died doing his duty for God, Country and his loved ones. He is listed on the Vietnam Memorial Wall, Panel 23w, Row 99. He is buried in the Green Acres Cemetery across from Walmart in Ermine, Kentucky.

SOURCES

http://army.togetherweserved.com/army/servlet/tws.webapp.WebApp?cmd=ShadowBoxProfile&type=Person&ID=47082&source=fold3

http://www.vvmf.org/Wall-of-Faces/14370/ANTHONY-DUTY#sthash.YvkN1qww.dpuf

http://thewall-usa.com/info.asp?recid=14369

http://www.virtualwall.org/dd/DutyAx01a.htm

http://www.recordsofwar.com/vietnam/army/

ARCHELOUS CRAFT
Revolutionary War Soldier
Patriot
Roaring River, Wilkes, North Carolina, USA
Buried in Crafts Colly, Letcher, Kentucky, USA
December 25, 1749-November 8, 1853

I am honored to write what I know of my ancestor. I am descended from Rainey Craft who married Hiram Blair. There are many thousands of descendents who know much more than me but nevertheless I feel it imperative to include him in Unsung Heroes.

Archelous was born on Christmas Day in 1749. He was the son of James and Sarah Hammons Craft. James (1714-1793) was the son of Henry Craft. Sarah (1718-1818) was born to William Hammon and Sarah Parsons (Note the S on Sarah's maiden name was added by someone). According to his sworn testimony, he was born in News County on Roanoke River in the State of North Carolina. NOTE: since a News County never existed Archelous possibly was referring to the Neuse River-New Bern, N.C.) He later moved to the Roaring River area, Wilkes County, North Carolina.

When American fought for its independence, Archelous heeded the call. He entered service in 1780, located near Brier Creek (Wilkes County, North Carolina). He fought with Captain Samuel Johnston's Company commanded by Colonel Gordon. Later he served under Colonel Ben Herndon and Colonel Locke. On August 7, 1780 he saw action in the Battle of Hanging Rock. Finally he served under Colonel Malmonday and finally under Colonel Locke again in the battle of Eutaw Springs, South Carolina on September 8, 1781.

According to Clara Shaw (Pine Mountain Chapter of the Daughters of American Revolution), he served three tours in the North Carolina Militia. "He volunteered for service in 1778 for three months and marched against the Indians who were assisting the British. In 1780 he enlisted again and fought in the Battle of hanging Rock as well as Eutaw Springs. He returned to farming but again in 1781 he enlisted for three months. He was discharged at Saulsberry, North Carolina."

After the war, he married Elizabeth Betsy Adams on December 1, 1785. He met her at a friend's wedding. She was born in 1770 (Loudon County Virginia) to John and Nancy Caudill. John Adams' first wife, Mary Boone, was the sister to Squire Boone. Squire was the father of Daniel Boone. No doubt Daniel visited his cousin's people when in the area. John Adams (1729-1815) is buried in the Mayking Cemetery.

Betsy was almost fifteen years old when she married him. He was almost thirty-six years of age. Betsy died in 1810 after being married to Archelous for twenty-five years. Archelous lived forty-three more years after her passing.

In 1804, they embarked upon an epic journey into Kentucky. They walked for weeks until they reached the place they wished to settle. They began building a house and clearing the land. Archelous would farm the land and hunt the forest to provide for his family. They were very hardy and believed in working the soil. They also were very religious, as was most during those days when freedom was not taken for granted. The party, which included his father-in-law, John Adams, decided they needed to form a church. They met at Isaac Whitaker's (another settler) homestead and farmed the Indian Bottom Church. Included in the group were several of my other ancestors including Henry Back, Elizabeth Hoffman Back, James Caudill, Stephen Benjamin Webb, John Dixon, Mary Caudill, and others. They formed the first Baptist church in the area.

On November 15, 1833, he was awarded a pension of $3.90 per month for his service during the Revolutionary War. His yearly salary would be $46.66! Given the era, most of his income came from what he raised and what he was able to barter with others. The pioneers were known for their hardiness. Family tradition says that on his one hundredth birthday he split one hundred rails.

Archelous was the father to the following twelve children: Mary Nancy Craft (Born: 1784-1877). Drucilla Craft (Born: 1787), Ezekiel Craft (Born: 1789-1789), James Washington Craft (Born: 1790-1867), John Wilhelm Craft (Born: 1792-1856), Sarah "Sally" Craft (Born: 1794-1880), Stephen Craft (Born: 1798), Simon Craft (Born: 1800-1880), Archelous "Cheed" Craft (Born: 1802-1853), Malinda Craft (Born: 1804-1804), William Craft (Born: 1807-1898), and Charity Craft (Born: 1810-1850).

After the death of his first wife Betsy in 1824, he married Sena Craft (Note the dates of her death are conflicting: one is 1824 and the other is 1835). He was seventy-five years of age at her passing. Archelous lived to be one hundred four years of age. His descendents number in the hundreds of thousands. ALL are proud of being a son or daughter of a revolutionary soldier.

There is a historical marker across from the turnoff at Letcher County Central High School (highway 119) marking the mouth of Crafts Colley. His grave is behind the Craft Colley Missionary Baptist Church. The property is owned by a private party.

SOURCES

http://adkinsmetcalffamily.wordpress.com/2009/01/27/archelous-craft-1749-1853/

http://www.findagrave.com/cgi-bin/fg.cgi?page=gr&GRid=47279508

http://www.findagrave.com/cgi-bin/fg.cgi?page=gr&GRid=47279508

Archealous Craft-Revolutionary War Patriot; Bicentennial Feature; by Pine Mountain DAR

ARLIE BLAIR
Sergeant First Class (SFC)
Veteran World War II and Korean War
29th Infantry Regiment
24th Division
Attached to the 19th Infantry Regiment
Bronze Star for Valor & Purple Heart Recipient
By Russell Blair & Dave Chaltas
February 8, 1916-January 14, 1972

Our family comes from a long line of veterans and we are extremely proud of that fact. One of my uncles who served in Korea was Arlie Blair. He married Molly Gay Blair. They had three sons (Arlin James, Russell and David) and two daughters (Deanna and Janet). Arlie's older brother Charlie served in World War II, along with a younger brother by the name of Arnold Blair. Their services are included in this book.

Arlie was assigned to the 29th Infantry Regiment, 24th Division and attached to the 19th Infantry Regiment. On Saturday, June 24, 1950, United States Secretary of State Dean Acheson informed President Truman by telephone, *"Mr. President, I have very serious news. The North Koreans have invaded South Korea."*

Preparation for war began. Troops, supplies, and planes began arriving at bases.

The first significant battle took place on July 5, 1950, involving five hundred forty men of the 24th Infantry Division. It was known as the Battle of Osan. One hundred eighty Americans were captured, wounded or dead. A general retreat of American forces was at hand. The 24th suffered three thousand six hundred two men killed in action or wounded. Two thousand nine hundred sixty-seven men were taken as prisoners of war. This included the commanding officer, Major General William F. Dean. Twenty-nine bombers and eighteen fighters were also shot down by the North Koreans. This was a devastating blow to moral and the war effort.

On July 27, 1950, an intense exchange between the North Korean Army and the United States forces occurred. Arlie was actively involved in the fight. They were ordered to hold off the enemy until reinforcements arrived. The raw troops were limited on ammunition and supplies, fighting a well trained North Korean force. The fighting turned into a fiasco. One battalion lost four hundred ninety-five of its seven hundred men in one afternoon. Such was the intensity of the fight.

Arlie was seriously wounded on July 27, 1950, the same day the army was almost decimated. The battle was a shocking rout of United Nation forces, who expected the North Koreans to be ill equipped and ill-trained. They had been ill advised. The American casualties were staggering and the commanding general was captured. Arlie recovered and returned to active duty on October 16, 1950. He remained in the military and upon retirement returned to Letcher County for the rest of his days.

SOURCES

http://www.ocregister.com/articles/says-254107-rodriguez-29th.html

http://en.wikipedia.org/wiki/29th_Inhttp://en.wikipedia.org/wiki/Korean_War Infantry_Regiment_(United_States)

http://en.wikipedia.org/wiki/Korean_War

http://aad.archives.gov/aad/record-detail.jsp?dt=230&mtch=1&cat=WR27&tf=F&q=Blair%2C+Arlie&bc=sl&rpp=10&pg=1&rid=53628

Note: The **19th Infantry Regiment** (Rock of Chickamauga) is a United States Army infantry regiment which is assigned to the US Army Training and Doctrine Command, with the assignment of conducting Basic and Advanced Infantry Training.

ARNOLD BLAIR
Company L
22nd Infantry Regiment
9th Armored Division
U.S. Army
Recipient of 3 Bronze Medals
March16, 1922-December 10, 1992

The following saga of my Uncle Arnold Blair is compiled from a portion of the research by Anthony Blair. Pertinent information came from Arnold Blair's grandson, Scotty K. Caudill. A few personal items are from my memory. Truly this man is an unsung hero.

Arnold Blair was the sixth child of Jim and Anna Back Blair. He had eleven siblings and was raised in the right hand fork of Perkins Branch, located in Letcher County, Kentucky. The old homestead is no longer in existence. The farm was the victim of mountain top removal.

Arnold worked at slaughter pen (Wardrups), Adams Plumbing and Heating Company, and also he was a custodian at Letcher High School. He was also a good carpenter. I recall him remodeling my room in our old house with paneling. He also designed a nice closet with sliding doors. I was very proud of that room as a young man. Arnold married Rena Mae Caudill. They had two children: Margaret Ann Blair and Sam Blair. They lived at Sycamore Loop and later in life moved to the right hand fork of Doty Creek.

At the onset of the war, Arnold decided to join the army. According to Scotty Caudill, his grandson, Arnold enlisted into the army as a private on October 6, 1942. He entered service at Fort Thomas, Kentucky, and separated from his military duties on November 13, 1945, at Fort Sumter. His Army serial number is 35488125. According to Fold 3, he enlisted in Huntington, West Virginia. But I have found in my research discrepancies due to the fact that anyone can put information on that site.

Arnold Blair specialty was a rifleman with the U.S. Army's 9th Armored Division. On March 7, 1945, his division captured the Ludendorff Bridge, which is better known as the Bridge at Remagen. This infamous railroad bridge was one of only two remaining useable bridges that crossed the Rhine River into Germany; the German military had destroyed the rest. The Germans had damaged the Ludendorff Bridge in their failed attempt to destroy it. After its capture by the Americans, the German military made an all-out effort to destroy the bridge to prevent the Americans from crossing the river into their homeland. The Germans attacked with frogmen, heavy artillery, fighter planes, and even V-2 rockets. However, the Americans successfully defended the bridge.

While the battle for the bridge was still ongoing, members of the 9th Armored Engineers Battalion removed the unexploded German ordinances and hastily repaired the bridge and Arnold Blair and the 9th Armored Division began crossing it that night, becoming the first invading force to cross the Rhine River into Germany since Napoleon in 1812. Soldiers, tanks, trucks, and other war supplies continued crossing the bridge for the next few days. The overworked and weakened bridge fell on March 17, 1945. The movie <u>The Bridge at Remagen</u> was filmed in 1969.

Arnold Blair participated in the Rhineland and Central European Campaigns and in the Ardennes Counteroffensive which is better known as the Battle of the Bulge. According to Wikipedia, "The Battle of the Bulge, (16 December 1944–25 January 1945) was a major German offensive campaign launched through the densely forested Ardennes region of Wallonia in Belgium, France and Luxembourg on the Western Front. The surprise attack caught the Allied forces completely off guard and became the costliest battle in terms of casualties for the United States, whose forces bore the brunt of the attack. It also severely depleted Germany's war-making resources."

Arnold likely was in Czechoslovakia when the war in Europe ended on May 8, 1945. Arnold Blair brought home an 8mm Mauser rifle that he had removed from a dead German soldier. The rifle is now in the possession of his great nephew and it still shoots great. Arnold Blair's dog tags were found in a field in Belgium and are on display in a small museum there. The museum owner sent the Blair family a photo of the displayed dog tags.

During the heat of combat, Arnold Blair threw a grenade into a foxhole containing German soldiers who were waving a white flag. To us Americans sitting in the comforts of our living room, a white flag is a signal of surrender or, at least, of a temporary stoppage of hostilities. However, the American troops had been taught that to a German soldier, a white flag meant something entirely different: it was a signal calling for their fellow German soldiers behind them to fire in the direction of the flag. So, Arnold Blair did what he was trained to do—he threw the grenade—because, after all, he who hesitates is lost, especially during active combat. His throwing the grenade haunted Arnold for the remainder of his life: were the young soldiers directing fire toward him and his comrades or were they surrendering?

The following was taken from this compiler's memory (Anthony Blair). It is a story told to him by his mother (Vina Hampton Blair).

"The American forces had captured a bridge from the Germans (perhaps it was the Ludendorff Bridge). In order to determine the strength of the bridge, the commanding officer called for the heaviest piece of equipment in his command to move forward and cross the bridge first. If the bridge held up under this heavy weight, then it likely would hold up for the remaining equipment and troops. If the bridge failed under this weight, then the commander's forces would still be intact and not divided on two sides of the river. If his forces became divided, then his forces could be more easily attacked by the enemy. The bridge did not collapse, so the commander's forces successfully crossed the bridge."

The following information was given to Anthony Blair by Scotty K. Caudill (grandson of Arnold Blair:

"I've got a Stars and Stripes about the bridge taking, and some other info I can scan and email to you. He had several stories, including how families kept the cattle inside the homes in Luxembourg, how dirty Paris was. He was haunted by having thrown a grenade in a foxhole....the young soldiers inside were waving a white flag. However, they were taught that was a directional signal for soldiers in the rear to fire.

"I've got German postcards, and a pamphlet detailing their operations in Belgium and Flanders. I used to have a Nazi youth armband and Mothers Cross he brought back, but have lost track of them. Among the medals he received were 3 Bronze Battle Stars."

SOURCES

Personal interviews by Anthony Blair

Scotty K. Caudill (grandson of Arnold Blair)

http://en.wikipedia.org/wiki/Battle_of_the_Bulge

http://www.fold3.com/s.php#s_given_name=Arnold&s_surname=Blair&offset=9&preview=1&t=829,825,765,893,823,896,750,796,858,831,848,95,493,878,894,476,477,489

Photos courtesy of Scotty K. Caudill

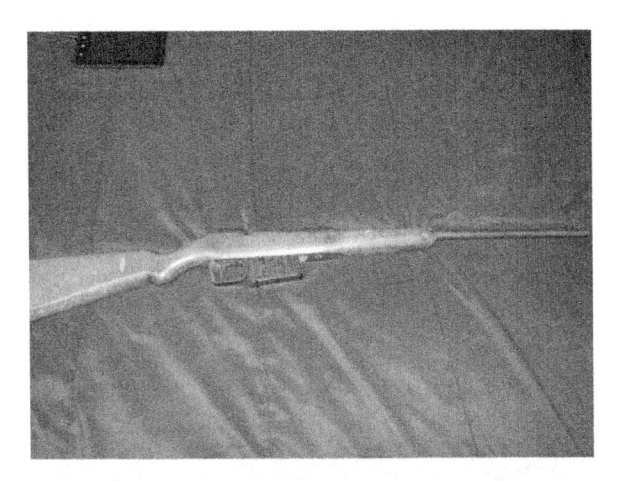

(Arnold's Rifle)

A SPECIAL TRIBUTE:
HONORING A TRUE AMERICAN HERO
Ben Buster Taylor
Command Sergeant Major
SGM E-9; U. S. Army, Special Forces

"To serve has been an honor and I would do it all again with pride, dignity and honor."
By Richard G. Brown and David Chaltas

I chose to add this current day American hero in an effort to pay homage to all those unsung warriors of yesterday and today. I recall several stories that he related to me but seldom did he discuss his contributions in preserving our freedom and heritage. When he did so, I felt they were for my ears only. I can still hear him call me his 'Little General' and honored me with a salute wherever he went. He was a modest man who served a cause in which he deeply believed while loving his southern heritage with the pride of a true southerner. In some ways he reminded me of Robert E. Lee, though I know he would quickly dismiss such a comparison. DPC

There are those that are born to be heroes. There are times when a man's shadow casts a much larger silhouette than others. Sometimes a hero comes along that is bigger than life. He was a hero that does not sing of his laurels nor rested upon them. He was a hero of the people that did all to serve others while denying himself. He was a hero that we all can emulate and be proud to say that we were honored by his presence. Sometimes a man overshadows his peers by his willingness to sacrifice all for what he believes. Such was the character of Ben Buster Taylor.

Ben Buster was a humble man of the mountains. He was born in a small community known as Millstone. It is in the southeastern portion of Kentucky, in Letcher County. It was a remote coal town that boomed as the coal industry blossomed and wielded when the coal was gone. Ben was born on June 20, 1928, to Ben Troy Taylor and Mattie Bates Taylor. Ben's father died when he was very young. According to an interview with Joe Bates, a lifelong friend Taylor was in the same line as Blaine Taylor in Whitaker (above Seco, KY). His mother was Mattie Bates Taylor. She was in the same Bates line as Martin Bates of Thornton, Kentucky.

Ben Buster was the grandson of C.R. Taylor and Sara Sergeant on his paternal side and William J. Bates and Lettie Hammons on his maternal side of the family. He was raised and grew up in the Millstone area, running the hills and hollers with his friends. He attended Millstone Grade School located 'only a stone's throw' from his boyhood home.

Joe Bates stated that Ben's mother, "Raised Ben and his sister by having a one room store on the old road in millstone in competition with the southeast commissary and she did well. Her little store was still going when the commissary closed."

Joe continued with the interview stating, "I moved to Millstone when I was twelve years old. Ben was eighteen or nineteen years old. He rode an Indian motorcycle. He was good to me and let me ride behind him, and from then on I admired him. He joined the army in 1948, on the way to Louisville to be sworn in he got into a fight on the bus, he bit the other fellow's fingers off and he was sent back to Millstone until 1949. Ben and I would come home on leave at the same time and spent most of our time in The Pound or Norton, Virginia, drinking and fighting whoever cared to take us on. We were both single until I was 30 and he was older before we settled down."

Upon reaching High School age, he attended Whitesburg High. But due to the hard times, dropped out and worked in the coalmines like his father and his father's father. He worked for Doc Bentley and Ben Bentley at the Consolidated Coal Company. He worked in what was known as the pony mines because ponies were used to pull the buggies in and out of the mines. He became disenchanted and quit that job and found employment with South East Coal Company near his home.

Ben had been impressed at seeing several men come home from World War II in their sharp uniforms. He especially liked the 'shiny boots'. When the Korean Conflict began he contemplated his next adventure. The mines were dangerous work and when he heard the Army paid $47.50 a month, he enlisted in the army at Whitesburg, Kentucky.

Ben was transported to Fort Knox, Kentucky, where he received basic training. After graduating basic training, he was sent to Fort Benning, Georgia, for Jump School. Upon completion of jump school, Ben decided to attend Ranger School, which was held at the same base. After successfully completing the training he was assigned to Fort Campbell with the 11th Airborne Division. In

October of 1950, he was sent to Korea as a member of Company A of 15th Regiment, 3rd Infantry Division. He served admirably in Korea from 1951-1952. Note the Korea War began on June 5, 1950, and ended on July 27, 1953.

Upon arrival in the Chron Valley (only railroad in Korea, ran north and south) he was thrust into combat the next day as a Rifleman, Private First Class. He soon became a squad leader. At that time, there were three main outposts for American soldiers in Korea: Tom, Dick and Harry. Ben was stationed at outpost Harry, which was west of White Horse Mountain and east of Old Baldy Mountain (American names). His first commander was Captain Eisenhower, son of President Eisenhower. Shortly thereafter, the captain was assigned to be a S3 Operation Officer.

The weather was bitterly cold; many days were below zero degrees. They were not adequately prepared for the cold, as they had not been issued appropriate winter clothing or equipment. They immediately constructed bunkers and trenches to be able to defend their position. At least twice a week the North Koreans and Chinese soldiers would conduct morning raids just before daylight. They would attack screaming, hollering and playing bugles, hoping to panic the American soldiers. When Ben was there, the American defensive perimeter lines were never broken. Ben would stay in this same area for most of the year.

After several weeks, Ben and his company finally received winter clothing, equipment and boots. The North Korean soldiers had better winter clothing than the Americans (Americans used heavy trench coats left over from World War 2) but their boots were not as good. The North Koreans also had better headgear with fur-lined hats and flaps that were better suited for the cold weather. One advantage of the steel pot helmets of the Americans though, was the use of being turned into heating ovens. The Americans would burn charcoal in the helmets to heat rations and to stay warm. Also on a positive note, the Americans sleeping bags were better than the Koreans or Chinese.

The enemy was equipped with AK 47 machine guns, rifles, and burp guns (these guns held 30 or 60 round clips). All of the enemy weapons performed well in the harsh winter conditions. The Americans were equipped with M-1 Garrands (nine round clip), M-30 carbines and one BAR (Browning automatic rifle) per company. The M-30 and M-1 were very dependable in the harsh conditions, but the BAR had to be kept clean and the ammunition kept clean to make it a dependable weapon. This was hard to do in bad weather. But through the summer months, all of the American's weapons were dependable.

To help counter the enemy attacks, the Americans started training South Korean soldiers to fight alongside them, placing a couple to each company. The main advantage of having Korean soldiers with the Americans was that they knew the language the enemy used. Most of the time before an enemy attack; the embedded Korean soldiers would hear the enemy's orders and inform their American counterparts. The drawback to having the Koreans with them was the Koreans never bathed and smelled bad. Their favorite food called 'Kimchi' had a foul order that seemed to permeate the pores. But the Koreans said that Americans smelled like 'spoiled milk'.

The company would stay on line for thirty to forty days, before being relieved for a couple of days. Also every thirty days the company would be resupplied and even less when they had been involved in heated conflicts with the enemy. No one would be permitted leave due to the Americans always being outnumbered. After being on the defensive line for several months, Ben was finally given five days of R & R and was sent to

Kurkia, Japan. The Japanese people treated the American soldiers very good and did not seem to have any animosity against them from World War II. The Company Ben served in did not have any fellow Letcher Countians in it and he hardly ever saw a familiar face from back home.

The enemy always greatly outnumbered the Americans and their leaders had no qualms about charging the American perimeters, knowing that there would be great loss of life. The outnumbered and outgunned Americans had to come up with something to even the odds. Ben had been a coal miner before joining the Army and had a working idea of explosives. He had seen the Air Force drop napalm on the attacking enemy during the day, warding off attacks. This resulted in the enemy attacking only at night when the planes could not be of much benefit to the American defenders. Ben requested a drum of the napalm to be delivered to his company.

As Ben had shown to be a resourceful soldier, his commander was agreeable to this request. Ben placed the drum of napalm several yards downhill from his defensive line and pointed the lid of the drum down the slope. He then placed detonating cord around the lid and a half of pound of TNT behind the drum. The detonating cord would blow open the lid of the drum and the TNT would force the napalm out plus igniting it. The first time this device was used against an attacking enemy force was a huge success. After that the device was set up all along the defensive lines of the Americans. After several episodes of this fiery weapon was used on the enemy, the attacks dropped off drastically. Even the Chinese couldn't afford to lose that many men plus it was getting harder and harder to get their men to charge up the slopes.

Unfortunately for Ben, when the regiment commander learned of his knowledge of explosives, he was assigned to clear mine fields. These mine fields were very dangerous and were usually not marked very well, even the ones that the Americans had placed. Ben soon learned to use "Bangalo" torpedoes to clear these mine fields. He would attach five or six of these torpedoes together, slide them into the minefield and detonate them. This was extremely dangerous work. Another technique to locate explosives was to use dogs. These dogs were held in the rear until needed, managed by their handlers. The dogs and handlers became intensely loyal to each other. This was apparent to Ben once when his squad was ambushed while using a dog team. The dog alerted the squad in time to save everyone but the dog handler. The intensiveness of the attack drove the squad back to the MLR (Main Line of Resistance), leaving the body of the handler and the dog. Ben and his squad went back to retrieve the body of the dog handler, after the attackers were driven off. The dog was still alive and would not allow anyone to touch or get close to his master's body. Apparently even the enemy soldiers had respect for such loyalty and left the dog alive to stay with his master. The body was only retrieved when a handler that knew the dog was allowed to attend to the situation.

After his stint at clearing minefields, Ben was given a squad to set up ambushes of the enemy at night. This would lead to one of his first reprimands. Vision at night in the mountains was very poor, especially on moonless nights. On one of these moonless nights, Ben and his squad set up an ambush on a road that was well known as the enemy route. During the night, the soldier that Ben had placed on point saw a large company of the enemy preparing to attack them. He shouted for help and the squad opened up on the alleged threat with everything that they had. When the morning sky began to lighten enough to see, there was no sign that an enemy force had ever been in the area. Squad Leader Taylor had a lot of explaining to do to a very angry company commander.

The first time that Ben would be involved in intelligence field was when he was ordered to report to an S-2 Intelligence Officer. Ben was ordered to ask some of his South Korean soldiers to volunteer for spying behind enemy lines. The assignment was extremely dangerous to the South Koreans that volunteered but the pay was very good which usually convinced them to accept the mission. The only condition was the money would not be given to them until they returned from the mission. The mission was dangerous for the Americans that retrieved the South Koreans at the MLR as well. Sometimes the South Koreans would be captured and persuaded to be a "turncoat" and switch loyalties. When they did this, the turncoat would bring an enemy squad with them that would ambush the Americans sent to retrieve them. Such is the price of fighting for one's country.

Late in the war, the Army began to establish PX for the soldiers to obtain personal items. One day a Bolivar watch was displayed. So many men wanted to buy it (including Ben) that the Commissary Officer put all of their names in a hat and drew one out. Ben was not the lucky name but he would later see the watch again. On his next mission, Ben approached a half-track armored vehicle that had taken a direct hit. On the arm of one of the victims was the watch that so many soldiers had wanted. Apparently the watch contained no luck.

Bill Powers was a fellow Korean War Veteran. He was from Winter Haven, Florida; He documented the following story as told to him by CSM Taylor.

"Sergeant First Class Ben Buster Taylor suffered more mental trauma than anyone I've ever known. He took me down to the personnel office and showed me the words written by a psychiatrist on his behalf. To paraphrase it, 'This record should show that Sergeant Taylor loves the Army, and has suffered beyond imagination for the pride he has in being a soldier. When he has problems, it should be remembered that he has this condition and it should be regarded as a badge of courage.' I had the good fortune to have had Taylor confide in me prior to a night jump when he was afraid. It made me feel so good to be able to assist this giant of a man.

"Once, when Ben Taylor and I were sitting around talking, and he was telling me about his old unit, the 7th Infantry Regiment of the 3rd Division, he told me of a tragic experience. He said that they were on patrol in the area of the Iron Triangle north of Pyongyang, and there were cliffs on one side of the trail. Taylor said that they could hear movement in a cave as they approached it. He said,

"You know, when they're in a solid rock cave, a fragmentation grenade often won't hurt them." The men in the patrol were all whispering to each other, "Willy Peter.....Willy Peter." Willy Peter is military slang for white phosphorous. So Taylor said that the patrol leader took a WP grenade and lobbed it inside the cave. He said they waited a few minutes, ready to shoot whoever came out of the cave. They were shocked to see two small children crawl out on fire. He said the patrol leader couldn't control the horror within himself for making such a terrible mistake. He said that he repeated, "I didn't know they were in there, did you?" And he kept repeating it again and again. They took the two children and the patrol leader back to an aid station."

In the winter of 1952, Ben received orders to report back to the United States because his enlistment would soon be up. He figured it was fitting that he arrived in winter and that he would leave in winter. When he left Korea, Ben had accumulated over $1,600. He had nothing to spend his pay on while stationed there and was looking forward to taking it home with him. He and other soldiers from various regiments boarded a huge troop transport ship that would take them across the Pacific Ocean to the United States. While traveling on the ship, life got boring and Ben began to gamble with his pay. Unfortunately he was not a very good gambler and by the time he arrived at San Francisco, he was completely broke. He had to wire his parents requesting money to be able to afford to come home on leave. It was a valuable but costly lesson and he did not gamble anymore.

After his leave was through, he returned to Fort Campbell, Kentucky, to rejoin the 11th Airborne again. He was offered a three hundred sixty dollar bonus if he would re-enlist for six years. As he was still broke from his gambling, he thought that was a lot of money and took the Army up on their offer.

When Ben arrived at Fort Campbell, he immediately began parachute training again. On his first jump back, he accidentally slapped his reserve chute along with his main chute, opening both. This naturally got him a chewing out when he landed on the ground. Things hadn't started off good for him but at least he had made it to the ground safe. During this time he was promoted to Sergeant First Class. He spent from 1953 to 1955 training at Fort Campbell and during this time applied for acceptance into the Special Forces. To be qualified for this newly formed unit, the requirements were very stringent. The applying soldier had to have secret clearance, been in combat, been a Ranger, and had been in Airborne.

The Green Berets were activated on September 16, 1953, at Fort Bragg, North Carolina. The first commander was Lieutenant Colonel Jack T. Shannon. The United States Army Special Forces are commonly known as the Green Berets due to the distinct color of their headgear. The Berets are made up of small groups of highly trained officers and non-commissioned officers, whose mission is to conduct "behind-the-lines" operations in enemy territory, reconnaissance, target acquisition and damage assessment, and precision strikes on strategic targets. Special Forces units have another unique mission. That mission is to train and operate insurgency and counter-insurgency units in the field. They carried out this mission with precision in Vietnam. They are well-schooled in foreign languages and customs, and are the units of choice when a training mission is done in another nation.

All of these requirements required cross training in many fields including weapons, demolitions, and intelligence. Ben had met all of the necessary requirements by his service in Korea and in 1956 was accepted as one of the first Special Forces candidates.

He was transferred to Fort Bragg, North Carolina, and was assigned to the 77th Special Forces Regiment. That entailed rigorous physical demands, which test the limits of endurance along with other skills necessary for survival. Special training in nonconventional warfare is the soul of being a Green Beret. He learned combat search and rescue, extraction, reconnaissance, counter proliferation, security, counter-mine operations and other skills needed to become a Beret. Ben Buster Taylor soon demonstrated that he would accept the dangers, hardships, being away from his family for the good of his beloved country to 'Free the Oppressed.' He earned his green beret and his wings.

The following information was retrieved from the 77th Special Forces Website: *"In 1960, the 77th was reorganized and re-designated as the 7th Special Forces Group. In the 1960s, the need for mobile training teams exceeded the capability of the US military, so the 7th Group provided the cadre for the 3rd and 6th Special Forces Groups. The 7th Group was active early in the Vietnam War, first operating in Laos (Operation White Star), and later in other Cold War operations in addition to South East Asia (Laos, Thailand, and South Vietnam)."*

The command structure is as follows: A Colonel is selected to be over the Battalions. Assisting the Colonel was the Command Sergeant Major (CSM). The group was usually made up of five battalions. Four of the battalions were Special Forces and one was the Support Battalion. They offered intelligence, medical and other pertinent services to the other Battalions.

Ben would spend the next three years training in several schools and locations. At Fort Benning, Georgia, he received advanced weapons training, at Fort Belvoid, Virginia, and training in demolition. At Fort Hollandbird, Virginia, he was assigned to training in intelligence. At Fort Bragg, North Carolina, once again he received training in parachuting, HALO (High Altitude and Low Opening) and at Key West, Florida, training in under water demolition. At Montera, California, he attended language school, learning Burmese, (he would later be in Burma).

In 1959, his first mission would be code named *White Star* (Operation Hot Foot), which was a classified assignment in Laos. Project White Star utilized the skills of the berets to train Royal Laotian Army and tribesmen to fight communism and later the North Vietnamese Army. LT. Colonel Arthur D. "Bull" Simons commanded the 107 man training team. Since Laos was considered 'neutral', the men did not wear military attire.

Ben's second mission would be in 1960, when he was dropped off the coast of Okinawa by a submarine (the USS Swordfish) that had originally picked him up in Japan. The five men crew paddled a raft to the Okinawa shore where they completed their mission, then paddled back into the ocean where they lassoed the periscope of the USS Swordfish. The submarine then rose up out of the water and picked up the squad. His next few missions would be parachute jumps into Thailand, Taiwan, Korea, and the Philippines. (While in Thailand he made friends with a monkey. The monkey had jumped on the train that he was riding).

Ben served two tours on Okinawa, one of eighteen months and one of twelve months. During this time he was stationed in a Special Forces camp that had been set up in bunkers that had been used during World War II to store kamikaze planes. Ben and other members of the Special Forces were the only people allowed to parachute onto Okinawa due to the winds. These were some of the scariest jumps that Ben participated in. While stationed here, Ben helped train Marines on the northern end of the island. Most of these trainings would be considered war games.

Ben stated that the island was one of the most beautiful places he had ever seen. He also would train and travel into Burma from Okinawa. He thought that Burma was as pretty as Okinawa. During his stay on the island, he weathered a few typhoons. These typhoons were very scary and Ben and his comrades of the Special Forces would lock themselves in their bunkers and get drunk, hoping to forget about the terrible storm churning outside. After a typhoon had passed, the air, and the water would be extraordinarily calm. The water would be so still and clear that you could see ships and planes that were on the ocean floor.

THE VIETNAM YEARS

Ben served four tours of duty in Vietnam. One of my favorite stories he shared was not of the war but of his pet monkey named Herman, the German. I recall two stories regarding Herman. One was that a monkey befriended him while he was on a train. He would come out of the trees and allow Ben to feed him. He climbed on Ben's shoulders and would chatter if someone got too close to his 'friend'.

My favorite story though is about Barney, the bear. While on patrol in Bien Hoa with the 5th Special Forces Contingent, he came across Malayan Sun Bear cubs. He took them back to their base. Unfortunately all of them died except for Barney. Being so young, Ben had to bottle feed him. Before long Ben's mother was shipping Letcher County honey for Ben to feed the bear cub. Ben and his bear soon received notoriety. The 5th were well known for their animals, including a tiger. It was later shipped to a zoo in Atlanta. Ben would not even consider having Barney placed in a zoo. Through his connections he was able to get Barney sent to Fort Bragg where he lived for several years as their mascot. Barney and Ben were even featured in a 1970 edition of a Green Beret magazine! Fort Bragg thought so much of Barney that when he died, they had him mounted and can still be seen at the Special Forces museum.

On June 20, 1952, the first of the Special Forces groups, the 10th Special Forces Group, was activated at Fort Bragg, North Carolina. It became the nucleus of the Special Warfare Center, now known as the John F. Kennedy Center for Military Assistance. It is located at Fort Bragg. The next unit to be formed was the 77th Special Forces Group, which was also activated at Fort Bragg, on September 25, 1953.

By July 1954, the U.S. Military Assistance Advisory Group MAAG), Vietnam, numbered three hundred forty-two. Ben was among those numbers. In October of that year President Dwight D. Eisenhower promised direct aid to the government of South Vietnam. From 1954 to 1956 Viet Minh cadres were forming action committees to spread propaganda and to organize the South Vietnamese to oppose their own government. In July of 1955 the People's Republic of China announced an agreement to aid the Viet Minh, and the Soviet Union announced aid to Hanoi.

U.S. Special Forces troops officially worked in Vietnam for the first time in 1957. On June 24, 1957, the 1st Special Forces Group was activated on Okinawa, and in the course of the year a team from this unit trained fifty-eight men of the Vietnamese Army at the Commando Training Center in Nha Trang. The trainees would later become the core, as instructors and cadre, for the first Vietnamese Special Forces units. CSM Taylor four tours of duty in Vietnam served the cause of America's call to arms with honor and dignity worthy of an American icon.

I would be remiss if I did not share a couple of personal stories told to me by 'Jake', or as I prefer to call him, 'Uncle Ben'. One dealt with Ben being home and went to Wise with his dog. During the course of the evening gaieties, he got into a fight and whipped a couple of men before being taken to jail. The next day he talked to the sheriff. Being well known, the sheriff stated something to the affect that Ben had given those boys a run for their money. Ben apologized and asked what the fine was. The sheriff said 'nothing.' Ben then inquired about his dog and the sheriff said, "Oh he is in the next cell." Ben asked if he could get him back and the sheriff smiled and said, "Sure, his fine is five hundred dollars."

Another story told by others to me was regarding Ben when he was very sick with brain cancer. He treasured his lovely wife Mona and believed in chivalry. He had taken her to a restaurant to eat and as she was getting a salad, a man rudely reached over her plate. Ben took exception to that and informed the man of his rudeness. The man became defiant and Ben told him that after he ate his dinner he would gladly talk to him outside. The man waited with a friend on Ben. Ben excused himself from his lovely bride and proceeded to teach a lesson desperately needed on rudeness and appropriate protocol in the front of a lady. Both men licked their wounds on their way back to their car. This was just prior to his passing. It gives insight into the creed of a green beret.

Army Career Span: 1949-1972
He served admirably in Korea from 1951-1952.
Selected by President John F. Kennedy for Special Forces Ranger Unit

Ben Buster Taylor also served in the following units:

11th Airborne Division
101st Airborne
187 R.C.T. Ranger Company
3rd Division Korea

Served in the following countries:
Japan, Okinawa, Korea, Burma, Philippines, Taiwan, Laos, Vietnam, Cambodia

Combat Time:
Burma-3 months
Kano, Nigeria-2 months
Laos-1 month

Two Wars:
Vietnam War-4 tours
Korean War-14 months

State Side Duty:

Ft. Campbell, Kentucky 11th Aabn
Ft. Bragg, N. C. 77th Ranger School
Ft. Devens, Massachusetts, 10th S. F. G.
Camp Hale, Colorado Mt. Climbing School
Key West Florida Scuba Diving School
Ft. Bragg, N. C. Halo School
Ft. Blevins, Virginia Demolition School

Ft. Benning, Georgia Weapons School
Monterey, California Language School

He was a Paratrooper, Ranger and served in the Special Forces for 22 years.

Ben had over 300 jumps under his belt. Jumps included 25,000 ft

Ben received many awards including: Bronze Stars (4), ribbons (18), medals (24) and decorations (Oak Leaf Clusters, Soldier's Medal) during his career. The one he was most proud of was being selected as an honor guard for President John F. Kennedy's Funeral. His letters from distinguished Veterans such as General W. C. Westmoreland and General William Evans-Smith (Special Forces Commander) were treasured by him.

I once asked him what he would consider to be his greatest moment. Uncle Ben paused for a moment to gather his thoughts. He looked at me and then into the distance. He said that his finest moment was also the saddest. It was when he received word of the assassination of President John F. Kennedy on November 22, 1963. America's innocence was shattered on that day.

Ben Buster Taylor was in a mess hall eating with other members of the 7th Special Forces Group when a radio station announced that President John F. Kennedy had been assassinated. Less than two and one half hours later, he and thirty-four other Green Berets were boarding a plane from Ft. Bragg, North Carolina, for a flight to Washington, D.C... There they were assigned to stand guard over Kennedy's coffin. They were issued complete new uniforms and new boots. Ben stated that the men had to stand up the entire flight so that they would not get their uniforms wrinkled.

Sergeant Taylor said his mind ran with imaginings of a possible conspiracy and what if our country would be invaded by a foreign power. He didn't have time to really think. He was also notified that he had been selected as one of the six honor guard for the funeral procession. Kentucky's finest had been given the last honor by the Kennedys who had supported and created the berets.

Sergeant Taylor and most of the other Green Berets who helped guard the President had just returned to the United States from a mission in Southeast Asia. While Special Forces troops didn't usually participate in such occasions, Taylor said they served as part of President Kennedy's honor guard, "Because his brother (Senator Robert Kennedy) requested us to. President Kennedy was proud of us and considered us as his unit."

In fact, it was President Kennedy who authorized use of the Green Beret as a symbol of courage. Prior to this the beret was considered not to be of a uniform and the men could be disciplined if caught wearing one. In 1962, when President Kennedy visited Ft Bragg, Colonel William Yarborough greeted him wearing a beret. The hat impressed the president. By executive order he made the beret something to aspire to earn.

When asked about the honor of escorting the president the final mile, Ben gave me a copy of the article written in the Mountain Eagle. He said it exemplified his position. *"It was a pleasure and an honor for me to be chosen, but it was a very, very sad situation."* He said. *"We were trained to be hard core, but it was tough to keep from getting all choked up, especially the night Caroline (President Kennedy's daughter) came in and kneeled down and kissed the coffin."* Taylor also recalls John John (President Kennedy's son) coming into the "rotunda with his mother. He was dressed in a little brown coat and short pants."

Among the things Uncle Ben remembered most about the four days were a lack of sleep and, *"The pain of having to stand at attention so long."* While Kennedy's body lay in state inside the Capitol rotunda, his coffin was guarded by five soldiers representing the five branches of the military. Taylor said they had to stand at full attention and count to one hundred, then stand at parade rest and count to one hundred, until a changing of the guard that occurred every thirty minutes.

Sgt. Ben Taylor said the closest he came to making a mistake during the ceremony was while he was marching near the front of the caisson that carried Kennedy's body to Arlington National Cemetery in Virginia. Blackjack was the Caparisoned horse, which is always riderless and follows the caissons (six white horses pulling the cart carrying the remains of the fallen). Blackjack had a grand cavalry saddle, sword, and backward boots in the stirrups. This symbol represented our fallen leader, President Kennedy. Uncle Ben stated that the horse was acting up and difficult to handle. They had a hard time controlling Blackjack, which made it hard to keep in step because the horse kept attracting the marching soldiers' attention.

The honor guard practiced to perfection and upon that sad day they attended to the casket, as they walked beside the caisson pulled by a team of horses. He recalled offering his condolences to Mrs. Kennedy and how his heart ached for the Kennedy children. He told me that the muffled sound of the drums somehow added a somber dignity to the procession. The boots hitting the pavement offered a forlorn rhythm to the occasion. He told me he did not notice the thousands upon thousands of people lined up along the procession route. His mind was upon the higher calling and wanted to make the Kennedy family, along with the nation proud of his small part in honoring our fallen President. Such was the humbleness of this warrior.

He talked of Blackjack and the manner in which his handler was beaten up from that spirited animal. He touched the boots turned backwards in the stirrups, which represented our fallen president, He recalled the salute of a child to his father.

Though 'hard core', Uncle Ben dropped his head as he fought back tears. He told me that the realization of what had transpired when they made it to Arlington. He struggled to state that America would never be the same. Then he straightened up his aging body. I for a brief moment glanced into the eyes of history. Not a word was spoken. I saw before me not an aged warrior but rather a warrior's spirit and one who would give his life for his country. I saw an undeclared pride in that he was honored and humbled to be a part of history's immortal moments.

I choked back the tears as I recalled being in my junior high school history class when Mr. Back came into the room and announced that the President of the United States had been shot. I let out an involuntary groan and said, "What: no." Everyone cried. Here, in front of me was a man who lived the experience. He had touched the caisson and casket. He had shaken the hand of the Kennedys and offered his condolences. He saluted the fallen president as he was laid to rest in that beautiful cemetery once belonging to the Lee family. He was a true American hero. He was a Green Beret.

In the November 20, 2013, edition of the Mountain Eagle, a special front page tribute to Sgt Taylor was given fifty years after the procession. This was two days after the assassination of the President of the United States. A picture of the six white horses, caisson and the coffin of the late president showed the Letcher County Green Beret as the third person marching behind the horses.

The eagle reported that, "He served as an honor guard in the procession going from the White House on Sunday to the Capitol rotunda. He marched beside the caisson bearing the President's body on Sunday and again on Monday. When the cortege reached Arlington cemetery, the Special Forces Group, which included Sgt. Taylor, stood by the grave site where the Kennedy family, statesmen and kings and queens walked to the President's grave.

"Sgt. Taylor, who is not stationed at Fort Bragg, recently returned from Vietnam. He is with the Special Forces Group in the Army.

"After returning from Washington, he called home and said words could not express the deep respect and sorrow shown for the President."

I had the honor of reading the comments of one. General Evans-Smith wrote, *"You have personified the high degree of image of the Special Forces trooper and have demonstrated to your colleagues and the general public the mark of a true professional and dedicated soldier. Be assured that the pride and appreciation you felt in personally being able to honor our fallen President was mirrored by Special Forces personnel the world over, and most especially by your comrades in the 7th Special Forces Group. You have displayed your badge of honor, the Green Beret, to the highest echelons of our government, the heads of foreign countries and the world's populace."*

"To Serve has been an honor and I would do it all again with pride, dignity and honor."
Ben Buster Taylor

The Honorable Senator from Kentucky, Mitch McConnell, paid tribute to the heroics of 'Uncle Ben'.

Ben would have been humbled by such accolades. The following are his words.

"Mr. President, I rise today to pay tribute to an outstanding Kentuckian, Ben ``Buster'' Taylor, a retired Special Forces sergeant major and former Letcher County Sheriff. Sergeant Major Taylor is not one to brag about his accomplishments, but he should be honored for his courageous and selfless acts during the two decades he spent serving this Nation in the U.S. military.

"In 1950, inspired by the heroism of World War II veterans, Taylor joined the United States Army's 11th Airborne Division at Camp Campbell, KY, which is now known as Fort Campbell. As he worked his way through various divisions, the Army began organizing its Special Forces Branch, the Green Berets. Taylor enthusiastically joined the Green Berets and spent the better part of two decades serving with his comrades in Japan, Korea, Thailand, Taiwan, the Philippines, Burma, China, Laos, and Vietnam.

"Taylor's missions exemplified his bravery and altruism. During his tours of duty, he was awarded 24 medals and 18 ribbons, among these four bronze stars. With each honor, a story revealing his heroism is told. He has notebooks full of citations and commendations that tell of the many times he risked his own life to save others. But of all these honors, the one most memorable to Taylor is the role he played in the funeral of President John F. Kennedy. Taylor was selected to represent the Green Berets at President Kennedy's funeral. He walked alongside the casket of the fallen

Commander in Chief. Today I ask my colleagues to join me in honoring and recognizing a true American hero, Sergeant Major Ben Taylor."

One of the many officers who had met Command Sergent Major Taylor was G. D. Guthrie, Colonel, U. S. Army. Colonel Guthrie is a veteran with over twenty-two years of service. He was Director of Center for Army Leadership, and served three and half years as a government contractor. He was a government contractor with two major defense companies. His role was Project Officer and Project Manager. Colonel Guthrie wrote a letter to the Mountain Eagle which captures the very essence of Ben's character and love of country.

Remembering Ben 'Buster' Taylor
To the Editor:

"On January 4, 2008, it was my privilege and honor to witness the burial of CSM (R) Ben "Buster" Taylor in plot 64 of Arlington National Cemetery. It was clear, cold, windy day unable to shake or quiver the professionalism of the soldiers from the 3rd U.S. Infantry (the Old Guard) and the Masons that helped to lay to rest Ben Buster.

"As I stood there, I wondered if the citizens of Letcher County realized what a tremendous loss to our nation the passing of Ben Taylor was.

"Around me were men Ben had served with in the fields of Vietnam. I wondered what stories they could tell about the experience of serving with "Jake". Ben told me the first time I met him in the old Whitesburg Post Office (former site of the Letcher County Veterans Museum) that his nickname when he was a soldier was "Jake."

"Ben was in the first U.S. Army unit designated as a Special Forces unit. Special Forces are often the first in and last out. They operate in 12-man teams working with indigenous forces trying to mold and shape U.S. foreign policy. Their tasks are thankless and their motto is "de oppresso liber" - free from oppression. They are the silent warriors that protect our nation and its way of life. Ben was one of the founding members of this elite group of warriors that today serve across the world helping to liberate from oppression.

"As many folks in Letcher County know, Ben was selected to be the Army Special Forces representative to help escort President Kennedy's caisson from the U.S. Capitol building to its interment. In the visitor center of Arlington National Cemetery is a picture of President Kennedy's casket (on the caisson) with members of the Department of Defense escorting it. If you look real close, you can see a Green Beret (Ben "Buster" Taylor). In an organization of so many special people (all volunteers), what kind of man is selected to represent a unique breed of warrior? What kind of soldier represents those silent professionals is arguably one of the greatest moments of grief in our nation's history - the funeral of President John F. Kennedy? The answer is Ben "Buster" Taylor.

"Ben went on to achieve the rank of command sergeant major (CSM), the highest enlisted rank a soldier can achieve. In order to achieve that rank he was promoted nine times. In order for an officer to be promoted nine times he/she would have to achieve the rank of lieutenant general. How many people get promoted nine times in their job? Ben "Buster" was a silent warrior and his career as a soldier epitomized those special and unique abilities required for success as a Special Forces professional.

"I only met Ben twice (both times in Whitesburg). He was older and did not move as fast as he once did, but his eyes were intense and focused. He was a soldier that served four tours in Vietnam and one in Korea. Five years away from his beloved eastern Kentucky in a 22-year career."

"I have served in four wars (Operation Just Cause, Operation Desert Shield and Desert Storm, Enduring Freedom and Iraqi Freedom) and I know what a soldier looks and acts like. I have led men into combat and seen what men must do in war. I was humbled to be in his presence. Only time and cancer could do what no man was able to do to this silent warrior - defeat his body.

"Our nation is lesser because of his loss. I only hope there is some young man or woman in the hills of eastern Kentucky that will pick up the torch of freedom that Ben "Buster" so courageously carried.

"My greatest fear is when my day of reckoning comes and I meet my maker, I see CSM Ben "Buster" Taylor guarding the pearly gates. Before I can get to see God and stand before the book of life, I must pass through Ben "Buster". I only hope my life as a soldier and a man can stand up to the scrutiny of a Special Forces soldier that lived, loved and served our nation as honorably and courageously as he did. "Ben "Buster", until we meet again, may God hold you in the palm of his hand."

Uncle Ben, your silver wings have now been replaced with ones of gold. DPC

Ben's legacy lives on through not only the Military Museum but through those he continues to inspire. One such person is a young lady by the name of Shai Boyd. When she was a senior she spent a few months interviewing Veterans, people who knew the Sergeant Major and Ramona Taylor, Ben's lovely wife. She won first place in the senior exhibit category at the state National History Day Competition in Frankfort with her exhibit entitled, Ben Buster Taylor: Legend of Letcher County. In an interview with the Mountain Eagle Shai stated, "There are a lot of people who deserve to be honored and if I had to pick one it would be Ben Buster Taylor," she said. "He is the ultimate soldier. He was just so humble about everything he did. "

After leaving the military, Taylor owned and operated a trucking company before being elected sheriff of Letcher County. In 2004, he established the Letcher County Veterans Memorial Museum, where he spent countless hours gathering military related memorabilia for public viewing. I recall being in the museum and Ben on the phone to somebody in the military telling them what he needed. Within a couple of weeks whatever he asked for arrived including a tank, jeep, deuce and a half, rocket launcher and other countless items.

Ben Buster Taylor died December 12, 2007, after a long battle with cancer. He was seventy-one years of age. His ashes were buried with full military honors on January 4, 2008, at Arlington National Cemetery. An empty chair will forevermore be placed at the table to honor and pay homage to a Letcher County giant of a man who walked amongst us.

SOURCES

http://news.google.com/newspapers?nid=2218&dat=20071226&id=rt4kAAAAIBAJ&sjid=gxAGAAAAIBAJ&pg=1821,3921265

http://www.themountaineagle.com/news/2008-01-30/opinion/020.html

hbehttp://books.google.com/books?id=ZGb80RBLHxcC&pg=PA17033&lpg=PA17033&dq=command+sgt+major+ben+buster+taylor&source=bln-taylor/

http://usacacblogs.army.mil/cgscstudentblog/2012/08/285/

p://capitolwords.org/date/2004/07/22/S8646-2_tribute-to-sergeant-major-ben-taylor/

http://usacac.army.mil/cac2/cal/repository/GuthrieBio.pdf

Interviews with SGT MAJOR TAYLOR by David Chaltas/Richard Brown

http://www.koreanwar-educator.org/memoirs/powers_bill/

http://www.themountaineagle.com/news/2009-06-03/features/064.html

http://www.eglin.af.mil/units/7specialforcesgroup/index.asp

http://www.eglin.af.mil/library/factsheets/factsheet.asp?id=19911

http://en.wikipedia.org/wiki/Operation_White_Star

http://ky-family.blogspot.com/2008/12/ben-buster-taylor.html

The Mountain Eagle; November 1963

Letcher Soldier was there 50 years ago; The Mountain Eagle; Wednesday, November 20, 2013; Volume 106; Number 38

"Taylor Recalls Four Days Guarding Kennedy Casket," Ben Gish; The Mountain Eagle, November 23, 1988

"Remembering Ben 'Buster' Taylor;" Guthrie, Lt. Colonel G.D. U.S. Army. The Mountain Eagle, January 30, 2008; Section A, Page 5.

http://en.wikipedia.org/wiki/Korean_War

http://en.wikipedia.org/wiki/Vietnam_War

BENNETT JONATHAN ADAMS
3rd BN, 6th Marines
Kilo Company WPNS PH
Unit 73300
EPO-AE-09509-3300
Anti Tank Assaultman
US Marine
By Tammy Baker Cook (mother)

I vividly remember Jonathan. He was the son of my former aide and fellow educator. He and his sister Amanda came into our classroom every evening when attending West Whitesburg and Whitesburg Middle School. He was full of life and I do believe I taught him a few pranks to play on his sister. On occasion they played them on me. They grew up under my feet and became a part of my heart. As a young boy he stated he wanted to become a Marine. He fulfilled his dream with honor.

U.S. Marine Bennett Jonathan Adams graduated Feb. 24, 2004, from Marine Basic training at Parris Island, S. C. He left on March 23, 2005, for first tour in IRAQ. He returned home in seven months in October, 2005. He was stationed in Jacksonville, North Carolina, for seven months and deployed for second tour in Iraq May, 2006.

His military education was Anti Tank Assaultman CRS (035), 2006 and Tan Belt CRS (MMB) 2005. He received an HONORABLE discharge in release Certificate in 2008 with Period Commences.

Adams is a 2003 graduate of Whitesburg High School and attended the School of Infantry East at Camp Geiger at Camp Lejeune, North Carolina. Adams primary specialty in Iraq served as Assaultman for two years and eight months.

While deployed Adams received the following awards:

Combat Action Ribbon (Iraq)
Sea Service Deployment Ribbon (2nd award)
Iraq Campaign Medal (with one Bronze Service Star)
Global War on Terrorism Service Medal
National Defense Service Medal
Navy Unit Commendation, Rifle Qualification Badge (Expert)
Pistol Qualification Badge (Sharpshooter)
Good Conduct Medal

Bennett Jonathan Adams is the son of Tammy and Steve Cook, Bennett and Paula Adams of Ermine, He is the Grandson of Bennett and Brenda Adams of Ermine, and Gertrude and the late Gene Baker of Camp Branch. He has three sisters and one brother.

(Bennett Jonathan Adams, Bennett Shade Adams and Gabriella Howard Adams)

BILLIE McFALL
Private First Class
?-August 1, 1950

The Mountain Eagle covered the dedication of the Millstone Bridge on August 1, 2008. The bridge honors the memory of Billie McFall who was killed in action while serving in the Korean War.

A re-dedication ceremony and ribbon-cutting for the Private First Class Billie McFall Bridge on KY 113 at Millstone has been set for Friday, August 1, at 11 a.m. at the site of the new bridge. The date is exactly 58 years after McFall, a Letcher County native, died on the battlefield in Korea. What used to be called the Millstone-Democrat Bridge was re-named by the Kentucky Transportation Cabinet at the request of Letcher County veterans groups. Veterans asked the Letcher Fiscal Court for a resolution naming the structure the PFC Billie McFall Bridge.

> PFC McCall was the first Letcher County native confirmed to have been killed in action during the Korean War. He "gave his all" on August 1, 1950.

The ceremony will begin and end with canon fire conducted by the Sons of Confederate Veterans of Letcher County. The keynote speaker for the event is James Duncan, himself a Korean War veteran and the only surviving Letcher County native held as a prisoner of war during the conflict. He shared his experiences while a POW in a Chinese Prison Camp. Duncan was in captivity for thirty-two months.

SOURCES

Mountain Eagle July 23, 2008

http://korean-war-casualties.findthedata.org/l/1994/Billie-E-Mcfall

http://kdl.kyvl.org/catalog/xt7xwd3pwg1d_1/text

BILLY WAYNE BRIDGEMAN
Sergeant
B Company
5th Battalion
7th Cavalry
1st Cavalry Division
Medical Specialist
October 5, 1946-May 3, 1968

I couldn't find very much about Billy except through his friends who posted things about him. I will continue my search in order to honor this unsung hero. One comment was from a high school friend. *"I remember Billy Wayne as we called him from school days at Virgie Hi. He was a good kid and it is so sad for his family to have lost him. I think of him often especially anything I see concerning Vietnam. May God bless"*. Jimmie Bates Louisville, Kentucky. A cousin posted, *"Dear Billy, I just thought I would send you a letter to heaven to say we all miss you, you were my*

2nd cousin. I remember the summer you came and spent with us in Catlettsburg, and I was 12...Like so many, you were so young, too young to die. love-your cousin," M. Diamond. Bob Camp stated, *"Billy my thoughts are about you and Jesse and that terrible day in the A Shau Valley. You were a good man and took care of us well...I will always remember you."*

The letter which touched me most was from the girl who was going to marry Billy upon his return from Vietnam. The following is by Mae Johnson Bentley: *"Billy and I were to be married as soon as he got home. We were counting the days. I know it has been over 31 years, but I still love him with all my heart. I would love to hear from people who knew Billy.*

From such letters, one can build a picture of Billy Wayne. He was a typical young man; filled with promise. He was friendly and well liked. He had aspirations of being married and becoming a family man. He was interested in the military and moved up in rank quickly. He was well liked by the men in his platoon and company. Billy Wayne was from Virgie, Kentucky. His service number is 51644094. His tour date was November 16, 1967.

Sergeant Bridgeman was assigned to Headquarters Company, 5th Battalion; 7th Cavalry. For some reason Sergeant Bridgeman was in the field with Bravo Company. During the mission they encountered the enemy and a firefight occurred. Sergeant Bridgeman, along with Corporal Jesse Carmona of Bay City, Michigan, died from hostile gunshot wounds while in Thua Thien. Two other men died on that Friday, May 3, 1968 date. They were Private First Class Dervin J. Keisling from Ephrata, Pennsylvania. He was twenty-three years of age. Private First Class John E. Manson was twenty-one at the time of his death. He was from Des Moines, Iowa.

Sergeant Bridgeman's body was recovered and he is buried in the Frank Martin Cemetery, Pike County, Kentucky. The cemetery is located on State Route 122, Indian Creek .Take graveled road beside house Number 762, Indian Creek Road. Cemetery is on the right side. Sergeant Bridgeman's name is listed on Panel 54E, Line 022 of the Vietnam Memorial Wall. He is an unsung hero…

SOURCES

http://www.virtualwall.org/db/BridgemanBW01a.htm

http://www.fold3.com/page/93135737_billy_wayne_bridgeman/

http://vietnam-asualties.findthebest.com/l/36798/Billy-Wayne-Bridgeman

http://www.vietnamwarcasualties.org/index.php?page=directory&rec=5598

BOBBY GEORGE FIELDS
Staff Sergeant
Charlie Company
1st Battalion
7th Cavalry
1st Cavalry Division
USARV
Army of the United States
Blackey, Kentucky
Vietnam Memorial Wall, Panel W7, Line 83
November 29, 1944-September 22, 1970

While surfing the internet and the Vietnam Memorial Wall for basic information regarding Bobby George Fields, I was aghast as to the lack of data available. There was a brief summation of his name, rank and other data but one could not conjure up an image of his character. I felt compelled to do so.

I had known Bob most of my life. He was a close friend to my uncle Charlie, Granville, and Dennis. He visited with them often. I was living with them at the time and recall sitting around listening to them talk. One of his artworks still proudly hangs on the wall of their house. It is a picture of a woodpecker that Bobby drew while in high school.

Bob's parents live between the bridges, on route 7. Their house was only a couple of miles from Blackey, Kentucky. They also owned a home in the Detroit area.

My uncles had a store next to Jean's Dairy Bar and for some reason relocated their grocery store between the bridges. Bob's home was in close proximity and he hung around there as most of us did in our youth.

Bobby went to school at St. Robinson and when the new high school was built, he attended Letcher High School. It was within walking distance from his home but most of the time he rode the bus. He was an upper classmate, being three years older than I. Most of us came to school early. I walked because I lived in a holler close to the school. The distance was just under a mile. When I arrived at school I would hang out in the halls with all the guys and girls. I floated from group to group at times and on occasion be with Bobby, Joe Duke, Joe Steely, James Crase and others. Of course I was the young one and picked on but it was all in good fun. I must admit I did my share of picking and pranks. I used to get into their lockers and fix the books so they would fall out on the floor when they opened them. I greased the handles of their lockers. Bob and Joe would get so mad and chase me but I was swift of foot. At least he made me feel that way. It was a great game.

I recall my graduation and not having any plans. I didn't know what I was going to do. Bob came up to my uncles while I was visiting them (I was now living in my own house) and stated he was going to Detroit for the summer. He mentioned he wanted company on his trip to Michigan. I said I was interested and before I knew it, we were traveling to Detroit. We went to his home and I stayed that night. The next morning I went to Ecorse and got a job as a stock boy for a local store. I even had a one room apartment. Within a week I had another job making bullets for a little known war called Vietnam.

Bob came out on occasion and we visited White Castle, which was next to the Detroit River. I worked that summer and wondered what I was going to do. Bob came to see me and stated the next weekend he was going back to college at Pikeville. He wondered did I want to go back to Kentucky. I was ready because I did not like the city life. On the appointed day he came and got me. We went to his parents' house and ate. His mother packed up the left over's and off we went.

I will never forget the trip. It was so hot. We traveled with the windows down but the air offered little relief. That night the fog was so thick it was hard to drive due to the poor visibility. I could feel the moisture from the fog on my hand whenever I stuck it out the window. As we traveled we talked and Bob mentioned Pikeville College. He asked had I thought of going to college and I told him I had but didn't have the money. He told me about how you could work and pay on your tuition. I told him I would think about it.

We arrived in the early morning hours. I didn't want to wake up my uncles so I went on up to the old house. I admit I was scared because of having to walk up the hill and it being dog days for snakes. I ran up to the porch and went inside. I slept in the side room with a fan in the window until about eleven that day.

I saw Bob on and off the next few days. I stopped at my usual haunt, Jean's restaurant. She inquired about my attending college and I said I wasn't sure. That was not good enough answer for her. She said I needed to go to school so I could make a living. I said I would think about it.

The Sunday before Pikeville started I was up at my old shack. I got busy doing something and before I knew it, I hear a knock on my door. I went to it and standing there was Darrell Hampton, Jean's husband. He said she wanted to see me. I knew I had to go because she wouldn't take no for an answer. I went with him in his Rabbit to their home. Jean greeted me with that beautiful smile and asked me why wasn't I in school. I didn't tell her I didn't have the money to go and made up a bogus excuse. She told me to get in the car. She and her husband took me out of the holler and talked to me about the importance of an education. They said they would watch my old home place and before I knew it we pulled up to the college. Darrell went to talk to someone and apparently they had papers for me to attend showing I had completed my senior year of high school. Within a little while I was enrolled. Jean opened the trunk area and had a suitcase. Darrell gave me $100 and said I couldn't pay him back except by getting an education.

I was in shock. I was taken to my room and Wayne Bowling, who had graduated with Joe Duke, was my roommate. The next morning I found out that Bobby and Joe roomed down the hall from me. I discovered several of my old friends were there. Richard Smith, Gary Caudill, and Rick Caudill were in close proximity.

There wasn't a day I didn't go to Bob and Joe's room. I must admit I tortured them! Their room was very close to the showers and I would 'visit' them. Once I had a box of salt wrapped in a towel and as they studied, I allowed the salt to 'sprinkle on their sheets. That night I woke up to a loud knock and when I opened the door, a gallon of water went everywhere. Wayne made me mop it up because he knew I had pulled a prank on someone. That year we continued little games until one of them would get mad and run us off for awhile.

I rode home with Bob on occasion. I do recall college graduation and him receiving a degree in art. Joe Duke was class president and had a promising career ahead of him. Wayne went on and became a lawyer. Bobby decided to teach.

He was hired by the Perry County School System and taught there as an art instructor. Then the draft was implemented. The last time I saw Bobby was at my uncle's home. He came and informed us that he would be leaving for the army in a couple of days. He gave Uncle Dennis a picture he had painted and talked about the days we spent at the store, playing football in Martin Joe Adams' house, riding with him to Detroit, going to Pikeville College, and our conversations at Uncle Granville and Dennis's store and/or the house.

I emailed Regina Blair Brown (Bob's niece) and she contacted Doreen Calhoun (Regina's mother who is Bob's sister). Mrs. Calhoun stated the following: *"I appreciate that article you have written about Bobby. Just a few notes: He graduated from Eastern State University, if my memory serves me correctly. He was an avid fisherman and hunter. While working in the factory in Detroit, he took a correspondence course in art and I think that is mostly what made his mind up to go into art. In his papers after his death was a letter from the Perry County Board of Education to the Draft Board. They asked that Bobby be exempted because art teachers were so scarce. Bobby told me before he let that he wasn't going to turn it in because he felt like it was his duty to go to the army. He said that too many had fled to Canada to avoid the draft. Thanks for everything."* Mrs. Doreen Calhoun

If I ever had any doubts on Bob's character (which I did NOT) that statement of love of duty, honor and country says it all about the man. I do not believe I would have become the man I am this day if it had not been for Bob's inspiration. My cousin, Russell Blair recalls the following: *"Bobby Fields and Bobby Steely were in basic at Knox together. I was able to visit them a few times while there. We all went to Ireland Army Hospital at Ft. Knox to visit Joe Steely who was there recovering from a leg wound."*

Bob was born on November 29, 1944. He was the son of Johnny and Oma Hampton Fields. Bob was never married. He was a Baptist in faith. He gave his life for his country on September 22, 1970, in Military Zone 3, Phuoc Long, Vietnam. His body was recovered and now rests at the Whitaker Cemetery, just off Route 7. Whitaker Cemetery is located between the bridges. He was twenty-five years of age. The Ben Caudill Camp #1629 erected a flag pole by his grave to honor his memory. The cemetery contained a Veteran from every war at the time the flag poles were set. They fly proudly over many unsung heroes.

POSTSCRIPT: A grave injustice has been given to Bobby. He is listed as being killed by friendly fire. Men such as Peyton Reynolds, who served with Bobby, stated he died when the NVA fired upon a helicopter and missed but unfortunately hit Bobby's location. They were there and know what happened. He deserves at least a Bronze Star if not a Silver one.

SOURCES

Interview with Darlene Calhoun (sister)

Personal recollections: Russell Blair & D. Chaltas

http://www.fold3.com/page/631175469_bobby_george%20fields/details/

http://thewall-usa.com/

http://vietnam-casualties.findthedata.org/l/31745/Bobby-George-Fields

http://www.vetfriends.com/memorial/honoree.cfm?hindex=54897#.UzMv3KhdUzI

http://www.vi

BRENT WOODS
SERGEANT
Company B
9th U. S. Cavalry
Buffalo Soldier
Indian Wars
Recipient of the Medal of Honor
1855- March 31, 1906

Brent Woods was born in Pulaski County, Kentucky, in 1855. He was a slave on a farm near Somerset. He lived as a slave for the first ten years of his life when the thirteenth amendment of the Constitution was passed. He died a free man while proving himself on a national scale. One article stated that he joined the army at age eighteen while another said he was twenty-four. He walked to Louisville and was assigned into what would become the renowned Buffalo Soldiers. He was in Company B of the 9th Cavalry.

This youthful Kentucky man was sent out west to fight Indians. He was paid thirteen dollars a month to do so. His job entailed escorting wagons, protecting settlers from raids, working on the telegraph lines and attempting to keep frontier towns from self destruction. Noting that prejudice and racism still abounded as far away as the west, it is amazing how well the Buffalo Soldier fought for America. They had something to prove and prove they did!

On August 19, 1881, Sergeant Woods was on patrol with seventeen soldiers. They were escorting civilians out of dangerous territory. While going through the Gavilan Canyon, New Mexico, they were ambushed by Mescalero Apaches. Their leader was a well known Apache by the name of Nana. Lt. G.W. Smith was killed instantly and Sergeant Woods received a wound to the arm. Though wounded Sergeant Woods made his way to the ridge and rained fire down upon the Apaches. Men testified that, *"If it had not been for him, none of us would have come out of that canyon."*.

On June 21, 1894, Sergeant Brent Woods was given the highest award the nation could offer for his bravery. Sergeant Woods went on to serve in the Philippines in 1899. Sergeant Woods served twenty eight years and nine month when he finally retired. He returned to Pulaski County where he resided with his wife. He lived approximately four years after he retired. He lived in obscurity and was buried in an unmarked grave in Somerset but thanks to the efforts of Lorraine Smith, he is now buried in Mills Springs National Cemetery, Nancy, Kentucky, row A; grave 930. He was given full military honors befitting this unsung hero.

SOURCES

http://en.wikipedia.org/wiki/Brent_Woods

http://www.wdwn-tampa.org/About-Brent-Woods.html

http://www.somerset-kentucky.com/local/x681542730/Civil-War-hero-from-Pulaski-to-be-honored

http://www.somerset-kentucky.com/local/x681542730/Civil-War-hero-from-Pulaski-to-be-honored

http://www.somerset-kentucky.com/local/x681542920/A-Day-for-Remembering

http://www.nytimes.com/1984/10/29/us/former-slave-has-rites-of-a-hero-80-years-later.html

http://www.9thcavalry.com/history/woods.htm

http://army.togetherweserved.com/army/servlet/tws.webapp.WebApp?cmd=ShadowBoxProfile&type=Person&ID=272619

http://www.geni.com/people/Brent-Woods/6000000012676701937

BROWNIE HALL
Staff Sergeant
C Company
1st Battalion, 12th Cavalry
1st Cavalry Division
USARV
October 15, 1928-December 23, 1966

Brownie was from Deane, Kentucky. I recall hearing of his death when I was attending Pikeville College. I remembered it because of his name, Brownie and he was the first casualty I had heard from Letcher County, Kentucky. Brownie was born on October 15, 1928. He enlisted and served as an 11Bravo 4 P. He was infantry and airborne qualified. He was a Light Weapon Infantry soldier. His ID number was 16257994. He was a sharpshooter. He was making a career out of the military, having served a total of eighteen years. During his eighteen years of service, he earned the rank of Staff Sergeant (E6).

Sergeant Hall's tour of duty in Vietnam began on March 28, 1966. He lost is life in South Vietnam on December 23, 1966. The casualty report stated he died outright due to hostile action. Casualty detail was due to suffocating or drowning. He was thirty-eight years of age at the time of his demise. His body was recovered and returned to Letcher County for burial. His faith was Protestant. He is listed on the Vietnam Memorial Wall: Panel 13E Line 74.

SOURCES

http://www.virtualwall.org/dh/HallBx02a.htm

http://www.fold3.com/s.php#s_given_name=Brownie&s_surname=Hall&preview=1&t=848,485&p_place_usa=KY,none

http://www.fold3.com/page/632049105_brownie_hall/details/

http://www.usfallenwarriors.com/index.php?page=directory&rec=18491

BURRISS NELSON BEGLEY
Colonel
421st TAC FTR SQDN
388th TFW
7th AF
United States Air Force
November 06, 1925-April 04, 1978

He was born on a Friday in 1925 in the small town of Hyden, Kentucky. The area is known for the musical legacy of the Osborne and the hospital founded by Mary Breckinridge. Burriss wanted to fly as a young man and when he was able he joined the Air Force. He served his country with honor and continued to rise in the ranks. He served in World War II, Korea and Vietnam. His MOS was 1115E Pilot and his ID number was 404249649. While flying a mission he was lost and reported as missing in action. The incident occurred on Monday, December 05, 1966. The family was notified and never gave up hope that he was captured as a prisoner of war. On Tuesday, April 04, 1978, the Air Force upgraded his status from missing to 'dead while missing'. He was forty-one years of age when he disappeared. Attached is the narrative found on line:

> Narrative :
> On 5 December 1966, Maj Begley was flying an F105D aircraft in a flight of four aircraft. The aircraft was shot down by a MIG aircraft and crashed in the vicinity of WJ 138865, Vinh Phu Province, near Tay Quan Village. In his last radio transmission, Maj Begley stated his aircraft was losing power and altitude and he was going to eject. The other members of the flight were taking evasive action from attacking MIGs and did not observe a parachute. Electronic beacons were not heard. SAR efforts were not initiated due to the location of the downed aircraft and proximity of enemy aircraft.

The following narrative is from the Senate Select Committee. It is the Final Report on
Burris N. Begley
(0542)

"On December 5, 1966, Major Begley was the pilot of an F-105, one in a flight of four aircraft on a combat mission over North Vietnam. Their flight was attacked by hostile MIG-17 aircraft while en route to the targets and Major Begley's aircraft was hit by hostile fire. Another flight member observed his aircraft apparently hit in the tail: debris and his drag chute were seen falling away from his F-105. Major Begley reported he was losing power and altitude and would be heading across the Red River. He later reported he would be ejecting, but aerial combat between the F-105 and MIG-17 aircraft prevented U.S pilots from tracking Major Begley. His aircraft crashed in Phu Tho Province, south of the Red River, and approximately 15 miles from the river town of Yen Bai. There was no chute observed and no radio or beeper signals. Major Begley was declared missing in action. Returning U.S. POWs had no information on his precise fate. In April 1978 he was declared killed in action, body not recovered, based on a presumptive finding of death. In November 1974, U.S. intelligence received a report from a People's Army of Vietnam defector describing the shoot down of a U.S. aircraft and the landing and capture of a pilot in Phu Ninh District circa January 1967. DIA concluded that this report might correlate to one of three U.S. airmen lost in this area, one of whom was Major Begley. Another report from a former People's Army soldier described the downing of a U.S. jet in Phu Tho Province circa November 1966 and the source reported human remains at the crash site. This report was also placed on Major Begley's file. In

November 1986, Vietnam repatriated remains it asserted were those of Major Begley. U.S. officials determined that there were insufficient remains for biological identification and they could not be correlated to Major Begley."

On Wednesday, November 26, 1986, the remains of what they thought were his body was sent home. Colonel Begley was identified on Thursday, April 18, 1996, as Colonel Begley. The agony of the waiting and wondering was over but the price the family paid was high. His name is listed on the Vietnam Memorial Wall: Panel 13E, Line 013. Colonel Burriss Nelson Begley was buried in Arlington National Cemetery, Arlington County, Virginia, USA. His plot is as follows: Plot: Section 60 Site 7141.

Kevin Schwartz, from Paradise City, Arizona, wore his name on a POW/MIA bracelet. He state that his mother was born in Kentucky and his father's brother (Vince Schwartz) was lost in WWII. The body was never recovered. When visiting the wall, Kevin etched his name in honor of his service and sacrifice.

SOURCES

http://www.virtualwall.org/db/BegleyBN01a.htm

http://www.pownetwork.org/bios/b/b015.htm

http://www.findagrave.com/cgi-bin/fg.cgi?page=gr&GRid=15526894

CARL NELSON GORMAN
Kin-Ya-Onnybeyeh
Navajo Code Talker
U. S. Marine
(Washindon be Akalh B-kosi-lai)
WWII
October 5, 1907-January 29, 1998

There are many people in my life who have left an impression. Few have touched me as much as Mr. Gorman. I remember being in awe of him the first time I met him. He had a gentle manner about him and the way his snow white hair glistened while in the traditional head wrap immediately caught my eye. I have always referred to him in person as Mr. Gorman due to my deep respect and reverence for the man.

I first met Mr. Gorman while attending a Chapter House meeting in Fort Defiance. He was very cordial and I remember the sparkle in his eyes. He greeted me with the traditional 'Yah Tah Hey' and smile. I was impressed with his humble dignity and his great sense of humor. He lived in and worked out of his trailer in Ft. Defiance, Arizona. I lived in the teacherage close to his home. The common ground we shared was Good

Shepherd Mission and other locations where the Code Talkers met. Mr. Gorman was the president of the Navajo Code Talkers Association. Later in life he had to move to Gallup due to health issues. During my six year stay he took me under his wing as I learned to walk upon the right road.

I vividly recall having the honor of walking in the parade honoring the Code Talkers. It was in 1982. I remember the reverence, pride and the eerie silence of the crowd when those unsung heroes passed by. Then the crowd exploded with applause and war shouts. I still get chills as I remember walking with legends.

Mr. Gorman was born on the Navajo Reservation in Chinle, Arizona. Chinle is the location of the famed Canyon De Chelly. He was a member of the Black Sheep (Khinyá' áni) Clan. His father, Nelson Gorman, and mother, Alice Peshlakai, founded the first Presbyterian Mission at Chinle. His father was a cattleman and a trader. Alice, his mother was a renowned weaver. She also worked with Presbyterian missionaries translating religious hymns into Navajo. Mr. Gorman was a man who was brought up in two worlds; Navajo and Anglo. His reluctance to accept the English language was evident when he attended Rehoboth Mission School. He was beaten for speaking Navajo instead of English and was locked in a basement. He was ten years old at the time. He ran away with his younger brother.

Later he attended the Albuquerque Indian School. He graduated with a keen love for his culture still in tack. Mr. Gorman took classes at Santa Monica Technical School and South Bay Adult School. During his free time he would draw horses much like he did when he lived in Chinle. He and his brother started a trucking business. In 1936 he worked as a range rider, land manager and clerk at a Native American jewelry store. Then came the war...

When the military learned of the possibility of using the Navajo language as a code they asked for volunteers. Mr. Gorman was one of the original men who answered that call. He was thirty-four (oldest of the Code Talkers) and lied about his age in order to get into the Marines. Training began and the Navajos began devising a code within a code. For example a turtle meant a tank. Their mission was top secret until it was declassified in 1968. Even after that date many of the Code Talkers were reluctant to share their experiences. On July 26, 2001, President George W. Bush presented Congressional Gold Medals to the original 29 Navajo Code Talkers to acknowledge their development of the unbreakable code. Of the twenty-nine original Code Talkers, only four lived to receive their medals. Such was their sacrifice for their country. Now their long overdue accolades can be told to the rising generations.

Once the code was developed and trial runs proved to be successful, the Code Talkers were dispersed to different areas of the Pacific. The battles of different islands such as Tinian, Guadalcanal, Saipan (he contracted Malaria and was shipped to Pearl Harbor for treatment), Tarawa, and Iwo Jima could not have been successful if it wasn't for the unbreakable code used by the Code Talkers. They coordinated movements of ships, troops and weaponry. Mr. Gorman said the Code Talkers were on front lines with radio in hands giving details to their counterparts so it could be given to the officers.

Mr. Gorman's patriotism and love for country was demonstrated by his actions, along with four hundred other Code Talkers. He once stated, *"Many people ask me why I fought for my country when the government has treated us pretty bad, but before the white man came to this country, this whole land was Indian country and we still think it's our land, so we fight for it. I was very proud to serve my country."*

After the war Mr. Gorman used the G I Bill to further his education. He attended Otis Art Institute in Los Angeles where his God given talents blossomed. He became a technical illustrator for Douglas Aircraft. He went on and organized a silk-screen design company and taught Native American art at the University of California. He returned home and worked out of his studio in Ft. Defiance. His love of horses became a prominent theme in his art. He worked with others on a Native-healing project as well. Another of his accomplishments was having oral interviews with the elders of the tribe.

In 1998 a bust was unveiled of Mr. Gorman. The bust was created by his son, R.C. Gorman. It pays tribute to all of the Code Talkers who served their country. It is located on the Northern Arizona University located in Flagstaff, Arizona. Also the Carl Nelson Gorman Museum is dedicated to his memory.

Mr. Gorman's selfless dedication to his people is best summed up in his own words: *"I want to help my Navajo people preserve their beautiful arts and crafts, which are rapidly vanishing. Indian art is dying out and we Navajo people must do something to prevent this great loss. Our young Navajo people do not realize the valuable heritage they have. They need training and help."*

Mr. Gorman died on Thursday, January 29, 1998, while hospitalized in Gallup, New Mexico. Funeral services were held at Sacred Heart Catholic Cathedral. He is survived by his wife Mary, Zonnie Gorman (daughter) of Gallup, New Mexico, and Donna Scott of Chinle, Arizona. He has three grandchildren. Mr. Gorman's son, R. C. Gorman was a renowned artist. R.C. had a studio in Taos, New Mexico and was world famous for his art. He was considered to be the premier Native American of his time. He was called the "the Picasso of American Indian art". He died on November 3, 2005. Zonnie, Dr. Gorman's daughter, continues to carry the torch as she lectures across the country on her walk with heroes. Safe Journey Grandfather.

THE TWENTY-NINE ORIGNIAL NAVAJO CODE TALKERS

They are all gone now but I can still see them in my mind's eye. I can feel the sense of pride as they rode by. Whenever there was a parade and the Navajo Code Talkers were there, when they came past the people, there was a silence which can only be explained as deep respect and pride. My eyes watered whenever I saw them in uniform or was in there presence.

These original Navajo Code Talkers created what became the impregnable code that defeated the Japan. In honoring the original twenty-nine, I wish to honor ALL Native Americans who served as code talkers and as soldiers.

Chester Nez is the last living original member. His words speak for All Native Americans who have served, are currently serving and will serve.

"It is important that my people take pride in their heritage, especially the young people, I hope that learning about the Code Talkers will help them to do that. It is also important that non-Navajos learn how a culture so different from theirs contributed to the U.S. victory in World War II."

1. Chester Nez
2. Lloyd Oliver
3. Charlie Y. Begay
4. Roy L. Begay
5. Samuel H. Begay
6. John Ashi Benally
7. Wilsie H. Bitsie

8. Cosey S. Brown
9. John Brown, Jr.
10. John Chee
11. Bejamin Cleveland
12. Eugene R. Crawford
13. David Curley
14. Lowell S. Damon
15. George H. Dennison
16. James Dixon
17. Carl N. Gorman
18. Oscar B. Ilthma
19. Alan Dale June
20. Alfred Leonard
21. Johnny R. Manuelito
22. William McCabe
23. Jack Nez Link
24. Joe Palmer
25. Frank Denny Pete
26. Nelson S. Thompson
27. Harry Tsosie
28. John Willie
29. William Dean Wilson

THE BEAUTY WAY

In beauty I walk.
With beauty before me I walk.
With beauty behind me I walk.
With beauty around me I walk.
With beauty above me I walk.
With beauty below me I walk.

SOURCES

http://www.nytimes.com/1998/02/01/us/carl-gorman-code-talker-in-world-war-ii-dies-at-90.html

http://centennial.ucdavis.edu/timeline/history/namesakes/gorman.html

http://articles.sun-sentinel.com/1998-02-02/news/9802010085_1_navajo-code-talkers-mr-gorman-gallup

http://en.wikipedia.org/wiki/R._C._Gorman

http://www.ncdemocracy.org/sites/www.ncdemocracy.org/files/docs/FFD_EducGuide_11_Carl_1.pdf

http://www.westerngraphics.com/carlgorman.htm

http://www.askart.com/askart/g/carl_nelson_gorman/carl_nelson_gorman.aspx

http://myvintagephotos.com/product_info.php?products_id=975

http://savvycollector.com/artists/1308-carl-nelson-gorman

http://www.findagrave.com/cgi-bin/fg.cgi?page=gr&GRid=22269864

http://www.apbspeakers.com/speaker/zonnie-gorman

http://www.lapahie.com/carl_nelson_gorman.cfm

CHADWICK A. GILLIAM
Lance Corporal
2nd Battalion, 6th Marines
2nd Marine Division
II Marine Expeditionary Force

As a teacher you have so many students that their names become lost but you recognize them by their face. Chad was not one of those. It may have been his decision to join the Marines that made him stand out in my mind. Or maybe it was the tribute that Mr. Billiter, his home room instructor offered to the news media when he heard of Chad's death. "There is not one of those kids that I had in my home room that I could tell one bad thing about because I have nothing but great fond memories of him. He was definitely a big part of that. He was a big part of who we were." Or maybe it was that his sacrifice and my class listing the names of those Kentuckians killed in service to their country touched me. Whatever it was, his demise had an effect upon me.

According to Mr. Scotty Billiter, Gilliam was always involved in activities. Football, Spanish class to other extracurricular events. Chad's goal was to be a Marine and was a natural when it came to leadership. Chris Damron, his brother-in-law, stated that, "All the

Marines seemed to really look up to Chad. He was a leader in the Marine Corps,"

Lance Corporal Gilliam was from Mayking, Kentucky. He attended Whitesburg High School. He enlisted in the Marines and was assigned to Camp Lejeune, North Carolina. He died on January 3, 2008, while serving in Kuwait. He was 29 years of age. His parents are Paul and Mary Gilliam.

The following RESOLUTION adjourned the Commonwealth of Kentucky State Senate in loving memory and honor of Lance Corporal Chadwick A. Gilliam.

With deepest respect and admiration, we pay homage and tribute to Lance Corporal Chadwick A. Gilliam, and we pause in silent reverence for his soul.

WHEREAS, Lance Corporal Chadwick A. Gilliam was born on November 2, 1979, in Whitesburg, Kentucky, and he traversed these earthly bounds January 3, 2009; and

WHEREAS, Chadwick A. Gilliam was the son of Paul Gilliam and Mary Ellen Cook Gilliam; he was the husband of Corinne Marie Stewart Gilliam; he was the brother of Paula Regina Damron and Michael Wayne Gilliam; he was preceded in death by his paternal grandparents Willard and Belvia Holbrook Gilliam and his maternal grandparents Arlie and Edna Sergent Cook; and he also leaves behind many other family members who loved him dearly; and

WHEREAS, Lance Corporal Chadwick A. Gilliam graduated from Whitesburg High School in the mid 1990s; and he graduated from Lindsay Wilson College with a Masters Degree in Counseling and Human Development; and

WHEREAS, Lance Corporal Chadwick A. Gilliam enlisted in the United States Marine Corps as an infantryman; he was assigned the 2nd Battalion, 6th Marines, 26th Marine Expeditionary Unit, Camp Lejeune, North Carolina; and he deployed to Iraq in support of Operation Iraqi Freedom; and

WHEREAS, the life of Lance Corporal Chadwick A. Gilliam ended prematurely from an apparent cardiac arrest at Camp Buehring, Kuwait; and

WHEREAS, Lance Corporal Chadwick A. Gilliam gallantly served his country with honor and distinction; and he was laid to rest on January 12th, 2008; and

WHEREAS, the Commonwealth of Kentucky has the highest respect for Lance Corporal Chadwick A. Gilliam and is deeply grateful for the sacrifice he made for the freedom of all Americans and to ensure the freedom of the Iraqi people; and

WHEREAS, the passing of Lance Corporal Chadwick A. Gilliam has left a void that cannot be filled, and he is mourned across the length and breadth of the Commonwealth;

NOW, THEREFORE,

Be it resolved by the Senate of the General Assembly of the Commonwealth of Kentucky:

Section 1. The Senate does hereby express its profound sense of sorrow upon the passing of Lance Corporal Chadwick A. Gilliam and extends to his family and many friends its most heartfelt sympathy.

Section 2. When the Senate adjourns this day, it does so in loving memory and honor of Lance Corporal Chadwick A. Gilliam.

Section 3. The Clerk of the Senate is hereby directed to transmit two copies of this Resolution to the wife of Lance Corporal Chadwick A. Gilliam, Corinne Marie Stewart Gilliam, and to the parents of Lance Corporal Chadwick A. Gilliam, Paul Gilliam and Mary Ellen Cook Gilliam, PO Box 169, Mayking, Kentucky 41837.

SOURCES

http://projects.militarytimes.com/valor/marine-lance-cpl-chadwick-a-gi6

http://legacy.suntimes.com/obituaries/chicagosuntimes/obituary.aspx?n=chadwick-a-gilliam&pid=122304980#fbLoggedOut

CHARLIE HASSEL CAUDILL
Private
WWII
September 26, 1913-January 3, 1982

They found it after a flood. It was lying on the bank of the river just below Blackey, Kentucky. It intrigued the couple on how a stone of that size could be washed away and rest next to the bank by their home. Was it discarded, thrown into the river on purpose or simply allowed to be displaced by the elements? They began looking for answers.

Nicole Rogers sent a picture of the gravestone to me via Facebook. It was an upright U.S. Military Marker. The name, rank, date and WWII was very plain but the elements had done their job.

She asked me did I know anything about the marker. I checked Fold 3 and after looking through several files, I discovered that Charlie had enlisted on July 15, 1940, and had been discharged on July 15, 1945. His Social Security Number was 228-32-7236.

That meant he was in the army during the bulk of World War II. I emailed Ben Gish, Letcher County Historical Society and began searching in earnest for the burial place of this unsung soldier.

We discovered that he was the son of Mary Caudill. She was born about 1896. Mary was seventeen years old when Charlie was born. She lived in lower Rochouse according to the 1920 census. His sibling was Hazel Caudill. Charlie was sixty-eight when he died. Now for the questions without answers.

How time fades the memory of a loved one. Surely someone has knowledge of this man and where he is buried. There are rumors he was murdered in the Woodrock area just above Blackey, Kentucky. There is another stating that his gravesite washed away with the last flood. NONE of these stories can be substantiated at the time of this publication. The search continues and will continue for this unsung hero.

SOURCES

http://www.fold3.com/?home=b&s_tnt=67932:1:0

http://www.rootsweb.ancestry.com/~kyletch/cemetery/records/index.htm

CHARLES ROBERT MARSHALL
Sergeant
579th BS
392nd Bomb Group
Waist gunner on a B-24 Bomber
U. S. Army Air Corps
November 24, 1924-July 21, 1944

For almost seventy years the family waited and wondered. They never gave up hope nor did they quit the vigil. They knew he would return. One May 31, 2013, he came home to his childhood sweetheart, his son, Robert David and family. This is his story.

Charles R. Marshall always wanted to be an aeronautical engineer. This was his dream. He grew up in Martin, Floyd County, which is located in the mountains of eastern Kentucky. He went to school and graduated from Martin High. He married his childhood love. Her name was Dixie Ratliff Marshall Hyden. They had a son named Robert David. He became the executive judge of Floyd County.

Charles was accepted into one of the more prestigious ivy schools in the nation; Duke. After his first semester he felt the need to serve his country and enlisted in the U.S. Army Air Corps. His widow stated, *"The night before he left to go we went to the jewelry store, and he picked this bracelet up and asked if he could get some names on it. About 10 minutes, he had Dixie and Bob on the bracelet. He put it on in the jewelry store and said when I come home I will take this off."*

The next morning he went to fight against the Axis forces that attempting to conquer the world. On July 21, 1 944, Sergeant Marshall was on a mission. The following report is from Lieutenant Brownfelder, navigator: *"The ship had been in the Group bombing mission formation just before being hit by enemy fighters near Munich at 1045 hours, altitude 25,500 feet. At about (30) miles west southwest of the target area, they left the bomber formation and were forced to abandon the aircraft due to severe damage. All members excepting perhaps one Waist Gunner and the Tail Gunner, both of whom were wounded, managed to bail out and he believed two men went in with the plane and were killed. He related further that the rest of the crew members were captured when they landed in their chutes in a (10) mile radius of Starnberg and that (1) gunner, Sgt. Glickman was found dead as a result of his parachute failing to open (a fact he learned later from Co-Pilot Ziegenhardt). Co-Pilot Ziegenhardt's later account added some more details regarding their ordeal: that the Engineer later told him that Waist Gunner Marshall had been wounded by a 20mm cannon shell from enemy fighters, and was attempting to don his chute when the Engineer bailed out of the aft hatch, waving the latter out first before him. The Co-Pilot added, that later, he was taken to the crashed and burned plane, and he did see one shoe and foot and bits of flesh scattered over a wide area which he believed to be the remains of Sgt. Marshall. He also noted that at a pre-takeoff inspection, Sgt. Marshall did advise the Co-Pilot that he did not have his dog tags with him for this mission. Another crew survivor's report on Sgt. Glickman, who at the time was flying as Top Turret Gunner rather than in the Waist Gun position, stated that Sgt. Glickman had been wounded in the left side* during the fighter attacks and flak barrages, but that the Sgt. had managed to bail out of the bomb bay opening. This surviving member related further that he saw Sgt. Glickman lying on the ground afterwards, noting that perhaps his chute did not open, or that Glickman did not manage to pull his rip cord before striking the ground. The Co-Pilot in his report went on to say: "...Soon after my capture by the Germans I was taken by car to where a body lay on the road. By signs the Germans informed me that I was to search the body. I did, and the body was that of Bertram Glickman. I removed one of his dog tags which the Germans wanted. He had bailed out at about 17,000 feet and his parachute was not opened. He struck the ground face down and most of the bones in the body were broken. His face was pushed back to about his ears but I recognized him by a bald spot on the rear of his head. Positive identification was made from the dog tags. This was about 3-4 miles from Sternberg, Germany on July 21, 1944". An added note to this statement by the Co-Pilot stated that the Navigator, Lt. Brownfelder, had returned after their liberation from POW status to Germany and had related that he found this man's (Glickman) grave. Pilot Carey in his statements covered most all of the above points concerning the crew's downing, but adding that on the bombing run their formation box had been hit by fighters and when he saw the gunners of their Lead ship firing, he asked his own Tail Gunner if he was firing as well. His Tail Gunner had replied "they are 51s" - and he then ordered him to fire at these attackers, that being the last that the Tail Gunner was heard from as the plane then was hit by flak and went on fire with the controls shot out. On Sgt. Glickman, the Pilot stated that it was positively determined that the ripcord on the former's parachute had not been pulled during his bail out procedure." It was reported that Marshall had been hit by 20mm fire and when last seen was adjusting his parachute.

In July 1945, Lieutenant Brownfelder returned to Munich, Germany, to continue the search for Sgt. Glickman's grave. The following is his account of his search: *"I located Sgt. Glickman's grave. He is (or was as of August 1945) buried in the village church yard at a town called Hadorf which is about (4) miles ENE of a larger town of Starnberg on the north tip of the Starnberger See. His grave was in excellent condition having been given special care by the villagers. When I left Germany I made certain that the grave was properly marked and also turned a report in to the Graves Registration authorities."* Unfortunately the location of Sergeant Marshall's remains lay dormant.

Sergeant Marshall was classified as Missing in Action but later changed to Killed in Action. For over six decades his remains laid on foreign soil. The family waited for some kind of news, praying that he would be brought home. Then Doc Marshall received a phone call from a Markus Mooser. He was from Germany and had news that he thought he might have found his father's remains. The German continued corresponding with Doc and finally the results of the DNA tests came back confirming it was his father. *"It took four years, but it took 69 years before that,"* said Doc Marshall. *"It means everything. You know you always wonder everyday what might have been or something, but it's good to know and just let it go now."* Sergeant Marshall's dog tags were returned. The most emotional gift of all was the return of the sacred bracelet with Bob and Dixie engraved on it over seventy years ago. His son, widow, and other family member were at Cincinnati/Northern Kentucky Airport to witness the Honor Guard escorting the remains off the plane. *"It was a very emotional ceremony,"* said R.D. "Doc" Marshall, who was one year old when his father was killed. *"It's just been an incredible journey and it all culminated today when finally my dad got to come home.*

On June 6, 2013, Sergeant Marshall's coming home was held at Davidson Memorial Gardens with full military honors and news coverage worthy of an unsung hero. He now rests in the land that he loved. Welcome home hero!

SOURCES

http://www.wkyt.com/wymt/home/headlines/WWII-remains-found-almost-70-years-later-209744731.html

http://www.b24.net/missions/MM072144.htm

https://www.facebook.com/powmia.us/posts/587293877971403

http://www.dtic.mil/dpmo/news/news_releases/2013/release_marshall.pdf

http://www.kentucky.com/2013/06/01/2662060/sixty-nine-years-later-floyd-county.html

http://army.togetherweserved.com/army/servlet/tws.webapp.WebApp?cmd=ShadowBoxProfile&type=Person&ID=338525

CHARLES YOUNG
Colonel
9th Cavalry
10th Cavalry
25th Infantry
'Buffalo Soldier' Commander
March 12, 1864-January 8, 1922

Charles Young was born in May's Lick, Kentucky, near Maysville. Noting that his birth year was 1864, Charles was born a slave. Charles father's name was Gabriel. Gab had been a slave but in 1865, he crossed the Ohio River to enlist in the 5th Regiment of Colored Artillery. Charles mother's name was Aminta. She had been taught how to read and write prior to being declared free.

After the War Between the States had ended, the family lived in Ripley, Ohio where young Charles attended an all-white high school. He graduated at the youthful age of 16 and was 1st in his class. He went into the field of teaching and taught at an all black school. In 1884 he won an appointment to West Point and in 1887 he graduated, being the 3rd black to graduate from that prestigious institution.

After his commission, he was assigned to the 10th U.S. Cavalry. He served with the 9th, 10th, 25th Infantry, and 'Buffalo Soldiers' in Nebraska and Utah. At the onset of the Spanish American War, 2nd Lieutenant Young began duty of training recruits at Camp Algers, Virginia. After the war he was assigned to the 10th Cavalry 'Buffalo Soldiers' in Cuba.

Later in his career he was assigned as an attaché in Port Au Prince, Haite. He was responsible for training and exercises conducted at that location. In 1903 he was assigned to the Sequoia National Parks as acting Superintendent. His work helped open up the national treasure to the public.

In 1908, he was assigned to the Philippines, where he was stationed until 1912. He was appointed attaché to Liberia. In 1916, he was chasing Pancho Villa in Mexico. His heroics led to once again being recognized as a leader. He was promoted to Lieutenant Colonel.

When World War I began Lt. Colonel Young was the highest ranking black soldier and the first to achieve such a rank in the army. He wanted to serve overseas but during a physical it was 'discovered' he had high blood pressure. Speculation is that due to his rank he would have been over several white officers and noting the year, this was not politically acceptable. On June 22, 1917, he 'retired' under protest.

A year later he rode five hundred miles on horseback to Washington D.C., proving he was fit for combat duty. He was reinstated but assigned to Grant, Illinois. He was then assigned to Liberia, and on January 8, 1922, while on a research expedition in Lagos, Nigeria. He died. He was given a full military funeral held at the Memorial Amphitheater at Arlington National Cemetery. He is buried in Section 3 of the famous national cemetery.

Charles Young was the 3rd African American to graduate from West Point. He was the 1st black U.S. National Park Superintendent. He was the 1st black military attaché, 1st black to achieve the rank of colonel, and the highest-ranking black officer in the United States Army until his death in 1922.

SOURCES

Black Cadet in a White Bastion: Charles Young at West Point, Brian Shellum, Lincoln, NE: University of Nebraska, 2006, pp. 6-13,

Brian G. Shellum, *Black Officer in a Buffalo Soldier Regiment: The Military Career of Charles Young*, Lincoln, NE: University of Nebraska, 2010, p. xx, a

James T. Campbell, *Songs of Zion*, New York: Oxford University Press, 1995, p. 262,

Colonel Charles Young. *Buffalo Soldier*. Davis, Stanford L. 2000.

"Lost Battalions: The Great War and the Crisis of American Nationality," (2005), pp. 41-2;

"Military Morale of Races and Nations," by Charles Young (1912).

CHARLIE BLAIR
Sergeant
WWII
November 18, 1911-April 4, 1966

This is a picture of my Uncle Charlie. How little I know of him though I lived with him on and off until he died. Charlie was the eldest son of Jim and Anna Back Blair. His siblings were Arlie, Eslie, Les, Arnold, Granville, Dennis, Goldie, Ellie, Dana (my mother) and Pearlie. They lived in the very head of Perkins Branch. The road to the house was nothing more than a sled path but they traversed it daily. They lived on a working farm, planted and hoed the crops, tended to the livestock and kept the mountain fields clear. On my first visit that I can recall, I thought it was paradise.

Due to the poverty of the region, Charlie worked at the side of his father. He was in the coal mine when a timber began cracking. My grandfather Jim knew too well the sound and bumped into Charlie, knocking him out of harm's way. My grandfather was not so lucky. He died while inside the Tea Cup portal #9. His body was brought out of the mine of Christmas Eve, 1931. Uncle Charlie would cry when he talked of that day.

One of the regrets I have in life is not listening intently to my elders' stories. I vividly recall Uncle Charlie. He was always nice to me. There were days when he didn't have much money but he would manage to give me a dime for school.

I used to sit on the front porch as Charlie played the guitar and Dennis played the banjo. Marion Sumner would visit and bring his fiddle on many occasions. Sometimes Lee Boy Sexton dropped by and the music flowed up and down the mountain.
I always looked forward to those evenings because I never knew who might come in to play blue grass music with my kinfolk.

Charlie enlisted on March 10, 1942, at Ft. Thomas, which is located in Newport, Kentucky. His Army Serial Number was 35133312. His enlistment was for the duration of the War or other emergency, plus six months, subject to the discretion of the President or otherwise according to law. He was wounded in the thigh on September 28, 1944. One of the things we remember (Arlin James, Russell Blair and I) as young boys is Uncle Charlie talking about being the drill instructor for Audie Murphy. I remember seeing a letter from Mr. Murphy but have no idea what happened to it.

The 3 fighting Blair brothers
(Charlie, Arlie, & Arnold)

SOURCES

http://aad.archives.gov/aad/record-detail.jsp?dt=893&mtch=6&cat=all&tf=F&q=charlie+Blair&bc=&rpp=10&pg=1&rid=5496768&rlst=193362,6170027,4894093,5331101,5496768,7277690

CHESTER BROWN
Seaman 1st Class
Navy
U.S.S. Halsey Powell
Task Force 58
3rd Fleet
November 23, 1925- December 13, 2003

Chester Brown was born in the little community of Crown (located in the Loggy Hollow area). His parents were Larkin and Susan Brown. He was one of six children in the family. Chester was a typical student and attended Whitesburg High School his freshman year. In 1944, Chester enrolled in Jenkins High School for his sophomore year but was drafted. He chose to join the Navy instead of going to the Army. He was eighteen years old at the time of his entering service.

Chester went to Great Lakes, Illinois, for his basic training. Afterwards he was sent to California and on to Pearl Harbor, Hawaii. There he was assigned to a destroyer (Halsey Powell). He would serve on that ship for fifteen months.

In 1945 he found himself in the middle of a world war! He was on the U.S.S. Halsey Powell (Task force 58). On March 20, 1945, he was in the Pacific Theatre and his ship was engaged in the first invasion of Saipan. From there they went to Tinian and Guam. Then the Battle of Leyte Gulf began. Imagine seeing Japanese suicide planes attempting to hit the ships, dropping bombs and the noise of the gunfire. The smell would also be overwhelming to the senses.

Chester recalled the battle in which he was wounded. They were nearing Okinawa when he saw the planes and heard the explosion of bombs. The destroyer's stern was hit and the Zero crashed on deck. He could not shake the thought of the twenty-eight injured (he was one of those wounded) and the nine men who were killed. He talked about the burials at sea. All of these events caused Chester to have issues with PTSD later in life.

According to Wikipedia, *"On 20 March, Halsey Powell was alongside Hancock when Japanese aircraft attacked. As the destroyer was getting clear, the aircraft overshot the carrier and crashed Halsey Powell. Her steering gear jammed, but alert action with the engines averted a collision. Fires were put out, and although 9 were killed and over 30 wounded in the attack the ship reached Ulithi on 25 March."*

The U.S.S. Halsey Powell was reported as sunk by the Japanese. Somehow the massive ship limped into port. Even when damaged, the ship was able to shoot down four enemy planes. Such was the tenacity of the American sailors.

The Mountain Eagle reported on April 5, 1945 that, "Chester Brown has been in the Pacific since March, 1944. He writes to his father of the good work they are doing. He was in the invasion of Siapan, and Tinian, screen around Guam, and back down to the Marshalls and also took part in the second battle of the Philippines and is still seeking the end of this war. Chester attended Whitesburg High School. We wish all our boys the best of luck. Seaman Brown is a son of Mr. and Mrs. Larkin Brown of Whitesburg."

Chester was sent to California to heal for the wounds on his back and right leg. From there he was sent to Crane, Indiana. He was discharged in 1946, having been active in seven major battles. He returned home.

He became a miner and married Fleta Mae Hatton in February of 1947. She was the daughter of John and Mattie Hatton. They lived in Whitco, just outside of Whitesburg, Kentucky. Fleta and Chester had ten children…

In 1952, Chester left the mines and worked at the Main Street Service Station. That is where I became acquainted with him. I used to stop and get gas there and have my truck serviced. Again this unsung hero didn't discuss his injury or war experience in my presence. The gas station was located across from the Courthouse (parking lot by Letcher Funeral Home). He was employed there for twenty-two years and bought the filling station in 1974. In 1983 he had to retire due to his injuries but he continued to hang around the station that was run by his sons.

Chester Brown died on December 13, 2003. He was seventy-eight years of age. He was interred at the Green Acres Cemetery. He is remembered as a good man who loved his community.

SOURCES

"Brown Narrowly Escaped Kamikaze Plane," William T. Cornett; the Mountain Eagle, June 28, 1989, Page10

http://www.locategrave.org/l/2307810/Chester-Brown-KY

http://www.fold3.com/s.php#s_given_name=Chester&s_surname=Brown&offset=41&preview=1&p_place_usa=KY,none

http://kdl.kyvl.org/catalog/xt7v416szc7h_1/text

http://en.wikipedia.org/wiki/USS_Halsey_Powell_(DD-686)

http://www.navsource.org/archives/05/686.htm

CHESTER NEZ
Lance Corporal
The Last of the Original Navajo Code Talkers
382th Platoon
U.S. Marines
Jan. 23, 1921-June 5, 2014

He was born in obscurity on the Navajo Reservation in the vicinity of Cousin Brothers Trading Post. . Yet his contributions to America will live on through history. He was one of nine children who lived approximately fifteen miles from Gallup, New Mexico. He spent his youth in a place known as 'among the oaks' or Chichiltah in Navajo. It was also referred to as 'two wells'. He grew up in the Navajo way and practiced the traditions of the Dinah. He was sheep herder. He was given the white name of Chester when he was young. When he was nine years of age he went to Tohatchi Boarding School. There he was taught in the white man's language and forbidden to speak his own. He was punished for speaking in his native tongue.

When he was eighteen he went to boarding school in Fort Defiance, Arizona, Gallup, and Tuba City. Visits home were few and far between but he never forgot nor did he forsake his roots. While at Tuba City, Arizona, he was recruited. He was in the tenth grade. Mr. Nez decided to join the Marines and was taken back to Fort Defiance in May of 1942. Training began upon arrival at Camp Pendleton, California.

Mr. Nez stated in an interview, *"After boot camp training was over they sent us to Camp Elliott, and that's where we started doing the code. It was kind of hard work, but it didn't take us too long to develop the code."* The code entailed using the Navajo language in a doubly encrypted system. It took thirteen hard working weeks to create a code. An alphabet was developed (ant-wol-la-chee) became A or be-la-sana, which is apple in Navajo). They substituted military terms for such items as Iron fish (submarine), potato (grenade). A fighter plane was a humming bird and a shark was a destroyer.

Once the code was developed, it was committed to memory. The Navajo history is an oral tradition; therefore it came natural to the warriors. They practiced long hours with their team mate until they became proficient in sending and translating messages. They were tested and proven to be much more effective than the codes utilized (and broken by the Japanese) by the military. A team of decoding experts was given the challenge of breaking the code and after several days of attempting to do so they finally gave up the quest.

When they went to the Pacific their skills proved to be superior to the Japanese ability to crack the code. The Code Talkers success was so great that they recruited over 400 hundred more Navajos plus other tribes. Mr. Nez was present on most of the campaigns but was always under guard. Thirteen code talkers were killed in action. In an interview, Mr. Nez spoke of his faith in time of war. *"Tábaahjii' nihil nida'iiz'éél, Nááts'ósí nidaaztseedgo ákóó nideeztaad. We would land on the beaches, which were littered with dead Japanese bodies,"* Nez says in Navajo. *"My faith told me not to walk among the dead, to stay away from the dead. But which soldier could avoid such? This was war. War is death. I walked among them."*

After serving gallantly Lance Corporal Nez spent time in a San Francisco hospital recovering from the exhaustion of constantly being on guard and moving from one location to another avoiding capture by the Japanese. He was reactivated in 1951 and left the military life in 1952. All code talkers were under strict orders not to discuss their mission or code. They kept their word until their saga was declassified in 1968.

Mr. Nez went back to the reservation. There was no heroes' welcome, no parades, nor anyone singing of his laurels. He thumbed to the Cousin Trading Post and was given a ride to the road of his father's Hogan. Simple words of affection by his father greeted him, *"Hello my son"*. With these words Chester was reaffirmed into the order of his people and the balance was realized.

Mr. Nez decided to go back to school. He enrolled in Haskell Institute (Lawrence, Kansas) where he obtained his GED. There he met Ethel, his bride-to-be. She returned with him to the reservation and was married in 1953 at St. Michaels, Arizona, which is only a mile or so from Window Rock, Arizona. Later they divorced. He worked for several years as a painter. Several of his artworks are on display at the Raymond G. Murphy Veterans Medical Center. Mr. Nez lived with his son Mike and family. Though confined to a well chair because of diabetes (he has lost both of his legs from the knees), and loss of much of his hearing, the warrior spirit still danced in his eyes, as he was the last of the original twenty-nine Navajo Code Talkers.

In 2001, fifty-six years after the war had ended, five of the surviving code talkers were honored by receiving a gold medal from President Bush for their contributions to victory in the Pacific and the war effort.

His love of country was evident during the ceremony when the president presented him with the medal. Instead of shaking his hand, Mr. Nez saluted him. He saluted the president for all those men and women who could not. He in essence paid tribute to the land, the people and the nation he loved; America.

*POSTSCRIPT: It was with great sadness that on June 6, 2014, I learned of the passing of the last living original Navajo Code Talkers: Chester Nez. He, along with twenty-eight of his brothers, created not only an unbreakable code but also an unbreakable bond. Through their sacrifices and sufferings, the Native American has finally received the recognition and respect they so rightly deserve. It was long overdue. Now, they rest in the land of their fathers.

We cannot repay their contributions to our freedom. We can only bow our heads in homage to the true American heroes and pray they continue to walk the red path in the other world. Safe journey Grandfather!

SOURCES

http://nativeamerican.lostsoulsgenealogy.com/biographies/chesternez.htm

http://www.washingtontimes.com/topics/chester-nez/

http://indiancountrytodaymedianetwork.com/2013/03/04/last-surviving-original-code-talker-chester-nez-speaks-during-northland-colleges

http://inamerica.blogs.cnn.com/2011/12/04/decoding-history-a-world-war-ii-navajo-code-talker-in-his-own-words/

http://www.stripes.com/navajo-code-talker-chester-nez-telling-a-tale-of-bravery-and-ingenuity-1.253099

http://www.koat.com/news/film-to-tell-story-of-last-living-navajo-code-talker/25013652

http://www.infosecnews.org/documentary-to-be-filmed-on-the-life-of-the-last-original-navajo-code-talkers-chester-nez/#.U3PJ19JdX5s

http://www.barnesandnoble.com/w/code-talker-chester-nez/1110865217?ean=9780425247853

http://www.tricitytribuneusa.com/wwii-vet-chester-nez-teaches-students-code-that-helped-win-the-war/

http://www.azcentral.com/news/native-americans/?content=codetalker

http://www.armchairgeneral.com/interview-with-navajo-code-talker-chester-nez.htm

http://www.nytimes.com/2014/06/06/us/chester-nez-dies-at-93-his-native-tongue-helped-to-win-a-war-of-words.html?_r=0

CHRISTOPHER ANDREW LANDIS
Specialist
2nd Battalion
3rd Special Forces Group (Airborne)
October 28, 1986-February 10, 2014

When Drew was born I was working on the Navajo reservation. For some reason when I encountered his story, I felt a kinship to this young twenty-seven year old who gave his life for our freedom. I felt compelled to offer a tribute to him.

Christopher (Drew) was the son of Edward and Carol Jeanne Landis. He was born in Jakarta, Indonesia. He had two brothers and one sister. Their names are Adrian, Ted and Andrea. The family lived in Independence, Kentucky. Drew was a typical young man who enjoyed baseball, basketball, playing with his siblings and friends. He enjoyed reading. He also enjoyed the great outdoors, and mountaineering in several states.

He was the product of being home schooled until his tenth grade. In 2004, Drew graduated from Calvary Christian School (I went to Calvary College in Letcher County, KY). He went on mission outreaches to Colorado and even as far as India. After the tragic tsunami which devastated Sumatra in 2005, he volunteered to work with Samaritan's Purse. Such is the giving heart of a true warrior and unsung hero.

Drew earned money by being a door to door salesman for the Southwest Book Company and attended Gove City College. He earned a history degree and decided to attend law school at Salomon Chase School of Law.

In March of 2011, he heard the call of service and joined the elite Special Forces. He went through at Fort Jackson, S.C., and attended the Defense Language Institute at the Presidio of Monterey, California, where he became a cryptology linguist specialist. He was assigned to Goodfellow Air Force Base in Texas, and finally to Fort Bragg's 3rd Special Forces Group.

Specialist Landis was deployed in August of 2013, as part of Operation Enduring Freedom. He served with honor. On February 10, 2014, he died at Bagram Airfield, Afghanistan. The cause was from injuries received from an enemy attack while he was on patrol. The insurgents fired a rocket-propelled grenade killing him instantly while in Kapisa Province, Afghanistan. This was his first deployment.

His body was recovered and returned home for full military honors. Services were held at the Grace Fellowship Church in Florence, Kentucky. His parents, siblings, sister-in-law (Sarah Jayne) and nephews Judah and Eli are left behind.

AWARDS

Purple Heart
Afghanistan Campaign Medal (Campaign Star)
Army Commendation Medal
National Defense Service Medal
Global War on Terrorism Service Medal,
Army Service Ribbon
Overseas Service Ribbon,
North Atlantic Treaty Organization Medal
Combat Action Badge
Parachutist Badge.

SOURCES

http://www.legacy.com/obituaries/cincinnati/obituary.aspx?pid=169777883

http://www.wlwt.com/news/local-news/news-northern-kentucky/nky-soldier-killed-in-afghanistan/24462222#ixzz331ADIQME

http://www.wlwt.com/news/local-news/news-northern-kentucky/nky-soldier-killed-in-afghanistan/24462222

http://www.fayobserver.com/military/article_c4b3923c-0960-5c53-88ab-d57f844fb363.html

http://www.fayobserver.com/military/article_c4b3923c-0960-5c53-88ab-d57f844fb363.html?mode=image&photo=1

htp://www.legacy.com/obituaries/cincinnati/obituary.aspx?pid=169777883#sthash.unAKZEnW.dpuf

CLARENCE BRUCE VARNELL
Private First Class
Company C
81st Wildcat Division
321st Regiment
By Roger Campbell Kelly

This citizen-soldier of the famed Wildcat Division was born in the foothills of the Great Smoky Mountains of eastern Tennessee on the day after Christmas in 1917. The first great World War was still raging in Europe when Clarence "Bud" Varnell opened his eyes for the very first time. He was the son of Ben and Daisy M. Varnell of Jefferson County, Tennessee.

Clarence grew up on the family farm along with nine sisters and a younger brother. As all young farm children did in those days, he worked alongside his siblings and parents as they managed a living from God's good earth. Clarence grew into a strong young man hoeing tobacco and planting corn, milking cows and getting in firewood for winter. He attended school and church and developed a sociable and pleasing personality.

At the end of the Great War, the world wasted little time in its attempts to heal itself and find an everlasting peace. Outside the calm and quiet confines of the Great Smoky Mountains, the world was churning itself into another frenzy of hate and confrontation. In 1939, under the leadership of Adolf Hitler, Germany without provocation attacked its neighbor Poland and the Second World War was underway.

America entered the fighting in 1941. A national draft was implemented and thousands of male citizens were brought into the ranks of the United States Army and Navy. The whole country mobilized for the fight that everyone knew would be long and bloody.

Clarence Varnell waited his turn at home on Shields Ridge. That wait would not be a long one as induction papers arrived in early 1942. Clarence passed all his physical requirements and was sent to Fort Oglethorpe, Georgia where he became a soldier. As part of the Tennessee contingent, he was assigned to the old 81st Infantry Division, nicknamed the "Wildcats". The 81st Infantry had been established at Camp Jackson in South Carolina, during World War 1 and was the very first fighting Division in the United States Army to wear a shoulder patch distinguishing it from other units. The original 81st had been mustered out of active service at the end of hostilities in 1918, but was hurriedly re-activated in June of 1942.

A brand new army post called Camp Rucker was built in Alabama especially for the newly formed 81st Division. Clarence Varnell was sent there from Fort Oglethorpe to advance his training and to help fill out the ranks of the Wildcats.

On June 28, 1942, Clarence wrote his first letter from Fort Rucker to his Mama back home in Tennessee.

Dear Mama....

I thought I would write you a few words to let you know where I am and how I am. I left Ft. Oglethorpe Thursday and am now stationed at Camp Rucker, Alabama. I am feeling fine and am being treated good.

I hope you all are feeling fine. I am thinking about you all every day. I don't want you all to worry about me any more than you can help for I am not here to take up bad habits, but make as good a soldier as I can.

I will be writing to you all more when I get time. Tell the girls that are away from home where and how I am and tell all of my friends hello for me. I guess I had better close for this time.

Your son

Clarence Varnell

During his time in the army, Clarence would write many such letters, trying to reassure his family back home of his well being and of his deep devotion to them. Many of those letters have been lovingly preserved by the family.

The 81st Infantry Division would spend many months of hard training within the 65,000 acres of Camp Rucker. The men would be separated into battalions and regiments. Clarence would be placed as a private first class into the ranks of the 321st regiment, Company C.

Early in its establishment as a fighting division, no one knew for certain where the 81st would be needed most in the war effort; therefore training was extensive and varied in its nature. From Fort Rucker, the Wildcats were sent up to Tennessee for its first real taste of field maneuvers. They remained there from mid-April to the end of June, marching and fighting mock battles day after day in the mud and rain of early spring.

The next stop for the Wildcats would take them clear across the country. The men of the 81st would find themselves in the deserts of Arizona. There they would face not only a bleak landscape, but temperatures that would reach well above the 100 degree mark. Despite the difficulties of life in the desert, some came to enjoy life at Camp Horn and most of the boys found life in the west to be somewhat interesting. Desert training would last from July to the middle of November when the Division would make a move that would bring them still closer to the west coast and the Pacific Ocean.

Camp San Luis Obispo, about halfway between Los Angeles and San Francisco, was probably the most well situated of all the camps the 81st had been assigned to. Here the men were well fed and there was very little mud or dust storms to contend with. There were towns nearby to visit and USO shows arrived with celebrities such as Kay Kyser and Rudy Vallee to entertain. Here the men were taught to swim and to acclimate themselves to the ocean and all of the amphibious maneuvers associated with beach landings. The Division remained here until the end of April 1944.

From Camp San Luis Obispo, the Wildcats would make their final training stop on the North American continent when they arrived at Camp Beale, California. Here the Division resumed its physical conditioning and emphasis was placed on individual rifle marksmanship. It was here that Clarence's regiment, the 321st, won the prestigious Wildcat Division baseball championship. They would go on to hold that title for the entire length of the war. It was a matter of great pride for the men.

Embarkation was the next step for the 81st Infantry Division. On the 26th day of June 1944, the Wildcats packed up their equipment and boarded a variety of ships. They were on their way to the Hawaiian Islands.

The 321st regiment arrived on the island of Oahu on the 7th day of July. From here the men of the regiment would receive their last and perhaps their most important training. For a period of six days, they would learn the deadly details of jungle living and fighting. The men of the 81st would be taught firsthand by several veterans who had already seen action on Jap held islands. This training was invaluable to the men.

In spite of the shortness of the stay on Oahu and all the intense training, many of the men did find a little time for some local sightseeing and relaxation on the famous Hawaiian beaches. Perhaps the biggest treat of all for the men was the outstanding USO show that was staged by Bob Hope and his troupe of entertainers.

The military operation that the 81st Division had been training for since the early days of Camp Rucker was coming to a dangerous head by late summer of 1944. It was decided that the Caroline Islands would be the target for American advancement. The islands of Angaur, Peleliu, and Ulithi would serve as the air and sea bases for the push into the western Pacific, if they could be taken.

The ship convoy that carried the 81st Division steamed into the Palau Islands area at dawn on the 15th of September. The day was sparkling clear and visibility was unlimited. The men on board the ships got their first look at Japanese held territory. The island of Angaur was but a small dot in a very expansive ocean, but it loomed large in the minds of the men who looked at its rough terrain.

Two days later, in the early pre-dawn hours, a loud crash woke the men of the 81st as the navy unleashed a tremendous barrage that covered the island from one end to the other. Battleships, cruisers, and destroyers pounded the Japs who watched helpless from their concealed positions.

At the first dim light of dawn, the Wildcats were taking their places in the landing craft and preparing themselves for the fight ahead. No doubt many a whispered prayer was sent up to heaven as the war was about to break full force upon the men of the 81st Division. The naval gunfire intensified and black smoke billowed up from the island in all directions as the smaller boats circled and made their way beachward. Suddenly, an ominous quiet settled over the entire scene as the big navy guns went silent to make way for the landing.

Rifle and mortar fire met the Americans as they waded ashore on Angaur, but once a beachhead was established, bulldozers were brought on shore to cut roads into the thick jungle. This allowed tanks and heavy equipment to move inland as the infantry slugged their way yard by yard into the unknown.

The Japanese defenders of Angaur made the most of their concealed bunkers and dug-out caves. Many a good soldier lost his life in the push inland. The fighting on this little speck of land was vicious and often hand to hand. For three days and nights the fighting raged between the Americans and the Japanese. Finally on the 20th of September, the island was officially secured. All organized resistance had collapsed and the enemy was hopelessly defeated. But there remained the dangerous job of mopping up. There were still pockets of Japanese soldiers who remained alive and willing to die to defend their small patch of ground. Clarence Varnell and the men of Company C of the 321st regiment were given the additional task of annihilating these remnants. This they did with military precision. The soldiers, who crawled, sweated, bled and battled in, over and sometimes thru this area, wouldn't hesitate to label this place as the toughest area in the Pacific. It was later learned that the Japanese who were defending Angaur were crack troops of the 14th Division. These troops were considered the elite of the Imperial Japanese army.

While the battle had been raging on Angaur, another fight was taking place on the island of Peleliu. The 1st Marine Division had been going at it tooth and nail since the 15th of September in an attempt to secure this strategic island. The 26,000 American troops had been weakened by considerable casualties and fatigue. It was then decided that re-enforcements were needed.

The 321st regiment of the Wildcats had proven themselves a tough fighting unit, so they were assigned the job of giving the Marines a helping hand. The arrival of the 321st on Peleliu was to begin the battle to drive the Japs from the Umurbrogol Mountain, known as Bloody Nose Ridge. There were still some 5,000 Japanese defending this area of the island.

Clarence Varnell and the 4,000 men of the 321st left Angaur on the 22nd of September and spent the night aboard ship where they received a much needed secure night of undisturbed sleep. By noon of the next day, they unloaded onto the beaches of Peleliu. These men were now battle tested veterans, sure of their fighting abilities and anxious to demonstrate to the Marines their prowess as infantrymen. And that's exactly what they did as they quickly took their positions opposite the Japanese, sending out patrols to determine the best point of attack.

On the morning of September 24th, the Wildcats started their move against the Jap positions on Umurbrogol Mountain. They were met with stiff resistance, but continued on toward their regimental objectives. The Japanese forces counterattacked, but couldn't break the lines of the tough Americans. The successes scored on the 24th of September by the 321st Combat team were truly notable. This part of the island had defied penetration for over a week by the Marines, but on the first day of fighting the Wildcats had advanced approximately a mile and a half.

For the next several days and nights, the 321st regiment was in the thick of things. Fighting along their lines was almost constant. Always they moved forward, gaining ground with the precious blood of its soldiers.

On the third day of October, a storm approaching typhoon strength was causing a number of supply problems for the Americans on Peleliu and the surrounding islands. However, the sharp clashes between soldiers of the Wildcat Division and the Imperial Japanese troops continued on without interruption. It was on this day and under these circumstances that Clarence Varnell lost his life. During a break in the fighting, Clarence decided to slip away to look for water. It was said that he wanted to do some personal laundry. On his way back to the defensive perimeter, a nervous GI mistakenly fired and hit Clarence thinking that he was a Japanese soldier. The gunshot was fatal and Clarence "Bud" Yarnell became a casualty of the war in the Pacific. He gave his all for the nation he loved, helping to preserve our sacred freedoms.

In accordance with family wishes, the body of Clarence Varnell was shipped back home to Jefferson County, Tennessee. His mortal remains lie in rest in the church cemetery at Wesley's Chapel, a short distance from the home he grew up in. Clarence was 26 years, 9 months, and 12 days old at the time of his unfortunate death. A younger sister, Ella, fully expects to see her brother Clarence again one day in that land where war has ceased to exist and death is no more.

CLARENCE J. DANIELS
Private
Bataan Prisoner of War & Survivor
WWII

Mr, Anthony Blair, a fellow veteran, mentioned this individual to me and had noted he was a POW at Bataan. He found the following information in the Mountain Eagle, which has always been not only a great place for news but always honor our American heroes. Private Daniels service and sacrifice must be remembered by a grateful nation.

Fold 3 has Clarence being born in 1919 in Letcher County, Kentucky. He enlisted into the Signal Corp on February 27, 1941. He enlisted in Roanoke, Virginia and was assigned to the Philippine Department. His service number is 13015219. (Information in box number 0114; film reel number 1.114)

Private Clarence J. Daniels was among the one thousand thirty-five prisoners aboard the 'hell ship" known as the Noto Maru. Ted Cook was another Letcher County native onboard that ship. James Monroe Combs and Daniel O. Webb were also part of the prisoners. The Letcher County natives were taken to the Philippines and then to Japan.

He and his fellow POWS became slaves and labored in the steel mill. Conditions were hard and they were treated poorly. This lasted until Japan's surrender.

In January of 1946, Private Daniels wrote a letter to the famed Mountain Eagle. He talked of the conditions he found while being a Prisoner of War (POW). He said, *"In Bataan we had eaten, among other things, lizards, monkeys, and horse meat...At Cabanatuan (a POW camp), we ate, if we could get them, dogs, cats, snakes, and water buffalo. Our main diet usually consisted of rice and thin watery soup. Lugaw, by the way is boiled watery rice, and there were plenty of worms and weevils in what we got."*

Here is another unsung hero for our area. Letcher Countians have always been proud to serve and we are proud of them for their serve and sacrifices.

SOURCES

http://www.fold3.com/s.php#s_given_name=clarence&s_surname=daniels&offset=8&preview=1&p_place_usa=KY,none

http://www.fold3.com/page/83729754_clarence_j%20daniels/stories/

Mountain Eagle, 1946

CLAYTON SHEPHERD
Seaman
BM2C Operational Specialist
U.S. Navy
World War II
Recipient of
3 Silver Stars,
Purple Heart
4 Gold Stars
November 19, 1917- October 26, 2011

I remember him very well. I was great friends with his son Phillip and daughter Carol. We went to school together. We all ran around together in the Letcher/Jeremiah area and hung out at Jean and Darrell's restaurant. His wife was kin to my mother. My first cousin, Roland Blair, married his daughter. Phillip married Karen Adams, who was my next door neighbor. Karen was the daughter of Monroe and Maggie Adams. She died in a tragic car wreck not long after Phillip was killed. They were all wonderful people. I never heard him talk about his service nor did I know that he was an unsung hero until I was a grown man.

Mr. Clayton Shepherd was a product of eastern Kentucky. He was born halfway up Pratt Branch Mountain on Mill Branch, close to Roxana. He lived close to Narce Whitaker's homestead. His father and mother were R.B. and Verda Crase Shepherd. R. B. was a logger and worked hard to provide for his large family of ten. R. B. had five sons and five daughters. In 1929, R.B. passed away. Clayton was either eleven or twelve years of age at the time of his father's passing.

The Great Depression made life hard and the Shepherds suffered along with other impoverished families in Appalachia. Somehow they survived and in 1932, Verda married Lee Adams. The family moved to

Jeremiah, Kentucky, just across the mountain, and a few miles above Pratt Branch.

The children enrolled in school at Stuart Robinson and Whitesburg High School. He graduated in 1937. Finding employment was hard but Clayton worked for Southern Bell putting up telephone lines. After that job, Clayton went to work in Indiana on his uncle's farm. He got a job in a canning facility in Austin. While working there he received notice that he was to report to Louisville, Kentucky, to take more tests to join the Navy. He had taken the basic tests earlier while with a few of his friends. They did so more or less as a fluke but not opportunity called.

Clayton decided to go and after the assessments he was in the Navy. He enlisted on August 16, 1938. His service number is 2872642. He reported to Norfork, Virginia, for basic training. He was stationed aboard the U.S.S. Enterprise in 1938. This aircraft carrier was the pride of the fleet and Clayton found himself a proud seaman working aboard this massive ship. He stated that the first time he say the aircraft carrier, "It looked big as a mountain," and "Once I got on board I had never seen anything so spotlessly clean. It was better kept than any house I had ever been in." He served aboard the Enterprise from November, 1938, until the summer of 1941.

With World War II looming in the foreground, Seaman Shepherd found himself at the Brooklyn Naval Yard. He helped train new recruits for duty on the U.S.S. North Carolina. Once the crew was trained, the U.S.S. North Carolina patrolled from Iceland to North Africa. Seaman Shepherd was there. Their mission was to monitor Nazi activity on the high sea.

On December 7, 1941, the Japanese attacked Pearl Harbor. Shepherd was one of thousands who went to the South Pacific as Task Force 58. They arrived at

Guadalcanal in early 1942, just after a terrible battle had taken place there. A strategy of island hopping, called Operation Cartwheel was put into action. They bypassed certain islands to reach other strategic targets. Soon Shepherd was in the middle of the fight at New Georgia, Bougainville, New Caledonia, Gilbert, Solomon and the Marianas Islands.

He recalled being scared and *"Praying a lot particularly since we hadn't started using a zigzag course yet, but went dead straight. We were sometimes just like sitting ducks. The Japanese ships and subs were our worst enemies—more so than their planes. But when we started changing course every 45 seconds, as they should have done in the first place, to prevent the enemy from having sufficient time to zero in on us, I began to think we'd surely win. After about eight months we really had them on the run. They always lost more in battle than we did. This part of the war was about who had the supremacy of the sea, and we soon had it."*

Clayton received special amphibious assault training and after being from home for so long, he received a thirty day leave. He wasted no time. On March 7, 1944, he married Bertha Caudill. Upon his return to the Navy, he was assigned to a light landing craft. After being on such huge ships as the Enterprise and North Carolina, this must have been a big change. The dangers were there. There job was to escort Marines to the beaches.

During one of those missions, his craft was hit and fifteen men were killed. Clayton was able to down the plane before being knocked unconscious from the explosion. The craft sank and men were taken aboard other ships. Clayton's legs were bleeding profusely yet he wanted to continue the fight. He had lost a couple of his friends and his blood was up but he had to have medical assistance before he could go back into action.

When the word spread that the war in the Pacific had ended, Clayton was in Memphis with his wife. His words best describe how our soldiers, sailors and Marines felt: *"You can barely describe the joy that day of surrender. We were in a park and everybody just went wild when the news broke loose. I never saw so much hugging and kissing."*

He was discharged on September 11, 1945, on Long Island, New York. This boy from the mountains came home an honored hero. He returned to Jeremiah and he and his wife Bertha stared a family. They had two children, Philip Lindsay and Evelyn Carol. Their son Philip was killed in November, 1971, in a car wreck. He was a Vietnam Veteran. Their daughter Evelyn Carol married Roland Blair. Roland is also a Vietnam Veteran. They lived next door to the Shepherds and have two lovely children. He worked for Blue Diamond, Kona, and Beth-Elkhorn mines for years. He retired in February, 1973. He received a pension and black lung for his labors.

Clayton Shepherd received three Silver Stars and four Gold Stars and several other medals and citations. He was given the honor of becoming a Kentucky Colonel and a special forestry award for identifying the largest pignut hickory tree ever discovered in Kentucky. He enjoyed hunting and fishing.

One of the things Mr. Shepherd wanted to do in his life was to revisit the U.S.S. North Carolina, which is moored in Wilmington, North Carolina. Carol and Roland took her father to the U.S.S. North Carolina museum. Clayton Shepherd died October 26, 2011. Funeral services were held at the Mt. Olivet Old Regular Baptist Church. He now rests close to his house in the Shepherd Family Cemetery. He was a genuine icon and unheralded warrior. Lest we forget...

SOURCES

"Story Worth Knowing," William T. Cornett, The Mountain Eagle, January 11, 1989, Page 10 & 15.

http://en.wikipedia.org/wiki/Island_hopping

http://en.wikipedia.org/wiki/Pacific_War

http://www.fold3.com/image/305042778/

http://www.fold3.com/image/301267417/

http://www.fold3.com/image/305680808/
http://wc.rootsweb.ancestry.com/cgi-bin/igm.cgi?op=GET&db=dmohn&id=I105727

DAKOTA MYERS
Sergeant U. S. Marine Corps
Embedded Training Team 2-8
Regional Corps Advisory Command 3-7
June 26, 1988-Present

CONGRESSIONAL MEDAL OF HONOR RECIPIENT

Dakota was born on June 26, 1988, in Columbia, Kentucky. I remember that date because I was born on June 27. I recall watching him receive his Medal of Honor from the President of the United States and the sense of pride I found within my spirit as a fellow Kentuckian and Veteran. He made us all proud on that September 15, 2011, day.

Dakota grew up in Columbia, Kentucky, and graduated from Green County High School. He enlisted into the Marines in Louisville, Kentucky, and went to the famed Parris Island for training. In 2007, SGT Meyers was deployed to Fallujah, Iraq. He was with the 3rd Battalion, 3rd Marines and served in the capacity as a Scout Sniper. While in Kunar Province during his second tour of duty, he learned of Marines and a Navy corpsman being missing. Without thought of personal safety he went into that area known for as a hot bed for insurgents. He searched until he located the bodies of the four men who were killed.

With assistance from Afghan soldiers, he recovered the bodies. The Americans who gave their lives for their country were 1st Lt. Michael Johnson, (a 25-year-old from Virginia Beach), Staff Sgt. Aaron Kenefick (30, of Roswell, Georgia), Hospital Corpsman 3rd Class James R. Layton (22, of Riverbank, California), and Edwin Wayne Johnson Jr., a 31-year-old Gunnery Sergeant from Columbus, Georgia. A 5th man, Army Sgt. 1st Class Kenneth W. Westbrook (41, of Shiprock, New Mexico) died from his wounds. According to reports and personal accounts, an Afghan translator known as "Hafez" charged into enemy fire to help U.S. Marine Cpl. Dakota Meyer rescue wounded Americans. Dakota Meyers also helped with the evacuation of twelve friendly soldiers close to a village by the name of Ganjgal. Twenty-four other Marines made it to safety due to his altruistic actions. Such is the nature of a hero.

On September 15, 2011, Sergeant Meyer was awarded the Medal of Honor in a ceremony at the White House. As of the writing of this book, he is one of the seventy-nine living recipients of the highest decoration given by the United States honoring heroism. His citation follows:

Citation

"Corporal Meyer maintained security at a patrol rally point while other members of his team moved on foot with two platoons of Afghan National Army and Border Police into the village of Ganjgal for a pre-dawn meeting with village elders. Moving into the village, the patrol was ambushed by more than 50 enemy fighters firing rocket propelled grenades, mortars, and machine guns from houses and fortified positions on the slopes above. Hearing over the radio that four U.S. team members were cut off, Corporal Meyer seized the initiative. With a fellow Marine driving, Corporal Meyer took the exposed gunner's position in a gun-truck as they drove down the steeply terraced terrain in a daring attempt to disrupt the enemy attack and locate the trapped U.S. team. Disregarding intense enemy fire now concentrated on their lone vehicle, Corporal Meyer killed a number of enemy fighters with the mounted machine guns and his rifle, some at near point blank range, as he and his driver made three solo trips into the ambush area. During the first two trips, he and his driver evacuated two dozen Afghan soldiers, many of whom were wounded. When one machine gun became inoperable, he directed a return to the rally point to switch to another gun-truck for a third trip into the ambush area where his accurate fire directly supported the remaining U.S. personnel and Afghan soldiers fighting their way out of the ambush. Despite a shrapnel wound to his arm, Corporal Meyer made two more trips into the ambush area in a third gun-truck accompanied by four other Afghan vehicles to recover more wounded Afghan soldiers and search for the missing U.S. team members. Still under heavy enemy fire, he dismounted the vehicle on the fifth trip and moved on foot to locate and recover the bodies of his team members. Corporal Meyer's daring initiative and bold fighting spirit throughout the 6-hour battle significantly disrupted the enemy's attack and inspired the members of the combined force to fight on. His unwavering courage and steadfast devotion to his U.S. and Afghan comrades in the face of almost certain death reflected great credit upon himself and upheld the highest traditions of the Marine Corps and the United States Naval Service."

SOURCES

http://en.wikipedia.org/wiki/Dakota_Meyer

http://www.cmohs.org/living-recipients.php

http://freebeacon.com/the-abandoned/

(SGT. Meyers Receiving his medal)

DAN BULLOCK
Private First Class
2nd Squad
2nd Platoon
Company F
2nd Battalion
5th Marines
1st Marine Division
December 21, 1953-June 7, 1969

How deep is your love for your country? What would you do for what you believe? Would you give your life freely for your principles? One young man like so many others did so. The only difference was that he was just fifteen years of age. This is his story.

All he ever wanted to do with his life was to be a Marine. Dan Bullock was born to Mr. and Mrs. Brother Bullock in Goldsboro, North Carolina. He has a younger sister by the name of Gloria. When his mother (Alma Floyd Bullock) died, he and his sister moved to Brooklyn, New York, to live with their father. Dan was only twelve at the time. He did not like New York and wanted to better himself along with helping his younger sister. He wanted to join the Marines.

Dan's desire to join the Marines was so intense that he changed his birth date to December 21, 1949, which made him eligible to join. He did so with those forged papers on September 18, 1968. Did his father realize he joined the Marines is a question unanswered at the time of this writing.

Dan went to boot camp at Parris Island, South Carolina, and held his own. He was a member of platoon 3039. No one suspected that he was only fourteen years old. On December 12, 1968, he graduated basic training. From there he went on to advanced training which lasted five months.

Private First Class Bullock was sent in country on May 18, 1969. He was assigned to Fox Company, 2nd Battalion, 5th Marines. Captain Kingrey was his company commander. They were stationed in An Hoi Combat Base, An Hoi, and Quang Nam Province.

On June 7, 1969, a night assault occurred and PFC Bullock recognized the intensity of the barrage. He knew that ammunition would soon be depleted so he took it upon himself to gather it for the men. Captain Kingrey wrote to his family the following: "The recent death of your son, PFC. Dan Bullock, United States Marine Corps, on June 7, 1969 An Hoa Combat Base, Quang Nam Province, South Vietnam is a source of great sorrow to me and all the members of Company F. Dan was assigned as a Rifleman in the 2nd Plt of Company F. During the early morning hours of June 7, Co. F was in night defensive positions on the perimeter of the An Hoa Combat Base. An assault of the lines started at approximately 1:00 a.m. Dan immediately realized that the attack was stronger than usual and that the ammunition supply was becoming depleted. He rushed to get more ammo for his unit. He constantly exposed himself to the enemy fire in order to keep the company supplied with the ammunition needed to hold off the attack. As the attack pressed on, Dan again went to get more ammunition when he was mortally wounded by a burst of enemy small arms and died instantly at approximately 1:50 a.m."

PFC Bullock's body was recovered and sent home. He was buried in Goldsboro, North Carolina. For thirty years he would go unmarked and his story untold, save for those who knew of his actions.

Now here is the rest of the story. When the news media discovered that Dan was only fifteen and had enlisted at the age of fourteen, eyebrows were raised. The Marines could not acknowledge his service because of the uniform military code of justice. That didn't stop the bullet which took the life of a youthful patriot. Neither did it detour Franklin McArthur on his quest for justice. He was in the same platoon as PFC Bullock and was with him in Vietnam. He learned of his age by reading a paper. A foundation in honor of PFC Dan Bullock was established and through the efforts of former Marines, Frank McArthur, Rolling Thunder, Sally Jessey Rapheal, Nam Knights and Police Departments he was given his headstone. They left Brooklyn and rode caravan style to Goldsboro, North Carolina to place his marker.

Ironically the request for a military funeral was denied by the Marines. The reason was that Dan forged the documents leading to his service. Thereby they were considered to be falsified. I wonder if the life he gave was unworthy because of his conviction to be a Marine. He gave his life for his convictions and probably saved lives by his heroics. Where is the JUSTICE in that we cry? The U.S. Air Force was contacted and they performed the ceremony.

Currently efforts are being made to have this boy warrior recognized and given the acknowledgment he deserves. The New York City Council in 2003 renamed a section of Lee Avenue (where Bullock had lived) in his honor. A statue is being planned by another man who remembers Bullock. Piscitelli was there on that fateful night and recalled that he had broken his thumb and Bullock traded places and went to the front lines. He is designing a statue with the young warrior holding an M-16 in one hand and a grenade ready to be tossed in another. Dan Bullock was the youngest man to die in the Vietnam War.

SOURCES

http://articles.philly.com/2000-10-30/news/25586235_1_boot-camp-parris-island-vietnam-memorial

http://en.wikipedia.org/wiki/Dan_Bullock
http://thewall-usa.com/mboard.asp?curpage=43&searchtext=killed

http://thewashingtonsyndicate.wordpress.com/tag/marines/

http://thewashingtonsyndicate.wordpress.com/tag/marines/

http://www.inquisitr.com/168102/only-the-good-die-young-in-memory-of-pfc-dan-bullock/#sMItDADP0u0oSfeo.99

http://www.findagrave.com/cgi-bin/fg.cgi?page=gr&GRid=22940838

DANNY WEBB
Sergeant
B Battery
4th Battalion
60th Artillery Defense Artillery
Duster Tank Commander
Recipient of the Bronze Star

There are men and women who have served our country with distinction but upon their return to stateside, they seem to fade into the mist and continue helping the people. They don't talk about their service. A true hero never does. Danny Webb is to be counted in that number. He has been a servant of the people from the time he entered the military all the way up to the writing of this book. He has been a captain and served in Letcher, Elizabethtown, Henderson and Pikeville. He retired from the Kentucky State Police in 2001, but was called to serve again. This time he was elected as sheriff of Letcher County in 2003. He has been in that position through the writing of this book.

His military service began when he was drafted and on February 5, 1969, he entered into Basic Training. After graduating from Basic he attended Advanced Infantry Training (AIT) at El Paso, Texas. His assignment was fort Bliss and there he began training on air defense, such as HAWK and Niki Herc missiles. He was offered NCO training and was assigned to M42 40 mm self-propelled anit-aircraft 'Duster' tanks. The Duster is an armored light air-defense gun. Beginning in the fall of 1966, the army deployed, "Three battalions of Dusters to the Republic of Vietnam. The battalion consisted of a headquarters battery and four Duster batteries, and each augmented by one attached Quad-50 battery and an artillery searchlight battery." The battalion structure was fashioned like the ADA missile system. The duster was used in Korea. According to an interview with Sheriff Webb, Jim Duncan (POW) was on a crew during his service in Korea before he became a prisoner of war. Sergeant Webb was in the Pleiku region and was what was referred to as a 'shake and bake' non commissioned officer. He was an E5 but served as an E6. Bottom line is you had a promotion without the pay.

Sheriff Webb has been a visionary for the region. He has chosen to serve the people of his area. He is modest, unassuming, and unpretentious. In fact he was recently surprised when he received a package from the Army. It was the Bronze Star, the fourth highest honor that could be bestowed upon a soldier. He received his citation in 1969 but it took almost forty-five years for it to be in his possession. It was allegedly lost in the mail. Sheriff Webb stated in an interview by the Mountain Eagle, "It was very emotional because it brought back memories that were a big part of my life at that time. It was special to get that." For his service he also received the national Defense Service Medal, Distinguished Rifleman Medal, Vietnam Service medal, Combat Action Badge, and the Army Good Conduct Medal.

He has also been recognized for his forty years plus service in law enforcement. He was recently honored by having a portion of highway 15x (from Rite Aid through town to Pizza Hut) was renamed Sgt. Danny R. Webb U.S. Army Vietnam Vet. Letcher County Sheriff

Highway. In an interview with WYMT and the Mountain Eagle Sheriff Webb's humble nature was evident. "It's an honor. I don't know if I am deserving of this. I have really enjoyed serving the people of Letcher County." Sheriff Webb is a member of the Kentucky Sheriffs Association and a board member of the Appalachian HIDTA (High Intensity Drug Trafficking Areas) program. His sheriff department has also worked with several programs, including the Senior Citizens Program, Child Identification Program, School Safety Program, Neighborhood Watch Programs and Drug Education Program.

SOURCES

http://www.wkyt.com/wymt/mobile/headlines/Letcher-County-officials-name-highway-after-sheriff--207460551.html

http://www.themountaineagle.com/news/2013-05-15/features
"Bronze Star Medal finally makes way to Sheriff Webb'; The Mountain Eagle; Volume 107, Number 1, March 5, 2014

Phone Interview with Sheriff Webb

http://en.wikipedia.org/wiki/M42_Duster
http://www.ndqsa.com/duster.html

http://unitpages.military.com/unitpages/unit.do?id=103604

http://www.dtic.mil/dtic/tr/fulltext/u2/505494.pdf

DANIEL O. WEBB
Sergeant
Coast Artillery Corps
60th B
1918-?

There are those men who endured the tortures of imprisonment. They were brave men who looked into the eyes of the enemy and saw no compassion, no humanity and no desire to follow the Geneva Convention rules. They were haunted by the horrors of the war and the ill treatment they received at the hands of their captures. Danny Webb was one of the many men who saw that fate and yet survived to tell the tale.

Daniel O. Webb was from Mayking, which is located in Letcher County, Kentucky. He had completed three years of high school. When the war began, he decided to serve. He enlisted on January 30, 194----. After training he was sent to the South Pacific Theatre. He was another Letcher County native who was captured when the Philippines were overran by the Japanese.

He suffered the same fate as several of his comrades and was shipped in cargo holds of 'hell ships' and transported to Japan where he worked at slave labor at a steel mill. The name of the ship was Tottori Maur and it departed on October 8, 1942. He was liberated after Japan surrendered in August of 1945. The October 14, 1947, edition of The Eagle carried the news that Sergeant Webb had survived the inhumane treatment at Bataan. In all there were over one hundred forty-three thousand men held captive by Japan or Germany during World War II. His service number is 6943867.

SOURCES

http://www.ww2pow.info/index.php?page=directory&rec=142510

http://kdl.kyvl.org/catalog/xt7m901zdd3p_7/text

http://eris.uky.edu/catalog/xt77d7957h19_8/text

http://www.mansell.com/pow_resources/camplists/Nagoya/nag_06_nomachi/nag-06b-partial%20roster.html

http://www.japanesepow.info/index.php?page=directory&rec=20596

http://www.fold3.com/s.php#query=daniel+o.+webb&preview=1&t=831

D. STANLEY HOLLAN
Lieutenant
Killed in Action
World War II

Unfortunately at the writing of this book, the information regarding this unsung hero is very limited. The following is a small notice in the Mountain Eagle. Fold 3 or other sources did not have any pertinent information. Yet his story must be found and shared for the rising generations. The search continues;

"A telegram notified Mrs. Rosemarie Zimmerman Hollan that her husband, Lieut. D. Stanley Hollan had been killed in action. Complete details are lacking."

SOURCES

Mountain Eagle, April 12, 1945; Volume 38, Number 40

DARRELL C. POWERS
SERGEANT
Easy Company
2nd Battalion
506th Parachute Infantry Regiment
101st Airborne Division
March 13, 1923-June 17, 2009

He was simply called Shifty and was a product of the southwestern portion of Virginia. He was a mountain man destined to serve his country and leave a legacy few could contest. He only lived a few miles from where I lived but it took Shifty's War to bring this unsung hero to be remembered as a true freedom warrior. This is a synopsis of his story.

Darrell was born in Clinchco, located in Dickenson County, Virginia. His parents' names were Barnum and Audrey Colley Powers. He was one of five children. Due to the Great Depression the family relied on animals they father killed in order to feed his family. His father Barnum, who was a renowned shot, taught him at an early age the secrets of firing a weapon. Allegedly Darrell could toss a coin high into the air and hit it before it reached the ground. Such was his skills as a marksman. They hunted together and enjoyed the simple life of rural Appalachia.

It was reported that Darrell earned his nickname 'Shifty' from his basketball days in which he was 'shifty' and moved so rapidly from one direction to another. Darrell attended school and after graduating decided to become a machinist. He attended vocational school in Norfolk.

When Japan attacked Pearl Harbor, Darrell was outraged. He stated, *"After the Japanese bombed Pearl Harbor, they (the government) moved all of us from the school over to the Navy Shipyard at Portsmouth, to do work on the ships there. I worked there as a machinist for a while. My buddy "Popeye" (better known as Robert Wynn, a fellow Virginian from South Hill) and me wanted to join the military so we went and signed up for the Army before we got stuck at the shipyard. We volunteered for paratrooper school."* On August 14, 1942, Darrell realized his dream and enlisted at Richmond, Virginia. He was sent to Camp Pickett, Virginia and then shipped out to Camp Toccoa, Georgia

Darrell was assigned to Easy Company and soon his skills as a sharpshooter became apparent. In an interview, he commented about the skills needed to be a crack shot: *"People think hunting's just being out walking in the woods, but its lots more than that. You see things, you hear things. You learn to know everything that moves around you. Might be a squirrel, deer, turkey, grouse, or another man. So you aim well, and aim for the eyes. It means a smaller target, but you have to promise me this – quick, clean kills only."*

Mr. Powers was well liked by all the men and by the end of the war, he was revered. During his training, he was given a three day pass but didn't have the money to go home. His fellow soldiers passed the hat and gathered more than enough for him to visit his family before being deployed. Little did they realize Sergeant Powers would repay them many times over by saving their lives.

Sergeant Powers was in several engagements. He participated in D Day. He fought in Carentan. He participated in Market Garden conducted in the Netherlands. He was a sharpshooter during the Battle of the Bulge. His keen sense of terrain proved to be a lifesaver. He reported to his sergeant that a tree had not been present on the landscape the day before mysteriously appeared. It turned out to be a camouflaged antiaircraft battery. His observation saved many lives on that day.

Another incident recorded in Band of Brothers, showed his ability along with his heart. On January 13, 1945, while attacking Foy, a German sniper had pinned down several men. Sergeant Powers spotted the tale-tale gun signature and struck the sniper in the middle of the forehead. While in the Ardenes, a German sniper had killed three Easy Company men. Sergeant Powers was summoned. He watched for the man's breath and fired. The German sniper was no more. Powers later recalled the incident and stated, *"We might have had a lot in common. He might've liked to fish, you know, he might've liked to hunt. Of course, they were doing what they were supposed to do, and I was doing what I was supposed to do. But under different circumstances, we might have been good friends."*

After the war ended He was ready to go home but did not have enough points to rotate stateside. A lottery was devised, which allowed on man to go home. Every single soldier in the lottery had his name pulled so that the only number was that of Sergeant Powers. Shifty was not wounded in action but ironically was involved in a crash to the airport.

After several months in the hospital, Darrell finally returned home. He took up his old vocation as a machinist for the Clinchfield Coal Corporation. He married a lady by the name of Dorothy. He lived in California for three years but returned home.

Darrell C. Powers, an icon and legend from Dickenson County, Virginia, died of lung cancer on June 17, 2009. He is buried at Temple Hill Memorial Park, Castlewood, Russell County, Virginia.

OBITUARY

Darrell "Shifty" Powers, 86, of Shifty Lane, Clinchco, VA, passed away Wednesday June 17, 2009, at Wellmont Regional Hospital, Bristol, Tenn., after a courageous battle with cancer.

He was a charter member of Clinchco Missionary Baptist Church. Shifty was a veteran of World War II, having served in the 101st Airborne, 506 Parachute Infantry Regiment. He was a member of the famed Easy Company whose exploits received worldwide recognition in "Band of Brothers," a book by historian Stephen Ambrose, and miniseries produced by Tom Hanks and Stephen Spielberg. Shifty dropped behind enemy lines in Normandy on D-Day. He also participated in all of Easy Company's battles including Operation Market Garden, Battle of the Bulge, and the capture of Hitler's Eagles Nest.

Darrell was preceded in death by his parents, Barnum and Audrey Colley Powers, brothers, James, Barnum and Frank Powers, and a great-grandson Gavin Johnson.

Survivors include his loving wife of sixty years, Dorothy; son, Wayne (Sandy) Powers of Clinchco, VA, daughter, Margo (Seldon) Johnson of Bristol, Va., sister, Gaynell (Clair) Sykes of Roanoke, VA.; sisters-in-law, Ann Powers of Clintwood VA., Betty Powers of Greenville, Tenn.; four grandchildren, Clay (Kayla) Powers, Dove Powers, Jake (Dawnyale) Johnson and Luke (Amanda) Johnson; two great-grandchildren, Caden Powers and Cooper Powers; several nieces and nephews; several great-nieces and nephews; and special family friends the Robinettes, Carol, David and Tammy and Suzanne Axtell.

Pallbearers will be Jake Johnson, Luke Johnson, Clay Powers, David Robinette, Johnny Sykes, Mike Strouth and John Wesley Hawkins. Honorary pallbearers will be Ben Sutherland, Claire Sykes, Tim Thomas, Wayne "Pappy" McCowan, Shang-Hi Nichols and Mickey Taylor.

A song service was held at the Mullins Funeral Home Chapel, located in Clintwood VA. Funeral services were conducted on Saturday June 20, 2009 at 1:00 p.m., with Pastor Randy Moore officiating. Graveside services with Military Honors were conducted by Francis Marion VFW post 4667 at Temple Hill Cemetery. Public awareness of his heroics must be accomplished for one (if not all) of the band of brothers.

MEDAL AND DECORATIONS

Bronze Star with 1 Oak Cluster
Presidential Unit Citation with 1 Oak Leaf Cluster
Good Conduct Medal
American Defense Medal
American Campaign Medal
European-African-Middle Eastern Campaign Medal
(With 3 service stars and arrow device)
World War II Victory Medal
Army of Occupation Medal
Croix de Guerre with palm
French Liberation Medal
Belgian World War II Service Medal
Combat Infantryman Badge
Parachutist Badge with 2 combat jump stars

SOURCES

Shifty's War; Brotherton, Marcus; Penguin/Berkley-Caliber; 2011

http://wikiofbrothers.wikia.com/wiki/StSgt._Darrell_C._Powers

http://www.examiner.com/article/darrell-powers-was-easy-company-s-shifty-sharpshooter

http://www.examiner.com/article/darrell-powers-was-easy-company-s-shifty-sharpshooter

http://www.truthorfiction.com/rumors/s/shiftypowers.htm#.U5iFkXJdX5s

DARRELL O. HOLBROOK
Staff Sergeant
Company C
3rd Battalion
8th Infantry Regiment
4th Infantry Division
Recipient of the Silver Star

I have never met the man but when I accidentally stumbled upon his story I knew I had to offer a salute to his heroic actions. Darrell Holbrook was born and lives in Springboro (Clear Creek, Twp), Ohio. He graduated from high school in 1960.

In 1969, Holbrook found himself in the middle of a war in a place called Vietnam. On May 6, 1970, Sgt. Holbrook found himself the highest ranking soldier in the field. The officers had been dropped into an unsecured area inside Cambodia. Recognizing the severity of the situation, Sergeant Holbrook took command. According to documentation, *"Holbrook continually exposed himself to intense hostile fire as he moved from position to position directing his men in establishing a secure perimeter."* The men were separated and had to wait until nightfall to combine their forces. Sergeant Holbrook also, *"Organized a night defensive perimeter and maintained security throughout the night."* They were surrounded and the firefight was continuous. *"I didn't think we would live to see the next day. I don't think anybody else did either."* The next morning the Air Cav (helicopters) came in and rescued the men. Out of the forty men, three were killed and eleven were wounded.

CITATION
General Orders: No. 4510
September 2, 1970
Headquarters, 4th Infantry Division

"The President of the United States of America, authorized by Act of Congress, July 8, 1918 (amended by act of July 25, 1963), takes pleasure in presenting the Silver Star to Staff Sergeant Darrell Holbrook, United States Army, for gallantry in action while engaged in military operations against an armed hostile force in Cambodia. Staff Sergeant Holbrook distinguished himself while serving with Company C, 3d Battalion, 8th Infantry Regiment, 4th Infantry Division. On 6 May 1970, Company C was inserted into an unsecured landing zone inside the Cambodian border. Staff Sergeant Holbrook continually exposed himself to intense hostile fire as he moved from position to position directing his men in establishing a secure perimeter. When gunships arrived on station, Sergeant Holbrook adjusted their fire on the entrenched enemy force. Assuming command when the Company Commander was killed, Sergeant Holbrook organized a night defensive perimeter and maintained security throughout the night. Staff Sergeant Holbrook's personal bravery, outstanding leadership and exemplary devotion to duty are in keeping with the highest traditions of the military service and reflect great credit upon himself, his unit and the United States Army."

After his tour of duty, Sergeant Holbrook came home. Darrell and his wife Mary raised two children, Alison and Matt. Darrell Holbrook served on the Springboro City Council and worked for Reynolds and Reynolds for twenty-eight years. He is retired and has written a book entitled, Twelve Days in May: The Untold Story of the Northern Thrust into Cambodia by the 4th Infantry Division. He is an inductee into the Ohio Military hall of Fame for his heroism.

Darrell encourages other Veterans to write of their experiences so that future generations will grasp the sacrifice given for their freedom. If we don't, "That part of history will be lost forever." He is right. If we do not record the heroic deeds of those who have served we will forget and soon America, the home of the brave and land of the free will be no more.

SOURCES

http://www.daytondailynews.com/news/news/local/vietnam-vets-heroic-story-finally-being-told/nNC26/

http://www.omaha.com/apps/pbcs.dll/article?AID=/20130527/NEWS0802/705279989/1677

http://projects.militarytimes.com/citations-medals-awards/recipient.php?recipientid=24405

www.cambodiaincursion.com

DARWIN K. KYLE
2nd Lieutenant
Company K
7th Infantry Regiment
3rd Infantry Division
June 1, 1918–February 16, 1951
Recipient of the
Bronze Star
Silver Star
MEDAL OF HONOR

He was the bravest man I ever saw."
Sgt. James Yeomans

Letcher County has an unsung hero who received this country's highest award, the Medal of Honor! He also was the recipient of the Bronze Star and the Silver Star. Yet what do we know of him? This fielder asks has his image faded so quickly. Are we truly a grateful nation for his sacrifice? Let us rekindle our desire to honor all who served and learn of their stories. This is what I know to date.

Darwin "Gus" Kyle was born in Jenkins, Kentucky. His parents were Charles and Pearl Keffer Kyle. Charles worked in the little mining town during World War I. When Darwin was young the family moved to West Virginia. He grew up in Midway, Boone County, West Virginia.

Darwin chose a life with the military. After graduating from high school he fulfilled his dream. He enlisted at Racine, West Virginia, in November of 1939. He was twenty-one years old. He proved to be a gallant soldier. Sergeant Major Darwin earned a Silver Star and Bronze star for his heroism. This was due to, "*Single-handedly carrying out an operation in which several tanks were destroyed and which saved the lives of several comrades.*"

He later married Betty Alice Totten on July 15, 1944. They became the proud parents of Donna Kay and Nancy Carol.

Master Sergeant Kyle distinguished himself by acts of heroism during World War II. He earned a Silver Star and a Bronze Star while in France and Germany. For his actions he also received a battlefield commission along with a Soldier's Medal. To his credit was countless lives saved by his single-handed action of destroying several tanks.

When the Korean Conflict began, Gus went to serve the cause of democracy. In the winter of December 1950, Kyle directed the removal of the wounded from the Hungnam beachhead. He did so while under fire and was recognized for his gallantry. On February 16, 1951, Lieutenant Kyle was leading an attack on Hill

185, and during the charge his platoon came under attack.

According to sources documented, the following account exemplifies his bravery:

"*After hostilities broke out in Korea, Master Sgt. Darwin Kyle, with Company K, 7th Infantry Regiment, 3rd Infantry Division, proved his valor again. In December 1950, Kyle directed removal of the wounded from the Hungnam beachhead while under fire and was recognized for his gallantry. He received a battlefield commission as a lieutenant, his lieutenant bars being presented by Lt. Gen. Matthew B. Ridgeway. He also was awarded the Bronze Star and the Silver Star. On February 16, 1951, Lieutenant Kyle was leading an attack on Hill 185, and during this charge his platoon came under heavy enemy fire. At one point Kyle charged the position and was killed by submachine fire. For his gallantry and self-sacrifice Lt. Darwin Kyle was awarded the Congressional Medal of Honor, the citation stating:*

CITATION

"Second Lieutenant Kyle, distinguished himself by conspicuous gallantry and intrepidity above and beyond the call of duty in action against the enemy. When his platoon had been pinned down by intense fire, he completely exposed himself to move among and encourage his men to continue the advance against enemy forces strongly entrenched on Hill 185. Inspired by his courageous leadership, the platoon resumed the advance but was again pinned down when an enemy machinegun opened fire, wounding 6 of the men. Second Lieutenant Kyle immediately charged the hostile emplacement alone, engaged the crew in hand-to-hand combat, killing all 3. Continuing on toward the objective, his platoon suddenly received an intense automatic-weapons fire from a well-concealed hostile position on its right flank. Again leading his men in a daring bayonet charge against this position, firing his carbine and throwing grenades, Second Lieutenant Kyle personally destroyed four of the enemy before he was killed by a burst from an enemy submachine gun. The extraordinary heroism and outstanding leadership of Second Lieutenant Kyle, and his gallant self-sacrifice, reflect the highest credit upon himself and are in keeping with the esteemed traditions of the military service."

At the onset of the Korean Conflict, Sergeant Major Kyle was given a field commission as 2nd Lieutenant for his role in evacuating Marines from Hungnam. He was killed in action on February 16, 1951. He was rewarded our nation's highest honor posthumously his actions on February 16, 1951, near Kamil-ni, Korea.

On September 27, 1951, the mortal remains of Lieutenant Darwin K. Kyle returned home with full military honors. He was thirty-three years of age. He is buried in Sunset Memorial Park in South Charleston, West Virginia. A school and a bridge proudly bear his name as a fitting memorial to his bravery. In 1992, the Letcher County Historical Society set a historical highway marker.

SOURCES

http://en.wikipedia.org/wiki/Darwin_K._Kyle

http://www.findagrave.com/cgi-bin/fg.cgi?page=gr&GRid=7194211

http://www.history.army.mil/html/moh/koreanwar.html

http://www.wvculture.org/history/wvmemory/vets/kyledarwin/kyledarwin.html

Cathy Schultz from history.army.mil

http://en.wikipedia.org/wiki/Darwin_K._Kyle

http://www.cmohs.org/recipient-detail/3144/kyle-darwin-k.php

http://www.homeofheroes.com/photos/7_korea/kyle.html

http://explorekyhistory.ky.gov/items/show/234#.Uuf-ttIo5kg

http://www.communitywalk.com/location/1906_lt_darwin_k_kyle/info/5726786

DELMER VIRGIL ASHBROOK
Sergeant
HQ Co,
2nd Battalion
39th Infantry
9th Division
March 19, 1948-March 17, 1969
Sergent, Kentucky
Vietnam Memorial Wall
Panel 29W Line 065

Delmer V. Ashbrook was born on Friday, March 19, 1948, at Sergent, Kentucky.

He was in the United States Army, serving as a Radio Operator (MOS: 05B20). He was with the 2nd Battalion, 39th Infantry, and 9th Infantry Division. He went to Vietnam on Thursday, June 20, 1968. He was in Vietnam for nine months. On March 17, 1969, Delmer became involved in a firefight in Dinh Tuong, South Vietnam. He was killed in action by small arms fire. His body was recovered. In the April 3, 1969, edition of the Mountain Eagle, the following was noted:

"Letcher County Friday buried its second victim of the war in Vietnam within a two-week period. SP4 Delmer Virgil Ashbrook was killed near Saigon on March 18, the eve of his 21st birthday."

What do we know about his unit or his service? The following information came from the source listed at the bottom of the page: *"From 1967 on, one of the division's brigades (the 2d Brigade) was the Army contingent of the Mobile Riverine Force. This brigade lived on the ships of Navy Task Force 117, and were transported on their infantry missions throughout the Mekong Delta on World War II landing craft supported by various other armored boats some of which mounted flame-throwers (called zippo after the lighter); had mortars in their holds; and even 105mm cannons on their bows (called monitors). The mobile riverine force was often anchored near the South Vietnamese city of Mỹ Tho, or near Dong Tam, the Division base camp, and they conducted operations in coordination with the Navy Seal teams, the South Vietnamese Marines, units of the ARVN 7th Division and River Assault Groups. Following the Tet offensive in 1968, General Westmoreland stated that the 9th Infantry Division and the Mobile Riverine Force saved the Delta region from falling to the North Vietnamese Army forces. In 1969, the division also operated throughout the IV Corps Tactical Zone."*

Darvin L. King wrote on the Virtual Vietnam Veteran Wall the following. *"We grew up together in Sergent Hollow, in the mountains of Letcher County, Kentucky. The memories of the great times we spent together will never be forgotten. You and I were cousins, but I always called you Brother. You were my best friend from the beginning of my life, and will be my brother forever."*

This we know. Sgt Ashbrook died bravely facing the enemy while actively engaged in preserving our way of life. He is an unsung hero. He is buried in the Evergreen Cemetery in Whitesburg, Kentucky

SOURCES

http://en.wikipedia.org/wiki/9th_Infantry_Division_(United_States)

- See more at: http://www.vvmf.org/Wall-of-Faces/1556/DELMER-V-ASHBROOK#sthash.Jqsw5cu1.dpuf

DEMMER RICHMOND
Private First Class
Company D
166th Infantry
42nd Division
WORLD WAR I

The early years of the 20th century found most of the civilized countries involved in World War I, known as the "The War to end all Wars". The United States managed to avoid sending her young men off to battle in the first few years of the war. With the war going badly for France and England, the United States finally became involved when President Woodrow Wilson declared war on April 17, 1917. The United States military force was ill equipped and undermanned at the time of the Declaration of War. The number of soldiers in the United States Army was at an all time low, with most soldiers depended upon to protect the country being in their respective state militias, now called the National Guard. Though Kentucky was not a densely populated state, the militia had no trouble filling its ranks with young men from the mountains and bluegrass areas. Private Demmer Richmond, from the mountains of eastern Kentucky, was one of many young American boys that would sail for Europe as a "doughboy", willing to fight for the preservation of freedom.

Demmer was born in March of 1897, near the head of Little Colley Creek in Letcher County, Kentucky. He was the son of Owen Richmond and Susan Collins Richmond. Demmer had grown up in the mountains listening to war stories told by both of his grandfathers who had fought in the Civil War. His grandfather on his father's side of the family, Jonathan Richmond, had served in the 64th Virginia Mounted Infantry of the Confederate Army while his other grandfather, Henry Collins, served in the 14th Kentucky Cavalry of the Union Army. Young Demmer no doubt heard differing viewpoints on the War Between the States from the two old soldiers that had at one time been enemies. Hoping to encounter adventures of his own, Demmer enlisted in the Kentucky Militia at Fort Thomas, Kentucky, on July 6, 1916. At that time, the young volunteer did not know that he would receive more than he had bargained for.

The young mountain boy easily adapted to military life, finding that the discipline and respect demanded there was no different than was expected in the hills of Kentucky. Also, like most country boys, he had grown up with a rifle in his hands, having done his part to keep food on the table. For almost two years Demmer and his fellow soldiers trained and enjoyed traveling the country during the uneasy peace. In the spring of 1918, his company of Kentuckians was transferred to the 166th Infantry of the 42nd Division of the newly formed American Expeditionary Force. The 42nd was known as the "Rainbow Division" and had been formed from militia units from 26 states. This nickname is generally credited to Douglas MacArthur's statement that the division "would stretch over the whole country like a rainbow". Major General C.T. Menoher commanded this newly formed division.

As a boy, he had floated up and down the Kentucky River near his home, pretending he was at sea. No longer would Demmer have to pretend as he and his fellow Letcher Countians soon found themselves sailing in a transport ship across the huge and rough Atlantic Ocean. Arriving in France, they were immediately sent to help in the defense of Champagne Marne. The Germans knew that the Americans were coming and had begun a huge offensive, hoping to win a decisive victory before their arrival. However, the Germans miscalculated the length of time that it would take for the Americans to take their positions. They anticipated that the Americans would be slow moving, much like the French but the Doughboys moved quickly into the Western Front battle line. On July 15, 1918, the last German offensive of the war began with a withering artillery barrage.

Demmer and his fellow Doughboys fought ferociously and stopped the German attack in three days of hard fighting. It was now time for the American Expeditionary Force to begin fighting on the offensive.

On July 18, the Aisne Marne offensive attack began. Several American Divisions spearheaded the attack but due to their losses in the last battle, the 42nd was held in reserve until July 25. That morning, Demmer and the 42nd crossed the Marne River and engaged the German defenders in desperate fighting. The color guard for the 42nd was Hank Gowdy, the hero of the 1914 World Series whom had volunteered to fight in the 166th. Gowdy had a batting average of .545 in the series as a player for the Boston Braves. Carrying Old Glory at the front of the advancing battle line, Gowdy and the 42nd took the town of Sergy. Counter attacking with mustard gas, the Germans retook Sergy. Donning their gas mask, the 42nd again charged, retaking the town. Fighting toe to toe for almost two weeks, the German army finally withdrew on August 6, leaving the town in ruins. The Aisne Marne offensive was considered an Allied victory but had cost the 42nd more than 5,500 men. Demmer and his fellow Letcher County comrades had now been exposed to one of the brutalities of war, the use of chemical weapons.

The Doughboys spent the next two weeks digging their trenches deeper and fortifying their position, waiting for another attack from the Germans. Unknown to the Allied commanders, the German forces were too weak to mount an offense. They spent the same time fortifying the area around St. Mihiel. The overall American commander, General John Pershing, had studied the trench warfare that the Allies and the Germans had fought up to this time. He was a firm believer in an offensive attack and decided to use a new concept of warfare that he and his staff had been devising. Breaking from tradition that all attacking forces would be commanded from one command center, he would allow his front line commanders to be independent and use their own initiative to confront problems arising in the attack. He also was impressed with his new armor commander, Colonel George S. Patton, a hard charging and independent officer. He advised his other field commanders to emulate Patton's style.

Having prepared his officers for the St. Mihiel offensive, Pershing decided on a time and date for the attack. Unfortunately, his European counterparts did not comprehend the importance of secrecy and allowed this information to become public. Ironically, one Swiss newspaper published the date and time of the attack. Upon learning of the leak, General Pershing asked his front line commanders their opinion of continuing with the attack. Colonel Patton and the other field officers all reported that their doughboys were eager to get out of the mud and water soaked trenches. Hearing this, Pershing ordered the attack to continue as planned.

On the morning of September 12, 1918, Demmer and his fellow Americans rose out of their trenches and surged forward. The doughboys were inspired by the aggressive style of leading from the front shown by Patton and other field officers and moved quickly all along the battlefront. This cavalry-style attack caught the German defenders off guard and resulted in their being pushed back. By September 16, the Allied forces controlled the St. Miheil area. Though this style of attack was successful for the Allies, in later years the lesson taught to the Germans would come back to haunt them. During World War II, German officers used this same lightning style of attack to defeat their neighboring countries.

The Allies were content with spending the next two weeks in their trenches fighting off several determined German counter attacks. During this time, Demmer once again felt the burning effects of mustard gas. He learned quickly that his most important possessions were his gun and gas mask. Meanwhile, General Pershing was already planning the Allies next offensive. This would be the greatest offensive of the war and would occur in the area between the Meuse River and Argonne Forest. Not only would taking the area split the German defenses, it would deprive them of the two rail lines that supplied them. The Germans were confident they could defend this section as the nature of the Meuse-Argonne terrain made it ideal to defend. The heavily wooded and tangled forest and the river presented natural obstacles.

General Pershing had learned a valuable lesson from the St. Mihiel operation about the importance of secrecy. This time, only a select few officers knew of the details of the plan. At this time, one of the most skillful and amazing events of the war occurred. The French soldiers along the front line were replaced with 600,000 American soldiers without the Germans knowing that there were any Americans in the area! The largest battle ever fought by American troops up to that time in history was about to begin. Demmer and his fellow Letcher Countians were about to be part of this historical event.

At 2:30 A.M. on September 26, 2,700 pieces of artillery commenced a barrage of fire that lasted for three hours. At the end of the barrage, the doughboys surged forward in a frontal attack. Due to the surprise and ferociousness of the attack, the Germans were pushed back six miles in the first four days of the offensive. The German Army was far from being defeated and soon began to stubbornly resist the American attack. German reinforcements poured into the area, mostly troops brought in from other battlefields. From September 30 to October 4, the attack stalled against the determined German defense. During this time, Demmer and his fellow Americans fought back several fierce German countercharges.

On October 4, the doughboys were ordered to charge once more. With their flags snapping briskly in the air, they surged forward and began to push the Germans slowly back. Each time the Americans would stop to allow ammunition and supplies to catch up, the

Germans would counter attack. The counter attacks were unsuccessful however, and by October 7, the hard charging doughboys had captured the Argonne Forest. The next day they crossed the Meuse River. Here the desperate Germans brought up all available reinforcements and managed to slow the assault down to a crawl. By mid October the Germans managed to stop the Allied attack. The remainder of October saw the two armies dug in and facing one another, each trying to bring itself back to enough strength to mount an attack.

General Pershing was successful in bringing up enough reinforcements to once again go on the offensive. In the early morning hours of November 1, the bugles called for a charge once more. Sensing victory, field officers all along the battlefield ordered their heroic doughboys to fix bayonets and charge across the cold and muddy fields in front of them. The Germans were battle-seasoned veterans and stubbornly gave ground to this onslaught. By November 4 however, most of the German Army was in full retreat and pulled back to the city of Sedan for one last stand. The end seemed to be in sight.

At this time Demmer and the 42nd Division dug in and fortified their position, hoping to discourage a counter attack. Now stationary, men of the 42nd became targets of the most feared of German soldiers; the sniper. Each day the unseen sniper killed and wounded several of Demmer's comrades. Demmer and the other doughboys desperately tried to spot the sniper but had no success. By this time of the war Demmer had made a reputation as one of the best shots in the regiment and was called upon by his comrades to takeout the sniper. Try as he might, Demmer could never spot the hidden sniper. On November 11th, war officially ended when the Treaty of Versailles was signed. For the men in the trenches, the sniper kept up his deadly work until word of the treaty was spread up and down the lines. Hearing that the war was over, the elusive and deadly sniper stood up from his hiding place. Demmer was immediately encouraged by his fellow soldiers to take the hated soldier out, though it would be against regulations and decency. They probably thought there was no possible way he could hit the sniper as he was almost out of rifle range. Taking steady aim, he fired and amazingly, the sniper fell. Immediately, several officers demanded to know who had fired but no one seemed to know.

The war had been a costly one for the doughboys, having suffered at least 122,000 casualties in the Meuse-Argonne Battle alone. In an attempt to thank the Americans for their sacrifice, the French designed a cemetery to bury slain American soldiers. The cemetery was named the Meuse-Argonne American Cemetery and has 14,246 interred soldiers. They also built the Sommepy Monument to commemorate the American's sacrifice at Champagne and St. Mihiel. To commemorate American involvement in the Meuse-Argonne Battle, they constructed a beautiful monument called the Montfaucon Monument. With the war now over, Demmer and his fellow doughboys were anxious to go home and were not interested in staying any longer for celebrations.

Once again Demmer and his comrades of the 166th Infantry crossed the rough Atlantic Ocean on a troop ship; the USS Leviathan. Though seasick most of the trip, Demmer did not complain, as he was glad to be alive to make the trip, many of his comrades had not been as fortunate. Arriving back in the United States, Demmer was stationed at Camp Zachary, Kentucky. On May 13, 1919, he was discharged and told he could go back home to the mountains. He did not have to be told twice. Having gotten attached to his old Army rifle, he could not resist the temptation and slipped it out of the barracks and took it home with him. His days of being in the military were now officially over.

Arriving back in his beloved mountains, he soon married a local girl by the name of Grace. They soon had a daughter and named her Cleta. The small family lived in a small coal camp outside Whitesburg named Whitco. Demmer entertained the neighborhood boys by shooting fish with his old army rifle. For the remainder of his life, he would be in and out of hospitals. He eventually lost one lung due to having been gassed during the war. He supplemented his Army pension by buying white oak staves to be used for whiskey barrels. Tragically, he was gunned down in an ambush on July 15, 1939. Having survived all that the Germans could throw at him during the war, he had became a victim of the violence of mountain feuding. He is buried beside his parents at the Sandlick Cemetery in West Whitesburg.

(Left to Right Matt Caudill, Avery Caudill, Demmer Richmond, Willie Collins, Melvin Cornett All Letcher Countians)

SOURCES

Richmond Family Records through present (October, 2004)

U.S. National Archives & Records Administration, Fall 1998, Vol. 30, No. 3; Yockelson, Mitchell

Rainbow Division Veterans Memorial Foundation, Inc. (www.rainbowvets.org) updated, June, 2004

Letcher County Court Clerk's Office, Veterans Discharge Records, World War 1, 1917-1919

Original pictures given to Richard Brown by Richmond descendants

Letcher Countians during World War 1
(Demmer Richmond is in the center)

Packed in Like Sardines in a can. We were Homeward Bound on "The U.S.Leviathan"   April 18, 1919.

DENNIE NEACE
Sergeant
Eleven Bush-Infantry
Company C
1st Battalion
12th Cavalry
1st CAV DIV
Army of the United States
August 03, 1947-31 May 31, 1967

Dennie, though I never met you, your story touched me. I was ashamed after researching you to see how little was written. I offer the following as a tribute to you and those brave men who died with you, as well as to ALL who gave their lives for our country. I will visit your grave to pay my respects in the near future. That is the least I can do.

Sergeant Dennie Neace lived just outside of Hazard, Kentucky, in the small community of Bonnyman. He enlisted into the army and served two years, achieving the rank of sergeant. He went in country on 2/16/1967. Three months later he was killed in action in Quang Tin (An Qui Bong Son Plain), South Vietnam. This was conflict Military Zone 1. Research reveals several operations going on during this time. From all indications the mission he was on was a search and destroy type task.

Sergeant Neace's body was recovered and returned home. Full military honors were afforded the family at the funeral. He was buried in Grapevine, located in Northern Perry County on Highway 15, nine miles north of Hazard. The name of the graveyard is Neace Cemetery. On his behalf, his family was presented with Sergeant Neace's Purple Heart, Vietnam Service Medal, National Defense Metal, Republic of Vietnam Campaign, Gallantry Cross citation.

He was nineteen years of age at his passing. According to the information found on line, Dennie was not married. His service number was 15712057. He was a Baptist. He is listed on the Vietnam Memorial Wall, Panel 21E Line 024

The following moving tribute by his cousin was found on Wall of Faces; posted 10/16/03: *"Not everyone has forgotten you!! Not your mom - not your dad and not me. Dennie, you and I grew up together before you went in the Army. I went to your funeral but stayed only while your coffin was still in your home. (It was) draped with the flag over it and the Purple Heart attached to it. I couldn't stay to see them put you in your grave so I went back to Newport, Ky. I later joined and went to Nam and was assigned to the November Company 75th Air-borne Rangers to work out, if you know what I mean. I thought that you may want to know the names of your buddies who died with you! 1. Hervey Allen Harris, 2.Randy Arbogast 3. Harold A Beaverson Jr. 4. Nathaniel Collins, 5.Teddy Rex Dunn, 6. William Wallace Money, and 7. Jerald Anthony Vokish. Your mom moved to Falmouth, Ky, close to me after your dad died. She died a few years back. Now you are together and can rest easy and be at peace. Your Cousin Ron (Combs) 158 N Grand Ave Ft. Thomas, Ky 41075.*

Donna, Dennie's cousin, wrote the following on the Virtual Wall honoring the fallen. *"We shall never forget you. Your smile was so heartwarming and contagious. Though you were only a cousin, you felt like a brother because of all time you chose to spend in our home. God needed you for a reason, so we had to let you go. You will always remain in our hearts."*
Love, Donna

SOURCES

http://www.virtualwall.org/dn/NeaceDx01a.htm

http://www.fold3.com/page/632073371_dennie_neace/details/

http://army.togetherweserved.com/army/servlet/tws.webapp.WebApp?cmd=ShadowBoxProfile&type=Person&ID=62133&source=fold3

http://www.fold3.com/s.php#query=dennie+neace&preview=1&t=830

http://www.usfallenwarriors.com/index.php?page=directory&rec=17472

http://genealogytrails.com/ken/perry/vietnamcasualties_perry.html

http://www.vvmf.org/Wall-of-Faces/37444/DENNIE-NEACE

http://en.wikipedia.org/wiki/12th_Cavalry_Regiment

http://www.youtube.com/watch?v=3dappJDVKzs

DESMOND THOMAS DOSS
Corporal
U.S. Army Medical Detachment
307th Infantry
77th Infantry Division
February 7, 1919-March 23, 2006

There are several types of heroes. Those who wear their medals on their chest and possess such pride in what they have done for their country. This is rightly so. There are those who refuse to talk of their heroism and maintain they were not a hero but did what they were called to do for their country. Then there was Desmond Thomas Doss.

Desmond was born in Lynchburg, Virginia, located in Walker County. He was a small man in stature (5'6") but a giant of a man in spirit. As a young man he had a bad experience with a gun. His father was arguing with Desmond's brother and the quarrel became inflamed. The father pulled a gun and the mother stepped between them. The father relented and the mother told Desmond to hide the gun before the police came. It was at that moment he vowed never to handle a gun again.

As a young man he became a Seventh-day Adventist. One item that inspired him was the Ten Commandments that his father had purchased at an auction. He studied them and became convicted that he would not break them. Another picture his father has bought showed Cain holding a club over the lifeless body of Abel, his brother. Later in life Corporal Doss stated, *"And when I looked at that picture, I came to the Sixth Commandment, 'Thou shalt not kill,'* in a documentary called Beyond Glory, he stated, "*I wondered, how in the world could a brother do such a thing? It put a horror in my heart of just killing, and as a result I took it personally:* 'Desmond, if you love me, you won't kill.'" Desmond kept his promise all his life.

When World War II began, Desmond felt it his duty to serve. Yet he did not believe in killing. In April 1942, this slime built twenty-three year old man enlisted and received a 1-A-O (Conscientious Objector) status. During basic training he refused to qualify using a weapon, which caused him to be chastised and ridiculed by fellow soldiers. He stuck to his beliefs. He sought and was granted a position as a medic. In the summer of 1944, Corporal Doss was sent to the Pacific Theatre where he received a Bronze Star as a combat medic on Guam and Leyte, Philippines.

In the spring of 1945, during the battle for Okinawa, his faith was put to the ultimate test. The island was well fortified with seasoned Japanese troops. The Maeda Escarpment was the objective. On May 5, 1945, the men were ordered forward. There they faced a four hundred high ridge when the Japanese counterattacked. In a counter attack by the Japanese, several soldiers were driven off the ridge. Many of the wounded could not escape. With Hercules strength, PFC Doss began carrying them one by one and lowered the men on a rope supported litter. He was oblivious to the enemy's fire. Trip after trip he made carrying wounded warriors. Some say he saved over one hundred. The official record stated seventy-five men were rescued.

Continued fighting during the next couple of weeks led to PFC Doss being wounded by shrapnel from a grenade. While being carried off on a litter, he saw a man who seemed in worse shape and he yielded his stretcher to that soldier. Such was the courage of this man who refused to fight. Later he was shot and his arm was fractured. He found a rifle stock and made a splint. He crawled to where he was able to get assistance. Doss left the army in 1946.

Due to the severity of his injuries and having tuberculosis, he spent five years back and forth in hospitals. He was unable to work but served his faith daily while living in Rising Fawn, Georgia and then Piedmont, Alabama.

Desmond T. Doss was the only person to receive the Congressional Medal of Honor for non-combat achievements in World War II. He was also the first conscientious objector to receive the medal. The medal was presented to him by President Truman on October 12, 1945.

In an interview with the Richmond Times Dispatch in 1998, Desmond's humble nature came through once again. "From a human standpoint, I shouldn't be here to tell the story. All the glory should go to God. No telling how many times the Lord has spared my life." Another statement giving a testimonial of his sterling Christian character was when the army thought about giving him a discharge. "I'd be a very poor Christian if I accepted a discharge implying that I was mentally off because of my religion. I'm sorry gentlemen, but I can't accept that kind of a discharge." The brave medic without a gun died on March 23, 2006, still serving his God and his country.

SOURCES

http://www.nytimes.com/2006/03/25/national/25doss.html?_r=0

http://www.homeofheroes.com/profiles/profiles_doss2.html

http://en.wikipedia.org/wiki/Desmond_Doss

http://www.outsidethebeltway.com/desmond_doss_pacifist_medal_of_honor_recipient_dies_at_87/

http://myhero.com/go/hero.asp?hero=Desmond_Doss_HAS_06

DOYLE JANNOW
Private First Class
Company H
2nd Battalion
318th Infantry Regiment
80th Division
WWII
October 16, 1920-December 4, 1993

Sometimes you encounter a story bigger than life. On occasion we find out about men of legend. Usually the story entails valor, heroism, and self sacrifice. All the elements and many more are part of the saga of this unsung hero from Letcher County, Kentucky.

While talking to my friend, Steve King (Jeremiah Post Master), I mentioned the book I was writing regarding unsung heroes. He immediately related a story of his father-in-law who served in World War II. I was mesmerized by the saga of Doyle Jannow and knew I had to research him. When I returned to my office I began searching. To my dismay I found little information and soon realized that this had to be rectified for this unsung hero. I contacted Steve and he called his wife. She offered the following information about her father, a true American hero.

During an interview she talked about her father with such pride, love and passion that afterward I felt I had met the man through her. I offer his story through her words regarding this American hero.

"If I had to say one thing about my daddy, he lived a full life before I was born. It was a good life. He worked hard and loved me more than anything. He worked in the coal mines after his service. He loved both because of the camaraderie he felt while serving his country. He was featured in Life Magazine. The picture showed him and Elkaney Potter on a tank.

"When I was young I would ask him questions. If he didn't want to answer he would simply say his name, rank and serial number. I still know them to this day. He had a great sense of humor. If mother said something to him, he would salute and wink at me. He met my mother when she was walking down the road. He offered her a ride and it was love at first sight. Mother's name is Willa Mae Salouis.

Doyle Jannow Jr. was born in Daisy, Tennessee. He moved to Kona, when he was young. There he grew up. When the war came he wanted to do his patriotic duty. He enlisted on July 7, 1942, at Camp Forrest, Tennessee. After he was trained he was assigned to the elite 80th Division.

The 80th Division became immortal during the western offensive. They earned their reputation in such offenses as the closing of the Argentan-Falaise Gap, smashing the Van Rundstedt Drive, crossing the Rhine and smashing the resistance in Southeast Germany. They broke the Germans Seventh Army.

During November, the 80th penetrated into German position and outflanked them, paving the way for Metz capture. By the 25th of November, the Maginot Line was breeched and the next day the 80th was in Saar Basin.

PFC Jannow served in France from late 1943, until he was wounded at Metz, France, on November 22, 1944. He and his comrades volunteered for a reconnaissance mission through Metz and were fired upon by a German Panzer. The jeep's gunner was killed instantly when the jeep flipper over from the blast. PFC Jannow was trapped under the jeep with both legs crushed. He kept fighting until he was airlifted to a hospital in Paris, France. He stayed hospitalized for several months. He was later flown to the Wakeman Convalescent Hospital at Camp Atterbury, Indiana. He spent an additional year there. He walked out on a cane. He was honorably discharged November 1, 1945. He was awarded the Purple Heart with two bronze clusters, European Campaign Medal, Good Conduct Medal and the Victory Medal.

He returned home to Cromona, Kentucky, and worked in the mines for forty plus years. He was employed as a miner for the Southeast Coal Company. He was nicknamed Junebug by his fellow miners. He was well liked and had a great sense of humor. He was seventy-three at his passing. His legacy lives on through family, friends and neighbors reflections.

SOURCES

http://www.fold3.com/s.php#s_given_name=doyle&s_surname=jannow&ocr=1&t=all&tx=830

http://www.death-record.com/d/n/Doyle-Jannow/Kentucky

U.S., Department of Veterans Affairs BIRLS Death File, 1850-2010

Interview with his daughter

http://www.ancientfaces.com/person/doyle-jannow/56224476

http://www.ancientfaces.com/person/doyle-jr-jannow/156468135

EDMOND A. HARJO
Private First Class
Battery A 195TH
Field Artillery Battalion
Seminole Code Talker
November 24, 1917–March 31, 2014

Another American icon now walks upon the wind. During his life he served his people and country with pride and sacrifice. He is truly an unsung hero whose passing ends a segment of an era for the greatest generation. His name was Edmond Harjo and he was a Seminole Warrior. He became a code talker. This is his saga.

Edmond was born on November 24, 1917. His parents were Yanna (Grant) and Tony Harjo of Maud, Oklahoma. He attended school and when World War II began he found himself in the service of his country. He enlisted on May 26, 1942, in Tulsa, Oklahoma. (Source: Box Number: 1292 1; Film Reel Number: 6.5). Note that FOLD 3 has his year of birth as 1916.

In 1944, he was walking through an orchard in the southern part of France. He saw some soldiers under a tree. As he approached them he realized that they were Native Americans singing a traditional song. He joined in and talked in the Creek dialect. Sometime later, a captain heard a couple of men talking in their native tongue and knew they would be a valuable asset to the war effort.

After the war, Mr. Harjo became a school teacher with the Maud Schools. He also worked with the Justice Schools and Picket Center. He was a well-known concert pianist. He was a longtime member/elder of his church. He never married. He died at the age of ninety-six in Seminole, Oklahoma. He was buried in Ada, Oklahoma, while at Mercy Hospital. Swearingen Funeral Home Chapel was in charge of the arrangements. The place of burial was in the Seminole Nation Veterans Memorial Cemetery.

Congressman Tom Cole (Oklahoma 4th District), a tribal citizen of the Chickasaw Nation, issued the following statement regarding Mr. Harjo's death: *"I was deeply grieved to hear about the loss of a true military hero and inspirational figure to generations of Native Americans. During the Congressional Gold Medal ceremony last year that honored code talkers from 33 tribes, I had the opportunity to meet Edmond Harjo and participate in the ceremony that recognized his bravery during World War II. Because he took great pride in his unique heritage, Harjo and other Native American soldiers were able to encrypt and transfer wartime messages and ultimately prevent highly-sensitive information from being intercepted by the enemy. His service and bravery will surely live on."*

During the ceremony, House Speaker Boehner said of Private First Class Harjo: *"Edmond and his brothers were at Normandy and Iwo Jima and they mobilized the weapon of language to thwart the fiercest enemy the free people have ever known and made a difference... join me in applauding their perseverance and the deeds that have been relegated to legend and may they now live in memory,"*

He is survived by nephews and nieces, other family members and friends to mourn his loss. Yet we must honor his contributions to our freedom by honoring his Seminole legacy. He walked the path of a warrior and now walks upon the wind. He was the last of the Seminole Code Talkers.

MEDALS AND AWARDS

- Congressional Gold Medal
- Good Conduct Medal
- EAME Service Ribbon
- Silver Service Star

SOURCES

http://nativenewsonline.net/currents/last-seminole-nation-code-talker-edmond-harjo-walks/

http://www.latimes.com/obituaries/la-me-passings-20140410,0,7261753.story#axzz2ybxc5irJ

http://www.foxnews.com/us/2014/04/09/edmond-harjo-one-last-remaining-native-american-code-talkers-dies-at-6-in/

http://www.indianz.com/News/2014/013200.asp

http://indiancountrytodaymedianetwork.com/2014/04/05/congressional-gold-medal-recipient-and-code-talker-edmond-harjo-walks-154332

http://www.tributes.com/notable/obituaries/EdmondHarjo

http://www.fold3.com/s.php#s_given_name=edmond&s_surname=harjo&offset=4&preview=1

http://www.fold3.com/title_831/wwii_army_enlistment_records/

EDWIN C. JENKINS
Lieutenant
B-24 Bombardier
World War II
Recipient of the Silver Star
Distinguished Flying Cross
Air Medal with 2 Oak Leaf Clusters

At the writing of this book I have been searching for information on Lieutenant Jenkins. He was a B-24 bombardier with over forty raids under his belt. According to the following article, he had three hundred combat hours. Yet very little is written about this unsung American hero.

"First Lt. Edwin C. Jenkins is in Whitesburg on a 20-day leave after spending 16 months in the war zone in the Middle East. A bombardier on a B-24, Lt. Jenkins has taken part in 40 raids over Sicily, Italy, Burma, Crete, Tripoli, Tunisia and other places and has 300 combat hours to his credit.

Medals he has won include the Silver Star, Distinguished Flying Cross, and Air Medal with two Oak Leaf Clusters. The son of Mrs. A.F. Stroud of Whitesburg, he was commissioned while overseas.

SOURCES

With permission from the Mountain Eagle; September 2, 1943; Volume 37; Number 7

ELI WHITT
34th Battalion Cavalry
Captain E. V. Harmon's Company,
McDowell Partisan Rangers, Virginia Volunteers.
February 13, 1846-February13, 1889
Written by Janice Busic

According to family legend, Eli Whitt was a single man when he came from Tazewell County to Buchanan County Virginia with his young son, George. Eli had been married to an Indian woman who had died when George was a young child. Eli buried George's mother and left the area, bringing George with him. They settled in the Garden Creek area where Eli married Hannah Bailey and had seven children. This information was passed down to great-grandson Lawson Blankenship by his grandmother, Mary Jane Short, wife of George Whitt.

A question posted on an internet genealogy forum got a reply from a fellow researcher in Sun, West Virginia. According to the writer, her grandmother told a story of a couple who lived "back on the mountain" in that area. This is her story, "The couple, a white man and an Indian woman, had a small son named George. The woman got sick and died and was buried on the mountain where they lived. The man took his son and left the area. The community never knew what became of them."

By combining anecdotal records with factual accounts, this seems to be the Eli Whitt family. Eli Whitt married Nancy Lester in March of 1857. Their marriage is recorded in Tazewell County, Virginia. Nancy was the second great granddaughter of Abner Alexander Lester and Martha Rebecca "Patsy" Arthur. Martha Rebecca was the daughter of Gabriel Arthur and Hannah Rebecca "Nikitie", no last name, a "Cherokee woman."

Much has been written about Gabriel Arthur. Some say he came to this country as an indentured servant. His record says he was uneducated but very intelligent. In the mid sixteen hundreds he was a long hunter who explored with James Needham. They were the first recorded English explorers who came to North Carolina and the New River Valley of Virginia. The research laboratory at the University of North Carolina has a collection of letters written by Abraham Wood that give details of the "Journey of James Needham and Gabriel Arthur."

During the War Between the States, Eli joined the Confederate Army. His military service record, which is located in the National Archives, show that he enlisted on July 10 at Gap Store by Captain Harmon. Eli answered roll call on July 15, 1862 in the 34th Battalion Cavalry, Captain E. V. Harmon's Company, McDowell Partisan Rangers, and Virginia Volunteers.

Again, according to family legend, Eli died of a gunshot wound. He was shot because of a long standing disagreement with a man who vowed as a child to kill Eli when he grew up. He carried through with that promise when he was about 20 years old. Eli lived several months after being shot but never recovered. He died on his birthday, 13 February 1889, at the age of 53. He is buried in the Whitt Cemetery on Drill Mountain in Buchanan County, Virginia. The inscription on his tombstone may give an indication of who Eli Whitt was. It reads, "His ways were evil, His deeds were kind, a host of friends he leaves behind."

ELMON GRADY POTTER
Private First Class
Paratrooper
HQ3/506th Parachute Infantry Regiment
3rd Battalion
101st Airborne Division
Recipient of the Purple Heart and the Bronze Star (3 battle stars)
October 5, 1922- September 27, 1991

This story of a Letcher County mountain boy turned man exemplifies tenacity of spirit and bravery under fire. Elmon proved to be a brave soldier and represented his county well. His life story is one of achievement and overcoming challenges. He is truly an unsung hero.

Elmon Grady Potter was the son of Roosevelt (Velt) and Hattie Collier Potter. He was the oldest of the six siblings. He was born at Craftsville near Millstone, Kentucky, on October 5, 1922. The family moved to Seco when he was young. Elmon attended Seco Elementary school. He was a typical young lad. He was small for his age but full of grit. Though fun loving and care free, Elmon would hold his own if pushed.

When he was fourteen years of age Hattie died due to accidently being given the wrong medication. She had poison ivy and a few days later had a couple of teeth pulled. She was in pain and sent for a prescription. Thinking it was a refill for poison ivy, they gave her medicine for that. Unknowingly she took it and became violently ill. She was taken to the Seco Hospital but died on March 13, 1937.

Elmon was considered to be a 'wild and free spirit.' He would leave home for days and show up at a relative's home. He was a hard worker and collected metal to sell. He worked in gardens, picked berries, chopped wood, bundled corn for fodder. He also was a paperboy, delivering the Knoxville News Sentinel to neighbors.

Elmon attended Fleming Neon in 1938. He went to school there for three years. Roosevelt, Elmon's father, remarried (Laura Belcher) and they relocated to Shelby Gap, which is located in Pike County, Kentucky. Elmon went to Dorton High School for a brief time.

When the winds of war began to blow, he felt it was his duty to enlist. He was too small and had to take the physical twice. Before the second physical, Elmon ate bananas and drank water. He joined the Army Air Corps in September 25, 1941. He was sent to Shepherd Field, Texas. When the Air Corps was divided he decided to go with the paratrooper training. He went with the famed 101st Airborne in 1942. He found himself in Camp Claiborne, Louisiana

He was deployed to England in September of 1941. There he with his brother soldiers prepared for the largest land invasion in the history of warfare. On D Day they jumped into France to liberate that country. The 101st made more jumps and in the winter found himself fighting beside his friend, Raymond Smith in the Battle of Bastogne, Belgium. From December 19,

1944, to December 26, 1944, fierce fighting occurred. The situation was extremely perilous and at one juncture the Germans order the Allied Forces to surrender. General McAuliffe uttered those immortal words, "Nuts" and the fighting continued.

PFC Potter fought hand to hand and received bayonet wounds. On February 23, 1945, once again he was wounded in the line of duty. The war ended soon after and He was released on October 21, 1945. Elmon returned home and graduated in 1947.

He decided to finish his high school education and graduated in 1947. He then attended school in Hot Springs, Arkansas and earned a degree in business. He returned home, fell in love and in August of 1950, he married Doris Creech. She was a school teacher from Skyline (Linefork), Kentucky.

For some reason they moved to Dearborn, Michigan, and Elmon found employment at the Great lake Steel Company. He worked for them for twenty-two years and became Superintendent. He retired in 1973. That year they moved back to Skyline with their three children, David Wayne (September 1951), Ricky Elmon, (November 1952), and Linda Susan (November 1963). Mrs. Potter found a job as the postmaster and her husband became the manager of Dawahare's. He served in that capacity for twelve years.

Elmon was a man of great diversity and talent. I recall his wife along with him. My aunt lived in Skyline and I used to drive a school bus up in that area. I also remember Elmon working at one of the Dawahare stores.

Mr. Potter was an avid UK fan, enjoyed the tournaments and loved the Detroit Tigers and Lions. He was a Kentucky Colonel, member of the VFW along with the American Legion. He was a proud member of the Association of the 101st Airborne Division. He is buried in the Mountain Home National Cemetery located in Johnson City, Tennessee (section LL; row O, grave number 259). He was sixty-eight years of age.

On September 29, 1991, funeral services were held by the following friends of Elmon: I.D. Back, Jim Fields, and Elwood Cornett. The next day the VFW Post #6875 offered a full military tribute with Chaplain Arnold Hanson officiating.

SOURCES

"101st Airborne Trooper Remembered," Enoch Potter, contributed by Elmon Potter's daughter Linda Potter.

http://www.findagrave.com/cgi-bin/fg.cgi?page=gr&GRid=1089300

http://www.nps.gov/history/nr/travel/national_cemeteries/Tennessee/Mountain_Home_National_Cemetery.html

http://www.fold3.com/s.php#s_given_name=elmon&s_surname=potter&preview=1&offset=3

http://www.fold3.com/title_848/veterans_affairs_birls_death_file/

"Joe, yestiddy ya saved my life an' I swore I'd pay ya back. Here's my last pair of dry socks."

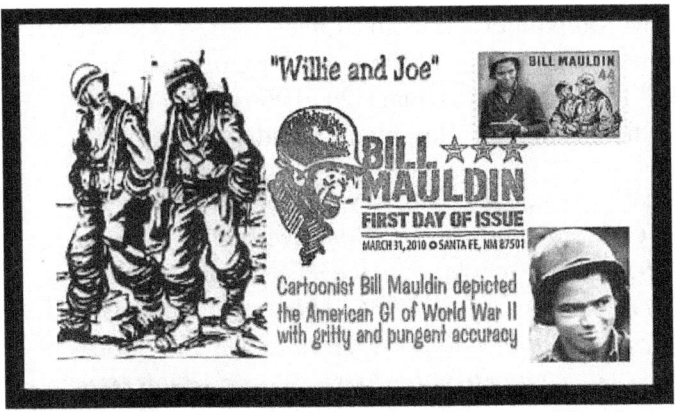

(Bill Mauldin, a true American Unsung Hero)

EMMITT COLON ADAMS
Private First Class
A Company
13th Signal Battalion
1st Cavalry Division
USARV
September 21, 1942-February 20, 1966

As I searched for information, I was appalled at the lack of it for so many of our unsung heroes. Our country owes so much to these men and women yet they seem to have faded from our memories. It is my sincere prayer that upon reading this you will become active in finding your local heroes and posting them so others can recall their deeds. I would love to obtain a picture of PFC Adams for this book and for our area's history.

Emmitt was born in Isom, Kentucky. He went into the service. His service ID number was 52625935. After basic he became Private Adams trained in the field of 31M2D (Mulitchannel Transmission Systems). He was twenty-three years of age at the beginning of his tour in Vietnam. The date was January 29, 1966. Twenty-two days later he would be killed by a grenade.

The Casualty Incident Summary states the following: *"Emmitt Colon Adams from Isom Kentucky had the rank of Private First Class in the U.S. Army when he was a Grenade casualty in 1966. This occurred during the Vietnam Conflict, South Vietnam. Marital status was never married. Private First Class Adams was enlisted as Multichannel Transmission Systems through Selected Service in the Army."* Private First Class Emmitt Colon Adams is honored on the Vietnam Memorial Wall; panel 5E, Line 54. He is buried at the Adams Family Cemetery or the Shade Adams Cemetery in Isom, Kentucky.

SOURCES

http://www.virtualwall.org/da/AdamsEC02a.htm

http://www.findagrave.com/cgi-bin/fg.cgi?page=gr&GRid=102064110

http://www.vvmf.org/Wall-of-Faces/215/EMMITT-C-ADAMS

http://army.togetherweserved.com/army/servlet/tws.webapp.WebApp?cmd=ShadowBoxProfile&type=Person&ID=37817

http://www.usfallenwarriors.com/index.php?page=directory&rec=77284

http://genealogytrails.com/ken/letcher/vietnamcasualties_letcher.html

EULIS RAY ADKINS
US Navy/Army
January 4, 1954-July 5, 2012

(Colonel Adkins on right)

There are very few men who are made out of a superior mode. I have known only a few. One man stands out in my mind. His metal was tested by fire in his youth and he proved to be worthy of the test. His name was Eulis Ray Adkins.

I first met Ray at, appropriate enough, a reenactment. Something drew me to him. He was a sergeant with the 6th Kentucky and possessed all the military skills of a sergeant. I soon realized that he was indeed a Veteran, having served with honor in Vietnam. I met his lovely wife, Debbie (Ray lovingly referred to her as the Secretary of War), and found she too possessed those intrinsic characteristics that speak volumes of a Christian upbringing.

There are so many precious memories. The long talks around the campfire, the practical jokes we all pulled on each other, the drills and dinners we had together and the sharing of our belief in Christ. One of my favorite memories is a baptism at the Battle of Barbourville. I vividly recall standing in a pond at Barbourville. I recommitted my life to Christ and before long several came forward (a total of 28) proclaiming the need to be saved and baptized. Brother Ray shouted for JOY on the banks of the shore. His words echoed louder than the others. He continued saying, 'Praise the Lord" while his hands were outstretched, as if welcoming the lost lamb to the fold. Standing beside him as always was his wife, Ms Debbie. He greeted each person who came out of the water with a hug. Truly Ray is a man after God's heart. It was a moment that forever is committed to my mind.

Ray, Mr. Gaddis, Les Williamson, Ronnie Bowling, and I began the 5th Kentucky years ago. Our purpose was to perpetuate the good name of our ancestors and to share our common bond of brotherhood, as we all had ancestors who fought in the Orphan Brigade, 5th Kentucky, 10th Mounted Rifles and 13th Kentucky Cavalry. I was so impressed with our mission statement of serving God first in all things, country and honor. The fifth has grown until it was the largest company in Kentucky. Colonel Adkins was instrumental in bringing events to eastern Kentucky and promoting local, as well as regional history during that time frame.

Through all his trials, Ray never lost his faith. Prior to losing his leg, the colonel wrote: "Most of you know I have been through a lot in the last two years, cancer, pad, (toes removed and part of my foot, bladder and prostate removal 10 surgeries in all). I want to Praise the Lord that I am still here, and getting better each day. I pray that by spring I will be the healthy man I was (the Good Lord willing). I owe him so much and he has brought me through many storms. I also know that YOUR prayers meant a lot. I would not be typing this now if the thousands of prayers had not been prayed." He still possessed the same unshakable faith to the end.

Eulis Ray Adkins was buried with full military honors with his Airborne Beret and Confederate Kepi on a stand with the American flag and the 5th Kentucky battle flag next to him. The 5th Kentucky Infantry his beloved unit stood guard for two days. Reenactors from Virginia, Tennessee, and Kentucky came and paid their final respects. Over 10 units Confederate and Union were represented. After the eulogy by Pastors Mark Partin and Rick Partin, Ray's brother in laws. One by one the D.A.V., Patriot Guard and all the reenactors present passed the casket with a slow final salute. Two hundred people, over a period of eight hours, paid their final respects. Members of the 5th Kentucky past and present gathered around the casket and sang Dixie accompanied by Moses and Evelyn Hamlin just as Ray would have wanted it. The DAV and the Patriot Guard escorted him home. Ray loved motorcycles and was an avid rider in the past. As requested a fully dressed Harley led the way with a full sized Battle flag flying just as Ray wanted.

Ray was more than my friend; he was a fellow Veteran, SCV member and my Brother. Ray's deep faith in God carried him through many painful months and his courage was something most people just strive for and never receive. We will miss Ray but we have the comfort in knowing he is no longer ravaged by the pain of cancer brought on in part by Agent Orange and the horrors of Vietnam.

EULOGY

Mr. Eulis Ray Adkins age fifty eight of Artemus, Kentucky, departed this life on Thursday, July 05, 2012, at his home. He was the husband of Debra (Partin) Adkins and the son of Wilma Jean Adkins born on January 4, 1954, in Middlesboro, KY.

He was a member of the Roadside Baptist Church and was a Veteran of the United States Army and Navy. He served his country during the Vietnam War. Mr. Adkins had been a warehouse supervisor at Jackson MSC and later was employed with the Knox County Board of Education. He enjoyed Civil War reenactments and was the "Colonel" of the 5th KY Infantry. He was a member of the Daniel Boone Festival Committee, Vice President of the Knox Co. Cancer patient fund, a member of the Sons of the Confederate Veterans, a KY Colonel and was a published author.

Mr. Adkins is preceded in death by his mother, Wilma Jean Adkins, his grandparents, Carl & Nola Adkins, a sister, Margaret Diann Klusman, his mother and father in law, John & Alma Partin and a brother in law, Doug Partin.

Survivors include his wife Debra Adkins of Artemus, Kentucky, his daughter Wendy Bunch a son-in-law Jimmy Bunch two sons, Jason Adkins and Kevin Miles, a daughter in law, Falina Adkins, grandchildren, Morgan Bunch, Tanner Bunch, Cassie Miles and Aliyah Miles, a sister Linda Raines, a brother, Billy Klusman and wife Linda, sisters-in-law Cathy Landrum, Zella Ledford, Judy Bowling and husband Ronnie, Pam Clines and husband Danny, brothers-in-law, Mark Partin and wife Pam, Johnny Partin and wife Michelle and Rick Partin and wife Sherry. He also leaves behind many special nieces, nephews, aunts, uncles and cousins and very special caregivers Mark & Pam Partin.

Funeral services for Mr. Eulis Ray Adkins were conducted at the Roadside Baptist Church in Barbourville on Sunday, July 8, 2012, at 2:00 p.m. with Rev. Mark Partin and Reverend Rick Partin officiating. He was laid to rest in the Abner Stewart Cemetery at Artemus.

Pallbearers were Tony Landrum, Alvin Brown, Brian Brown, Keith Partin, Chris Partin, Jeremiah Partin,

Randy Partin, Joel Partin, Nathan Warfield, Chris Bowling, Josh Partin and Daniel Clines. Honorary pallbearers will be Members of the 5th KY Infantry, Nurses and staff of the Knox Co. Health Dept., Doctors, Lohe, Hasni, Jain and staff, Dr. Niazi and staff, all fellow civil war reenactors, Dr. Carl and nurses and staff. Hampton Funeral Home was in charge of all arrangements. Ray proudly served our country in the Navy as well as being an Army Veteran. He served his country during the Vietnam War. Respectfully submitted by Les Williamson and Dave Chaltas.

SOURCES

http://obits.dignitymemorial.com/dignity-memorial/obituary.aspx?n=Eulis-Adkins&lc=6780&pid=158404643&mid=5162243

http://www.tributes.com/show/Eulis-Ray-Adkins-94101349

EVERTT TIPTON CULP
Private First Class
Company C
11th Infantry
1st Battalion, 1st Brigade
'Red Devil Brigade'
5th Division Mechanized Army

Everett (Tipton) Culp was born on June 21, 1948, in Letcher County, Kentucky. He was the son of the late Ellis Culp and Stacy Irene Collier Halcomb (1924-2003).

Tip was drafted by the Selective Service on December 15, 1968. His MOS was 11B10. He was killed in the line of duty on March 27, 1969, in Province 2 of the Republic of Vietnam. He was twenty years of age. He was married and listed as Baptist in faith. His name is on the Vietnam Memorial Wall (Panel 28W-Line 058) and is listed as living in Columbia City, Indiana. Noted on the Vietnam Wall was the following: *"Private First Class Everett T. Culp was killed in action during Operation Montana Mauler on Hill 208 just North of Con Thien in Quang Tri Province, March 27, 1969."* The after action report stated he, *"Died as a ground casualty from multiple fragmentation wounds."* Also note the information stated his body was recovered. Another report stated that his body was NOT recovered. According to Roy Culp, Tipton's brother, his body was recovered and brought home with full military honors. Also the Vietnam Memorial Wall database page states his body WAS recovered.

The Mountain Eagle offered the following information about his death: *"The family of Gary Pace was informed this week that he has been killed in Vietnam. Services were held here Tuesday for Pfc. Everett Tipton Culp, killed March 27 on duty in Vietnam."* The website, Findagrave.com stated the following: *"Everett Culp was killed in South Vietnam during the Vietnam*

War. *His remains were never returned but his family placed a marker in the family cemetery in his honor, least he not be forgotten."*

Everett (Tipton) Culp, Private First Class, 5th Division Mechanized Army was killed in action on March 27, 1969. He is buried in the Halcomb Cemetery located in Eolia, Letcher, Kentucky.

While researching Tippy, I found the following note on the Virtual Wall. Listed below are the men who lost their lives fighting alongside of Tip.

"On 27 March 1969, elements of the 1st Battalion, 11th Infantry, assaulted Hill 208, located between Con Thien and the Demilitarized Zone. The Battalion lost 14 men as a result of the assault, 13 killed in action on 27 March and one, Captain Marvin Roberts, who died the next day of wounds received."

B Company, 1/11th Infantry

- CPT Marvin J. Roberts, Baton Rouge, LA (Dist Svc Cross)
- 1LT William D. Cody, Robinson, IL (Dist Svc Cross)
- SGT Louis K. Dixon, Mobile, AL
- SP4 Robert L. Anglin, Arista, WV (may have been C/1/11 Inf)
- SP4 Bobby J. Walters, Petersburg, IN
- SP4 Leslie W. Worl, Long Beach, CA
- PFC Oscar G. Johnson, Philadelphia, PA

C Company, 1/11th Infantry

- SP4 Dimitrios G. Arniotis, Jamaica, NY
- SP4 Joseph J. Dobynes, Marion, AL
- SP4 David E. Flannery, Muskegon, MI
- SP4 Allison W. Locklair, St Stephen, SC

- PFC Everett T. Culp, Columbia City, IN
- PFC Leonard C. Ivy, Terre Haute, IN

HHC, 1/11th Infantry

- PFC Rene A. Buller, Houston, TX

Mr. Smith's comment regarding incorrect coding in the 1993 casualty database is correct. The Virtual Wall notes that the 2003 DoD casualty file properly reflects Quang Tri Province.

On August 20, 2007, Past Commander David Chaltas noted in the Ben Caudill Journal that, *"Everett Tipton Culp, a Vietnam Veteran, will have the Red Star Bridge named in his honor."*

SOURCES

http://www.bencaudill.com/journal07.html
Coffelt Database volume 075, Certificate 37031

http://www.findagrave.com/cgi-bin/fg.cgi?page=pv&GRid=94347256

http://www.themountaineagle.com/news/2009-04-08/PDF/Page_05.pdf

www.ancestory.com

http://www.virtualwall.org/dc/CulpET01a.htm

http://www.virtualwall.org/dc/CulpET01a.htm

Interview with Ellis Roy Culp (brother) and Barbara Back Culp

FAST EDDIE
The Saga of Eddie Rickenbacker

They called him Fast Eddie. He was a man driven by the love of machines and speed. He loved them even at a young age. His passion was racing and before World War I he had competed in the Indianapolis 500 four times. When war was declared in 1917, Eddie joined the army but his love for machines soon gained him notoriety and he was selected to be an engineer officer. But he was determined to fly and after many challenges, he was awarded his wings. He became America's leading ace and reportedly had over 300 combat hours and twenty-six confirmed downing of enemy aircraft, and balloons. His fame grew.

Eddie started his own auto building company, bought the Indianapolis Motor Speedway, and formed Eastern Airlines. He also helped create a comic strip entitled Ace Drummond. He was also a well-known author. All was well in his life. On February 26, 1941, he was a passenger on a Douglas DC-3 airliner that crashed outside of Atlanta, Georgia. His injuries were so severe that those working to save lives left him for dead. His body was soaked in fuel, covered with debris and his physical injuries defied living. Yet he survived. God was not through with him yet.

When World War II began, he was selected to inspect troops and do all to support the war effort. On a trip to the Pacific Theatre, he carried a secret message to General McArthur. While on a Flying Fortress, navigation went haywire and they had to ditch the plane in the ocean. For twenty-four days they drifted in unknown waters. After the third day, there was no food, no water, or other supplies on the life raft. The sun was merciless. Hope was fleeting. Then came a sea gull and landed on the hat of Eddie. He grabbed the gull and quickly sacrificed it for the lives of those in the raft. From its entrails he made a crude fishing line. A shark was also provided and then the rains came. Miracles at sea! They drifted for close to a month before they were spotted and rescued. God wasn't through with him yet. One of the stories told about Eddie is he would on occasion go to the dock and offer shrimp to sea gulls thanking them for saving him from a certain death. Though unsubstantiated, it stands to reason that he would not only be grateful to the gulls, but more importantly to God for the rescue.

Upon his return and recovery he was given yet another mission. Fast Eddie was chosen to go to the USSR in 1943 and through his efforts was able to report back to Churchill and the United States Government of Russia support and alliance. His endeavors helped assure victory against the Axis.

After the war, he continued his writings, worked at his enterprises until he retired. He became a well-known speaker. On July 23, 1973, Eddie died leaving a legacy behind him few can duplicate. His legend lives on and the story of being adrift at sea has been told by several. Major Eddie Rickenbacker was the recipient of the Metal of Honor.

Some say there were two atheists on board the rafts. Yet I doubt there are many atheists adrift on the vast ocean or in foxholes. And what are the chances of a sea gull landing on a person's head or catching fish with parts of it? Did not God provide manna for the Israelites when they came out of bondage? Did God not feed Elijah in the wilderness (1 Kings 17:4)? Christ fed five thousand with what (Matthew 14:13-2)? Do birds worry about their daily meals (Matthew 6:26)? God works miracles for us everyday yet we are too blind to see or too stubborn to realize it. You cannot make me believe that those eight men did not pray to God for help? God answers prayers as evidenced by His Word. Note Psalm 66:19: "But God has surely listened and has heard my prayer."

Friend, God in His wisdom gives us examples and role models. They are people who have withstood the storms and are stronger for it. It is up to you to listen to His voice and truly believe that He will do for you what you cannot do for yourself.

SOURCES

For More Information about an American Legend go to:

Captain Rickenbacker's Story of the Ordeal and Rescue of Himself and the Men with Him; Eddie Rickenbacker

Eddie Rickenbacker: An American Hero in the Twentieth Century; Lewis, David

Fighting the Flying Circus; Eddie V. Rickenbacker

We Thought We Heard The Angels Sing; Whittaker, James, 1943

FRANCIS GARY POWERS
USAF Captain-GS12 CIA)
Pilot U-2 Spy Plane
468th Strategic Fighter Squadron
F-84 Thunderjet
August 17, 1929-August 1, 1977

Francis Gary Powers was the son of Oliver and Ida Powers. They lived in Jenkins, Kentucky. His youth was spent in Pound, Virginia, just across Pound Gap. After high school he went to Milligan College and then entered military service into the United States Air Force. Soon he was recognized for his abilities and was recruited by the Central Intelligence Agency. He became a seasoned veteran at flying secret missions over Russia in the latest high-tech plane known for the time: the U2 Spy Plane. It was equipped with sophisticated spy equipment and was thought it could not be shot down due to the high altitude that it flew.

In 1960, while flying over Russia, he was shot down by an S-75 Divina anti-aircraft missile. Francis could not trigger the self destruct mechanism and was forced to bail out of the plane. A total of eight missiles were launched. One hit a Russian jet and the pilot was forced to eject after he bravely stirred the damaged fighter away from a populated area.

Powers was captured and interrogated by the KGB. The U-2 plane was recovered virtually intact, resulting in the Russians being able to have access to the most modern technology of the era. The U. S. established a cover story and reported that the plane had strayed into Russian territory and was only there as a weather monitoring aircraft. Powers was tried and given seven years of hard labor, with three years imprisonment, but he was exchanged on February 10, 1962.

Upon returning home Powers loyalty was questioned to the point of being asked why he didn't take the 'suicide pill'. He was interrogated by the government and appeared before the U. S. Senate. They determined that he had acted accordingly and stated he was, "A fine young man under dangerous circumstances."

In 1963, Francis went to work for Lockheed. He worked for seven years but was 'let go' after he wrote a book entitled, <u>Operation Overflight: A Memoir of the U-2 incident.</u> In 1976, Lee Majors portrayed Francis in a movie. A year later, while reporting on a brush fire in Santa Barbara, California, his helicopter crashed. His last act of heroism came when he noted children playing in the area where he could land safely. Instead of endangering their lives, he chose to crash in an area without population. He is buried in Arlington National Cemetery.

A roadside plaque stands at the corner of the Courthouse in Whitesburg, Kentucky to honor Letcher County's native son. It reads:

FRANCIS GARY POWERS, 1929–1977
PILOT—SPY—HERO

"Francis Gary Powers and the "U-2 Incident" catapulted activities of the United States into world view. This Burdine native, with other pilots directed by

CIA, flew U-2's (high altitude jet gliders) over Russia photographing missile and industrial site and nuclear tests. On May 1, 1960, when his plane was disabled 1300 mi. over Russia, Powers parachuted to safety. Taken Prisoner, Powers stated his compass had malfunctioned on a weather flight. Finding film intact in plane's wreckage, the Russians told him he would stand trial for espionage. Sentenced to ten years imprisonment, Powers was released in 1962 in exchange for a Soviet spy. Later decorated by CIA. Died in civilian helicopter crash."

MEDAL AND AWARDS

CIA's Intelligence Star
Prisoner of War Medal
Distinguished Flying Cross
National Defense Service Medal
CIA Director's Medal
Silver Star

SOURCES

http://en.wikipedia.org/wiki/Francis_Gary_Powers

http://www.history.com/this-day-in-history/pilot-francis-gary-powers-charged-with-espionage

http://www.arlingtoncemetery.net/francisg.htm

FRANK WILLIAM JEALOUS OF HIM
Specialist 4th Class
Company B, 1st Battalion
46th Infantry
198th Light Infantry Brigade, American Division
May 5, 1947- June 9, 1969
Recipient of the Silver Star

Sometimes we fail to remember the sacrifices of our Native American brothers and sisters. While working on the reservations I was in awe of their love of the land and their patriotism. Every soldier was honored and must be given the rightful seat at the table. When I found Specialist Jealous of Him's story, I knew I had to include it. He was a true warrior in every sense of the word and an American icon.

Frank was born May 5, 1947, at Manderson, South Dakota. Manderson-White Horse Creek is located in Shannon County, South Dakota. The population was six hundred twenty-six at the 2010 census. Oglala Lakota tribesman, Kicking Bear, died here on May 28, 1904. The town is located on highway BIA 33. Frank was the son of Clayton and Eva (Mesteth) Jealous of Him. During his youth, his mother died and his father remarried. Her name was Bernice. He had a brother, Matthew (nicknamed Congo) and five half-sisters by the name of Clynda, Julie, Carol, Verla, and Kathy.

Frank dropped out of school and found employment at a head Start Center in the Wounded Knee District of Pine Ridge. Pine Ridge Reservation was considered to be the poorest place in America during those days and alcoholism was rampant. He was a teacher's aide. He worked on his GED during that time.

Frank was a talented young man and sang. He was also a good musician. His band, known as the Sioux Playboys, was very good and won a contest in Rapid City.

Frank Williams Jealous of Him enlisted into the military on February 1, 1968. From Sioux Falls, he was sent to Fort Lewis, Washington, for training. He did well on his assessments and was eligible to attend Officer's Training School. Frank chose to go to Fort Polk, Louisiana, for Advanced Infantry Training (AIT) instead. He was given a three week leave and was welcomed home by his tribe. They held a ceremony in which he received his warrior's name of Ana Kita (They Run To Him). Frank began his tour of duty on August 22, 1968, with Company B.

Specialist 4th Class Jealous Of Him wrote that he was a point man on several missions. He had an ability to sense and locate booby-traps. His advice to other soldiers should be considered to be accurate. *"Well, you got to use your feelings, your intuition, not be distracted for a minute. Chances of hitting a booby trap are greater than seeing any NVA...so watch the ground, then before you step, look up...really look at the trees. If there is a cluster of leaves or a dark spot that shouldn't be there, it could be a sniper or a wired shell. The wires are small, so move slow, keep an eye on the men to your flanks so we move at the same speed."* He saved a squad once simply by using his compass and map to bring them back to base. He was stationed around Da Nang (LZ Baldy) during this period.

On March 6, 1969, this Sioux Warrior received orders to report to Chu Lai (LZ Professional). It was located in the Quang Tin Province. Frank made friends easily and loved to joke with his friends. One of his conversations revealed the serious side of his thoughts. *"Whether I'm fighting for you whites or whether I'm just trying to get home alive, I'm not even sure. You white boys got a world to go back to. If I make it home, it will be to poverty."*

While on patrol on that June 9, 1969 evening, everything seemed quiet. As a point guard I am sure he was worried about the stillness. It was reported he once said, *"If anything bothers me, it's that either there's really no one out here, or they know we're here."* Somewhere along the trail they stopped for water. Karl Schofer volunteered to fill the canteens out of the river. Frank decided to go with him. Karl filled his canteens and as he was leaving the riverbank a shot rang out. It was a sniper and it found its mark.

Without thought of his personal safety Specialist Jealous of Him ran to his friend, picked him up over his shoulders and ran for the safety of the underbrush. *"I'm here, man, I'm here for you, white boy. Hang on to me; I'm going to get you out."* As he struggled with the weight of his friend, another shot rang out and the warrior fell to the ground to move no more.

Four days after he was killed in action trying to save his friend, his company was over run and wiped out with fifty-five men killed or wounded. It is my belief that Frank and Karl were killed by an advanced sniper of this impending assault.

Specialist Jealous of Him was returned home with full military honors. Rapid City held a memorial service in his honor. According to the resources listed below, *"Led by highway patrolmen, the hearse, escorted by 30 airmen serving as honor guards, made its way across the prairie toward Wounded Knee—with about 150 cars following and people lining the roads. After an emotional three-day wake, the body of Frank Jealous of Him was buried with military honors on June 24, 1969, at a cemetery at Porcupine."*

Frank Williams Jealous of Him exemplifies the best of men in the worst of times. He willingly gave his life in an effort to save a friend. He is a true unsung hero who must be remembered for his gallantry. Rest in peace.

SOURCES

file:///C:/Documents%20and%20Settings/dchaltas/Desktop/South%20Dakotans%20who%20gave%20their%20life%20in%20service%20during%20the%20Vietnam%20War.htm

http://freepages.genealogy.rootsweb.ancestry.com/~mikestevens/2010-p/p173.htm

http://www.virtualwall.org/dj/JealousFW01a.htm

http://www.vvmf.org/Wall-of-Faces/25663/FRANK-W-JEALOUS-OF-HIM

http://www.vvmf.org/Wall-of-Faces/25663/FRANK-W-JEALOUS-OF-HIM#sthash.C5ddCBK6.dpuf

I offer special recognition for the work done by Brady Cole Thelen, 8th Grader, Stanley County Middle School, Fort Pierre, South Dakota, and to Mrs. Hansen, Spearfish Middle School for their contribution in remembering an American hero.

Of Uncommon Birth; Dakota Sons in Vietnam; Mark St. Pierre; University of Oklahoma, August 3, 2003

FRANKLIN DOUG MILLER
Command Sergeant Major
5th Special Forces
1st Special Forces
January 27, 1945-June 30, 2000

Franklin Doug Miller was born in Elizabeth City, North Carolina. He attended school at St. Mary's in Albuquerque. In 1966, he joined the army. He enlisted from Albuquerque, New Mexico. His accolades are far too many for summation. He always had a mustache which was long and lanky in his youth. He was a man's man and served with pride as a Green Beret. In the listing below I offer some of his accomplishments. The following paragraphs are his military records and achievements.

In 1992, Franklin Miller retired from the Army as a Command Sergeant Major. He continued to serve his fellow veterans as a benefits counselor for the Veterans Administration. He developed cancer and died while living in St Pete Beach, Florida. His ashes were taken to New Mexico and scattered over his homeland. He was fifty-five years old at the time of his death. Through his outstanding book entitled, <u>Reflections of a Warrior: Six Years as a Green Beret in Vietnam</u>, his legacy lives on and his exploits become legendary. Frank 'Doug' Miller is survived by his son, Joshua, a daughter, Danielle and a brother by the name of Walter.

Walter also is a retired Command Sergeant Major. He was Colonel Bull Simons' radio operator on the Son Tay Raid, which was an attempt to free U.S. prisoners in North Vietnam. Range 37 of Fort Bragg was dedicated to Frank Doug Miller in 2002.

During one of his tours in Vietnam on January 5, 1970, Sergeant Miller was on patrol with an American. They were in the Kontum Province (enemy controlled territory). They were on long range recon when they were ambushed by the Vietcong.

He was leading a seven-man team, along with Montagnard Tribesmen (from Laos). A booby trap was triggered injuring five men. They were vastly outnumbered. Sergeant Miller held off an assault while obtaining Air Cav support for his troops. Though wounded in the chest he continued fighting until all the men were extracted. In an interview Sergeant Miller stated that he, 'felt like he was being drowned' and added, "I had something of a religious experience." He thought of Sgt. Bumgarner who told him to calm down. He did so and continued fighting because he was the only member of his patrol capable of firing. He stayed off the onslaught until a patrol came to his rescue. He and two others were the only survivors of the attack. For this action he received the Medal of Honor. He also was awarded two Bronze Stars, the Silver Star, six Purple Hearts and the Air Medal. President Richard M. Nixon awarded him the Congressional Medal of Honor on June 15, 1971.

According to military records, Sgt Miller *"Enlisted in the U.S. Army on February 17, 1965, and completed basic training at Fort Polk, Louisiana, in April 1965. After completing advanced Infantry training, Pvt Miller attended Special Forces Training at Fort Bragg, North Carolina, from July to December 1965, followed by service with Company C, 2nd Battalion of the 501st Infantry Regiment at Fort Campbell, Kentucky, from December 1965 to February 1966. His next assignment was as an infantryman with Company D, 2nd Battalion, 8th Cavalry Regiment of the 1st Cavalry Division in South Vietnam from March 1966 to February 1967, followed by service with Company B, 1st Battalion of the 506th Infantry Regiment at Fort Campbell from May 1967 until he left active duty on July 7, 1968.*

"SSG Miller returned to active duty on August 29, 1968, and then served as an Operations Sergeant and Reconnaissance Team Leader with the Studies and Observation Group in South Vietnam from September 1968 to February 1971. His next assignment was as a Reconnaissance Team Leader and Intelligence Sergeant with the U.S. Army Vietnam Training Advisory Group in South Vietnam from February 1971 to February 1972, followed by service as with the 90th Replacement Battalion in South Vietnam from February to December 1972. He served as a Section Sergeant with the 3rd Armored Cavalry Regiment at Fort Bliss, Texas, from December 1972 to March 1973, and then as a Light Weapons Infantry Instructor with the Advanced Individual Training Brigades at Fort Bliss from March 1973 to February 1974.

"SFC Miller served as a Platoon Sergeant with the 82nd Airborne Division at Fort Bragg from February 1974 to February 1976, and then as a Squad Leader and then Platoon Sergeant with Troop B, 2nd Squadron of the 9th Cavalry Regiment at Hunter Army Airfield and then at Fort Stewart, Georgia, from February 1976 to March 1979. His next assignment was as an

Instructor and then Chief Instructor at the Recondo School with the 25th Infantry Division at Schofield Barracks, Hawaii, from March 1979 to October 1982, followed by service as a Platoon Sergeant with Headquarters, Hunter Army Airfield, from October 1982 to January 1985.

"He served as Operations NCO with the U.S. Army Element of the United Nations Command in South Korea from January to April 1985, and then as Supply Chief with the 25th Infantry Division at Schofield Barracks from April to November 1985. 1SG Miller next served as 1st Sergeant for E Company of the 725th Maintenance Battalion, 25th Infantry Division, at Schofield Barracks from November 1985 to September 1986, followed by service as 1st Sergeant of B Company, 25th Supply and Transportation Battalion of the 25th Infantry Division from September 1986 to January 1988. After attending the U.S. Army Sergeant Major Academy, SGM Miller served as Senior Logistics NCO for the 1st Signal Brigade in South Korea from August 1988 to July 1989, and then as Command Sergeant Major for the 25th Supply and Transportation Battalion at Schofield Barracks from July to November 1989. His final assignment was as Senior Logistics NCO with the U.S. Army Logistics Assistance Office at Schofield Barracks from November 1989 until his retirement from the Army on December 1, 1992."

CITATION

"For conspicuous gallantry and intrepidity in action at the risk of his life above and beyond the call of duty. S/Sgt. Miller, 5TH Special Forces Group, distinguished himself while serving as team leader of an American-Vietnamese long-range reconnaissance patrol operating deep within enemy controlled territory. Leaving the helicopter insertion point, the patrol moved forward on its mission. Suddenly, 1 of the team members tripped a hostile booby trap which wounded 4 *soldiers. S/Sgt. Miller, knowing that the explosion would alert the enemy, quickly administered first aid to the wounded and directed the team into positions across a small stream bed at the base of a steep hill. Within a few minutes, S/Sgt. Miller saw the lead element of what he estimated to be a platoon-size enemy force moving toward his location. Concerned for the safety of his men, he directed the small team to move up the hill to a more secure position. He remained alone, separated from the patrol, to meet the attack. S/Sgt. Miller single-handedly repulsed 2 determined attacks by the numerically superior enemy force and caused them to withdraw in disorder. He rejoined his team, established contact with a forward air controller and arranged the evacuation of his patrol. However, the only suitable extraction location in the heavy jungle was a bomb crater some 150 meters from the team location. S/Sgt. Miller reconnoitered the route to the crater and led his men through the enemy controlled jungle to the extraction site. As the evacuation helicopter hovered over the crater to pick up the patrol, the enemy launched a savage automatic weapon and rocket-propelled grenade attack against the beleaguered team, driving off the rescue helicopter. S/Sgt. Miller led the team in a valiant defense which drove back the enemy in its attempt to overrun the small patrol. Although seriously wounded and with every man in his patrol a casualty, S/Sgt. Miller moved forward to again single-handedly meet the hostile attackers. From his forward exposed position, S/Sgt. Miller gallantly repelled 2 attacks by the enemy before a friendly relief force reached the patrol location. S/Sgt. Miller's gallantry, intrepidity in action, and selfless devotion to the welfare of his comrades are in keeping with the highest traditions of the military service and reflect great credit on him, his unit, and the U.S. Army."*

Command Sergeant Major Frank Doug Miller's
CREDO:

"Share your fears with yourself and your courage with others. You will inspire people to do things that are incredible."

SOURCES

http://en.wikipedia.org/wiki/Franklin_D._Miller

http://www.amazon.com/Reflections-Warrior-Franklin-D-Miller/dp/0891413871

http://www.veterantributes.org/TributeDetail.php?recordID=1604

http://www.mishalov.com/MillerFrank.html

http://www.sfalx.com/moh/miller_franklin_SF.htm

http://www.groups.sfahq.com/3rd/moh_former_3rd_membe_doug_miller.htm

http://articles.latimes.com/2000/jul/20/local/me-55731

http://www.sfahq.com/miller/

FRANKLIN RUNYON SOUSLEY
World War II
2nd Platoon
Company E (Easy Company)
2nd Battalion
28th Regiment of Fifth Division Marines
September 19, 1925–March 21, 1945

This is a tale of a family's triumph and tragedy. It is a story of endured hardship during a time when the greatest generation was youths. This is a saga legendary in the annuals of American history.

He was born on a rural farm in Fleming County, Kentucky. The name of the place where he lived was Hill Top. His father and mother were Merle Duke Sousley and Goldie Mitchell. He had an older brother who died when Frank was only two years of age. His death was caused due to appendicitis. His father died when Frank was nine years old. Franklin had a younger brother by the name of Julian, who was born when he was eight years of age. Their father was only thirty-five at the time of his passing. His death was caused by diabetes. Franklin became the man of the house and had the responsibility of helping his mother raise young Julian. He worked the crop, shared in the household chores in and around the cabin, and helped with the daily duties of farm life. During this time he became very close to his mother Goldie.

It was said he had a great sense of humor. One joke he played was on Halloween. He and a few of his friends rounded up some cows and 'fenced' them in on the porch of the general store. To insure they left something on the porch, the boys gave the cows a good dose of Epson Salts. Another story was told that while he was in boot camp, some of his fellow Marines came back to the barrack and noted a peculiar odor. They found young Franklin keeping the eastern Kentucky tradition of making moonshine out of raisins he had 'procured' while on KP!

There wasn't much to do in the rural area other than farm, fish, hang around the local store, hunt, be with some buddies and attend school. Franklin attended a two room school in the little via of Elizaville. Later he attended high school at Fleming County. Fleming County High School was near the small town of Flemingsburg, Kentucky. After graduating in May of 1943, Franklin went to work in a refrigerator factory in Dayton, Ohio.

He worked until he was drafted. Instead of going to the Army, Franklin chose to become a Marine. On January 5, 1944, he began his combat training and was assigned to the Fifth Marine Division. After boot camp he was given a furlough. He left Fort Pendleton, California, and arrived in Maysville via train. He looked, "Straight as a string" and went home. When he left his mother, he stated he would, "Come back a hero". He disembarked for 'Island X' on September 19, which happened to be his nineteenth birthday. The ship came to port in Hawaii and the Marines were given a brief furlough. PFC Sousley returned to the USS Missoula with a tattoo of the Marine globe and anchor proudly engraved on his arm.

By February 19, 1945, he found himself on a Japanese occupied island with fellow Marines. The Marines were instructed to take a hill which was five hundred fifty feet in height. A fierce battle took place. On February 23, 1945, fellow Marines, John Bradley, Ira Hayes, Rene Gagnon, Harlon Block and Michael Strank were instructed to post the colors on Mount Suribachi. A photographer by the name of Joseph Rosenthal captured the immortal image, which has become etched in the hearts of all Americans. The island was known as Iwo Jima. Franklin was positioned between Ira Hayes and Michael Strank.

According to documentation, *"Mid-morning on February 23rd the weather finally cleared. The brass ordered a four man patrol up the mountain just as the rain ceased. Those four men soon returned to report that, incredibly, they had been all the way to the top and encountered no resistance. Although that news seemed too good to be true, the Colonel ordered a larger force -- 40 men -- up the mountain. Almost as an afterthought, the Colonel handed one of the men a small (54" x 28") flag, saying, "If you get to the top, put this up." The Marine who took it remembered that the Colonel did not say "when, he said, 'if.'" That patrol also gained the top of the mountain. A Marine Corps photographer who accompanied them recorded the raising of the first American flag to fly over Japanese soil. Immediately after the flag went up, "all hell broke loose" as the enemy started popping out of holes and shooting. This was the first time many of the Marines had actually seen a Japanese soldier. They were able to see plenty then. For reason known only to them, the Japanese rushed the Marines in one of their suicide charges. The Marines accommodated.*

"Elsewhere on the island every American cheered when they saw the flag flying atop the mountain. Infantrymen stopped firing, laborers on the beach stopped loading and even the ships in the bay sounded their horns. At this point, fate took a hand in arranging a sequence of events that immortalized six men and one photographer."

Overnight fame came to all men, though they did not want it. Franklin toured with others in the iconic picture to help raise money for the war effort. PFC Franklin returned to battle and on March 21, 1945, while walking down a supposedly safe area, was shot in the back by a sniper. Reportedly, Franklin's mother did not have a phone. "Someone had to come from the general store to tell her that her son was dead. The neighbors report that they could hear her screaming all through that night. The neighbors lived a quarter-mile away." He was buried on Iwo Jima but later was brought back to his beloved Kentucky and buried in Elizabville Cemetery on May 8, 1947. Four years later her son Julian was killed in a car crash. Goldie lived to be eighty-four years old.

MEDALS AND RIBBONS AWARDED

Purple Heart Medal
Combat Action Ribbon
Presidential Unit Citation with silver 5/16 inch star
American Campaign Medal
Asiatic-Pacific Campaign Medal with bronze service star
World War II Victory Medal.

FLAG BEARERS OF IWO JIMA

1. <u>Mike Strank</u>: He was the oldest of the flag raisers. He gave the orders to find a pole, attach the flag and "put'er up!" His right hand is around the wrist of Franklin Sousley, helping the younger Marine push the heavy pole. Strank died on Iwo Jima on March 1, 1945. He is buried in Arlington National Cemetery.

2. <u>Harlon Block</u> : Harlon was born in Texas and enlisted with twelve of his Weslaco High School football players. On March 1, 1945, Harlon Block, was killed by a mortar just a few hours after Strank. He was twenty-one years old. When his mother saw the flag raising photo in the newspaper on February 25, she exclaimed, "That's Harlon," pointing to the figure on the far right. Block is buried beside the Iwo Jima Monument in Harlingen, Texas.

3. <u>Franklin Sousley</u>: Raised on a tobacco farm in Kentucky, Sousley enlisted at seventeen and shipped out his eighteenth birthday. He wrote a letter while in boot camp to his mother saying, "Mother, you said you were sick. I want you to stay in out of that field and look real pretty when I come home. You can grow a

crop of tobacco every summer, but I sure as hell can't grow another mother like you." Franklin Sousley died on Iwo Jima, March 21, 1945. He is buried at Elizaville Cemetery in Kentucky.

4. Ira Hayes: Ira was a Pima Indian from Sacaton, Arizona. His chief told him to be an "honorable warrior" and bring honor upon his family when he enlisted. He did so but could not live with the dark memories of Iwo Jima. Hayes was one of two survivors to return home from the war. He died in a shallow pool of water on January 24, 1955. He is buried at Arlington National Cemetery.

5. Rene Gagnon: Rene was from Manchester, N.H.,. He was the youngest Marine who carried the flag up Mt. Suribachi. He died in 1979, and is buried in his hometown.

John Bradley One of the men who 'lend a hand' was John Bradley. In his report to Congress the true humble spirit of a Marine was reviewed. *"People refer to us as heroes, I personally don't look at it that way. I just think that I happened to be at a certain place at a certain time and anybody on that island could have been in there, and we certainly weren't heroes, and I speak for the rest of them as well,"* His son wrote the immortal book entitled, Flags of Our Fathers. John H. Bradley died in 1994 while in Antigo, Wisconsin; the place of his birth.

America, remember their names and their deeds! They were the few, the proud, the United States Marines!

SOURCES

Shadow of Suribachi: Raising the Flags on Iwo Jima; by Parker Bishop Albee, Jr. and Keller Cushing Freeman

Flags of Our Fathers; James Bradley

From Hilltop to Mountaintop; Ron Elliott

http://jkhg.org/franklin_sousley.htm

http://en.wikipedia.org/wiki/Franklin_Sousley

http://huntington.patch.com/groups/around-town/p/bearers-of-the-flag

http://www.iwojima.com/raising/first.htm

FREDDIE STOWERS
Corporal
Company C
371st Infantry Regiment
93rd Infantry Division
World War I
January 12, 1896–September 28, 1918
Recipient of the Medal of Honor

(Composite from forensics of parents)

Freddie was a native of Anderson County, South Carolina. He was born in Sandy Springs, South Carolina. He was the grandson of a slave. He was married to Pearl (last name unknown) and had a daughter by the name of Minne Lee. He worked as a farm hand until he was called to service. Freddie was drafted on October 4, 1917, being twenty-one years of age. He went to Fort Jackson for his training.

Freddie was selected as part of a new division and fought alongside his fellow American soldiers though racism existed. But when in the trenches, vision was color-blind. He was part of the American Expeditionary Force.

On September 28, 1918, Squad Leader Stowers' group was the lead company during the attack on Hill 188, in the Champagne Marne Sector, France. One of the tricks noted by several soldiers during World War I was used during a cease fire. The Germans pretended they wanted to surrender. When the Americans pressed forward to within one hundred meters, the Germans ran back into their trenches and rained down deadly fire upon the exposed Americans. Between the mortar rounds, machine gun and German rifles, half of the men were cut to pieces. My Uncle Arnold stated they did the same thing during World War II.

Corporal Stowers took charge and through his brave actions restored order among the panic stricken soldiers. Corporal Stowers crawled towards the machine gun nest without regard to his own personal safety. His squad followed suit. A ferocious battle erupted resulting in the nest being destroyed. The brave corporal continued his assault against the enemy. He crawled towards the second entrenchment while encouraging men by his example to follow. A machine gun hit him yet he pushed forward towards the enemy. His wound was mortal and he died while facing the enemy and inspiring the men behind him. Hill 188 was captured and Corporal Stowers gallantry contributed much to that undertaking. His death was just six weeks before the end of hostilities.

Although recommended for the Medal of Honor, the nation's highest award for bravery was not given until April 24, 1991. Reports indicate that his recommendation had been 'misplaced'. The award was given to his sisters, Georgina and Mary, by President George H. W. Bush seventy-three years after his ultimate sacrifice. He is one of two Black soldiers to receive the coveted Medal of Honor during World War I.

CITATION

"Corporal Stowers, distinguished himself by exceptional heroism on September 28, 1918 while serving as a squad leader in Company C, 371st Infantry Regiment, 93d Division. His company was the lead company during the attack on Hill 188, Champagne Marne Sector, France, during World War I. A few minutes after the attack began, the enemy ceased firing and began climbing up onto the parapets of the trenches, holding up their arms as if wishing to surrender. The enemy's actions caused the American forces to cease fire and to come out into the open. As the company started forward and when within about 100 meters of the trench line, the enemy jumped back into their trenches and greeted Corporal Stowers' company with interlocking bands of machine gun fire and mortar fire causing well over fifty percent casualties. Faced with incredible enemy resistance, Corporal Stowers took charge, setting such a courageous example of personal bravery and leadership that he inspired his men to follow him in the attack. With extraordinary heroism and complete disregard of personal danger under devastating fire, he crawled forward leading his squad toward an enemy machine gun nest, which was causing heavy casualties to his company. After fierce fighting, the machine gun position was destroyed and the enemy soldiers were killed. Displaying great courage and intrepidity Corporal Stowers continued to press the attack against a determined enemy. While crawling forward and urging his men to continue the attack on a second trench line, he was gravely wounded by machine gun fire. Although Corporal Stowers was mortally wounded, he pressed forward, urging on the members of his squad, until he died. Inspired by the heroism and display of bravery of Corporal Stowers, his company *continued the attack against incredible odds, contributing to the capture of Hill 188 and causing heavy enemy casualties. Corporal Stowers' conspicuous gallantry, extraordinary heroism, and supreme devotion to his men were well above and beyond the call of duty, follow the finest traditions of military service, and reflect the utmost credit on him and the United States Army."*

SOURCES

http://raahistory.com/moh/worldwar1.htm
http://en.wikipedia.org/wiki/Freddie_Stowers

http://en.wikipedia.org/wiki/List_of_African_American_Medal_of_Honor_recipients
http://www.arlingtoncemetery.net/fstowers.htm

http://www.cmohs.org/recipient-detail/2595/stowers-freddie.php

http://www.cmohs.org/recipient-detail/2595/stowers-freddie.php

http://mojosteve.blogspot.com/2011/02/black-history-month-freddie-stowers.html

http://www.militarian.com/threads/freddie-stowers.6605/

FRENCH FORREST
Assistant Secretary of the Confederate Navy
War of 1812
Mexican American War
American War Between the States
October 4, 1796-December 22, 1866

French was a young man destined to fight in three wars and serve two nations. His dream as a child was to be in the Navy. He soon realized that dream. In fact he was a naval man who served in two navies.

French Forrest was born in St. Mary's County, Maryland, and at the age of fifteen he was a midshipman during the War of 1812. He was at the Battle of Lake Erie with Commodore Oliver Perry. He was also present during the battle between the HMS Peacock and USS Hornet, which occurred on February 24, 1813. After the war he rose in rank swiftly.

He was commissioned as a naval lieutenant on March 5, 1817. On April 18, 1831, he married Miss Emily

Simms Forrest. She was the daughter of John Douglas Simms. The newlyweds lived in Clermont (near Alexander), Virginia.

He continued to rise in rank and on February 9, 1837, he became a commander. On August 17, 1838, Douglas French Forrest was born. He was born in Baltimore, Maryland. He was destined to become a reverend even though he studied to be a lawyer at Yale and University of Virginia Law School. Following the footsteps of his father, he chose to fight on the side of the Confederacy. He was with the 17th Infantry Regiment, and was on the Rappahannock when the war ended. During this period Douglas kept a diary entitled Odyssey in Gray, which chronicles life as a Confederate sailor.

On March 30, 1844, Forrest received yet another commission. This time he was promoted to a captain. During the Mexican War he was commissioned adjutant general and commanded the forces which land at Vera Cruz, Mexico. He also was in charge of the Washington Navy Yard prior to the War Between the States.

After a distinguished career of approximately fifty years in the U. S. Navy, French resigned his commission and joined the Virginia Sate Navy. French was third in seniority. He served as commander of the Norfolk Navy Yard. He personally was responsible to inspect the ships of the fledgling navy (established on February 21, 1861) and he assisted in the construction work on the CSS Virginia (built from the USS Merrimack). In the third month of 1863, he was appointed as Flag Officer of the James River Squadron. He was appointed as assistant Secretary of the Confederate Navy until the end of the wary. He died a year later as a result of typhoid. He was seventy years of age.

SOURCES

http://en.wikipedia.org/wiki/French_Forrest

Inventory of the Forrest Family Papers; in the Southern Historical Collection, UNC-Chapel Hill.

John M. Coski (1996). Capital Navy: The Men, Ships and Operations of the James River Squadron. Campbell, CA: Savas Woodbury Publishers. ISBN 1-882810-03-1.

http://www.geni.com/people/Captain-French-Forrest-CSN/6000000001180184661

http://books.google.com/books?id=dIUaAAAAYAAJ&pg=PA63&lpg=PA63&dq=Asst+secretary+of+the+Confederate+navy+FRENCH+FORREST&source=bl&ots=0jZOJHs9Yw&sig=c0p9l8OpCdP9O12FNulev5X2zuQ&hl=en&sa=X&ei=IcCAU-6XFbesQTHgYLACg&ved=0CEgQ6AEwBg#v=onepage&q=Asst%20secretary%20of%20the%20Confederate%20navy%20FRENCH%20FORREST&f=false

http://uvastudents.wordpress.com/2011/05/26/douglas-french-forrest-17-aug-1838-3-may-1902/

GARY OWENS

Mother of a Soldier
By Janice Busic

I am the daughter, grand-daughter, great grand-daughter, great-great grand-daughter, and great-great great grand-daughter of a soldier, up to being the 5th great granddaughter of a soldier. Therefore, it came as no surprise when my sons joined the military.

Sending my sons off to Iraq was hard. Giving them that last hug and watching them walk down the runway to board a plane broke my heart. I had to wonder if I would ever see and hold that child again. I also had to believe that I would. I was extremely proud to see my little boys become men – men who were willing to step forward and defend their country.

My older son, Gary, is extremely patriotic. He was in New York and watched as planes hit the World Trade Center on 9/11. He watched as men and women jumped to their deaths. He stood in a park and held a little pre-school age girl and tried to calm her fears as she asked extremely difficult questions. He came away from that day angry and with a determination to go to Iraq. And he did.

Gary entered service on April 9, 1989. His basic training took him to Fort Leonard Wood, Montana. He served two tours of duty in Iraq, from 2004-2005. Then he returned for another tour in 2006-2007.

He was involved in some battles that came very close to ending his life. His wife and I stayed in close communication by email with other wives and mothers in their unit. One of the worst experiences, from my perspective, was when we received word that Gary's convoy had been attacked and there were causalities. We stayed online all that night awaiting word, waiting for the names. It was almost 24 hours before we learned that none of the troops in Gary's unit were killed. That was one of the lowest points.

Gary did return from Iraq with no physical injuries. Eventually his troop was called for deployment again, and he chose to go with them. These were young men and women he had trained and he would not send them in alone. During this deployment a lot of communication with families was limited. So we didn't know as much about what was happening. He retired in October of 2009, after twenty years of service.

GEORGE DEE HIGGINS
The Original Band of Brothers
U.S. Army

They were raised in a mining town community owned by a large coal company. Their roots were deeply entrenched in the mountain tradition of loving God, Country and Family. Five brothers so closely knit that when one decided to volunteer for service, they all went.

George D. Higgins had four brothers who also served during World War II. They were part of the greatest generation. They were Clarence Franklin Higgins (Army), Dillard Dennis Higgins (Army), Emmit Higgins (Army), and Charles Woodrow Higgins (Army). They were the sons of Charles Grover Higgins and Roxie McIntosh Higgins. The Higgins brothers were born and raised near the old Haymond Grade School, located in Haymond, Kentucky. In Letcher County, we are proud to call them the original band of brothers. They heard the sound of America calling their names and heeded the plea.

SOURCE

The News-Press Extra, Volume 6, Number 6, July 2013

GEORGE HOBERT NOE
Corporal
A Company
1ST Battalion
46th Infantry Regiment
198th Infantry Brigade
January 12, 1949-May 26, 1969

When I came across this man's story I could not help but note how young he looked. Yet he was a warrior; being twenty years of age at his passing. For some reason he reminded me of what I must have looked like. During my research I started getting a clear picture of a young man dedicated to the cause of America's call. His attributes rang out as a man possessed with a great personality, a wondrous smile, playful nature, loving you man who was devoted to God, Country and Family.

A cousin, who is not identified, wrote on the virtual wall the following: *"Hobie, I will always remember your loving wonderful smile, my dear wonderful cousin. You gave your life so that your fellow soldiers would live. That of course was you. What a wonderful husband and father you would have been. The world's best. I will always remember you and your wonderful smile and kindess. I miss you dearly every day. I love you, cousin."* These words speak volumes of this unsung hero.

George 'Hobie' Noe was born on a Wednesday, January 12, 1949, in Harlan County, Kentucky. His parents were Carl Dennis and Gertrude Stanton Noe. He lived and was raised in Cawood, Kentucky. He enlisted (selective service) into the Army as an 11B10 (Light Weapons Infantry), and awarded the rank of PFC (Posthumously). His ID number is 53760065. Corporal Noe never married. He listed being a Baptist as per his religious affiliation.

His tour in Vietnam began on May 8, 1969, and ended sixteen days later (May 26, 969). He was killed in Quang Tin, South Vietnam, due to 'hostile, ground casualty other explosive device'. His body was recovered. He was brought home and received a military funeral for his ultimate sacrifice. George Hobert Noe is buried at Resthaven Cemetery, Keith, Kentucky. He is listed on the Vietnam Memorial Wall, panel 24West, Line 112

What better tribute than those who knew him. On March 21, 2003, Monica Stanton Gibson, posted on 'together we stand' the following about her cousin: *"George Hobert Noe or Hobie as we called him is my hero. Hobie was a wonderful person with a wonderful sense of humor. Like so many of the other soldiers that were killed he will always be remembered. His death changed our family and his forever. He has truly been missed all of these years and I will never forget or let anyone else forget. He had a big huge smile and dumbo ears, but when he did his impression of Gomer Pyle and Barney Fife you can forget it. No one in the room could stop laughing. Hobie would have been a wonderful father and husband. Sadly he never got the chance to experience either one. I thank all of those who served* and died for my country there, and are defending my country now. I love my freedoms and I want to keep them. If not for men and women like my cousin and the others who died in Vietnam or the men and women who served or serve now I would not have them. I love you all and thank you from the bottom of my heart. I WILL NEVER FORGET ANY OF YOUR SACRFIC'S! So long dear cousin until we meet again!"

His brother David wrote the following moving synopsis about their childhood: *"I've never forgotten what a beautiful and wonderful brother you were. I still laugh at all the times you pretended to be Barney Fife and Gomer Pyle. We used to love to pest each other all the time. I am sure proud to call you my brother. The day we received the word of your death was absolutely terrible. No one could believe such a young, funny, loving and terrific little boy was gone. You sure have made us all proud and I miss you more than anyone will ever know. Say hello to Mom and Earl."*

SOURCES

http://www.virtualwall.org/dn/NoeGH01b.htm

http://army.togetherweserved.com/army/servlet/tws.webapp.WebApp?cmd=ShadowBoxProfile&type=Person&ID=62495

http://www.mocavo.com/George-Hobert-Noe-Corporal-Us-National-Archives-the-Coffelt-Database/16585445876664831288

http://vietnam-casualties.findthebest.com/l/42402/George-Hobert-Noe

http://www.usfallenwarriors.com/index.php?page=directory&rec=81997

http://thewall-usa.com/search.asp?curpage=12&name=&lname=&hometown=&homestate=&service=&age=&ssn=&ranknum=&dobmonth=1&dobday=12&dobyear=&casmonth=&casday=&casyear=&searchpanel=&casualtiesdate=&birthdaydate=&searchwoman=&casmonthfrom=&casdayfrom=&casyearfrom=&casmonthto=&casdayto=&casyearto=

http://www.vvmf.org/Wall-of-Faces/38020/GEORGE-H-NOE

http://www.fold3.com/search/#query=george+hobert+noe&preview=1&cat=252

GEORGE WILLIAM CASEY
MAJOR GENERAL
1ST Cavalry Division (Airmobile)
March 9, 1922-July 7, 1970
Arlington National Cemetery
Section 5, site 16

Generals too die in war. Such is the case of a brilliant general who served as the commander of the 1st Cavalry Division in Vietnam. The general was born a soldier. He was from North Scituate, Massachusetts.

He began his career by attending Harvard College and then transferring to West Point. There he graduated with a Bachelor of Science degree in 1945. He earned a Masters Degree in International Relations from Georgetown University and a master in business administration from George Washington University. He returned to Harvard and worked on post graduate degree in International Affairs. He did all this between wars, having served in World War II, Korea and then going to Vietnam. He fought at the famed Heartbreak Ridge that Clint Eastwood immortalized via the film.

The general was well liked by his men and was considered to be a rising star in the military. He was one of those generals who believed in visiting his troops and those wounded. He was actually captured by the Viet Cong but was rescued by daring men who are willing to offer their lives to do so.

This promising general was killed on July 7, 1970, along with six others, when his UH-IV chopper he was flying hit a mountain. Those who lost their lives with General Casey were: Major John Alexander Hottell III, Aide-de-Camp; First Lieutenant William Frederick Michel, Pilot; Command Sergeant Major Kenneth William Cooper, Division Sergeant Major; Sergeant William Lee Christenson, Door Gunner; Sergeant Ronald Francis Fuller, Crew Chief; Sergeant Vernon Kenneth Smolik, Aide & Stenographer. The general and his staff were near Bao Luc on their way to visit wounded Sky Troopers in Cam Ranh. Poor weather conditions were the official cause of the crash. Major General Casey was forty-eight years old. He was survived by his wife, Elaine Morton Casey, three daughters and two sons. The good general was buried with full military honors befitting his sacrifice.

Note that he is one of the three Major Generals who gave their lives in Vietnam. They were: Major General Keith Lincoln Ware and Major General John A.B. Dillard. Please also note that George William Casey, Jr, (son of George Casey Sr) served as the 36th Chief of Staff of the U.S. Army for four years (April 2007- 2011).

SOURCES

http://www.arlingtoncemetery.net/gwcasey.htm

"Gen. Casey to make West Point Center of Excellence for Ethics, Values"; Bartelt, Eric S.; U.S. Army News; April 26, 2007

http://whittier-daily-news.vlex.com/vid/corodimas-vietnam-war-hero-dies-69608794

"George William Casey, Major General, United States Army". ArlingtonCemetery.net.

G. WIX UNTHANK
WWII Paratrooper
509th Parachute Infantry Regiment
June 14, 1923-June 25, 2013

G. Wix Unthank was born on June 14, 1923, in Tway, Kentucky. He was the son of Green W. Unthank and Estelle Howard Unthank. They were teachers in the Harlan County Schools. He graduated from Loyall High School in 1940.

When World War II began, G. Wix Unthank felt it was his duty to enlist into the army. He served as a paratrooper in the 509th Parachute Infantry Battalion. According to Wikipedia, the 509th Parachute Infantry Regiment (509th PIR) was the first combat paratrooper unit of the United States Army formed during World War II. 1st Battalion currently serves as an opposing force at Fort Polk's Joint Readiness Training Center and 3rd Battalion is assigned to the 4th Brigade Combat Team, 25th Infantry Division, in Fort Richardson.

The 509th carried out the first US combat drop during the invasion of North Africa. The transport planes flew all the way from English airfields to the African coast. This first operation was unsuccessful, with seven of its thirty-nine C-47s widely scattered. Only ten aircraft actually dropped their troops, while the others unloaded after twenty-eight troop carriers, nearly out of fuel, landed on the Sebkra d'Oran, a dry lake near their target. The 509th marched overland to occupy its objective, and on November 15th, three hundred paratroopers successfully dropped on the Youks-les-Bains Airfield.

Forty-six Paratroopers from the 509th participated in the liberation of Ventotene, a small Italian island, on September 9, 1943. The German commander was tricked into surrendering to the weaker American force before realizing his mistake. An account of this is given in John Steinbeck's "Once There Was a War."

Later, the 509th saw two more combat jumps in Italy and Southern France. After landing, they were often used as elite mountain infantry in the Italian mountains and French Alps. Paul B. Huff, a member of the 509th, was the first American Paratrooper awarded the Medal of Honor on February 29, 1944, for action at Anzio, Italy.

During the Battle of the Bulge, the 509th fought in Belgium to blunt the German attack. An account of this battle is described in the book "Bloody Clash at Sadzot." The war ended for the 509th at the end of January 1945, near St. Vith, Belgium, with only about fifty remaining unwounded of the original seven hundred who entered the battle. At this time, the 509th was disbanded, and the men left were used as replacements for the U.S. 82nd Airborne Division. For his bravery Unthank was awarded the Bronze Star Medal and a Purple Heart as a result of injuries sustained from a German grenade (1943). He was honorably discharged in 1945 and returned home.

After the war, Judge Unthank attended law school at the University of Kentucky and earned his doctorate from the University of Miami Law School in Coral Gables, Florida. He served in several different positions, inclusive of ten years as Commonwealth Attorney and seven years private practice. In 1980 he was appointed U.S. Federal Judge for the Eastern District of Kentucky.

WYMT television reported that Tom Self, retired U. S. Assistant Attorney, stated, "He brought a decorum and respect for the federal bench that lasted and still lasts today," Bruce Stephens, a retired lawyer and personal friend, stated that Judge Unthank was, "An honorable man, a good judge, a good lawyer. He represented the people here in Harlan County as their judge and Commonwealth Attorney."

The Honorable Judge G. Wix Unthank died on June 25, 2013, being ninety years of age at his passing. He was a loving husband (married in 1953 to Marilyn Ward Unthank). He was a family man, servant of the people, faithful member and trustee of the 1st Presbyterian Church of Harlan.

SOURCES

http://www.wkyt.com/wymt/home/headlines/Community-gathers-for-judge-G-Wix-Unthank-funeral-213435971.html

http://en.wikipedia.org/wiki/509th_Infantry_Regiment_(United_States)

McConnell, Mitch. "Tribute to Judge G. Wix Unthank". *Congressional Record*

United States Government Printing Office.
The Harlan Daily Enterprise - Judge decorated WWII veteran dies

"Unthank". *Obituaries - June 26, 2013*. The Harlan Daily Enterprise. June 26, 2013.

"The Honorable G. Wix Unthank". Harlan County Public Schools.

G. MURL CONNER
1st Lieutenant
Company K
3rd Infantry Division
7th Army
June 2, 1919-November 5, 1998

Some of his land is flooded now by the Wolf Creek Dam. There lingers some land though where an unsung hero walked. He was awarded four Silver Stars (with three oak clusters), four Bronze Stars, seven Purple hearts and the Distinguished Service Cross. He also was awarded the Croix de Guerre (the French Medal of Honor). His friend, Sergeant York was also awarded France's highest honor during World War I. Lt. Conner was in battle for twenty-eight+ consecutive months. He was the second most decorated soldier in World War II and some say he served longer and was wounded more than the famed Audie Murphy. His name was Garlin Murl Conner.

There is a long standing petition to award him the Medal of Honor. On January 8, 2003, Kentucky Congressman Ed Whitfield introduced H.R. 327 in the

108th Congress, authorizing the President to award a Medal of Honor posthumously to Lieutenant Conner. It's yet to be done. In March of 2014, U.S. District Judge Thomas Russell ruled in an eleven page opinion that his widow, Pauline Conner of Albany, Kentucky, petition for the Medal of Honor, would be declined. Why? This is his story.

Fold 3 had listed several facts about Lt. Conner. He was born in Clinton County, Kentucky. He enlisted on March 1, 1941, at Louisville, Kentucky. He served until June 22, 1945. His Army Serial Number was 35101319 1. His MOS was 745 (Rifleman). His occupation was listed as general farm hands. Yet there is a void as to this hero. Who was this man who was wounded seven times yet refused the Purple Heart? One of the wounds was so severe that he was told he would never walk again. But they didn't understand the heart of a warrior! He had tenacity of spirit! He not only walked again but spent his life farming and was the president of Clinton County Farm Bureau. He and his bride, Pauline, leased a mule from his father and tended thirty-six acres next to the Indian Creek. He dismissed his heroism when asked and rarely talked about his years as an American warrior. Yet he was fearless in helping other Veterans get their pensions.

In 2001, The United States Army honored Conner's heroism by naming an Eagle Base in Bosnia-Herzegovina after him. 'He was a real hero,' said attorney Donald Todd of Lexington, who represents Conner's family. The Army knows a hero when they hear and see the deeds.

Yet, who was this man who was the second most decorated soldier of World War II and the hero to several that credit him with saving their battalion? What do we know of his person and what he did for our country? Why is it we readily recognize Sgt Alvin

York and Audie Murphy but have no clue as to the identity of Lt Conner?

Garlin Murl Conner was born on June 2, 1919, close to what is now Lake Cumberland. The area is known as Aaron. He lived on the border of Kentucky and Tennessee. Ironically Murl was an acquaintance of the Famed Sergeant York (World War I) and lived close to his farm at Pall Mall, Tennessee. In fact when Garlin Murl Conner came home, the area held a parade in his honor. One of the speakers was none other than Sergeant York! Also paradoxically Audie Murphy was in the 3rd Infantry Division!

Those who knew Lt. Conner said he was a quiet man. He was a small man, standing five feet five inches in height and weighed one hundred forty-five pounds. What he lacked in stature he made up for in courage. He was drafted in 1941, and within three months of combat he went from a sergeant to the rank of Lieutenant for his gallantry via a field promotion. He served in the following campaigns: African campaigns, Sicily, Italy, and France. He then went on to Berlin.

An example of his heroic nature occurred in France. On January 24, 1945, at 0800 hours, Lt Connors performed a phenomenon at Hussein, France. He had been wounded and was in the hospital but this did not deter him from rejoining his men. He left the hospital and went back to his men. He heard they needed someone to run communication lines within four hundred yards of the enemy. Without hesitation he, *"Grabbed the wire and off he went through the impact area of an intense concentration of enemy artillery fire to direct friendly artillery on a force of six Mark VI tanks and tank destroyers, followed by 600 fanatical German infantrymen, which was assaulting in full fury the spearhead position held by his battalion. Along the way, as he unreeled the spool of telephone wire, he disregarded shells which exploded 25 yards from him and set up an observation post. For three hours, Lt. Conner lay in a shallow ditch as wave after wave of German infantry surged toward him, at times to within five yards of his position. As the last all-out German assault swept forward, he ordered his artillery to concentrate on his own position, resolved to die if necessary to halt the enemy. Friendly shells exploded within five yards of him, blanketing his position but Lt. Conner continued to direct artillery fire on the assault elements swarming around him until the German attack was shattered and broken. Murl Conner was individually credited with stopping more than 150 Germans, destroying all the tanks and completely disintegrating the powerful enemy assault force and preventing heavy loss of life in his own outfit."* His bold action and lack of concern for his own personal safety saved countless American lives.

One of his superior officers stated, *"As the last all-out German assault swept forward, he ordered his artillery to concentrate on his own position, resolved to die if necessary to halt the enemy,"* Conner's commanding officer wrote. *"Friendly shells exploded within five yards of him, blanketing his position . . . but Lieutenant Conner continued to direct artillery fire on the assault elements swarming around him until the German attack was shattered and broken."* Yet he does not have the Medal of Honor! Why? The federal judge ruled that Pauline Connors, the widow of Murl, had waited too long to file. Several officers stated that they did not properly write Murl's heroics due to the constant fighting and there is enough evidence showing he earned the nation's highest honor. Lt Connors always took the point and the most dangerous positions; he would sometime be the only man reporting for a hazardous night mission within enemy lines. "I'm it!" when asked where were the rest of the men. This was a man's man; a true hero of the highest caliber.

On February 10, 1945, When Lt. Gen. Alexander M. Patch, Seventh Army Commander presented the Service Cross to Conner, he stated in part, *"For extraordinary heroism in action, on 24 January 1945 at 0800 hours, near Houssen, France, Lt. Conner ran 400 yards through the impact area of an intense concentration of enemy artillery fire to direct friendly artillery on a force of six Mark VI tanks and tank destroyers, followed by 600 fanatical German infantrymen, which was assaulting in full fury the spearhead position held by his battalion."*

Lt. Col. Lloyd B. Ramsey, (now retired Maj. Gen. Lloyd B. Ramsey) commanding 3rd Battalion, 3rd Division, 7th Infantry, 7th Army (General Patch commanding) wrote his father. He stated in part, *"I just sent one of my officers home. He was my S-2 (Intelligence Officer), Lt. Garlin M. Conner, who is from Aaron, Kentucky. I'm really proud of Lt. Conner. He probably will call you and, if he does, he may not sound like a soldier, will sound like any good old country boy, but, to my way of seeing, he's one of the outstanding soldiers of this war, if not **the** outstanding. He was a Sergeant until July and now is a First Lieutenant. He has the D.S.C., which could have been, I believe, a Congressional Medal of Honor but, he was heading home and we wanted to get him what he deserved before he left. He has a Silver Star with 4 clusters, a Bronze Star, Purple Heart with 6 clusters and is in for a French medal. On this last push, within two weeks he earned the D.S.C., a cluster to his Silver Star and a Bronze Star. I've never seen a man with as much courage and ability as he has. I usually don't brag much on my officers but, this is one officer nobody could brag enough about and do him justice; he's a real soldier."*

With this type of endorsement and the support of congress, does not Lt. G. Murl Connors deserve the Medal of Honor? He EARNED it! We must do all to insure he gets the recognition he rightfully deserves. Richard Chilton of Lake Geneva, Wisconsin is doing what he can to see that Pauline Connors receives the medal for Murl. Chilton was a Green Beret, who served with the 11th Division in Korea and in Desert Storm he was with the Israeli paratroopers.

Chilton began searching for information about his uncle (Gordon Roberts was killed in Anzio, Italy & was part of Lt. Connor's platoon) and began interviewing veterans who served with the 7th Infantry. He stated that the name of Garlin Conner kept coming up and *"They were amazed when they learned he had made it through the war and was still alive at that time, and they would go on to tell me what he had done."* When Chilton met Mr. Connors the old man was in a wheelchair and could not speak. Chilton stated that upon mentioning his uncle by name to Conner, he began weeping. Such is the heart of a humble hero; always thinking of others first.

After you have read this I ask you to write your congressman, representative and let us rally to give Pauline, Paul (Murl's son) and the grandchildren the medal that Lt. Conner earned. He gave so much of himself; can we not afford to do something to honor his sacrifice? Contact the Director of the Army Board for Correction of Military Records in writing, offer a petition and keep his legend alive on the social media. Also know that the military can also conduct a review at the behest of Congress.

"There is no doubt that Lt. Conner should have been awarded the <u>Medal of Honor</u> for his actions," Ramsey wrote. "One of the most disappointing regrets of my career is not having the <u>Medal of Honor</u> awarded to the most outstanding soldier I've ever had the privilege of commanding." Ramsey

SOURCES

The Courier Journal, Louisville Kentucky; Crawford, Bryon, June 11, 2000

http://www.kyphilom.com/www/murl.html

http://www.grunts.net/army/3rdid2.html

http://www.sacbee.com/2014/03/12/6231222/judge-decorated-soldier-wont-get.html

http://projects.militarytimes.com/citations-medals-awards/recipient.php?recipientid=30595

http://randyspeck.blogspot.com/2010/06/to-honor-hero.html

http://www.army.mil/article/88445/TACOM_FMX_dedicates_buildings/

http://www.fold3.com/s.php#s_given_name=garlin&s_surname=conners&ocr=1&t=all&tx=830&p_place_usa=KY,none

http://news.msn.com/us/judge-decorated-soldier-wont-get-medal-of-honor

http://www.dailymail.co.uk/news/article-2579429/Judge-Decorated-soldier-wont-Medal-Honor.html

http://news.google.com/newspapers?nid=1298&dat=20060708&id=wS4zAAAAIBAJ&sjid=fAgGAAAAIBAJ&pg=6590,2095385

http://muse.jhu.edu/login?auth=0&type=summary&url=/journals/register_of_the_kentucky_historical_society/v110/110.1.ridenour.pdf

http://www.warfoto.com/watch_Sep-Oct2012.pdf

http://www.newsmax.com/US/Conner-medal-honor-thwarted/2014/03/12/id/559174/

http://army.togetherweserved.com/army/servlet/tws.webapp.WebApp?cmd=ShadowBoxProfile&type=AssignmentExt&ID=570372

HAROLD GREGORY 'HAL' MOORE
Lieutenant General
1st Battalion
7th Cavalry Regiment
February 13, 1922-Present

Before this country was known as the United States, Kentuckians have always had a patriotic spirit and willingness to sacrifice for their state and country. There are those few who go above and beyond the call of duty, serving God, Country and Honor. Such is the case of the famed Lt. General Harold 'Hal' Moore. What a legacy he leaves for the rising generation.

Harold Gregory Moore was born on February 13, 1922. He was nicknamed Hal. He was born to Harold Sr and Mary Crume Moore in Bardstown, Kentucky. He was the oldest of four children. His father worked in the insurance business and his mother raised the children.

Hal showed an early interest in the military. He was determined to join and while in high school he got a job working in the U.S. Senate book warehouse. He was seventeen years old at the time. He was motivated and worked through the day while attending night classes. He graduated from St. Joseph Preparatory School with the class of 1940.

His dream was to attend West Point. It became his passion. He attended George Washington University for two years. He continued working at the book warehouse through the day. He was offered an appointment to the U.S. Naval Academy by Representative Ed Creal. Hal asked if he could trade that appointment for West Point, the focal of his ambition. Representative Eugene Cox of Georgia endorsed his candidacy. His dream was now a reality.

He entered West Point on July 15, 1942. During the summer he qualified expert on the M-1 Garand rifle, being the top scorer in his company. Due to the war, his class was to graduate in three years instead of four. Hal doubled up on his lessons and made it through. With determination, sacrifice and hard work, Cadet Moore graduated from West Point on June 5, 1945, and he was commissioned as a second lieutenant in the branch he wanted; the infantry. His career began to blossom and it is duly noted that Hal Moore was the first of the class of 1945 to be promoted to brigadier general, major general, and lieutenant general.

Lt. Moore went to Fort Benning, Georgia. There he met Julia B. Compton. She was a student at Chapel Hill and was visiting her parents, Colonel and Mrs. Louis J. Compton, at Fort Benning. They fell in love and were married on November 22, 1949. Their union has yielded five children (Gregg, Steve, David, Julie Moore Orlowsik, Cecile Moore Rainey. Two of his sons continued the tradition of serving in the military as officers.

From Benning, he was sent to Tokyo, Japan, with the 11th Airborne Division. From 1945 to 1948, he was with the 187th Glider Infantry Regiment stationed at Camp Crawford, Sapporo, Japan. In June of 1948, he was assigned to the 82nd Airborne. At Ft Bragg he volunteered to join the Airborne Test Section on a newly designed parachute. He made 150 jumps in the two year time frame.

In the summer of 1952 he was assigned to the 17th Infantry Regiment after completing yet another officer training course. The 17th was part of the 7th Infantry Division in Korea. Captain Moore commanded a company of heavy mortars. His star continued to rise as he served in the capacity of Assistant Chief-of Staff, Operations and Plans. He was promoted to major.

Major Moore became an instructor at West Point in 1954. He taught for three years and then attended the Command and General Staff College located at Fort Leavenworth, Kansas. After completion of that year long program, he reported to the Pentagon. He worked at the Chief of Research and Development. In 1960, he went on and graduated from the Armed Forces Staff College in Norfolk, Virginia. From there he served for three years as a NATO Plans Officer in Oslo, Norway. His greatest challenge lay in the coming year.

The year of 1965 saw Lieutenant Colonel Moore earning a master's degree in international relationships form his old college (George Washington University). He was assigned to command the 2nd Battalion, 23rd infantry based out of Fort Benning, Georgia. They were later designated as the 1st Battalion, 7th Cavalry, 1st Cavalry Division. They were deployed to South Vietnam on August 14, 1965.

On November 14, 1965, Moore found himself and his men in a battle for their lives at La Drang. Their battalion landed in what turned out to be a hornet's nest of North Vietnamese soldiers. They found themselves completely surrounded. General Custer's old command was once again fighting for their lives but this time the verdict was placed upon the leadership and the gallantry of his men.
They fought as warriors, liken unto the 300 Spartans. They fought as though possessed. Despite the fact that they were greatly outnumbered, they refused to give up the ground. The aftermath saw seventy-nine Americans

dead and several hundred of the North Vietnamese dead. For his valor, Colonel Moore was given the Distinguished Service Cross. He continued to tour Vietnam until 1967.

Upon returning to the states Colonel Moore had the following assignments: After Vietnam, Moore served as G-3 8th Army in Korea, Commanding General of the 7th Infantry Division; Commanding General of the Army Training Command at Fort Ord; Commanding General of the Military Personnel Center, and finally, Deputy Chief of Staff for Personnel, Department of the Army. He also earned another degree from Harvard during this period. He was promoted to Brigadier General in 1968. He became a Major General in 1970.

General Moore retired in 1977, after thirty-two years of service to his country. In 1990, he suffered a stroke. Upon recovery he became active in writing a book. He remained busy with authoring a best seller which was made into a movie starring Mel Gibson; <u>We were Soldiers Once</u>.

He was Vice President of the Crested Butt Ski Area in Butt, Colorado. He and his coauthor, Joe Galloway, wrote about the first major battle in Vietnam, known as LZ Xray (Ia Drang Battle). He is the founder of the National Endowment for the Public Trust. He continues to sign books, offers presentations and represents the finest of our American creed. He is an icon who gave more of himself to his country than he will ever know. A grateful nation can only say thank you for your service.

The true character of a man shines through when he can face his enemy and forgive him. He faced his nemesis, Vietnamese Lt. Gen. Nguyen Huu An, with gallantry and tenacity. Yet he held him no ill will.

Lt. General Moore's words ring so true for noble warriors. *"When the blood of any war soaks your clothes and covers your hands, and soldiers die in your arms, every breath forever more becomes an appeal for a greater peace, unity and reconciliation. It was Vietnam. I was their commander and accountable for them. We charged the enemy with bayonets fixed to our rifles in face-to-face combat. I still hear the ugly sounds of war... I still see the boots of my dead sticking out from under their ponchos, laces tied one last time by their precious fingers. ... I still carry the wounded to the helicopters as they bled, screamed and begged to live one more day ... and I still hold those who die in my arms, with their questioning eyes dreading death, as they called for their mothers ... their eyes go blank and my war-crusted fingers close their eyelids. The blood of my dead soldiers will not wash from my hands. The stains remain.*

When he met General Nguyen Huu An in 1993, he wrote the following: *"My unending thirst for peace and unity drove me to return to the "Valley of Death" in 1993. Some of my men accompanied me to meet with the man, along with a few of his soldiers, who had once endeavored to kill us all. Lt. Gen. Nguyen Huu An and I came face-to-face. Instead of charging one another with bayonets, we mutually offered open arms. I invited all to form a circle with arms extended around each other's shoulders and bowed our heads. With prayer and tears, we shared our painful memories. Although we did not understand each other's language, we quickly saw that the soul requires no interpreter.*

"*Gen. An and I then walked toward each other and shook hands. He kissed me on both cheeks! A communion of friendship was established that far outweighed past bloody memories. Later, Gen. An and I walked part of the battlefield. Together we surveyed the once blood-soaked terrain. Foxholes dug long ago were adorned with blooming wildflowers. No thunder of war filled the air. Instead, birds sang with a most beautiful "noise." Ever so gently, Gen. An placed his arm in mine. We had made a very long journey from war to peace. This was sealed through the reverent affection of one arm in the other."*

AWARDS and DECORATIONS

- Combat Infantryman Badge (2 awards)
- Basic Army Aviator Badge
- US Army Airborne master parachutist
- Original Air Assault Badge
- Vietnam Parachutist Badge
- Office of the Secretary of Defense Identification Badge
- United States Army Staff Identification Badge.

- 1st Cavalry Division - Shoulder Sleeve Insignia
- Distinguished Service Cross[4]
- Army Distinguished Service Medal
- Bronze oak leaf cluster
- Legion of Merit (with two bronze oak leaf clusters)
- Bronze oak leaf cluster (4 awards, including two for valor)
- Silver oak leaf cluster
- Air Medal with one silver and three bronze Oak Leaf Clusters
- Joint Service Commendation Medal
- Bronze oak leaf cluster
- Army Commendation Medal (with 2 bronze oak leaf clusters)
- American Campaign Medal
- Asiatic-Pacific Campaign Medal
- World War II Victory Medal
- Army of Occupation Medal
- Bronze oak leaf cluster   National Defense Service Medal (with bronze oak leaf cluster)

- Korean Service Medal with three bronze campaign stars
- Vietnam Service Medal with three bronze campaign stars
- Armed Forces Expeditionary Medal
- Vietnam Cross of Gallantry with Palm (three awards)
- United Nations Service Medal for Korea
- Vietnam Campaign Medal
- Republic of Korea War Service Medal
- Army Presidential Unit Citation
- Republic of Korea Presidential Unit Citation
- Vietnam Gallantry Cross Unit Citation with Palm (2 awards)

SOURCES

http://www.google.com/#q=hal+moore&safe=active

http://www.imdb.com/character/ch0010423/bio

http://www.lzxray.com/hmoore.htm

http://americanranger.blogspot.com/2008/05/hal-moore-is-better-man-than-me.html

http://militaryhistory.about.com/od/vietnamwar/p/Vietnam-War-Battle-Of-Ia-Drang.htm

We were soldiers once-and young: Ia Drang, the battle that changed the war in Vietnam; Harold Moore; Joseph Galloway; New York: Random House, 1992

http://www.commandposts.com/author/lt-gen-harold-g-moore/

http://www.google.com/search?q=lt+general+hal+moore&safe=active&source=lnms&tbm=isch&sa=X&ei=w5Q0U7e6K5DQsQSdlYHQBw&sqi=2&ved=0CAcQ_A

UoAg&biw=1024&bih=677&surl=1#facrc=_&imgrc=
ZrT3xH7dTkCg7M%253A%3BMAoZsq2NuBU9IM%
3Bhttp%253A%252F%252Fi1.wp.com%252Fpgoaame
ricanprofile2.files.wordpress.com%252F2011%252F05
%252Fk-hal-moore-
lessons_photo.jpg%253Fcrop%253D0px%25252C636p
x%25252C2410px%25252C1359px%2526resize%253
D487%25252C292%3Bhttp%253A%252F%252Fameri
canprofile.com%252Farticles%252Fleadership-lessons-
list-from-vietnam-veteran%252F%3B487%3B292

HARRY M. CAUDILL
Private
85th Division
5th Army
May 3, 1922-November 29, 1990

I remember him well. I was teaching for Hazard Community College and needed a speaker. By chance I happened to run into Mr. Caudill and since we were distant kin, we began talking. His mother was a Blair and his father a Caudill. I am kin to both sides of his lineage. I had always admired his writings and his ability to share stories. I asked him if he could spare some time and he was eager to do so. He became a regular speaker in my Appalachian Studies class. He was another person (James Still was another man of inspiration) who encouraged me to continue my career as an author. He became a man of legend, having served in the army, legislature, professor activist, and renowned author. This is a glimpse into his life.

Harry Caudill was born in the heart of the coal fields of Letcher County, Kentucky. The place he was born is called Long Branch and is located just below the town of Whitesburg. He was the son of Cro Carr and Martha Victoria Blair Caudill. Cro Carr worked for Consolidated Coal until he lost his arm in a mining accident. Harry took a lesson from this and decided an education was his way out of poverty.

According to Fold 3, Harry entered into the army on July 11, 1942. Other sources state he enlisted on April 5, 1943. Most documents state he indeed enlisted on April 5, 1943, because his basic training was at Infantry Replacement Training at Camp Croft, South Carolina, Then in November he was sent to Fort Dix, New Jersey. The 1943 time line matches. His Army Serial Number was 15305775. He enlisted in Lexington, Kentucky (Source: Box # 01941, Card # 31, and Film Reel # 2.531).

After his training he was sent to French North Africa in January of 1944. At that location he received more intense combat training in preparation of future engagements. In March of 1944 he was sent to Naples, Italy. On April 13, 1944, Private Caudill found himself on the front lines.

During an intense fight on May 16, 1944, near Santa Maria, Private Caudill was severely wounded. Shrapnel tore into his lower left leg, which resulted in permanent damage. He was sent to Europe and returned to the United Stated on July 2, 1944, for further medical procedures. He was sent to South Carolina and Nashville, Tennessee. Due to his injuries, he was discharged and returned home. But his war effort didn't end there.

He wrote a series of articles of the Mountain Eagle talking of his experiences. They covered from September 21, 1944 until November 16, 1944. The articles were entitled, 'My Experiences in the Army' and were detailed in their description. He felt it was his duty to tell his fellow Letcher Countians and the readers of the paper what a soldier went through in preserving America's freedom. Listen to his words: *Tonight there will be many a Letcher County man whose only bed is a muddy slit-trench. A slit-trench is a hole about eighteen inches wide, two feet deep, and five or six feet long. In the cold November rains the ground becomes muddy and two or three inches of water runs into the hole. During the night the water turns to ice. Yet at the front no Infantry soldier who hopes to see the sunrise can sleep on top of the ground. He must use his steel helmet as a pail and bail the water out of this trench for that muddy hole is his bed. He may spread his raincoat on the bottom of the hole and pull his overcoat over his body. In such a position, he must endure the night only to rise at dawn to face still greater hardships and dangers. Let us remember, my friends, to never allow ourselves to complain about our own little troubles. How would you like to sleep in his bed tonight?*

Harry M. Caudill went to law school at the University of Kentucky. There he met Anne Frye. They were married in 1946. Upon graduation they returned to Letcher County and began practicing law. He ran for the Kentucky House of Representatives and served three terms. He always had a gift for writing and in 1963 gained national attention for a book which literally changed the perception and brought attention to the poverty of the region. 'Night Comes to the Cumberland' was a best seller, though controversial. It brought attention to coal companies, greed, and the devastation of strip mining. Mr. Caudill continued writing and published six books, close to one hundred articles and spoke on the lecture circuit. He was also a professor at the University of Kentucky (history) and became an outspoken environmentalist.

Harry M. Caudill died of a self-inflicted gunshot wound to the head at the age of sixty-eight. He was in his front yard looking upon Pine Mountain. He was suffering from Parkinson's disease. His legacy lives on through his books, a library named in honor of him and his wife's work to preserve his contributions to eastern Kentucky as well as the world. The War on Poverty was a direct result of this man's writings.

SOURCES

http://en.wikipedia.org/wiki/Harry_M._Caudill

http://www.fold3.com/page/84274430_harry_m%20caudill/details/

http://www.nytimes.com/1990/12/01/obituaries/harry-m-caudill-68-who-told-of-appalachian-poverty.html

"My Experiences in the Army," Harry M. Caudill, The Mountain Eagle, September 21, 1944, Page 6; October 5, 1944, Page 4; October 26, 1944, Page 3; November 2, 1944, Page 6; November 9, 1944, Page 6; November 16, 1944, Page 3.

http://community.berea.edu/hutchinslibrary/specialcollections/saa74.asp

http://www.kentucky.com/2012/12/23/2452306/chapter-5-harry-caudill-inspired.html

HARRY M. REVENNE III
Captain/Major
138th Aviation Company
1st Aviation Brigade
224th USASA Battalion
USASA Group, Vietnam
Army Security Agency
September 29, 1937-November 15, 1966
Declared death date recorded as June 6, 1975

(Capt. Harry Ravenna atop the wing of his plane)

While searching the internet, I found this moving story on my cousin's facebook. I was moved by it and thought this saga must be shared with others in fervent prayer that we never forget the cost of freedom. I searched Fold 3 and found that he was from San Antonia, Texas but born in Houston. He was reported as not being married. He graduated from Thomas Jefferson High School in 1955 and St. Mary's University in 1960. He enlisted in the Army, attended Officer Training School at Ft. Sill, Oklahoma, and was assigned to duty in Vietnam in September 1966. Captain Ravenna was assigned to highly classified agencies and secret cover designations (RRU-Radio Research Units)

His specialty was Fixed Wing Aviator (U.S. Army). Please note that his casualty date is November 15,

1966, but his death date as recorded by the government is June 6, 1975. It also strikes me as strange that he is listed casualty type: hostile, died while missing and he died of an air loss crash-land (Ground Air Sea). The province and Military Region is listed as unknown, yet there was a flight plan recorded. The Loss Coordinates were: 162535N 1074619E (ZD150045). The official reports state that, "Ravenna and Keiper were last believed to be in South Vietnam about halfway between Da Nang and the city of Hue. Later investigation concluded that on his present course, had it been followed, Ravenna's aircraft would have impacted with the side of a mountain in that vicinity. The hostile threat in the area prevented extensive search, and all efforts to discover the fate of Ravenna and Keiper have failed." Dare we say this mission was and may still be classified. Intriguing! Harry Ravenna was thirty-seven years of age.

"On 15, November 1966, Capt. Harry Ravenna of the 138th Aviation Company, Army Security Agency, took off from Dong Ha, RVN (Republic of Vietnam), in a U-6A (Beaver-serial number #541723) after filing a VFR (Visual Flight Rules) flight plan at Da Nang.

"On board with him was Marine Cpl. John Keiper assigned to Helicopter Attack Maintenance Squadron 16, Marine Air Group 16, which was based at Dong Ha. Keiper assisted in the maintenance of aircraft temporarily based at Dong Ha. (NOTE: His role on this mission is unclear from public record.)

"At approximately 1430 hours Capt. Ravenna made radio contact with Da Nang. He said: "Lonely Ringer 723 (aircraft #541723), heading 125, 3000 feet, estimating Da Nang at 40, request radar, presently on instruments." Da Nang could not locate the aircraft on radar and requested his position. Ravenna radioed that he was forty-five nautical miles from Dong Ha. Da

Nang requested that he contact Dong Ha, and he acknowledged that request, but that was the last contact with the aircraft.

"It is believed that the plane went down in the Hi Van Mountains in South Vietnam, half way between Da Nang and Hue, but due to the hostile threat in the area at the time, an extensive search was not possible, and the actual crash site was never located. A later investigation concluded that if the plane had continued on its original course, it would have impacted with the side of a mountain in that vicinity.

"Harry M. Ravenna III was from San Antonio, Texas. He was a graduate of St. Mary's University and had graduated from OCS at Ft. Sill, Oklahoma. He was twenty-nine years old at the time of the crash.

"John Charles Keiper was from Renovo, Pennsylvania, and had enlisted in the Marine Corps in 1963. He was twenty-one years old.

"Former ASA intercept op David Adams of Tucson, Arizona recently wrote: "I was stationed in Da Nang when we were called the 3rd RRU Det. J. I was there from June 1965 until December 1966. I was a Morse intercept operator and flew in U-6s and U-8s. I flew with Captain Harry Ravenna on his flight from Da Nang to Dong Ha. His mission was to fly me to Dong Ha where we were supporting the Marines. The weather was terrible, and we barely got into the Dong Ha airfield. The Marine (Keiper) that was lost that day was on his way home on emergency leave due to a family emergency."

"Capt. Ravenna and Cpl. Keiper have never been found and are still listed as KIA/BNR (Body Not Recovered)"

Harry M. Ravenna is on the Vietnam Memorial Wall under Panel 12E, Line 72. May he be found and brought back home…

NOTE: As reported by the POW Network: "Keiper and Ravenna are among nearly 2500 Americans who did not return from the war in Vietnam. Today, thousands of reports have been received by the U.S. Government that indicate that men are alive still, held in captivity in Southeast Asia. Thus far, official policy is to state that "conclusive proof" is not yet available. Detractors state that proof is in hand, but the will to act on that proof does not exist. As long as even ONE American is alive, held against his will, we must do everything in our power to achieve his release."

SOURCES

"Unlikely Warriors" - Chapter 13, Pages 162-163

(Photo via B. DeHennis-findagrave.com)

http://www.fold3.com/s.php#s_given_name=harry&s_surname=Ravenna&preview=1&t=825,855,485

Government agency sources, correspondence with POW/MIA families, published sources, interviews. (Updated by the P.O.W. Network)

Vietnam Memorial Wall; Panel 12E, Line 72

HENRY TIMOTHY VAKOC
Major U. S. Chaplain's Corp
January 8, 1960–June 20, 2009

Sometimes we forget the importance of religion in war. A chaplain is called upon when someone is wounded or dying. The soldier asked the chaplain to pray for him/her as he/she goes into battle. He offers services whenever needed and is right in the heat of battle, serving God. These are true unsung heroes. There are many. The Four Chaplains of World War II are but a few examples. The following story is of Father Henry Tim Vakoc.

Henry was born on January 8, 1960, in Robbinsdale, Minnesota. He was the youngest of three siblings. He attended Benilde-St. Margarets' School and upon graduation enrolled in St. Cloud State University. While attending college he was called 'Hollywood' by his fraternity brothers. Little did his friends or family know the path he would take upon graduation from college.

He was accepted into St. Paul Seminary School of Divinity which is located in St. Paul, Minnesota. He was ordained as a Roman Catholic Priest on May 29, 1992. Four years witnessed Father Vakoc working in different Minnesota churches. He felt led to join the army and serve God by ministering to the soldiers.

He was stationed in Bosnia and Germany until 2003. He was ordered to Iraq. During the Iraq War he served faithfully. He was promoted to the rank of Major. He was known to travel throughout Iraq celebrating mass. He was a chaplain of the common soldier. On May 29, 2009, he was returning from a mass in the field to Mosul when his vehicle was hit by a roadside bomb. He was the first chaplain to sustain a serious injury in the Iraq War.

Father Vakoc was flown to Baghdad, Germany, and finally to Walter Reed. His injuries were severe. He was in a coma for six months with the fear of infection lurking over his torn body. He was paralyzed and had brain damage due to the explosion. According to his sister, Anita Brand, "He was heavily bandaged, hooked to tubes and monitors, shut out from the world. Even so, he had a special aura about him." One of the chaplains who visited him "He said, 'Tim, you are still a priest, and this bed is now your altar,' " Brand recalled. Staff members felt it, too, when they entered his room. "It's like being on holy ground." People began to hear of his plight via the internet and prayers for Father Vakoc poured unto heaven.

Progress was slow and setbacks were many but this man of God fought back but five years later, on June 20, 2009, he was called home to serve in a heavenly capacity. He was the first and only military chaplain to die due to injuries sustained in a war zone. He was awarded the Bronze Star and Purple Heart along with the Combat Action Badge.

SOURCES

http://mentalfloss.com/article/29695/12-heroic-us-military-chaplains#ixzz2lmXHdHG8
--brought to you by mental_floss!

http://en.wikipedia.org/wiki/Tim_Vakoc

http://www.catholic.org/national/national_story.php?id=33938
http://www.startribune.com/local/11586086.html

HENRY WILLIAMS
Technical Sergeant
5th Air Force
WWII

I attempted to discover information about Henry Williams but to date I have only found the following. It is courtesy of Ben Gish of the Mountain Eagle. I would be honored to obtain more information about this Silver Star recipient. He is truly an Unsung Hero.

CITATION

"Having been decorated four times for courageous service to his combat organization and given the Silver Star, the Oak Leaf Cluster, and the Air Medal, Technical Sergeant Henry Williams, son of Mr. and Mrs. E.L. Williams, arrived in Whitesburg Sunday night from eighteen months of fighting in the southwest Pacific area. Tech Sergeant Williams will be the guest of honor at the Rotary Club luncheon in Whitesburg on Friday. He received the Air Medal for his participation in an aerial flight over Vitiaz Straits. He and the other crew members on a B-17 bomber were part of a formation engaged in an attack on a Japanese convoy that was proceeding to reinforce Burma. Faced with intense anti-aircraft fire the crew continued to make bombing runs and scored a direct hit on a destroyer that later sunk."

Henry E. Williams, United States Army Air Forces, was awarded the Silver Star for conspicuous gallantry and intrepidity in action against an armed hostile force while serving with the FIFTH Air Force in the Pacific Theater of Action during World War II.

SOURCES

http://www.themountaineagle.com/news/2013-07-03/Columns/Clips_from_available_Mountain_Eagle_pages_since_ou.html?print=1

http://projects.militarytimes.com/citations-medals-awards/recipient.php?recipientid=50551

http://www.themountaineagle.com/news/2013-07-03/Columns/Clips_from_available_Mountain_Eagle_pages_since_ou.html?print=1

HERCULES MULLIGAN
Revolutionary War
Patriot
1740-1825

Few have heard his name. Few know of his story. He has been lost to antiquity. However I can think of no other patriot who had such an impact on our nation. His name was Hercules Mulligan. This is his story.

Hercules was born in Antrim, Ireland. When he was six he moved to New York City with his family. It has been recorded that he was a large Irishman with a round-faced capable of spreading the blarney with the best of men. He attended school at Kings College (Columbia University) and chose being a tailor as his vocation. This choice would put him in a position whereby his services to his country would become paramount.

Mulligan owned a shop on Water Street. It was located near Lower Manhattan's East River wharves. Later he owned a shop on 23 Queen Street (Pearl Street). His clientele included very prominent British officers and men of means. When the Revolutionary War began, Hercules became an activist. In fact he was a member of the Sons of Liberty prior to the war. He listened to the conversations of those purchasing items from his shop and he informed the freedom fighters. He actually became so involved that he fought in the Battle of Golden Hill. In 1775, he also helped steal muskets from the city armory. He was a member of the New York Committee of Correspondence. This group proved effective in opposing the British through their communications.

July 9, 1776, witnessed a group of patriots destroy the statue of King George III. Mulligan was attributed as their leader. The Sons of Liberty hacked the statue into pieces and used the lead for bullets. Such was the tenacity of the Irishman.

A man by the name of Alexander Hamilton became a boarder because of a letter he had in his possession from Hugh, Hercules brother. It was Mulligan's passion that persuaded Hamilton to join the cause of freedom. Hamilton went on and began an aide for Washington with the rank of Lieutenant Colonel. When in need of reliable information, Colonel Hamilton recommended Mulligan. This would prove to be George Washington's life saver. A British officer came to his shop late one night stating he needed a coat for an immediate mission. As he waited the officer stated, ""Before another day, we'll have the rebel general in our hands."

Gathering needed information he sent his servant to inform General Washington of the plan. The British had acquired knowledge of the General's location and was planning a trap. Luckily the information from Mulligan saved his capture.

A second attempt was averted by Mulligan and his brother Hugh. In February 1781, the English placed a large order of items needed immediately. It was soon discovered that three hundred dragoons were being sent to New London, Connecticut to capture Washington as he went to meet General Rochambeau. Having the plan reported, Washington changed his route through Rhode Island where he greeted the three hundred cavalrymen in an ambush.

Because Mulligan did all his work undercover, many people were resentful of him. George Washington made a personal trip to him so all could see that indeed Hercules lived up to his name in helping in the new birth of freedom. George even had a complete wardrobe made by this Irish tailor. Mulligan became known as the, "Clothier to Genl. Washington."

Mulligan continued his business with his wife, five daughters and three sons. He died at the age of eighty-five. He is buried in the Trinity Church in New York, where Alexander Hamilton rests.

SOURCES

http://www.foxnews.com/opinion/2012/07/04/this-july-4-let-thank-forgotten-revolutionary-war-hero/

"Secret Heroes: Everyday Americans Who Shaped Our World-He Saved Washington Twice; Martin, Paul; July 4, 2012; Fox News.com

H.T. NICHOLSON
Private First Class

Sometimes when researching unsung heroes you run into a brick wall of sorts. This is the case with PFC Nicholson. I wonder just how many are out there unheralded as their memories faded in the mist. Did he serve overseas during World War II? Was he home from leave? Where did he live in the Fleming area? Are any of his relatives still living and if so, what information could they offer?

The only information I could find was from an article sent to me by my friend Ben Gish. It is my desire and fervent prayer that more information will be discovered about this young warrior because of the publication of this book. The following obituary appeared in the Nov. 4, 1943, edition of The Mountain Eagle.

"PFC Harold Thomas Nicolson, 21 years old, stationed at Camp Mackall, North Carolina was killed October 29th, when the plane he was in crashed in trying to make a forced landing. The plane caught fire and PFC Harold was killed from injuries and burns from the burning plane. He was a son of Mr. and Mrs. L.F. Nicholson of Fleming, KY. Funeral services will be held at the Baptist Church of Fleming with Rev. Childers officiating. Burial was in the Fleming Cemetery. Craft Funeral Home was in charge."

HUGH J. HART
PFC
1st Infantry Division
North African Campaign
WWII
1925-March 31, 1943

Hugh was a boy from the mountains. He was proud of his roots and loved his country. He was a typical young man of eastern Kentucky.

On December 7, 1941, the Japanese bombed Pearl Harbor. War was declared and men were called forth to come to the aid of America. Young Hugh Hart was one of those men who heard the war drums of patriotism and went to serve his country.

When World War II broke out young Hugh enlisted at the age of sixteen. The date of his enlistment was January 2, 1941. He joined the army in Norton, Virginia. He attended basic training and was immediately deployed to the battlefields of North Africa. Hugh was assigned to the 1st Infantry Division. In the zestfulness of youth, he was a gallant soldier winning the respect of his fellow soldiers. The 1st Infantry Division was in combat in the North African Campaign from January 21, 1943 to May 9, 1943, helping secure Tunisia. For almost two years he served until he was killed in action.

PFC Hart received the Silver Star posthumously.

CITATION:

"J. Hugh Hart. 13015695, Private First Class, Infantry.

"For gallantry in action: When a concentration of enemy artillery fire destroyed his battalion's advance, Private Hart, although under direct fire, remained at his gun and placed accurate counter fire on enemy batteries until mortally wounded by an exploding shell. Trough out this action, the courage and determination displayed by Private Hart exemplified the highest traditions of the Service. Residence at enlistment: Whitesburg, Ky. Next of kin: Mrs. Millie Hart, Mother, Whitesburg, Ky."

"A previous award of the Purple Heart to Private Hart, for having made the supreme sacrifice in defense of his country, was sent to his mother by Major General J. A. Ulio, The Adjutant General. Dr. B. F Wright, County Judge, pointed out that nearly 4,000 young men from Letcher County were in the Service. The judge said that while the boys are making sacrifices on the battlefronts, the home folks should be willing to sacrifice on the home front. He paid tribute to Mrs. Hart as a mother who brought up her son to love the home country, as a fine citizen and Christian mother in Letcher County. J. L Hays, county attorney, presided at the American Legion program. In introducing Captain Ted G. McDowell, Post Public Relations Officer at Fort Knox, who in turn introduced Major Napier, Mr. Hays said that as a peace loving nation, strong Americans had imbedded in their hearts the strength to fight for freedom and the pursuit of happiness. He remarked that it was more honor to sacrifice and die in battle than to bow in defeat and disgrace on the home steps. Captain McDowell emphasized the peace and quiet of the mountains and the great love the people had for their way of living, but when the country got involved in war the young men would come voluntarily from the mountains and be the first in the lines on the battle fields. He said that mountain men were heroes in the Mexican war, in the War Between the States, in World War One and in World War Two; wherever there was a war, there would be mountain men, and wherever there were mountain men there would be men from Letcher County, remarked Captain McDowell. He said that the biggest honor that can come to any man is that he made the supreme sacrifice while protecting his company for his country when under fire. Rev. L O. Griffith gave the invocation and benediction. The Whitesburg high school glee club rendered several selections of patriotic songs.

The presentation of a Silver Star Medal was to Mrs, Millie Hart, of Whitesburg, Kentucky, in honor of her son who was killed in action during the African campaign. Approximately eight hundred people were present to honor the memory of Hugh Hart. The ceremony took place on August 30, 1943, at 10 o'clock a.m. The presentation was made by Major Guy J. Napier, Adjutant at Fort Knox, Kentucky. The ritual was sponsored by the American Legion Post of Whitesburg.

"In making the presentation, Major Napier, who fought with the First Infantry Division in World War One, the same Division of which Private Hart was a member; praised the work of the First Division. He remarked that its record for gallantry on the field of battle was made by men like Private Hart who made the supreme sacrifice while trying to protect his comrades when under fire."

At his funeral, the Mountain Eagle recorded that, "The

Letcher County Courthouse was filled to capacity Monday morning by people wishing to view the presentation of the Silver Star and Purple Heart to the family of a Letcher County soldier killed in Africa. The medals were received by Mrs. Millie Hart after being presented posthumously to Private First Class J. Hugh Hart by Major Guy G. Napier of Fort Knox, who read the citation noting Hart's gallantry in action while under direct enemy fire. The presentation ceremony was sponsored by Douglas Day Post 152 of the American Legion and is the first of its kind to be held in Letcher County."

Such is the pride of our mountain people. We honor those unsung heroes deeds and reflect upon their sacrifices with pride and devotion.

SOURCES

http://warmemorial.us/mediawiki3/index.php?title=HUGH_J._HART_-_Letcher,_KY_(PFC)_WWII

http://nyx.uky.edu/dips/xt7m901zdd3p/data/0261.pdf
http://eris.uky.edu/catalog/xt7nvx05xv8k_8/text

HUMBERT 'ROCKY' VERSACE
Captain
Detachment A-23
5th Special Forces Group
Intelligence Advisor, MAAG at Camau
July 2, 1937- September 26, 1965

Here is a story of a man living up to his calling and his nickname; Rocky. He never gave up, he never gave in and he never abandoned his cause or God. His story is one of inspiration and Christian character in the face of adversity. For God, Country and Honor!

Humbert Roque Versace was the son of Colonel Humbert Joseph Versace and Marie Teresa Rios Versace. Rocky was born in Honolulu, Hawaii. He was the first born. He grew up in Alexander, Virginia, where he attended Gonzaga College High School close to the nation's capital. He attended Frankfort American High School in Germany for his junior year and graduated from Norfolk Catholic High School.

Humbert J. was a graduate of the U.S. Military Academy of 1933. He and his wife (Tere Rios) are buried in Arlington National Cemetery. Tere Rios was the pen name for his wife. She was the author of three books, one of which the TV series, Flying Nun, was based (Fifteenth Pelican).

After graduating from high school Rocky followed the footsteps of his father and entered West Point. He graduated in 1959 and was commissioned as a second lieutenant. He entered Ranger School (Class 4-60) and graduated with the Ranger Tab on December 18, 1959. From there he enrolled into Airborne School where he earned his parachutist badge.

Lieutenant Versace was assigned to the 3rd Battalion, 40th Armor, 1st Cavalry Division. He went to Korea as an M-48 tank platoon leader. He served for over a year in that capacity. In the spring of 1961, Captain Versace was assigned to the 3rd U.S. Infantry as a tank platoon leader in Headquarters and Headquarters Company.

As the war in Vietnam began, Captain Versace volunteered for duty. He went through training at the Military Assistance Institute, the Intelligence course at Fort Holabird, Maryland. After completion of that he took the USACS Vietnamese language Course at the Presidio of Monterey. This six year Veteran's tour of duty began on May 12, 1962. He served in the capacity as an intelligence advisor.

Captain Versace decided that after his tour he was going to go into the priesthood (Catholic) and help with missionary work in Vietnam. Unfortunately that dream was cut short just weeks before he was to leave Vietnam. On October 29, 1963, Captain Versace volunteered with Detachment A-23 (5th Special Forces Group) with the South Vietnamese Civilian Irregular Defense (CIDG). Their objective was to gain control of a Vietnamese Command Post in the Mekong Delta. They went in without air cover and limited artillery support. While on patrol a VC Battalion ambushed them. Captain Versace provided cover fire for others to escape but he was captured. He was shot in the legs and back. He became a Prisoner of War (POW) with two other Americans (LT Nice Rowe and Sergeant Dan Pitzer-both Green Berets).

Rocky was not your typical prisoner of war. He refused to cooperate with the Viet Cong. He defied them and repeated the Geneva Convention over and over. He spoke French and Vietnamese fluently. Sergeant Pitzer heard him tell them they could, *"go to hell in three languages"*. He angered officers and guards alike by repeating his name, rank and serial number over and over. Another prisoner (LT Rowe) heard him shouting to those interrogating him: *"I'm an officer in the United States Army. You can force me to come here, you can make me sit and listen, but I don't believe a damn word of what you say!"* He would sing God Bless America and was removed from the other prisoners.

He attempted to escape on four occasions. Due to his injuries he didn't make it far. He was shackled, physically abused, and isolated. His will was never broken though they continued to try.

The last time Lieutenant Rowe heard Rocky's voice was when he sang God Bless America. The next day the VC showed him the blooded cell which had contained Rocky. The LT thought they had killed him. In fact they began moving Rocky to different sites in Vietnam. Almost a year had passed with LT Rowe (Rowe later escaped by clubbing a guard-he was inspired by Rocky's determination-Rowe was assassinated while in the Philippines 1989.) spotted him. This young man now possessed white hair, under nourished and appeared to have jaundice. Rowe later wrote: *"The Alien force, applied with hate, could not break him, failed to bend him; Though solitary imprisonment gave him no friends, he drew upon his inner self to create a force so strong that those who sought to destroy his will, met an army his to command..."*

Rescue efforts proved to be futile but there were sightings of Rocky. Tales of seeing Rocky paraded around by torchlight while he defied them in their native tongue. He would then be hit in the face with rifle butts as punishment for his defiance. One momma-son said after she saw him being assaulted. *"A bleeding Rocky Versace looked up to heaven with a smile, and echoing Jesus' words in the Gospels, asked God to forgive his captors."* He was paraded around the Delta in an effort to break him but instead several of the villagers began to admire this unbroken man. *"I heard from the people I spoke to that he was converting his captors,"* Nicholson said. *"I think that's why they decided they had to kill him."*

Because of his defiance and lack of cooperation he was murdered by the VC. His body has never been recovered. The date was September 26, 1965. He has a headstone in section MG-108 at Arlington National Cemetery. His name is inscribed on the Vietnam Veterans Memorial, Panel 01E, Row 033. He was awarded the Silver Star but later it was upgraded after years of petitioning. Due to the persistence of many known as the 'Friends of Rocky Versace', Captain Versace received the nation's highest award for valor for his self sacrifice and devotion to his country: The Congressional Medal of Honor. This was the first award ever given to a prisoner of war for his actions while captured. President Bush stated it well: *"In his too short life, he traveled to a distant land to bring the hope of freedom to the people he never met,"* Bush told the assembled crowed. *"In his defiance and later his death, he set an example of extraordinary dedication that changed the lives of his fellow soldiers who saw it firsthand. His story echoes across the years, reminding us of liberty's high price, and of the noble passion that caused one good man to pay that price in full."*

MEDAL OF HONOR CITATION

'For conspicuous gallantry and intrepidity at the risk of his life above and beyond the call of duty while a prisoner of war during the period of October 29, 1963 to September 26, 1965 in the Republic of Vietnam. While accompanying a Civilian Irregular Defense Group patrol engaged in combat operations in Thoi Binh District, An Xuyen Province, Republic of Vietnam on October 29, 1963, Captain Versace and the CIDG assault force were caught in an ambush from intense mortar, automatic weapons, and small arms fire from elements of a reinforced enemy Main Force battalion. As the battle raged, Captain Versace fought valiantly and encouraged his CIDG patrol to return fire against overwhelming enemy forces. He provided covering fire from an exposed position to enable friendly forces to withdraw from the killing zone when it was apparent that their position would be overrun, and was severely wounded in the knee and back from automatic weapons fire and shrapnel. He stubbornly resisted capture with the last full measure of his strength and ammunition. Taken prisoner by the Viet Cong, he demonstrated exceptional leadership and resolute adherence to the tenets of the Code of Conduct from the time he entered into a prisoner of war status. Captain Versace assumed command of his fellow American prisoners, and despite being kept locked in irons in an isolation box, raised their morale by singing messages to popular songs of the day, and leaving inspiring messages at the latrine. Within three weeks of captivity, and despite the severity of his untreated wounds, he attempted the first of four escape attempts by dragging himself on his hands and knees out of the camp through dense swamp and forbidding vegetation to freedom. Crawling at a very slow pace due to his weakened condition, the guards quickly discovered him outside the camp and recaptured him. Captain Versace scorned the enemy's exhaustive interrogation and indoctrination efforts, and inspired his fellow prisoners to resist to the best of their ability. When he used his Vietnamese language skills to protest improper treatment of the American prisoners by the guards, he was put into leg irons and gagged to keep his protestations out of earshot of the other American prisoners in the camp. The last time that any of his fellow prisoners heard from him, Captain Versace was singing God Bless America at the top of his voice from his isolation box. Unable to break his indomitable will, his faith in God, and his trust in the United States of America and his fellow prisoners, Captain Versace was executed by the Viet Cong on September 26, 1965. Captain Versaces extraordinary heroism, self-sacrifice, and personal bravery involving conspicuous risk of life above and beyond the call of duty were in keeping with the highest traditions of the United States Army, and reflect great credit to himself and the U.S. Armed Forces."

Rest easy brother!

SOURCES

http://www.stripes.com/news/soldier-who-stood-firm-against-viet-cong-captors-inspired-fellow-pows-earned-medal-of-honor-1.249628

http://www.arlingtoncemetery.net/hrversace.htm

http://en.wikipedia.org/wiki/Humbert_Roque_Versace

http://www.pownetwork.org/bios/v/v017.htm

http://www.somf.org/moh/versace_rocque_USA.htm

http://www.hawaiireporter.com/a-spirit-filled-life-cut-short-capt-humbert-roque-versace-u-s-army-medal-of-honor-korea-vietnam-1937-1965/123

http://www.touchthewall.org/Rocky.html

http://www.findagrave.com/cgi-bin/fg.cgi?page=gr&GRid=7531924

JACK V. COMBS
Sergeant
December 17, 1930- October 3, 1952

Here is another unsung hero who gave his life for the cause of freedom. Note that this young warrior was only twenty-two years of age, yet he was serving his second deployment. I searched Fold 3 but could not find anything other than navy listings and none from Kentucky. The following is taken from the Mountain Eagle, Volume 46, courtesy of Ben Gish.

"Mr. and Mrs. Cicero C. Combs of Seco have received word that their son, Sgt. Jack V. Combs, 22 was killed in action in Korea October 3, 1952. Sgt. Combs was in the eight month of his second tour of duty in Korea at the time of his death. He had first been sent overseas in April, 1949, serving in Korea, until June, of 1951. He was sent back to Korea in March of this year. He entered the army January 8, 1948, after graduating from the Fleming Neon High School. He was born at Seco December 17, 1930.

"Besides his parents, he is survived by six brothers, Harlan, Harvey, Frank and Wayne, all of Seco, Edgar, Chicago, Ill. and Edward of the U. S. Navy; and three sisters, Kathleen Combs, Anna Lee Combs and Sue Combs, all of Seco."

JACKIE COOTS
Sergeant
C Company
2nd Battalion
14th Infantry
25th Division
February 22, 1949-June 26, 1969

Jackie was from Cumberland, (Harlan County) Kentucky. He was drafted into the army and served as an 11B20 Infantryman. His military ID was 53758114. He began his tour on Friday, August 30, 1968, and was killed on Thursday June 26, 1969. The location of his death was Binh Duong, South Vietnam. He was twenty years of age at his passing. He was not married. He is listed on the Vietnam Memorial Wall, panel 21W-line 017. Jackie is buried at Huff Cemetery in Cumberland, Kentucky.

But what else do we know of this unsung hero? This we know.

SGT Coots was killed alongside his brothers-in-arms; SSG Roger L. Simpson (Belington, WV), Corporal Charles D. Ayers (Sneads, Fl) and Specialist John T. Ryan due to a hostile engagement with the enemy. Reportedly he died due to an explosive device.

James Hunt (his brother served with SGT Coots) stated on the virtual wall, *"Jackie, I didn't know you but my brother did (SGT Leroy Hunt). He said you were a fine person and one of his best friend over in Vietnam, so maybe you will find him in God's Country...he left us five years ago. Thanks for being his friend in a strange land."*

Diane Mills posted, *"Jackie, your family misses you and thinks of your great sacrifice often. You were a great soldier. You are in our hearts. We love our soldier of yesterday. May you continue to rest in God's holy peace."*

SOURCES

http://www.virtualwall.org/dc/CootsJx01a.htm

https://army.togetherweserved.com/army/servlet/tws.webapp.WebApp?cmd=ShadowBoxProfile&type=Person&ID=44485

http://www.vvmf.org/Wall-of-Faces/10428/JACKIE-COOTS#sthash.EGujVhb9.dpuf

http://vietnam-casualties.findthebest.com/l/42376/Jackie-Coots

JACOB LEE BUTLER
1ST Battalion
Headquarters Company
1st Battalion
41st Infantry Regiment
April 26, 1978-April 1, 2003

His father made a promise. It was a promise from a father to his son. It would not be broken no matter what happened.

Jacob was an all around good kid. You could say he was a typical American boy growing up in the heartland. Jacob was born in Merriam, Kansas. He was a twin. His brother's name is Joe. Jacob and Joe were born to James C. and Cynthia D. (Aune) Butler. He attended South Park Elementary until he was nine years old. When he moved with his family he attended Wellsville Schools. He went to Wellsville High School. He graduated in 1996.

Jacob loved to hunt and fish. Being in a rural area he enjoyed raising cattle and family life most of all. He worked at Nolkes Cash Saver and SMH in Olathe. Two years later Jacob joined the army. The date was November 13, 1998.

Jacob was very proud to serve his country. He joined the Association of the United States Army. He received his basic training at Ft. Hood, Texas. He became a cavalry scout. His training entailed going to the Mohave Desert and deployment to Kuwait in 1999, as a cavalry scout.

On March 23, 2001, he re-enlisted and was sent to Ft. Riley, Kansas. In April of 2002, he found himself back in Kuwait. His third deployment began March 2, 2003. He became part of Operation Iraqi Freedom. While stationed around As Samawah, a rocket grenade hit his vehicle and he was killed instantly. Jacob had written a letter a couple hours before he went out on patrol. In the letter he stated, *"Remember me. We'll all be together soon."* Upon hearing of the loss of his twin brother, Joe Butler said. *'"I just know for a fact that he died fighting for our freedom and doing something that he loves to do. That's really all I can tell you at this point in time."*

His father James knew he had to keep his promise. He had told Jacob that if anything happened to him while he was in the army, he would go and stand on the spot where he fell. He would breath the same air, taste the same water, walk on the same ground, and see with his own eyes what Jacob saw. In a moving six minute documentary, James shares the tragedy of loss and the triumph of flying in a black hawk helicopter close to where his son was killed. From the base he walked two miles and stood on the spot where his son offered up his life. The video is referenced below in bold.

Sergeant Butler's family received the following decorations for his sacrifice: The Meritorious Service Medal, The Army Commendation Medal (two oak leaf clusters), The Army Achievement Medal, The National Defense Service Medal, The Armed Forces Expeditionary Medal (service star), The Good Conduct Medal and The Purple Heart.

SOURCES

http://www.legacy.com/ns/obituary.aspx?n=jacob-l-butler&pid=149066677

http://www.legacy.com/obituaries/kansascity/obituary.aspx?page=lifestory&pid=93250

http://www.fallenheroesmemorial.com/oif/profiles/butlerjacob.html

http://www.findagrave.com/cgi-bin/fg.cgi?page=gr&GRid=10850023

http://freedomremembered.com/index.php/army-sgt-jacob-lee-butler/

http://projects.militarytimes.com/valor/army-sgt-jacob-l-butler/256581

http://cjonline.com/stories/040203/bre_soldier.shtml

http://search.cjonline.com/fast-elements.php?type=standard&profile=cjonline&querystring=%22JOE+BUTLER%22

2http://www.propublica.org/article/a-son-lost-in-iraq-but-where-is-the-casualty-report

JACOB WALTER BEISEL
Lance Corporal
3rd Battalion
8th Marine Regiment
2nd Marine Division
Marine Expeditionary Force
September 27, 1984-March 31, 2006
Killed In Action

Operation Iraqi Freedom

What constitutes a hero? Is it the size of the deed, price paid for the sacrifice, or is it something we do for others with no thought of reward for ourselves. It is all of these factors and more. It is the undying devotion to one's country and assisting others. It is overcoming fear and thought of losing your own life for the welfare of others. It is in essence the hundreds of thousands of unsung heroes' creed.

I first heard of Lance Corporal Beisel through a young man I watched grow into a fine marine and person of character. Ryan reenacted with us and he was always a step above the crowd. His demeanor was that of a soldier even before he joined the Marines. He contacted me and told me that today (March 31, 2014) was the anniversary of the death of Jacob and to pray for the family. That moved me to tears. I prayed and it donned on my being what better tribute than to put him in the book. This is what I discovered about this unsung hero.

Jacob was from Lackawaxen, Pennsylvania. The town is located in Wayne County. His friends recalled Jacob as a fun-loving young man. He was well liked and got along with everyone. He enjoyed goofing off with his friends and was very down to earth. He enjoyed hunting in the winter and fishing in the summer.

He attended Wallenpaupack Area High School. He was a good student and received top grades in his courses. Principal Joann Hudak said that Jacob was, *"The kind of student that everyone wants to have, quiet, went about his business, respectful, a really solid young man from a good family."*

Jacob dreamed of going to college after he served his country. From his younger days he dreamed of being a Marine. He decided to join the few and the proud while in high school. He did so and after graduating from high school in September of 2003, he was in the Marines. He went through boot camp and was stationed in Camp Lejeune, North Carolina. He became part of a weapons company. From there Lance Corporal Beisel was deployed to Iraq. He was on his second tour of duty when he was killed in action.

Lance Corporal Jacob Walter Beisel was mortally wounded while conducting combat operations in Anbar Province, Iraq. He died serving the country he loved. He was twenty-one years old at his passing. He is survived by his parents, Albert and Mary Beisel, and a younger sister by the name of Amanda. Jacob became the 13th local member of the military to have been killed in connection with the war in Iraq. He was buried at Lackawaxen Cemetery (Pike County), Pennsylvania.

SOURCES

http://projects.militarytimes.com/valor/marine-lance-cpl-jacob-w-beisel/1670322

http://www.youtube.com/watch?v=xXXnWm1kyPo

http://www.fallenheroesmemorial.com/oif/profiles/beiseljacobw.html

http://joshdevore.wikispaces.com/Lance+Cpl.+Jacob+W.+Beisel

http://www.pinterest.com/chetmanley/gone-but-not-forgotten/

http://www.findagrave.com/cgi-bin/fg.cgi?page=gr&GRid=13865091

http://newsmilitary.com/pages/3430449-marine-lance-cpl-jacob-w-beisel

http://www.fold3.com/s.php#s_given_name=Jacob&s_surname=BEISEL&preview=1&t=882&p_place_usa=PA,none

JAMES BREEDING, JR.
5th Division
WWII
POW
October 16, 1924-February 12, 2009

As a young boy I grew up in his shadow. Little did I know about the man. His son, Larry 'Poss' C. Breeding was one of my best friends. We were in the same grade, grew up together and ran around. In fact it was said that Posse's car couldn't start unless I was in it.

James Breeding's son Larry attended Berea College. On weekends Mr. Breeding would get off work and then drive to pick up him and others to bring them back home. On Sunday Mr. Breeding would take them back to Berea. Education was extremely important to Mr. Breeding. In fact, Larry graduated first in our class and went on to get his doctorate degree.

James was the son of James (Jimmy) and Vina Caudill Breeding. He was born in Jeremiah and delivered by a midwife. James had three brothers and two sisters. Venters (one of his brothers) and I were good friends and used to run around together.

Mr. Breeding lived at the top of Garner Mountain close to the Letcher County/Knott County line. I always thought the house was beautiful due to my living conditions. Mr. Breeding always was nice to me and he did not seem to mind the status of me being poor running with his son, the smartest kid in our class. On occasion he would slip me a 'little change' so I would have enough money to go to the movies, bowling or some other adventure with his son Larry. I always admired him and thought if I only had a father figure like Mr. Breeding or Mr. Benton Back.

James enlisted into the army on July 10, 1943, at the age of eighteen. He enlisted at Fort Thomas (Newport), Kentucky. His military number was 35870997.

His wife, Shirley Frazier Breeding, submitted an article written by James about his experiences. It was published in the Hazard Herald and then in the Kentucky Explorer (January 2014 edition).

His words rang out after his passing. "I went to the army in WWII. Before this I had gone to Michigan to work. When I turned eighteen, I came back to Kentucky to register for the United States Army."

Upon registering James discovered he had to wait so he volunteered and was sent to Huntington, West Virginia for the physical. From there he went to Fort Thomas and later transported by rail to Camp Fannin, Texas. He spent the next seventeen weeks in training. Sometime during that training he broke his leg. Because of the injury he did not graduate with his class. He was sent to Fort Howes and at that location was given the opportunity of volunteering to go to England. He jumped at the chance. He was with the Fifth Division.

Within a couple of weeks he found himself in southern France fighting Germans. During intense fighting Private Breeding and some men were in a bunker. The Germans were able to break through the lines and to horror of the Americans, they began melting the door. They tossed hand grenades into the bunker and the men had to surrender. Private Breeding and fourteen others became POWS. He was taken to Stalag 14 in Strousberg, Germany.

While there James volunteered to do farm work. He stated he did so out of hunger. The work was hard and the weather cold. The pounds seemed to drop off of him.

As the Russians invaded the area, the Germans decided to take the 2,500 some odd prisoners towards the American lines. James stated that he was in a weakened condition that he felt he couldn't go much further. When liberation came, James weighed only ninety-two pounds. He was in such bad shape that he spent five months in a VA Hospital in Louisville, Kentucky. In an interview he stated, "I spent three more months shell-shocked and would jump whenever something moved." This Post Traumatic Stress Disorder took its toll on James but finally he was able to eat.

After the war Mr. Breeding worked at Standard lab. His job was to sample coal. He also worked for Andy Adams and Golden Oak mines. He was a security guard. I think I remember his son saying that Mr. Breeding drove a taxi for awhile.

The Obituary obtained from the Letcher County Funeral Home stated, "He was a lifetime member of the Disabled American Veterans (DAV), Veterans of Foreign Wars (VFW), American Legion, the Whitesburg Masonic Lodge, and a member of the Isom Presbyterian Church. Surviving are his wife, Shirley Frazier Breeding; a son, Dr. Larry C. Breeding and wife Barbara of Canton, Miss.; two daughters, Sherie Caudill and husband Terry of Mayking, and Jackie Joseph and husband Mike of Smoot Creek; a brother, Vanters Breeding of Indiana; two sisters, Oma Sexton of Bonita Springs, Fla., and Opal Hogg of Isom; nine grandchildren, Hanna, Dustin, Zach, Sarah, Mary, Brad, Todd, Chad and Kim; and two great-grandchildren, Jasmine and Kate.

"James was preceded in death by his first wife, Marcelen Sexton; a daughter, Shirley Ann Breeding Sexton; and two brothers, Earnest Breeding and Venson Breeding." Full military honors were afforded at the gravesite by the Pound VFW. Mr. Breeding was buried in the Herb Maggard Cemetery at Rockhouse. He was eighty-four years of age."

One of Mr. Breeding's grandsons, Zach Joseph, wrote a very moving article that was published in the Mountain Eagle. Zach's last paragraph sums up what we sometimes take for granted about our Unsung Heroes. "As I sat down at my grandfather's funeral, I learned many things about his life that I had never known before. If I wanted to, I could make up an excuse for why I didn't know these things about his life like, "Oh, he went into the nursing home when I was seven and his mind wasn't very good after that." But the truth is I took him for granted. Now I understand why so many songs on the radio are patriotic. The people that wrote them understood how much the soldiers of America such as James sacrificed, and how little they can do in return to repay these soldiers. So please, if you know any veterans, ask them about their lives, and whatever you do, don't take them for granted like I did."

Looking back over the faded pages of my life, I too realize I stood in the shadows of greatness. I stood next to history and an unsung hero unaware. I am honored to have known this unsung hero and to have his son, Larry C., as one of my best friends in my youth.

SOURCES

http://www.fold3.com/page/89297635_james_breeding%20jr/details/

<u>Young James Breeding Spent a Winter as a Prisoner of War</u>; Breeding, James Jr.; Kentucky Explorer, Volume 28, Number 7; pages 28-29; January 2014

http://www.themountaineagle.com/news/2009-02-18/obituaries/041.html

http://news.google.com/newspapers?nid=1481&dat=20090218&id=Mj9lAAAAIBAJ&sjid=lZMNAAAAIBAJ&pg=382,5461371

Mountain Eagle; Jan13, 1993; Page B9.

http://www.themountaineagle.com/news/2009-03-04/columns/007.html

http://www.themountaineagle.com/news/2009-05-20/obituaries/054.html

JAMES E. CHAFFIN III
Captain
3rd Battalion
319th Airborne Field Artillery Regiment
1st Brigade Combat Team
82nd Airborne Division

Every morning before breakfast our school assembles and we discuss the news, weather, and remember those men and women who are currently serving or have served in the military. We always review the statistics of those men and women killed in Iraq and Afghanistan, prior to offering the Pledge of Allegiance.

Today I was sharing with the students that March 2014, was the first month in which we did not have a casualty in twelve months. I also discussed the cowardly shooting at Ft. Hood, Texas. Around 10:30 a.m., I received an update that we had lost another soldier. I shared the news with our school and thought to add his name and what I could find about him to Unsung Heroes. This is what I learned.

Captain Chaffin died while in Kandahar, Afghanistan, on Tuesday, April 1, 2014. His death is currently under investigation as a non-combat death. He was from West Columbia, South Carolina. He was twenty-seven years of age.

James went to school at Brookland-Cayce High and graduated in 2005. From high school he was accepted and attended the prestigious U.S. Military Academy at West Point, New York. Captain Chaffin was commissioned as a 2nd Lieutenant in May of 2009. He completed the Basic Officer Leaders Course and attended the Field Artillery Basic Officer Leader course at Fort Sill, Oklahoma.

He arrived at Fort Bragg on June 12, 2010, and was deployed to Iraq in May 2011. In August of 2013, he transferred to the 1st BCT. He with as a Fire Support Officer with Headquarters and Headquarters Company but served with the 2nd Battalion, 504th Parachute Infantry Regiment, 1st BCT. He was in support of Operation Enduring Freedom as a brigade liaison officer.

According to the news media release, Captain James Chaffin died of non-combat injuries. Lieutenant Colonel Phillip Jenison stated, *"We have suffered a great loss in the 3-319th Airborne Field Artillery Regiment and express our deepest condolences. Capt. Edward Chaffin was an exceptional officer and absolutely value added to our team. Our thoughts and prayers go out to his family and friends. We will never forget him."*

He is the 48th service member with ties to South Carolina that has died in the Southwest Asian country since the war began after Sept. 11, 2001. Another 64 service members with ties to South Carolina, have been killed in Iraq.

AWARDS AND DECORATIONS

- Bronze Star Medal
- Army Commendation Medal
- Army Achievement Medal
- National Defense Service Medal
- Iraq Campaign Medal with Campaign Star
- Global War on Terrorism Service Medal
- Army Service Ribbon
- Basic Parachutist Badge and Air Assault Badge.

SOURCES

http://www.wsav.com/story/25146897/sc-soldier-the-latest-casualty-in-afghanistan

http://www.wltx.com/story/news/2014/04/02/a-midlands-soldier-has-died-in-kandahar-afghanistan/7223253/

http://www.thestate.com/2014/04/02/3364122/west-columbia-paratrooper-dies.html

http://www.wistv.com/story/25146892/west-columbia-soldier-dies-from-non-combat-injury-in-afghanistan

JAMES KEELAN
Private
Thomas Legion
Defender of the Bridge
1818-February 12, 1895
Recipient of the Confederate Medal of Honor

James was born in Pittsylvania County, which is located in Virginia. The family moved to Tennessee when James was a young man. He was a descendent of Scots-Irish immigrants who came to America and farmed the rich land of East Tennessee. He made a living hunting, fishing and farming. Not much is known of his early years except for the writing of his kinfolk (refer to sources).

James was for secession and when the war came he promptly enlisted. He joined the famed Thomas Legion which was made up of mostly Cherokees who avoided the dreaded Trail of Tears because of the work of William Thomas. Now they fought for him and the possibility of freedom.

Private Keelan was forty-three years of age when he entered the Confederate army. One of the positions he held was to protect the bridges and telegraph lines of the area. William Carter was a federalist who wanted to remove the Confederate forces from the region. He came up with a plan of burning bridges and cutting telegraph lines to confuse and slow down the rebels. Then he would have soldiers from the border of Tennessee/Kentucky line (Cumberland Gap) invade.

President Lincoln approved the plan on November 8, 1861. Generals George Thomas and William Sherman were to coordinate the campaigns. General Zollicoffer received intelligence of a build up in the area and took his army in the direction of London, Kentucky. This effectively halted General Thomas (Union) but Carter continued with his plan.

They were able to burn five bridges. They then headed to Strawberry Plains to burn the bridge over the Holston River. Little did they know that some of Thomas Legion's men were waiting.

On that cold November night Private Keelan was on guard duty. William Pickens and nine men were working their way to the bridge. Pickens and Montgomery left the other men and crept towards the bridge with ill intent. At point blank range, Private Keelan fired and Pickens fell. The other men began firing in Private Keelan's direction. Soon it was hand to hand, as Keelan used his knife to defend himself. Keelan was able to kill another man and the rest backed off in order to fire in his direction. He was shot three times but he refused to yield his position.

The battle ended as quickly as it began. The would-be bridge burners left. Private Keelan was alone and bleeding profusely. He made his way to a house by dragging his body along the ground. He made it to the Elmore house. He called for help and was greeted by the home owner, William Elmore. He was able to get Dr. Sneed who took care of his wounds. He had three cuts on his head from a saber, been shot in the right hand, right arm and a bullet was lodged in the left hip. His left hand was in worse shape. It had to be amputated.

Private Keelan returned to the area he so loved and remained there doing what he knew best. But due to his injury he could only do this with one arm. As he began to age he had to apply for a pension from the government. His wife had died and he was the guardian of three grandchildren. It was granted and he survived off of it until his death. He is buried in Bristol's East Ridge Cemetery. His headstone reads: "James Keelan, Defender of the Bridge – The South's Horatius."

On August 20, 1994, James Keelan received the fortieth Confederate Medal of Honor. It is on permanent display in the Confederate Memorial Hall in Knoxville, Tennessee.

SOURCES

http://www.knoxnews.com/news/2011/nov/05/james-keelan-bridge-defender/

http://sunnytennessee.wordpress.com/2011/07/14/james-keelan-defender-of-the-bridge/

http://www.tennessee-scv.org/keelan2.htm

http://civilwartalk.com/threads/pvt-james-keelan-thomas-legion.82840/

http://www.tennesseehistory.com/class/Horatius.htm

http://books.google.com/books?id=V86_sen9bzsC&pg=PA59&lpg=PA59&dq=james+keelan&source=bl&ots=aPIVzKqT5j&sig=3ZCF7BHVsvalH5cGTncCxeQjfK8&hl=en&sa=X&ei=Kg4nU5rvDonaqQGgvIGwBg&ved=0CDMQ6AEwAzgK#v=onepage&q=james%20keelan&f=false

JAMES LEON LOLLAR
Master Sergeant-Captain
Weapons Maintenance
TDY to 72nd Strat Wing,
Anderson AFB Guam
U.S. Air Force
Recipient of two Distinguished Flying Crosses

What constitutes a hero? Is it based on deed, location, heroics and/or event? To me it is a combination of all of the things mentioned and more. This section of the book is dedicated to a man who is the epitome of a hero.

James was born in 1945, and was raised in the small town of Kilmichael, Mississippi. This is the hometown of blues guitar player, B.B. King. James attended school in the Montgomery County School District. He enlisted into the U.S. Air Force a few years after high school.

In August of 1967, he deployed to Phan Rang AB in South Vietnam. He was a bomb-loader on a B-57. He also served as a door-gunner for a UH-helicopter. After his tour of duty he volunteered for a second term. He was assigned to Ac-119, AC-47, and Ac-130 Gunships. He went on for flight training to be a Tail Gunner on a

B-52. He would fly on several missions into Laos, Cambodia, and North Vietnam.

In the winter of 1972, while being involved in Operation Linebacker II, his B-52 aircraft (72nd Strat Wing) was shot down over Hanoi, North Vietnam. Sergeant Lollar was the only one who survived but he became a prisoner of war. According to the latest update on Prisoners-of-war, the following information is pertinent and leaves many questions unanswered: "Ronald Perry's remains were returned exactly three years to the day from the day he was shot down. The remains of Randall J. Craddock, Bobby A. Kirby, George B. Lockhart and Charles E. Darr were returned six days short of the sixteenth anniversary of their shoot-down. The positive identifications of the second group to be returned were announced in August 1989.

"Another returned POW, Ernest Moore, mentioned that he believed Darr had been held at the "Zoo" in Hanoi, but the U.S. never changed Darr's status from Missing to Prisoner. There is every reason to suspect the Vietnamese knew what happened to all the crewmembers, but especially Charles E. Darr. Whose radios beeped in distress from the ground that day in December 1972? When and how did Bobby Kirby, Randall Craddock, Charles Darr, Ronald Perry and George Lockhart die? If any of them were prisoners of war, why did we allow the Vietnamese wait sixteen years to return their remains?"

Sergeant Lollar was sent to the infamous Hanoi Hilton and was a member of the 4th Allied POW Wing. He was released on March 29, 1973, after serving a total of ninety-nine days as a POW. Sergeant Lollar stated, *"I was held in several camps, all in the vicinity of, or in, Hanoi. First I was taken to a camp called the "Plantation" for a couple of days, then moved to a camp called the "Zoo" for a couple of days more. I then spent the remainder of captivity at the Hoa Lo Prison, popularly referred to by its inhabitants as the 'Hanoi Hilton."* He had flown fifty-two missions.

Upon being sent home he furthered his education and was commissioned as an officer. He served as an Internal Auditor for the USAF and was a team leader in investigating military contractors. When he retired (January 22, 1982) he started the Lake City Carpentry Company. He continues to be very active with various groups such as the American Ex-Prisoners of War Organization, along with several other organizations such as the Red River Valley Fighter Pilots Association. His accolades are too many to list; as this unsung hero does what most do: give to the people.

His medals include the following: Distinguished Flying Cross (1 Oak Leaf Cluster & 'V' device), Bronze Star (V device), Purple Heart (1 Oak Leaf Cluster), Air Medal (1 Oak Leaf Cluster), POW Medal, Vietnam Cross of Gallantry, Vietnam Campaign Medal (10 devices) and numerous Presidential and Unit Citations.

CITATION

The President of the United States of America, authorized by Act of Congress, July 2, 1926, takes pleasure in presenting the Distinguished Flying Cross with Combat "V" to Staff Sergeant James Leon Lollar,

United States Air Force, for heroism while participating in aerial flight as a Fire Control Operator near Hanoi, North Vietnam, on 20 December 1972. On that date, as a crew member of a B-52 engaged in one of the largest conventional bombing raids ever amassed in the recent history of aerial warfare, Sergeant Lollar received significant battle damage to his aircraft as the result of extremely heavy hostile fire. Sergeant Lollar and his crew were targeted against massed supplies, communications equipment, and transportation lines in order to eliminate the aggressor's capacity to initiate an offensive and despite receiving heavy battle damage and incurring grave personal danger, Sergeant Lollar and his crew were able to destroy the target even though the loss of the aircraft was imminent. The outstanding heroism and selfless devotion to duty displayed by Sergeant Lollar reflect great credit upon himself and the United States Air Force.

SOURCES

http://projects.militarytimes.com/citations-medals-awards/recipient.php?recipientid=42447

http://www.axpow.org/lollarjim.htm

http://www.pownetwork.org/bios/l/l088.htm

http://veterantributes.org/TributeDetail.php?recordID=45

http://www.couriernews.net/story/2010277.html

http://www.linebacker2.com/Those_Who_Lived_It.php

http://www.nampows.org/nampowslist.html

http://en.wikipedia.org/wiki/Kilmichael,_Mississippi

Compiled by Homecoming II Project 01 April 1991,
from
Raw data from U.S. Government agency sources,
Correspondence with POW/MIA families, published
sources, interviews.

JAMES MONROE COMBS
Sergeant
3rd Pursuit Squadron
Army Air Corps

Imagine being a young man from the mountains of eastern Kentucky and being thrust into a Japanese prison camp. Imagine seeing unthinkable evils committed upon your fellow man and being helpless to do anything about it. Imagine being so hungry that all you thought about was food.

James Monroe Combs was born in Letcher County, Kentucky. He was the son of Jim Combs, onetime sheriff of the county. He attended school in the county and graduated from Whitesburg High School in 1938. He went on to attend Morehead Teachers College.

In an interview with the Mountain Eagle, Sgt. Combs stated that, *"None of them (the Japanese) treated the Americans like humans but to a man were cruel and brutal.* He went on to say that, *"One who had been educated in America (a doctor), in a fit of rage knock down a fellow American who was not only ill but who only weighed 110 lbs."* To add insult to injury this so-called doctor owned property in Seattle, Washington. According to Sergeant Combs this incident occurred just prior to being liberated. Rarely did they get an opportunity to read. He recalled one shipment from the

Red Cross of reading material. Some men were in such bad shape they couldn't remember how to read. Another thing he despised was that no matter the rank, the prisoner had to salute the Japanese. It was a sign of superiority and demeaning to the Americans.

Sergeant Combs was the first Letcher County native to be released from being a Prisoner of War associated with the Battle of Bataan. The date was February 4, 1945. When liberated, Sergeant Combs weighed around one hundred thirty-five pounds. At one time he weighed one hundred ten pounds. His diet had consisted of rice and fish. His forced labor consisted of road building, repairing roads, airport construction, and farming. The work was back breaking and malnutrition caused several deaths while being imprisoned.

As the soldiers came through who freed the men, Sergeant Combs asked them did anyone know where Whitesburg, Kentucky, was located. A man spoke up and said he was from Whitesburg. His name was James Monroe Francis. The man had the same first and middle name of Sergeant Combs. Three other Letcher County natives would also return home from that prison.

SOURCES

http://kdl.kyvl.org/catalog/xt751c1tf87f_1/text

James M. Combs Returns After Two years in Jap Prison; Mountain Eagle; April 12, 1945, Volume38, Number 40

http://www.themountaineagle.com/news/2013-04-10/Columns/The_Way_We_Were.html

JAMES NELSON SPANGLER
First Lieutenant
919th ARS
4252nd Strategic Wing
SAC
April 4, 1942-March 19, 1966

James was a man of the mountains. He was born on Friday, April 4, 1942, to George and Hazel Spangler. He was raised in Mayking, Kentucky. The beautiful valley is in the shadow of the great Pine Mountain. He wanted to fly and after attending Berea went to the Air Force Academy in Colorado.

James joined the Air Force and became a pilot. His MOS was 1115 Pilot and his ID number was 407541294. He had not been in the service long until tragedy struck. On March 19, 1966, while flying in inclement weather, Lieutenant Spangler KC-135 was given clearance to take off. His plane was part of the

4252nd Strategic Wing in support of the troops serving in the Vietnam War. Due to the weather his plane crashed during take-off from Kadena Air Base, Okinawa. His body was recovered and brought home. He was twenty-four years of age. He is listed on the Vietnam Memorial Wall: Panel 08E, Line 007.

The following letter was sent to Valerie King who was attempting to gather information about her relative:

"James was a First Lieutenant when he died in the crash of a KC-135 refueling aircraft at Kadena Air Base, Okinawa on 19 May 1966, while performing copilot duties. Assigned to the 919th Air Refueling Squadron from Turner AFB, Georgia, Jim was on a TDY (temporary duty) tour to the 4252 Strategic Wing at Kadena, flying air refueling missions in support of the Southeast Asia effort (Vietnam War). The accident occurred during a routine training flight, with the aircraft crashing on takeoff.

"Memorial services were held at the Moore and Craft Funeral Home in Whitesburg, Kentucky, with burial at Green Acres Cemetery in Whitesburg at 1 p.m. on Saturday, 4 June 1966. Military honors were rendered by Air Force personnel from Guthrie Air Force Station at Charleston, West Virginia (l am sure Guthrie no longer exists). Jim is survived by his parents Mr. George N. and Mrs. Hazel K. Spangler of Mayking, Kentucky.

"It seems that Jim was placed in the status of "missing" from 19 May until 24 May 1966, the date of receipt of evidence by the Department of the Air Force Jim was deceased (which again casts a doubt that the aircraft crashed on takeoff) l would guess that this was a "cover' for the actual mission and crash, because if the aircraft crashed on takeoff, the remains would have been very quickly found and identified). [For your information, I was a boom operator on this same type

of aircraft from 1959 to 1967. The crew consisted of a pilot (usually a captain), a copilot (usually a lieutenant), a navigator (usually a captain or senior lieutenant), and a boom operator (an enlisted person usually a Staff, Technical or Master Sergeant).

"In a press release after graduation from pilot training: "BlG SPRING, Tex. - Second Lieutenant James N. Spangler, son of Mr. and Mrs. George N. Spangler of Mayking, Ky., has been awarded U.S. Air Force sliver pilot wings upon graduation from flying training school at Webb AFB, Tex.

"Lieutenant Spangler is being assigned to Turner Air Force Base, Ga., for flying duty. He becomes a member of the Strategic Air Command which keeps the free world's mightiest missile and jet bomber force ready to counter the enemy threat. The lieutenant, who attended Whitesburg (Ky.) High School and Berea (Ky.) Foundation School, was commissioned upon graduation from the U.S. Air Force Academy in 1964 where he also received his B.S. degree."

"There is also correspondence in his folder concerning his name being added to the Graduate War Memorial which stands in the Cadet Area by the flagpole. It turns out that the Air Force Report of Casualty (DD Form 1300), dated 27 May 1966, did not specifically indicate that Jim's mission was "in direct support of combat efforts in an arena of war," which was one of the criteria for being listed on the memorial. A fellow classmate, Capt. Joseph Driscoll, who was looking over the names of his classmates on the memorial, noted that Jim's name was not listed and wrote to the executive director of the then-fledgling Association of Graduates (our organization). Driscoll's letter of April 25, 1969: "Dear Capt. Metcalf, In looking over the names of the graduates for the War Memorial, I do not see the name of Lt James N. Spangler, who died on a mission in

direct support of SEA (Southeast Asia) (19 May 66). I hope this was only an oversight."

"Driscoll's letter sparked numerous pieces of correspondence between our association (AOG) and the Strategic Air Command (SAC) Personnel Center to determine if Jim's mission was in direct support of the Vietnam War. Unfortunately, because of the proximity of the requests for information and the war itself, SAC came back saying that this information was classified and would probably remain so for 10 to 15 years after the war ended. Finally in September of 1973, Capt. Metcalf sent a note to the Academy Superintendent, Lieutenant General A.P. Clark, asking his help in determining the nature of Jim's mission. General Clark, in turn, wrote a letter to the Strategic Air Command Commander, General John C. Meyer (later to become Air Force Chief of Staff) asking if the general could resolve the question, General Meyer then sent this letter of 1 Oct 1973 to General Clark (they were good friends, therefore the salutation): " Dear Bub, I am very sorry that your Association of Graduates has not been able to get the information on First Lieutenant James N. Spangler. This information regarding the mission in which Lieutenant Spangler participated is still classified. However, according to the criteria listed in your letter, we can state that Lieutenant Spangler was killed on a mission that was in direct support of our combat effort in SEAsia. The listing of his name on the War Memorial appears to us to be justified. "

"Also on 1 Oct 73, Capt. Metcalf took a telephone vote of the association's Executive Committee which had to approve Jim's name's addition to the memorial. The vote was unanimous that Jim's name should be added. On 2 October, Capt. Metcalf added Jim's name to a list of 15 others killed in the war to be added to the War Memorial. His listing reads: 1LT J.N. SPANGLER '64 19 May66. According to information we have on Jim as a cadet, he was a flight commander (Cadet Captain)

during his senior year, was a member of the ski club and squash team. That's pretty much what I found in Jim's folder. If you have any other specific questions, please let me know and I'll see if I can find the answer."

Best personal regards.
Tom Kroboth
Class News/Obituary Editor

On December 2, 2002, M. Saranell Caudill wrote the following tribute to her brother: "*James N. Spangler was a brother worthy to be remembered. His dream was to one day be an astronaut. If he had had the chance, I believe he would have made it. He was 8 years old when I was born and left home while still in high school to attend the Berea Foundation and then from there was accepted into the Air Force Academy in Colorado. I can remember when he would come home to visit when I was just a girl and I always thought he was so grand. He would always tell me to straighten my shoulders and walk correctly. He loved flying and was full of life. He was 1st lieutenant on an Air Force KC-135 fueler jet that fueled other planes while in the air when his plane was sabotaged and crashed in Okinawa on May 19, 1966. He was the brother of two sisters and four other brothers and we still miss him greatly.*"

Cheryl Wallace Hamilton, the daughter of Staff Sergeant Glen E. Wallace, maintains a memorial page for her father and provides the following crew list taken from the Memorial Service held May 24, 1966, at the base chapel at Kadena:

- Captain Benny T. Stowers, Pilot
- Captain Charles T. Hafendorfer, Navigator
- 1LT James N. Spangler, Co-Pilot
- 1LT Ronald W. Ringwall, Navigator
- TSgt Franklin Waters, Hydraulics Specialist
- SSgt Charles T. Stuart, Boom Operator

- SSgt Clyde H. Crow, E. B. U.
- SSgt Glen E. Wallace, Crew Chief
- A1C Kenneth Alston, Asst. Crew Chief
- A1C Marvin L. Dooley, E. B. U.
- A1C Thomas R. Annis, Hydraulics Specialist

SOURCES

http://www.virtualwall.org/ds/SpanglerJN01a.htm

http://airforce.togetherweserved.com/usaf/servlet/tws.webapp.WebApp?cmd=ShadowBoxProfile&type=Person&ID=81576

http://www.vvmf.org/Wall-of-Faces/29139/JAMES-N-SPANGLER

http://memwall.usafalibrary.com/files%5C643220%20Msn%201.PDF

http://kdl.kyvl.org/catalog/xt7gth8bgz0r_1/text

http://www.vietnamwarcasualties.org/index.php?page=directory&rec=49035

http://goldstarfamilyregistry.com/heroes/james-nelson-spangler

JAMES T. PECE
Private First Class
228th Field Artillery Group
(KIA)
Distinguished Service Cross
(WWII)
March 8, 1921-October 13, 1944

James T. Pece was born in Letcher County, Kentucky. He was the son of Edgar Poe Pece and Mary Ashley. His education was through grammar school and he never married. He enlisted on July 18, 1942, in Richmond, Virginia. His enlistment into the Army was for the duration of the war or other emergency, plus six months, subject to the discretion of the President or otherwise according to law.

CITATION

"Private First Class James T. Pece (ASN: 13065539), United States Army, was awarded the Distinguished Service Cross (Posthumously) for extraordinary heroism in connection with military operations against an armed enemy while serving with the 228th Field Artillery Group, in action against enemy forces on 13 October 1944. Private First Class Pece's intrepid actions, personal bravery and zealous devotion to duty at the cost of his life, exemplify the highest traditions of the military forces of the United States and reflect great credit upon himself, his unit, and the United States Army." General Orders: Headquarters, Ninth U.S. Army, General Orders No. 39 (1944)

The Following is a declaration for the President of the United States honoring PFC Pece's heroism.

"The President of the United States takes pride in presenting the Distinguished Service Cross (Posthumously) to James T. Pece (13065539), Private First Class, U.S. Army, for extraordinary heroism in connection with military operations against an armed enemy while serving with the 228th Field Artillery Group, in action against enemy forces on 13 October 1944. Private First Class Pece's intrepid actions, personal bravery and zealous devotion to duty at the cost of his life, exemplify the highest traditions of the military forces of the United States and reflect great credit upon himself, his unit, and the United States Army."

PFC Pece was buried with full military honors in Chattanooga National Cemetery, Hamilton County, Tennessee. His mortal remains rest in plot Section Y #258. He was twenty-three years of age at his passing. He rests as a true American hero from Letcher County, Kentucky. May his deeds be remembered by a grateful nation.

SOURCES

http://www.homeofheros.com/valor/1_Citations/03_ww
ii-dsc/army_p.html

Headquarters, Ninth U.S. Army, General Orders No. 39
(1944)

General Orders: Headquarters, Ninth U.S. Army,
General Orders No. 39 (1944)

J CLIFFORD JENKINS
Sergeant
E Company
1st Battalion
506th Infantry Regiment
101st Airborne Division
December 29, 1948-April 04, 1969

Like so many boys from eastern Kentucky, J. Clifford wanted to serve his country. He was the product of Corbin, Kentucky, and had instilled within his very fiber a strong love for his nation. When our nation called, he answered. J.C. was 11B4P Infantryman (Parachutist) with the 101st Airborne Division. His service ID number was 14913596. He served one tour of duty in Vietnam then returned on a Sunday, December 3, 1967. He was killed in action on April 4, 1969, in the Thua Thien, South Vietnam. His body was recovered and returned home for a military funeral. He was twenty years of age. According to posted records he was survived by his wife. J.C Jenkins is honored on the Vietnam Memorial Wall: Panel 27W; Line 010. Though the picture is poor in quality, I felt it imperative to offer a face to the man.

On May 23, 2004, Dave Sas, a Vietnam Brother, recalled Clifford as only one who had been there could do. He said, *"Clifford and I were in recon together during his first tour in Vietnam in 1967/68. Both of us were sent over to Vietnam from Fort Campbell, Kentucky, with the 101st Airborne Division in December of 1967. Clifford was going to be a career* soldier. He loved what he was doing and always accepted his orders and duties without argument. He was not wounded during our first tour, but lost his life during his second tour. He was an asset to our recon team in his first tour and I'm sure as well with his second tour. He gave his life for what he believed in and for his country.

Denny Liford wrote the following on the virtual wall: "I was 13 when J.C. was killed. His mom, Dorothy Wells, was our next door neighbor. I'll never forget the day the Army came to their house and broke the news; it seemed the grieving wail of his mother echoed all over Corbin. My brother had come back from Nam in 66, but Nam finally killed him in 2003. J.C. was one of 3 people who were neighbors of ours that lost their lives in Nam. His was the first military funeral I attended and although it was very sad, there was a sense of honor and enormous pride in the Taps. I have always had the deepest respect for our Vets, especially the Vietnam Vets. I visited the Wall in 02, and traced his name from the Wall along with Ralph McNew and David Miles, our other neighbors we lost."

SOURCES

http://www.virtualwall.org/dj/JenkinsJC01a.htm

http://vietnam-casualties.findthebest.com/l/8484/J-Clifford-Jenkins

http://army.togetherweserved.com/army/servlet/tws.webapp.WebApp?cmd=ShadowBoxProfile&type=DecorationExt&ID=331344

http://www.vietnamwarcasualties.org/index.php?page=directory&rec=25759

JEFFERSON SCOTT DOTSON
Captain
416th Tactical Fighter Squadron
31st Tac Fighter Wing,
7th AF
August 6, 1944-August 9, 1969
Reported dead-April 26, 1976
Remains returned December 11, 2001
Announced to the family September 4, 2002
Interred at Arlington on October 25, 2002

Sometimes heroes can be found living next door and you are unaware. In this case the hero lived just across Pound Gap, located in Virginia. Jefferson Scott Dotson was from the little town of Pound, Virginia, but his saga is epic in proportion.

For as long as the family could remember Scotty wanted to fly like his father. Before his death, Otis Edward Dotson Sr. taught Scott and his older brother Buddy how to fly when they were teenagers. Everyone knew that someday both would become pilots. Cantrell, the younger sister of the boys, became dear friends as they grew older. Scott taught her how to drive.

After graduating from high school, Scotty applied and was accepted into the prestigious Virginia Military Academy. After four years he earned an electrical engineering degree. The year was 1966. The following year Scott realized his dream and joined the Air Force. The Christmas of 1967, Cantrell flew home from Germany and spent what turned out to be the last time with her brother. Scott was deployed to Vietnam in the summer of 1968. His wife Mary Ann remained at home with their new three month-old baby daughter named Christa.

1st Lt. Dotson arrived in Vietnam and was stationed at Phan Rang Air Force Base. That was the base where his brother Buddy was stationed. Buddy maintained 'refuelers', runway sweepers and firefighting equipment on base. Scott lived his dream of flying. For the next five months they spent as much time as they could together. Before Buddy returned stateside in December of 1968, he tried to get his brother to come home after his tour. But Scotty was bound and determined to fly missions out of Tuv Hoa.

Captain Jefferson S. Dotson served with the 416th Tactical Fighter Squadron from Tuy Hoa Air Base, Republic of South Vietnam. The missions involved utilized the F100 Super Sabre to detect troop movement in Laos and to note supply routes.

The area was known as Oscar 8. It contained large jungle covered valleys with two main roads. One of the roads was named Highway 92 and the other 919. The Hoi is a river flowing through that portion of Laos. There was a power line parallel to one of the highways. The area was rugged and secluded.

This was a hot bed for the Viet Cong and North Vietnamese Regulars. General Vo Bam's 559th Transportation Group was embedded in that region. The sector also contained the largest North Vietnamese

Army storage facility found outside of North Vietnam. Plus the anti-aircraft artillery (AAA) was a formidable force. Finally the terrain favored the enemy and they were well acquainted with it.

The North Vietnamese played hit and run into the sanctuary of Laos. The Ho Chie Minh Trail was being used to transport needed equipment to those supporting the North Vietnamese. There were several planes shot down in this hot zone but rescue operations proved to be fairly successful in this section of Laos. Yet over six hundred men were not found or rescued. The search continues to this day.

On August 9, 1969, Lt Dotson and Captain Gourley left the Tuv Hoa base on a classified mission in central Laos. They were involved in a 'Misty' Forward Air Control (FAC) operation. He and Captain Gourley flew off base in their F100. Note that his F100 (Tail #45-3734; call sign 'Misty 31'), was not what was known as the Wild Weasel series introduced in 1965. His was equipped with advanced radar signal detectors though. Ironically they were not due to go out on that date because of the weather. The mission was one that was unannounced but had to be done. Their mission was to fly fast and low, look for targets and return with the data.

As the two men swept the area another aircraft picked up a transmission from their plane. "We've been hit, we're going to try to get out." The plane saw the flames shooting out of the F100 and also witnessed ejection of the pilot and rear seat. The plane smashed into the mountainside and burst into flames. The search and rescue (SAR) began but within a couple of days the two men were classified as MIA.

1st Lieutenant Dotson's last known coordinates in Laos were: 161800N 1063900E (XD762026). The last reported location placed Misty 31 on the south side of

Route 92. This was a primary east/west road that was a major artery of the Ho Chi Minh Trail. It ran along the southern side of a jungle covered mountain range. When the family was notified, they decided to not give up hope and kept a vigil. They wrote letters and sent packages to authorities in Laos. The United States Government ordered the families to quit sending items to the Laotian government. They continued their efforts in spite of the intimidation and also became active in attempting to obtain information about their loved ones and to determine their status. Noting that fighter pilots were called upon to serve their country and were prepared to die if need be it appears ironic that the same government would abandon them because of political rhetoric.

In 1973, five hundred ninety-one POW was released but not one was from Laos. One can only imagine the emotional drain it had on the families uncertain of their loved ones fate. Stories from refugees abounded about Americans being prisoners but the government did nothing to assist those men on Laos's soil.

On Wednesday, September 4, 2002, Barbara Elkins, Sheila Cantrell, Buddy Dotson, and Margery Dotson (Scotty's mother) were notified. It came by a knock on the door as they were informed that Captain Dotson's remains had been recovered and identified. Both men had allegedly died in the crash. But what about the reported parachute? According to Buddy, the remains of the pilot who was with his brother were found at the crash site. The crash was about ten miles outside the village of Sepone in the Savannakhet Province. His brother's remains, however, were found buried near a villager's hut. What happened? Why was his body not buried where he crashed? Was he still alive and was he held captive until his death? It is a mystery as to why they were removed from the crash site. It was a bitter sweet pill to swallow. His name is listed on the Vietnam Memorial Wall: Panel W20, Line 118

Captain Jefferson Scott Dotson was laid to rest at Arlington National Cemetery with full military honors on October 25, 2002. He was one of the eleven VMI graduates to be killed in Vietnam. Forty-eight of 'Brother Rats' VMI graduates from the Class of 1966 paid their respects at the funeral. He was thirty-one years of age. He is survived by his mother, Margery Lee Dotson; his daughter, Crista Renee Dotson Plikat; his two sisters, Barbara Elkins and Sheila Cantrell; his brother, Otis Edward Dotson; and his former wife, Mary Ann Hollyfield Dotson Goetzel. To honor her father, Christa became a pilot. He now rests in the land he loved. Welcome home brother.

Funeral Procession at Arlington

SOURCES

http://www.virtualwall.org/js/profile.htm

http://www.pownetwork.org/bios/d/d077.htm

http://www.arlingtoncemetery.net/jsdotson.htm

http://www.angelfire.com/va2/VAPOW/Dotson.htm

http://www.vvmf.org/Wall-of-Faces/13754/JEFFERSON-S-DOTSON

http://www.fold3.com/page/110513340_jefferson_scott_dotson/

http://www1.vmi.edu/airforce/events%20folder/funeral%20for%20capt%20jefferson%20scott%20dotson%20-%2025%20oct%2002/funeral%20for%20capt%20jefferson%20scott%20dotson.htm

Data compiled by Homecoming II Project from one or more of the following:
Raw data from U.S. Government agency sources, correspondence with POW/MIA
Families, published sources, interviews: Updated by the P.O.W. NETWORK 2002.

http://www.taskforceomegainc.org/d077.html

JESSE JAMES GILLIAM
Third Class
Storekeeper
U.S. Navy
December 12, 1920-June 19, 1942
World War II

There are many 'Jesses' who did not come home. They rest in foreign soil but their spirits have returned to the land that they loved. We must never forget them or their sacrifices.

Jesse James Gilliam was born in Letcher County, Kentucky, on December 12, 1920. He was most likely named for the famed Jesse James who allegedly lived in the Pike County area for awhile. Little is known of Mr. Gilliam until he joined the Navy (reference # 2874032) in 1940.

He was stationed in Hawaii. According to the article published in the Mountain Eagle, James wrote his half brother, Willard Gilliam about the beauty of the land. He described the beach, getting sunburn, eating a banana off the stalk and getting a haircut from a lady barber. In a letter home he stated he had passed a test and was promoted to Store Keeper Third Class. He seemed to be very proud of that fact. His pay per month was sixty dollars. He also asked about his father.

He was then stationed in Corregidor, a tiny Philippine island guarding the foyer to Manila Bay. He was captured on December 8, 1941 (four days before his birthday). He was officially listed missing in action (MIA) in the summer of 1942. For three years the family waited on word of their son. It came on October 4, 1945. The official document stated he died while in Cabanatuan (prison camp) of dysentery.

According to the article published in the Mountain Eagle on March 18, 1988, the camp was described as the closest thing to hell. *"Gilliam was joined by survivors of the Bataan Death March, which occurred about a month earlier after the Japanese captured the Bataan Peninsula in the Philippines and forced an estimated 70,000 prisoners to march 60 miles to prison camps. At least 10,000 to 18,000 of those prisoners were brutally murdered on the trip by their Japanese captors. Beheadings, throat cuttings, disembowelments, bayonet stabbings, and rifle butt beatings were commonplace. The prisoners were deliberately refused food or water while they were kept continuously marching in the tropical heat, resulting in many deaths caused by starvation or dehydration. Thousands of American prisoners being held at Cabanatuan later drowned at sea after the Japanese placed them on "hell ships." These ships were not marked as being prison ships and were bombed by American planes and submarines who thought they were Japanese supply ships returning home. Jesse James Gilliam's body was never recovered."*

Jesse James Gilliam is remembered by a tablet of the missing at Manila American Cemetery, Philippines. In March, 1998, fifty-six years after his demise, the Veterans Administration issued a bronze marker commemorating his death on June 19, 1942. The marker was attached to a marble monument and placed in a cemetery at Mayking, Kentucky.

We must remember the deprivations and hardships endured by our unsung heroes. For upon their sacrifices our freedom is sustained. Lest we forget…

SOURCES

"Memorial Will Honor Soldier Who Didn't Return from WWII;" The Mountain Eagle; March 18, 1998; Pages 1 & 11.

http://www.fold3.com/s.php#s_given_name=Jesse&s_surname=Gilliam&p_place_usa=KY,none

http://www.fold3.com/page/529955355_jesse_j%20gilliam/details/

JIM SAYRE
Kagnew Station
Signal Corps

I have a dear friend who portrays Abraham Lincoln. He has been an icon for over thirty years in offering presentations to schools, civic organizations, reenactments and other venues. He paired with Cliff Howard (portrayed President Davis) and they created a great debate between Lincoln and Davis. It was a debate that never occurred but entailed the 'what ifs'. It was well received all over the country.

Mr. Sayre is a true gentleman who loves history as well as his country. He is a family man and worked in the transportation business. He currently lives in Lawrenceburg, Kentucky, with his wife Mary. She portrays Mrs. Lincoln. They are the parents of Bo and Bart. Their daughter-in-laws are Darla and Suzanne. They have five grandchildren (Lisa, Adam, Caleb, Kelly and Heidi) one grandson-in-law (Les), one daughter-in-law (Andrea) and four wondrous Great grand children (Jude, Quinn, Elijah and Nehemiah).

The following are the words of Mr. Sayre: *"I received my draft notice in October 1957, and was to report to St Helens, Kentucky, for induction into the U.S. Army on November 26, 1957. I received basic training at Fort Knox, Kentucky. Basic training was difficult but not as bad as I had heard it would be. I was then sent to Fort Monmouth, New Jersey, where I attended signal school for twenty-six weeks. My wife went to New Jersey to be with me. We lived off post.*

"I graduated August 7, 1958. I was then required to have another medical exam and was vaccinated and received an immunization certificate that allowed me to go to a foreign country. I then received orders to report to Charleston, South Carolina, where I would then be sent overseas. Before I went to South Carolina, I received a thirty day leave. I took my wife back to Kentucky, and later reported to Charleston, South Carolina.

"I briefly served in these countries while in service Bermuda, Azore Islands, Spain, Libya, Saudia Arabia, Yemen, and Ethiopia. The greatest amount of my time was spent in Ethiopia. I was stationed in Asmara, Eritrea, Ethiopia. The altitude there in Asmara was seven thousand six hundred twenty-eight feet. The air was thin and required a few days to adjust to this high altitude.

"Duty was good where I served, and was well protected by ASA. It was a rare occasion that I would carry a weapon. I did nothing other than serve my country as I was instructed to do. My total commitment to our country was from November 26, 1957, until October 31, 1963. I have no regrets and was proud to serve THE GREATEST COUNTRY IN THE WORLD."

SOURCES

Interview with Jim Sayre/
Personal reflections

JIMMY DUNCAN
Private
Battery D
15th Anti-Aircraft Artillery Battalion
7th Infantry Division,
Chosin Reservoir, North Korea
POW
Silver Star Recipient
January 15, 1930-September 6, 2012

I remember Mr. Duncan well. He always stopped at Bill's Marathon and carried a large amount of money on him. But no one dared say anything to him about him carrying it in his pocket. He also carried protection and something told me he was not the type of man you would mess with. I really liked him and he liked me.

I enjoyed listening to him talk and recall the Veterans Day (November 11, 2011). We were invited to Letcher County Central High School to be honored. I sat a few feet from 'Jim' and he looked at me and winked. We were given a letter of appreciation for our service and Mr. Duncan received a plaque. The picture tells the story. He was honored to receive it but more importantly he was touched by the way the student body reacted.

Every Memorial Day he would be at the Whitesburg Military Museum and speak briefly to the crowd. I recall the last time I saw Mr. Duncan. He was sitting in a chair and seemed very frail. He was introduced and talked for a moment about being a POW in a Chinese Prisoner of War Camp for over thirty-two months.

The following excerpt is from the newspaper located in Letcher County, Kentucky, known as the Mountain Eagle.

Duncan, who was decorated with a Silver Star, died last week. Funeral services were held September 9 for a highly decorated veteran from Whitco who died last week at the Eastern Kentucky Veterans Center in Hazard.

James "Jim" Duncan, 82, who died September 6, was a Korean War veteran who served in the United States Army. He was a prisoner of war for more than thirty-two months (December 2, 1950 - August 14, 1953).

Duncan was presented with the Silver Star for his "gallantry in action" on November 28, 1950.

The citation on the award says the Silver Star was presented to Private Duncan by the President of the United States,

"For conspicuous gallantry and intrepidity in action against the enemy while serving with the Battery D, 15th Anti-Aircraft Artillery (Automatic Weapons) Battalion (Self Propelled), 7th Infantry Division, in action at the Chosin Reservoir, North Korea, on 28 November 1950.

"On that date, the Command Post of the 1st Platoon of Battery D was taken under heavy attack by the enemy, and the personnel at the Command Post were in grave danger of being overrun by the enemy. When the Battery Commander called for volunteers to join a patrol to go to the assistance of the Platoon Command Post, Private Duncan unhesitatingly volunteered. While crossing open ground in the attack on the enemy force, the patrol was pinned down by intense enemy fire from one of the flanks. Private Duncan, with complete disregard for his own personal safety, immediately ran toward the strong point from which the enemy was firing, and with his carbine and a hand grenade neutralized it.

"As a result of his gallant act, the patrol continued the attack on the enemy and succeeded in killing or driving off all those who remained. The personnel in the Platoon Command Post were thus rescued. Private Duncan's outstanding display of gallantry on this occasion was in keeping with the highest traditions of military service and reflect great credit upon himself, his unit, and the United States Army."

Duncan was on the Board of Governors of the Letcher County Veterans Memorial Museum. He was a member of the Whitesburg VFW post # 5829 and Whitesburg American Legion post # 152. Duncan was a member of the Graham Memorial Presbyterian Church and attended the Old Regular Baptist Church. Duncan was married to the late Fairy Mae Duncan. She died July 1, 2004. A son of the late Verna Duncan, he is survived by his son, Buger Duncan of Whitco; and special friends, Pat Richardson of Mayking and Amanda Parker of Whitco.

The Military Times noted his passing and his heroism during the Korean War.

"The President of the United States of America, authorized by Act of Congress, July 9, 1918, takes pleasure in presenting the Silver Star to Private James C. Duncan (ASN: RA-15197978), United States Army, for conspicuous gallantry and intrepidity in action against the enemy while serving with the Battery D, 15th Anti-Aircraft Artillery (Automatic Weapons) Battalion (Self Propelled), 7th Infantry Division, in action at the Chosin Reservoir, North Korea, on 28 November 1950. On that date, the Command Post of the 1st Platoon of Battery D was taken under heavy attack by the enemy, and the personnel at the Command Post were in grave danger of being overrun by the enemy. When the Battery Commander called for volunteers to join a patrol to go to the assistance of the Platoon Command Post, Private Duncan unhesitatingly volunteered. While crossing open ground in the attack on the enemy force, the patrol was pinned down by intense enemy fire from one of the flanks. Private Duncan, with complete disregard for his own personal safety, immediately ran toward the strong point from which the enemy was firing, and with his carbine and a hand grenade neutralized it. As a result of his gallant act, the patrol continued the attack on the enemy and succeeded in killing or driving off all those who remained. The personnel in the Platoon Command Post were thus rescued. Private Duncan's outstanding display of gallantry on this occasion was in keeping

with the highest traditions of military service and reflect great credit upon himself, his unit, and the United States Army."

SOURCES

http://www.funeralhomesweb.com/Everidge_Funeral_Home/webcast/6487

http://projects.militarytimes.com/citations-medals-awards/recipient.php?recipientid=25078

http://www.themountaineagle.com/news/2012-09-12/Families_(and)_Friends/Duncan_was_highlydecorated_Korean_War_prisoner_vet.html

JIMMY ELLISON TOLLIVER
Staff Sergeant
Marine Observation Squadron 6 (VMO-6)
Marine Aircraft Group 36 (MAG-36)
1st Marine Aircraft Wing
USMC
Place of Birth: Jenkins, Kentucky
Cromona Kentucky
Status: KIA
January 5, 1940-February 16, 1968

Sometimes heroes are made from circumstances. Sometimes heroism falls upon shoulders wishing not to carry the burden but do because of duty and honor. Then there are those born to a greater destiny. They are those born to die a hero. Jimmy Ellison Tolliver was such a person.

My first memory of Jimmy was when he was Killed in Action. I was attending Calvary College when we heard of a Letcher County Soldier being killed in combat. I don't think I ever met him but I knew his father-in-law. Jimmy was married to George Hampton's daughter. He was the postmaster at Jeremiah. I think this was the first time the Vietnam War came home to me. My cousin Charles Blair is married to Jimmy's sister, Margaret Tolliver Blair. Jimmy was a Letcher County native from Cromona. He attended Whitesburg High School and joined the Marines.

In an effort to save American soldiers' lives, an extraction was attempted by tunit VMO-6 from a Recon Area. While on an LZ (landing zone) the helicopter came under fire, as they took off. The enemy continued firing into the helicopter resulting in exploding. Five were KIA and two injured. One later died from wounds sustained during the action. The official summary stated: Shot down by AW fire while on an emergency extraction of a recon team. Incident Number: 68021666.KIA.

Bob Malloy (VMO-6 1966-67-68), a team brother, had the following to say about those who died in the crash. "They were my squadron brothers. 1st Lt Galbreath...1st Lt Jensen...and Staff Sergeant Tolliver were Killed in Action when the Huey crashed ... 2/16/68. Cpl Harry W Schneider survived for 2 days and died 2/18/68. From what I remember being told a couple of days later, he was pinned in the Huey and fought till the end."

SILVER STAR CITATION

"The President of the United States of America takes pride in presenting the Silver Star (Posthumously) to Staff Sergeant Jimmy Ellison Tolliver (MCSN: 1813850), United States Marine Corps, for conspicuous gallantry and intrepidity in action while serving with Marine Observation Squadron SIX (VMO-6), Marine Aircraft Group Thirty-Six (MAG-36), FIRST Marine Aircraft Wing, in connection with combat operations against the enemy in the Republic of Vietnam. On the afternoon of 16 February 1968, Staff Sergeant Tolliver launched as Aerial Gunner aboard an armed UH-1E helicopter diverted to support the emergency extraction of an eight-man reconnaissance team which was heavily engaged with a numerically superior North Vietnamese Army force six miles northwest of Dong Ha. Arriving over the designated area, he expertly directed a heavy volume of machine gun fire on the enemy positions during repeated strafing runs in support of the extraction aircraft. Although five Marines had been extracted, subsequent attempts to rescue the remaining men had failed due to a heavy volume of ground fire which had seriously damaged three helicopters. When his pilot volunteered to evacuate the surrounded men and made an approach to the hazardous area, the aircraft was damaged by hostile fire and forced to abort the approach. Realizing the seriousness of the situation, he again provided a heavy volume of machine gun fire during his helicopter's second attempt and, after landing, continued to deliver covering fire, enabling the three Marines to embark. Lifting from the fire-swept site, his aircraft was struck by a burst of enemy fire and crashed, mortally wounding Staff Sergeant Tolliver. By his courage, intrepid fighting spirit and steadfast devotion to duty, Staff Sergeant Tolliver upheld the highest traditions of the Marine Corps and of the United States Naval Service. He gallantly gave his life for his country."

The following report was submitted summating the action.

While surfing the internet for information regarding Sgt. Tolliver, I found this touching tribute to all who died on February 16, 1968. The place in Vietnam was known as Quang Tri.

The post is dated September 29, 2002.

"The Virtual Wall staff rarely sponsors a memorial to men that we did not personally know. On this day, however, we are sponsoring five of them ... for five Marines who died while trying to recover a 3rd Force Recon Company patrol force that was engaged with a far superior enemy force. Four of the Marines were air crewmen with Marine Observation Squadron 6; the fifth was a radioman with Bravo Company, 1st 1 Battalion, 4th Marines. Although the circumstances of their deaths is spelled out in some detail on the Box Score Memorial (linked below), Captain Bobby Galbreath was the pilot-in-command of a UH-1E gunship; 1st Lt Paul Jensen was his copilot.

"They made a desperate attempt to extract three Box Score team members who were surrounded by North Vietnamese Army regulars. Galbreath's effort failed; the UH-1E was shot down as he lifted off. Galbreath received the Navy Cross; Jensen the Silver Star. The Box Score Patrol The events surrounding the Box Score patrol's engagement and the efforts to extract the team are a glowing example of Marine heroism under fire and were recognized as such at the time. Five of eight Box Score Team members, four air crewmen from VMO-6, and one infantryman from Bravo 1/4 Marines died on February 16, 1968, and a number of others were wounded. The actions of the men involved in the engagement were recognized by one Medal of Honor, three Navy Crosses, five Silver Stars, and two Bronze Stars.

"The Virtual Wall takes pride in honoring the Americans who died in the Box Score engagement and through them the men who survived. Details of the engagement are published on the Box Score Memorial Page. The following Marines are honored on The Virtual Wall: From Team Box Score - 3rd Force Recon Company 2nd Lt Terrence Collinson Graves - KIA - Medal of Honor Cpl Robert Brian Thomson - KIA - Silver Star L/Cpl Steven Eric Emrick - KIA - Bronze

Star PFC James Earl Honeycutt - KIA - Navy Cross PFC Adrian Salome Lopez - Died of Wounds - Silver Star From VMO-6 (UH-1E BuNo 151291) Capt Bobby Frank Galbreath - KIA - Navy Cross 1st Lt Paul Andrew Jensen - KIA - <u>Silver Star SSgt Jimmy Ellison Tolliver</u> - KIA Cpl Harry Warren Schneider - KIA From Bravo 1/4 Marines: Cpl William A. Lee – KIA."

Jimmy Ellison Tolliver is honored on Panel 39E, Row 67 of the Vietnam Veterans Memorial. He was twenty-eight years old at his passing. He had been in the service for eight years. He was listed as a Protestant. His tour began on May 27, 1967. He was in country for almost nine months before being killed in action. His body was recovered.

SOURCES

<u>http://projects.militarytimes.com/citations-medals-awards/recipient.php?recipientid=41338</u>

<u>http://www.virtualwall.org/dt/TolliverJE01a.htm</u>

<u>http://vietnam-casualties.findthedata.org/l/11932/Jimmy-Ellison-Tolliver</u>

<u>http://www.vvmf.org/Wall-of-Faces/52240/JIMMY-E-TOLLIVER</u>

<u>http://www.vvmf.org/Wall-of-Faces/52240/JIMMY-E-TOLLIVER#sthash.gqUk.dpuf</u>

<u>http://www.weststpaulantiques.com/chapter12page2.html</u>

<u>http://www.homeofheroes.com/members/04_SS/5_RVN/citations/marines/tuv.html</u>

<u>http://www.vhpa.org/KIA/incident/68021666KIA.HTM</u>

JOHN CHAVIS
Revolutionary Soldier
5th Virginia Regiment
Presbyterian Minister
1763-June 15, 1838

The first time I had the honor of walking the campus of Washington-Lee College, I encountered an intriguing sign. The sign stated that John Chavis was a Black man who fought in the Revolutionary War. After the war he attended Washington College on a recommendation from George Washington. He went on and became a preacher, establishing churches for black and white students. This really caught my attention and I decided to do some research on the man. I found him to be a true Christian man who served the people honorably. The following is his story.

John Chavis was of African-American descent. He was born in Granville County, North Carolina. He grew up in Mecklenberg, Virginia. Not much is known of his youth except that he was a deeply religious man, professing Jesus Christ wherever he went. He also had a love for the classics throughout his life. Mr. Chavis enlisted in December of 1778, and served three years as a soldier. He served with the 5th Virginia Regiment and his commander certified in 1783 that Chavis had, *"Faithfully fulfilled his duties and is thereby entitled to all immunities granted to three-year soldiers."* In 1789, it is recorded that he owned a horse and was a free Negro. He was gainfully employed by the

Greenwood Estate as a tutor for orphans. He was the first Black to obtain a college education in America. He stated that he was a freeborn man and was proud of his service as a Revolutionary soldier.

After the Revolutionary war John entered school at the College of New Jersey (Princeton). The year was 1792. There he was tutored by the president of the college, John Witherspoon. Mr. Chavis transferred after the death of his mentor. In 1795, John enrolled into Liberty Hall Academy (the school was established with an endowment from George Washington-it later burned and was relocated and renamed after its benefactor), which is located in Lexington, Virginia. This was in spite of a federal law prohibiting the education of blacks! He learned Latin and Greek while attending classes as well as learning the rudiments of proclaiming Christ to others.

The minutes of the Presbytery of Lexington offers the following insight regarding John Chavis: *"At Timber Ridge Meetinghouse, the 19th. day of November, 1800, the Presbyn. of Lexington having received sufficient testimonials in favor of Mr. John Chavis, of his being of good moral character, of his being in full communion with the church & his having made some progress in literature, proceeded to take him through a course of trials for licensure & he having given satisfaction as to his experimental acquaintance with religion & proficiency in divinity, Presbyn. did & hereby do express their approbation of these parts of trial & he having adopted the Confession of Faith of this church & satisfactorily answered the questions appointed to be put to candidates to be licensed the Presbyn. did & hereby do license him the said Jno. Chavis to preach the Gospel of Christ as a probationer for the holy ministry within the bounds of this Presbyn. or wherever he shall be orderly called, hoping as he is a man of colour he may be peculiarly useful to those of his own complexion. Ordered that Mr. Chavis receive an attested copy of the above minutes."* He completed his studies at the school in 1799, the year that George Washington died. He was ordained as a Presbyterian minister.

John returned to his roots in North Carolina and began establishing schools for black and white children. The elite whites of the area entrusted him with the education of their children, including a future Whig senator Willie Mangum, Governor Charles Manly, and New Mexico Governor Abram Rencher. By 1809 he was living in Raleigh, North Carolina, and was a circuit rider and preached at several churches. He taught notables such as the future North Carolina He taught for the sum of $2.25 per quarter for white students and $1.75 per quarter for black students.

In Clement Eaton's book, <u>The Mind of the Old South</u>, the following notation was discovered about John Chavis: *"The Reverend John Chavis, a free Negro who taught a famous school for white children in the 1830s in Raleigh, North Carolina. . . . received an education in the classics and rhetoric in Washington Academy (now Washington & Lee University) and according to tradition had also studied at Princeton as a private pupil of President Witherspoon."*

The Raleigh Register contains an article dated April 22, 1830, regarding reverend Chavis. It was written by Joseph Gales and states: *"On Friday last, we attended an examination of the free children of color, attached to the school conducted by John Chavis, also colored, but a regularly educated Presbyterian minister, and we have seldom received more gratification from any exhibition of a similar character. To witness a well regulated school, composed of this class of persons-to see them setting an example both in behavior and scholarship, which their white superiors might take pride in imitating, was a cheering spectacle to a philanthropist. The exercises throughout, evinced a degree of attention and assiduous care on the part of the instructor, highly creditable, and of attainment on the part of his scholars almost incredible. We were also much pleased with the sensible address which closed the examination. The object of the respectable teacher, was to impress on the scholars, the fact, that they occupied an inferior and subordinate station in society, and were possessed but of limited privileges; but that even they might become useful in their particular sphere by making a proper improvement of the advantages afforded them."*

Mr. Chavis believed in the education of all children but especially Blacks. Yet he did not believe in immediate emancipation for fellow Blacks under the scourge of slavery. He possessed conservative views of the time. Some of his letters though are controversial to the modern day ear. Keep in mind that in the 1790s both Virginia and New Jersey were slave states. I offer them as a reflection of the period in which he lived. In 1805, Chavis met a well-educated black woman and afterwards noted, *"I joined with this my sister in saying that it is truly a matter of thankfulness to the black people, that they were brought to this country for I believe thousands of them will have reason to rejoice for it in the ages of eternity."*

In an 1836 letter to Senator Mangum, Mr. Chavis wrote, *"Immediate emancipation would be to entail the greatest earthly curse upon my brethern that could be conferred. . . I suppose if they knew I said this they would be ready to take my life, but as I wish them well I feel no disposition to see them any more miserable than they are."* Chavis knew the result of immediate emancipation would be poverty and great uncertainty. Noting the letter was in reaction to an abolitionist petition demanding emancipation of the District of Columbia. He wrote Senator Mangum: *"I am of the opinion that Congress has no more right to pass such a law than I have to go to your house and take Orange and bring him home and keep him as my servant. And I am astonished that the members of Congress act so much like a parcel of mullets nibling at bait upon fish hooks. Why don't they act like men who---come up boldly to the subject of those petitions and put their feet upon them and stamp them to the centre of the earth, in such a manner, that all the poweres on earth never could be able to raise them again....That Slavery is a national evil no one doubts, but what is to be done? It exists and what can be done with it? All that can be done, is to make the best of a bad bargain."*

Mr. John Chavis's death was under mysterious circumstances. It is not clear if it was attributed to his increased vocal condemnation of slavery in his later years. Before his death, Mr. Chavis was visited by several of his former students. They noted his hair was the color of snow but his demeanor the same as in the days of their education; that of a devout Christian. A park is named after him. There also exists a small roadside plaque across from the house of Mr. and Mrs. Robert E. Lee, located in Lexington, Virginia. He was survived by his wife, Sarah Francis Anderson, and son, Anderson (Note: another source stated he did not have children).

SOURCES

http://www2.wlu.edu/x30476.xml

http://www.ncdnpe.org/documents/hhh146.pdf

http://www.blackpast.org/aah/chavis-john-1763-1838#sthash.L5znjioQ.dpuf

Court Order Book, April 6, 1802. Rockbridge County, Virginia

Washington & Lee University Trustees Papers (Folder 21) Room Rent Book, 1794-95. Washington & Lee University Library, Lexington, Virginia.

Berlin, Ira. Slaves Without Masters: The Free Negro in the Antebellum South. Oxford, UK: Oxford University Press, 1974.

Brawley, Benjamin. Negro Builders and Heroes. Chapel Hill, NC: University of North Carolina Press, 1937.

Crenshaw, Ollinger. General Lee's College: The Rise and Growth of Washington& Lee University. New York: Random House, 1969.

Franklin, John Hope. The Free Negro in North Carolina, 1790-1860. Chapel Hill, NC: University of North Carolina Press, 1943.

Federal Writer's Program of the Works Progress Administration. The Negro In Virginia. New York: Hastings House, 1940.

Kaplan, Sidney & Emma Nogrady Kaplan. The Black Presence in the Era of Revolution. Revised edition. Amherst, Mass.: University of Massachusetts Press, 1989.

Quarles, Benjamin. The Negro in the American Revolution. Chapel Hill, NC: University of North Carolina Press for the Institute of Early American History and Culture, Williamsburg, Va., 1961.

Shaw, G. C. John Chavis, 1763-1838. Binghamton, New York: The Vail-Ballou Press, 1931.

Woodson, Carter G. Negro Makers of History. Washington, DC: The Associated Publishers, 1928.

Des Champs, Margaret Burr. "John Chavis as a Preacher to Whites." The North Carolina Historical Review 32 (April 1955): 165-172.

Hudson, Gossie Harold. "John Chavis, 1763-1838: A Social-Psychological Study." Journal of Negro History 64 (Spring 1979): 142-154.

Jackson, Luther Porter. "Virginia Negro Soldiers and Seamen In The American Revolution." Journal of Negro History 27 (July 1942): 247-28

Knight, Edgar W. "Notes on John Chavis." The North Carolina Historical Review 7 (July 1930): 326-345.

Savage, W. Sherman. "The Influence of John Chavis and Lunsford Lane on the History of North Carolina." Journal of Negro History 25 (January 1940): 14-24.

Virginia Soldiers of the American Revolution, Volume 1. compiled by Hamilton J. Eckenrode. Originally published in 1912 as List of the Revolutionary Soldiers of Virginia. Virginia State Library and Archives.

Weeks, Stephen. "John Chavis: Antebellum Negro Preacher and Teacher." Southern Workman (February 1914): 101-106.

JOHN CURTIS STRINGER II
Captain
Unit: Company B
1st Battalion
11th Infantry
1st Brigade
4th Infantry
January 12, 1946-November 30, 1970
Missing with Honor

During my research I have encountered several stories which touch the heart. When I came upon the story of John Curtis Stringer, I was moved. I thought how ironic his demise in the service of his country. I offer his saga to you dear reader in order to grasp a better understanding of the sacrifices made by our men and women who serve.

John was born in Ashland to Chris and Elizabeth Stringer. Chris was the principal at Prichard High School. John grew up in Grayson. His parents later moved to Hazard, Kentucky. He was very athletic in basket ball and baseball while attending Prichard High School, home of the Yellow Jackets. He was involved in the Boy Scouts and attended church at Bagby Memorial Methodist. He attended Eastern State University from 1964-1969. He was in the ROTC program. He was commissioned as a second Lieutenant upon graduation. John was also a member of the Sigma Chi Delta Fraternity He was sent to Vietnam.

According to reports with POW/MIA Network (1998), 1st Lieutenant Stringer was leading Company B, 1st Battalion, 11th Infantry. His company was approximately fifteen miles east northeast of Khe Sanh in Qunag Tri Province. The company came to a muddy river surrounded by dense jungle vegetation. Lt Stringer tested the river first. As they crossed a muddy river at Mai Loc, Lieutenant Stringer lost his grip on the rope midstream and plummeted into the water. The rope had been secured across the river with the aid of a helicopter.

The current was swift but somehow he managed to grab a branch overhanging the river. His men attempted to rescue him but unfortunately the branch broke before they could get to him and he was swept away. The men continued the search but could not find him. Rescue efforts continued for three weeks; until December 10, 1970. His body has never been recovered. His last known location was coordinates: 164118N 1065923E.

Tony E. posted on the Virtual Vietnam Veteran the following tribute: *"I remember Lt. Stringer as a happy man who always had a smile for everyone and a joke. When he got a picture of his child in the mail all he did was go around and show everybody. He was so proud of that child. My best to the family. He is always in my thoughts and prayers.'*

His disappearance is still a mystery. One site involving MIAPOW has not ruled out the thought that maybe he was captured by a VC patrol. With information still classified by the government about the several thousand MIA/POW, the family is still in limbo without full closure. This we know: Captain Stringer is truly an unsung hero, who ironically is still **unaccounted while serving his country.** His name is on the Vietnam

Memorial Wall: Panel 06W-Row 099. He was the only son of Mr. and Mrs. Stringer. They are buried at East Carter County Memory Gardens next to an empty grave reserved for their son. Let us pray that someday he comes home...

SOURCES

http://vietnam-casualties.findthebest.com/l/31946/John-Curtis-Stringer-Ii

http://va.eku.edu/heroes/wall/john-curtis-stringer-ii-

http://vietnam-casualties.findthebest.com/l/31946/John-Curtis-Stringer-Ii

http://www.pownetwork.org/bios/s/s162.htm

http://www.findagrave.com/cgi-bin/fg.cgi?page=gr&GRid=53407422

http://army.togetherweserved.com/army/servlet/tws.webapp.WebApp?cmd=ShadowBoxProfile&type=Person&ID=70570

http://www.vvmf.org/Wall-of-Faces/50300/JOHN-C-STRINGER-II

http://www.waymarking.com/waymarks/WMG5XY_Capt_John_C_Stringer_II_MIA_Hazard_KY

JOHN EDISON HAMPTON
Private First Class
C Troop
3rd Squadron
4th Cavalry
25th Infantry Division
Army of the United States
April 13, 1943-June 23, 1966

John was from Whitesburg, Kentucky. He was a product of Selective Service. His MOS was 11E10 Armor Crewman. His ID was 52625784.

John began his tour in Vietnam on Sunday, May 8, 1966, and less than a month later was killed in action in Pleiku Province, on Thursday June 23, 1966. It was reported that Rudolph died from injuries when the tank he was riding in was hit by an explosive device. He was considered a ground casualty. PFC John Edison Hampton was twenty three years of age. His name is listed on the Vietnam Memorial Wall: Panel 08E-Line 080.

14 July 2008, Jesse Hall (the son of a friend to John) wrote the following: *"It is funny how even though you never met someone they can have an affect upon you. Private Hampton died before I was born. I can remember his picture being displayed proudly in our home with a half dollar that he gave my grandmother before he shipped out. He told her that he would not be*

coming home, how true were those words. I don't know what happened that long ago day, I do know that it took his life. I used to look at that picture and wonder who that man was. He made such an impression on the family that hung with other members of the family. Since I moved away from the home many years ago, I have not seen the picture. I will never forget the time I visited the Wall and the feelings I had. Mr. Hampton, you live in my heart. I have heard you were a good man and a good friend to some of my kin. For all that and your sacrifice, I am grateful."

Two other men lost their lives on June 23, 1966, from Charlie Troop of the Fourth Cavalry. John's brothers-in-arms were: Staff Sergeant Francisco Luna, Victoria, Texas, and Private First Class Rudolph Whitaker of Wilson, North Carolina.

SOURCES

http://www.virtualwall.org/dh/HamptonJE01a.htm

http://www.vvmf.org/Wall-of-Faces/21085/JOHN-E-HAMPTON

http://army.togetherweserved.com/army/servlet/tws.webapp.WebApps?cmd=ShadowBoxProfile&type=Person&ID=51514

http://www.findagrave.com/cgi-bin/fg.cgi?page=gr&GRid=44139647

http://goldstarfamilyregistry.com/heroes/john-edison-hampton

JOHN ROBERT PARSONS
Lance Corporal
L Company
3rd Battalion
5th MARINES
1st MARDIV
III MAF
October 03, 1948-October 14, 1968

John R. Parsons was born in Combs, Kentucky. The quaint community is located just north of Hazard, Kentucky. I was married to a lady from Combs and I recall her dad talking about a Parsons man who was killed in Vietnam. He was younger than me and died when he just turned twenty years old.

John entered the Marines after high school and went through boot camp. He was a 0311 Rifleman. He was assigned to the 1st Marine Division. His tour of duty began on June 25, 1968. Less than four months later he was a casualty of that war. He was killed on October 14, 1968, in the Quang Nam Province of South Vietnam. He was a ground casualty and died outright. His body was recovered and returned to his home where he was buried with honors. His name appears on the Vietnam Memorial Wall, Panel W41, Line 62.

Donnie Feltner, a high school buddy wrote, *"Bobby is my friend and an inspiration to me and all of us who went to school at Combs with him and what a good basketball player he was."*

This was posted on Together We Served and I thought it most appropriate to honor Lance Corporal Parsons as well as ALL who gave their full measure. *"Thank you Marine for your service to this great nation and to our Corps...By Larry Isaacs: November 14, 2011."*

THE WALL

Standing here in front of the Wall
Silently reading your name
Solemnly I thank you one and all
Each of you different, yet the same

The list seems forever endless
But I remember your faces
You made the supreme sacrifice, I confess
As I walk slowly with measured paces

Each one of you answered the call
Willingly or not, you gave your lives
Rest easy, my Brothers - heroes all
The Nation still survives

"War drew us from our homeland in the sunlit
springtime of our youth.
Those who did not come back alive remain in perpetual
springtime -- forever young --
And a part of them is with us always."
--- Author Unknown ---
God Bless You

SOURCES

www.VirtualWall.org

ttps://marines.togetherweserved.com/usmc/servlet/tws.webapp.WebApp?cmd=ShadowBoxProfile&type=Person&ID=127356

http://www.vvmf.org/Wall-of-Faces/39610/JOHN-R-PARSONS

http://thewall-usa.com/guest.asp?recid=39583

JOHN VERDELL BACK
Lieutenant
United States Air Force
World War II
Silver Star Recipient

One of the families of Letcher County who offered their sons to fight in World War II for freedom was Mrs. Ella Back. She had three sons fighting. Major Blair Back, Lieutenant Harold Back (a bombardier), Klair Back (Instructor at West Point), and Lieutenant John Verdell Back who was a pilot. Their brother-in-law, John W. Adkins served with the engineers in North Africa.

At the writing of this article, I am not fully acquainted with the men but I am sure they are kinfolk. My grandmother was a Back and married a Blair. What I discovered is courtesy of Ben Gish and the Mountain Eagle. The following is what I have learned to date. It pertains to John Verdell Back. His brothers and brother-in-law remain unsung heroes at the writing of this book. I pray that someone will submit information regarding these heroes to either the paper or put in on ancestry.

John V. Back was a fighter pilot. He was sent to Sicily and almost immediately saw action. I am sure he flew many 'shorties' over the area and was involved in several dog fights. As a Letcher Countian I feel proud to know our men and women stand among the brace during times of national emergencies.

My friend, Ben Gish submitted the following information and gave me permission to use it. "Lieutenant John Verdell Back has scored a "victory" by downing an enemy plane during a dogfight over a beach landing in northern Sicily. Back was flying his plane about 5,000 feet above enemy planes before diving in on them from the side. The one he shot burst into flames.

The extract is from a letter John sent home during World War II. It vividly explains the action taken place in the skies over Sicily. "I'll tell you the story (in narrative form) about how I got my Victory. We were patrolling a beach landing on North Sicily when someone called out an enemy aircraft target over the radio. I looked in the direction indicated and saw enemy planes in flight for the first time. My flight was the closest to the enemy and we were about five thousand feet above them. We dived on them from the side and my flight leader and I were separated from the rest of the Squadron. We started to fire at the closest planes…our diving speed closed us in on them very fast. We fired on numbers three and four of the formation respectively (there were six of them) and numbers five and six, respectively, started firing at us. The one I fired at burst into flames and went in. We immediately turned to fire at the planes firing at us and they ran into the clouds for protection. Then another came back into the fight and it was then that my flight leader chalked up his victory. Our Squadron leader in the meantime had shot down another, making three for the afternoon. They were Focke Wolfe 190's which is one of the best air-planes of the enemy. None of our boys were hit by enemy fire."

SOURCES

Mountain Eagle; September 2, 1943; Volume No. 37

http://eris.uky.edu/catalog/xt77sq8qcc3k_7/text

http://www.themountaineagle.com/news/2013-09-04/Columns/Clips_from_available_Mountain_Eagle_pages_since_ou.html

JONATHON D. OWENS
Sergeant
Delta Troop
2nd Squadron
14th Cavalry
2nd Brigade Combat Team
25th Infantry Division
Tours of duty: Iraq and Afghanistan
By Janice Busic

When my youngest son, Jonathan announced his decision to join the Army I thought I knew what to expect. I didn't. Gary was still in Iraq when I watched Jonathan's plane leave.

Jon arrived at Camp Taji by a unique kind of jet drop that I still don't fully understand. Jon is a pilot and flies a UAV. He says he has a job that is "safe".

Gary was commander of truck convoys that transported items between army camps in Iraq. One highlight was when Gary called me and said, *"I'm in Camp Taji. Can you reach Jon and help us find each other? I immediately got Jon online while talking with Gary by phone. Gary used his rank to get Jon pulled away from the flight line for a couple of hours so they could get together. Taji is a big place and I was passing messages back and forth until they found each other. That was a highlight for all of us!"*

Jonathan is my "thinker". He and I discussed what makes a man choose to face death by becoming a soldier. I'll never forget his words. He said, *"Mom, it's because of the rose by the door."* Jon says patriotism is a part but the ultimate reason is home and family. I thought about that and wrote a poem, using the Civil War as the basis.

The Rose by the Door

Who are the men we honor today?
Why were they willing to give their lives away?
They rode off to war with a tear in their eye.
They told wife, children and mother the last goodbye.

They knew not the outcome of that terrible war
But they would fight for the southland and the rose by the door.
They left ole Virginia not knowing if they'd be back.
These brave southern men, carrying a quilt and haversack.

That quilt had stitches and remnants from home.
Scraps of cloth that reminded them of Nancy and John.
While the snow fell around them and the north wind did roar
They huddled 'neath the quilt and dreamed of the rose by the door.

Some men were injured and barely survived
Hospitalization and prison but they came out alive.
Finally going back home to their loved ones once more
At last, they could see the REAL rose by the door.

Copyright © May 2007
By Janice Busic

JOSEPH BOYD SUMPTER
Private First Class
D Company
11th Engineering Battalion
3rd Marine Division
1371st Combat Engineer
U.S. Marines
August 26, 1946-September 9, 1967

As I searched for more information, I found what I had inadequate. I have done the best I could. Yet I feel this unsung hero must be remembered and maybe someone who knew him could submit more information. I will gladly add to his testimony of service and sacrifice. That is the purpose of this documentary manuscript.

Joseph was born in Letcher County, Kentucky, on August 26, 1946. He was the son of the late Joe and Novella Sumpter. He had a sister by the name of Patricia Anne Sumpter Trent. He enlisted into the Marines. His military service ID number is 2233349.

There was a note on the wall telling of the 11th Engineer Battalion's Command Chronology for September 1967. It contained the following entry: *"9 Sept 1967: At 0945H, "D" Company's sweep team was ambushed on Route 1, YD215725 by small arms, mortar, and hand grenades. This action resulted in 3 KIAs and 7 WIAs to the sweep team plus 1 KIA and 3 WIAs on the Army's supporting truck mounted quad 50 machine gun."*

The four men who were killed were from D Company, 11th Engineering Battalion. They were Lance Corporal Guadalupe M. Alvarez (Donna, TX), Lance Corporatl John R. Vanderzicht (Pompano Beach, FL), Private First Class Joseph B. Sumpter (McRoberts, KY) and Sergeant James L. Tweed (Findlay, OH) of G Battery, 65th Artillery, US Army.

PFC Sumpter was killed by hostile mortar and artillery fire in Quang Tri, South Vietnam. He was twenty-one years old at the time of his demise. A monument has been placed and a walkway named after him in honor of Joseph's sacrifice.

He was given a military funeral with full honors. Joseph was a recipient of the Purple Heart He is buried at Green Acres Cemetery, Mayking, Kentucky. He is listed on the Vietnam Memorial Wall, Panel 26E, 040 to honor his supreme sacrifice for his country.

SOURCES

http://marines.togetherweserved.com/usmc/servlet/tws.webapp.WebApp?cmd=ShadowBoxProfile&type=Person&ID=120887

http://www.virtualwall.org/ds/SumpterJB01a.htm

http://vietnam-casualties.findthebest.com/l/19301/Joseph-Boyd-Sumpter

http://www.usfallenwarriors.com/index.php?page=directory&rec=31435

http://www.vetfriends.com/memorial/honoree.cfm?hindex=63444#.U2qS54FdX5s

JOSEPH E. GANTT
Army
Sergeant 1st Class
Battery C
503rd Field Artillery
2nd Infantry Division
MIA/POW
April26, 1924-Deceased in early 1951

She waited faithfully for his return. Though he told her if anything happened to him, she was to remarry. Yet Ms Clara waited for sixty-three years. Finally in December of 2013, he came home with a full military escort. His ninety-four year old wife waited at the Los Angeles terminal.

Joseph E. Gantt joined the army in 1942, and served his country while in the South Pacific of World War II. He remained in the service (#13072743). While traveling by train from Texas to Los Angeles, California, he met Clara. They fell in love and were married in June of 1948.

When the Korean War began, Sergeant Gantt was sent to Korea as a field medic. According to the official records (OR) of Missing Personnel Office (MPO) out of Washington, D.C., Sergeant Gantt was missing in action (MIA) on November 30, 1950. The 2nd Infantry Division was attacked by a superior force of Chinese near Kumu-ri, North Korea. The after action report (AAR) stated the division withdrew. Several men were unaccounted for during roll call.

In 1953, returning Prisoners Of War (POW) stated they had seen Sergeant Gantt. He had been captured by the Chinese. In early 1951, the former POWS stated he had died from lack of medical care and malnutrition. For over sixty-three years the whereabouts of his remains were unknown.

On an early dawn December morning, a ninety-four year old widow waited in the cold. It had been sixty-three years but the waiting was over. As she slowly walked to the flag-draped coffin, Mrs. Clara Gantt wept while the honor guard carefully carried his remains to the hanger. Ms Clara said, "He told me if anything happened to him he wanted me to remarry. I told him no, no. Here I am, still his wife," She went on to say, "Sixty-some odd years and just receiving his remains, coming home, was a blessing and I am so happy that I was living to accept him."

Mrs. Gantt never wavered in her devotion and loyalty to her fallen husband. "I was praying to the Lord,' she told CBS, "to let me live to see the closure with my husband. My husband was a wonderful man, he was a good husband."

Sergeant Joseph E. Gantt was buried with full military honors on December 28, 2013. His mortal remains lie in Inglewood, California. Gantt was awarded the Bronze Star with Valor, a Purple Heart and other honors. He is one less of the seven thousand nine hundred men unaccounted for from that war.

SOURCES

http://www.npr.org/templates/story/story.php?storyId=255890227

http://www.dailymail.co.uk/news/article-2530604/Funeral-Korean-War-vet-Joseph-E-Gantt-identified-63-years-death-held-Saturday-widow-never-remarried-attendance.html

http://www.dailymail.co.uk/news/article-2527501/Harrowing-moment-widow-finally-reunited-remains-Korean-War-POW-husband-63-YEARS-death.html

http://www.foxnews.com/us/2013/12/20/remains-joseph-e-gantt-korean-war-soldier-returned-to-us/
http://archiver.rootsweb.ancestry.com/th/read/GANTT/2013-12/1387644397

http://www.dailymail.co.uk/news/article-2527501/Harrowing-moment-widow-finally-reunited-remains-Korean-War-POW-husband-63-YEARS-death.html#ixzz2qOngNXeR

JOSHUA A. GRAY
Private First Class
10th Mountain Division
FORT DRUM, N.Y.
November 10, 1992-February 10, 2014

PFC Joshua Gray was from the little villa of Van Lear, Kentucky, made famous as being the childhood home of Loretta Lynn. He was a hometown boy, attended Johnson Central High School and voted by his classmates as most memorable. He was also prom king. He loved helping his fellow students, computers, and was on the academic team along with being a member of the Skills USA team.

According to his instructors, Josh was highly intelligent and very personable. He had an endearing one-of-a-kind personality and carried with him his mascot, Mr. Waddles, a stuffed penguin. Josh took music lessons under Angie Camere at Mountain Christian Academy in Martin, Kentucky. He reportedly had an ear for music and when he listened to a song he could play it. Josh graduated from Johnson County High School in 2011.

Josh could have become anything his heart desired and he did. He decided to serve in the military. Not surprising because of the way he was. He joined the army in November of 2012, and became a Satellite Communication System Operator Maintainer. His training was at Fort Jackson, South Carolina. He was assigned to Fort Gordon, Georgia and Fort Benning, Georgia. In 2013, during the month of October, he was assigned to the headquarters and Headquarters Battalion, 10th Mountain division at Fort Drum, New York.

The official report from the defense department stated that PFC Gray died from a 'non-combat related incident at Bagram Airfield'. This is the largest U.S. Military base in Afghanistan. It is located outside the city of Bagram. At the time of this tribute, little is known of the details. , He died, 'supporting Enduring Freedom.' The circumstances are under investigation.

Upon researching our fallen hero, I encountered the following article regarding U.S. reports four military deaths in Afghanistan. They were Army Specialist. John A. Pelham, 22, of Portland, Ore., (killed February 12 by small-arms fire in Kapisa province), Army Sgt. 1st Class Roberto C. Skelt, 41, of York, Florida, Army Specialist Christopher A. Landis, 27, of Independence, Kentucky (died Feb. 10 at Bagram Airfield after being wounded by a rocket-propelled grenade in Kapisa province) and Pfc. Joshua A. Gray, 21, of Van Lear, Ky., (died February 10, 2014, at Bagram Airfield in an incident unrelated to combat). At the writing of this article a question still looms if there was a connection between the death of Specialist Landis and PFC Gray.

Governor Cuomo of New York made the announcement. "On behalf of all New Yorkers, I extend our deepest condolences to the family and friends of Private First Class Joshua Gray," Governor Cuomo said. "We are saddened at the death of this young soldier, and we join with his fellow soldiers at Fort Drum in mourning his passing and honoring his service." Governor Beshear of Kentucky along with

Governor Cuomo of New York, ordered flags to be flown at half mast in honor of PFC Gray.

PFC Joshua A. Gray was twenty-one at his passing. He gave his life much like he lived: serving others and his country. He is survived by his mother and father. He is a true unsung hero from Johnson County.

The parents of Private First Class Gray received the following accommodations for their sons sacrifice: Army Commendation Medal, the Army Good Conduct Medal, the NATO Medal, the Overseas Ribbon, the Army Service Ribbon, the National Defense Service Medal, Global War on Terrorism Service Medal, the Afghanistan Campaign Medal and the Expert Marksmanship Badge.

On February 24, 2014, several people paid their respects by meeting PFC Gray's mortal remains at the Big Sandy Regional Airport. The Patriots Guard was there watching over the Johnson County native, like angels welcoming home loved ones.

Visitation for Gray was held on Friday, February 28, 2014, evening from five until nine. The memorial wake was held in the Johnson Central Middle School. The outpouring of love by the hundreds who attended the service was evidence of the impact this young man had made within the community, county and country. *"Well, we were all just deeply saddened. Of course, it kind of hits closer to home when it's someone of your own child's age, and same class and things along those lines,"* stated Tom Salyer of the Johnson County Schools system.

The funeral service was held on Saturday, March 1, 2014, at eleven. Burial followed at Highlands Memorial Park with full Military honors befitting a fallen hero. The gravesite was surrounded by friends, family and fellow soldiers bidding him goodbye.

SOURCES

http://www.wsaz.com/news/headlines/Johnson-County-Soldier-Killed-in-osn--245250511.html

http://www.nydailynews.com/blogs/dailypolitics/2014/02/army-private-1st-class-joshua-a-gray

http://www.watertowndailytimes.com/article/20140214/NEWS03/702149893

http://projects.militarytimes.com/valor/army-pfc-joshua-a-gray/6568550

http://www.dailyindependent.com/local/x1783668506/Pfc-Josh-Gray-remembered-as-brilliant-JCHS-student

http://www.kpbs.org/news/2014/feb/12/army-investigating-death-afghanistan-joshua-gray/

http://www.syracuse.com/news/index.ssf/2014/02/army_soldier_from_fort_drum_dies_in_afghanistan.html

http://www.kentucky.com/2014/02/13/3085905/soldier-who-died-remembered-as.html

http://www.kansascity.com/2014/02/15/4825969/military-deaths.html

http://www.wkyt.com/wymt/home/headlines/Eastern-Kentucky-soldier-dies-in-Afghanistan--245011221.html

http://www.wkyt.com/wymt/home/headlines/Eastern-Kentucky-soldier-dies-in-Afghanistan--245011221.html

http://www.jones-prestonfuneralhome.com/fh/obituaries/obituary.cfm?o_id=2435986&fh_id=11777

LARRY DWIGHT MAGGARD
Sergeant
HHD
89th Military Police Group
18th MP Brigade
USARV
January 20, 1946-June 6, 1968

Larry was born and raised in Isom, Kentucky. Unfortunately there is not much information regarding his youth. Louise Moore posted on line about him. *"My Mother & Larry's Mother were very close friends. Mom thought of Mrs. Maggard as her 'second Mother' as she grew up in Kentucky. I met Larry before he left for Vietnam and we wrote often until his death. His death was such a shock to us. He is thought of even now and I often wonder what he would be like today. One thing I know, he would still be a very special man. He had a beautiful smile, a sparkle in his eyes and a love for life, family and country that is rare today. He enjoyed the military and took pride in what he was doing. May his memory live on in those who knew and loved him."*

Sergeant Maggard's MOS was 95B40 (Military Police). His ID number was 15755003. He had been in the army for two years. His tour of duty in Vietnam began on March 27, 1967.

According to the after action report submitted by Colonel Francis E. 'Frank' Payne, the helicopter in which Sergeant Maggard was riding was shot down in Gia Dinh Province. The following is his official report: *"On Wednesday, 5 June 1968 SGT Maggard, age 22 of Hazard, Kentucky and SMG Kenneth E. Kidd age 40, of Orlando, Florida, accompanied Colonel Francis E. Payne, the 89th MP Group Commander on a helicopter flight to Saigon and the Delta Region.*

"The Colonel had received orders for a new assignment and was conducting a farewell inspection of the units

before leaving Vietnam. SGT Maggard had been the Colonels driver and body guard throughout his tour beginning as Commanding Officer of the 720th MP Battalion, and finishing as the 89th Group Commander. SGT Maggards tour started 27 March 1967 with B Company. From there he went to HQ Detachment, 720th MP Battalion, and followed COL Payne to the 89th MP Group as his driver.

"His tour was coming to an end in March 1968 and he requested an extension so he could return to the states with the Colonel in June. Both SGT Maggard and SMG Kidd were in the back seat of the Huey on the return flight to Bien Hoa Air Base. They had just passed over Saigon, the Colonel who had dozed off briefly, awoke startled by the pilot's frantic calls of Mayday. Within seconds the helicopter fell to the ground and crashed into a rice paddy. The force of the impact threw COL Payne and the pilot clear of the impact into the rice paddy, SGT Maggard and SMG Kidd were not as lucky, they were crushed when the helicopter motor came forward.

"The Colonel and the pilot were both kept alive by the quick actions of a doctor who was passing by in a jeep several hundred yards away and had witnessed the crash. The doctor managed to swim to them and assist their breathing until they could be evacuated to Saigon. Both were very seriously injured but survived.

"In the fall of 1968 COL Payne met with SGT Maggards family at a memorial service in their local church in Kentucky. At the service he presented SGT Maggard's parents with the Purple Heart, Army Commendation Medal and Bronze Star (meritorious service) Medal."

One of his brothers-in-arms talked about meeting Sergeant Maggard. "I had the pleasure of meeting Larry a few days prior to the helicopter being shot down and claiming his life. Larry and I spent an hour *or so sitting and talking in an MP jeep on Bien Hoa AFB. We had transported our Provost Marshal Colonel Payne to a meeting. Larry told me that he had extended his tour in Vietnam so he could return to the USA with Colonel Payne, who was due to leave during the summer of 1968. I was impressed with the attitude and esprit-de-corps of Larry and really enjoyed our short time together. It was heartbreaking to hear about the helicopter being shot down, severely injuring Colonel Payne and the Pilot, and killing Larry along with CSM Kidd."*

Larry is buried at Johnnie Collins Cemetery in Isom, Kentucky, with full military honors. He is also honored on the Vietnam Memorial Wall; Panel W60, Line 19.

SOURCES

http://www.virtualwall.org/js/profile.htm

https://army.togetherweserved.com/army/servlet/tws.webapp.WebApp?cmd=ShadowBoxProfile&type=Person&ID=58632

http://www.vvmf.org/Wall-of-Faces/31940/LARRY-D-MAGGARD

http://www.honoredmps.org/maggard-larry.html

http://www.honoredmps.org/maggard-larry.html
www.vvmf.org

http://www.usfallenwarriors.com/index.php?page=directory&rec=17677

LEIGH ANN HESTER
Sergeant
617th Military Police
503rd Military Police BN (Airborne)
18th Military Police Brigade
January 12, 1982-Present

Imagine being nineteen years old and deciding to join the National Guard. Imagine going to Iraq and being involved in the liberation of that country. Imagine how you would feel and how it would affect you. Leigh Ann Hester was that young woman of destiny.

Leigh Ann Hester was born in Bowling Green, Kentucky. She was sports minded and played varsity basketball and softball during high school. After high school she worked in a retail store for awhile. At the age of nineteen, she enlisted into the National Guard in April of 2001. She was assigned in a unit out of Richmond, Kentucky. She was later deployed to Iraq.

On March 20, 2005, she found herself in a life altering fire fight. A supply convoy had been ambushed near Salman Pak, Iraq. Sergeant Hester's squad made up of three Humvees (eight men and two women) charged forward into action. They were met by roughly fifty insurgents firing upon the convoy. Realizing the severity of the situation, Sergeant Hester led her quad through the kill zone and was able to flank the insurgents. They had to remove a sniper who was causing havoc up and down the ambush. With the assistance of Sergeant Tim Nein, they were able to clear the trenches. The fire fight lasted thirty minutes or more. The casualty list was twenty-seven insurants killed, one captured and six wounded.

For their heroic actions and disregard for their personal safety, Sergeant Hester, Specialist Jason Mike, and Nein were awarded the Silver Star. Specialist Ashley J. Pullen from Danville, Kentucky, also won the Bronze Star. Her citation stated that she "Exposed herself to heavy AIF fires in order to provide medical assistance to her critically injured comrades."

Upon the end of her tour, Hester became a police officer in Nashville, Tennessee, but in 2010 duty called and she returned to active service. She was the recipient of the Silver Star, Army Commendation Medal, NCO Professional Development Ribbon, Army Service Ribbon and Combat Action Badge. In 2007, she was recognized by the Army Women's Museum (Ft. Lee, VA) where depicted in a life size model of Raven (unit). Also she was honored at the Women's Memorial where her saying is now immortalized in writing. She served her country today with pride and honor of being a soldier.

Sergeant Hester is the first woman to receive the Silver Star since World War II. She is the first woman ever to be cited for valor in close quarters combat. We salute this reluctant hero. Her citation reads:

CITATION

The President of the United States of America, authorized by Act of Congress July 9, 1918 (amended by an act of July 25, 1963), takes pleasure in presenting the Silver Star to Sergeant Leigh Ann Hester, United

States Army, for exceptionally valorous achievement during combat operations in support of Operation IRAQI FREEDOM, on 20 March 2005, in Iraq. Sergeant Hester's heroic actions in Iraq contributed to the overwhelming success of the Multi-National Corps-Iraq mission. While serving as the Team Leader for RAVEN 42B in the 617th Military Police Company, 503d Military Police Battalion (Airborne), 18th Military Police Brigade, Sergeant Hester led her soldiers on a counterattack of anti-Iraqi Forces (AIF) who was ambushing a convoy with heavy AK-47 assault rifle fire, PRK machine gun fire, and rocket propelled grenades. Sergeant Hester maneuvered her team through the kill zone into a flanking position where she assaulted a trench line with grenades and M-203 rounds. She then cleared two trenches with her Squad Leader where she engaged and eliminated 3 AIF with her M-4 rifle. Her actions saved the lives of numerous convoy members. Sergeant Hester's bravery is in keeping with the finest traditions of military heroism and reflects distinct credit upon herself, the 503d Military Police Battalion (Airborne), the 18th Military Police Brigade, and the United States Army. NARRATIVE TO ACCOMPANY AWARD: Sergeant Leigh A. Hester is cited for conspicuous gallantry in action against an armed enemy of the United States while engaged in military operations involving conflict with anti Iraq forces (AIF) as a team leader for Raven 42B, 617th Military Police Company, 503d Military Police Battalion (Airborne) stationed at Camp Liberty, Iraq on 20 March 2005, in support of Operation IRAQI FREEDOM. The team's mission was to assist Raven 42 in searching the Eastern Convoy Route for improvised explosive devices (IEDs) and provide additional security to sustainment convoys traveling through their area of responsibility. While patrolling Alternate Supply Route (ASR) Detroit, Raven 42B was shadowing a sustainment convoy consisting of 30 third country national (TCN) semi-tractor trailers with a three vehicle squad size escort, call sign Stallion 33, traveling from LSA (logistics support area) Anaconda to CSC (convoy support center) Scania. The weather for this ASR patrol was 75 degrees and sunny with a 10 knot breeze from the southwest. While traveling on ASR Detroit approximately 50 AIF ambushed the convoy with heavy AK47 fire, RPK heavy machine gun fire, and rocket propelled grenades (RPGs) from the southwest side of the road at 1140 hours. The AIF were utilizing irrigation ditches and an orchard for the well planned complex attack. The AIF had cars combat parked along a road perpendicular to the ASR with all doors and trunks open. The AIF intent was to destroy the convoy, to inflict numerous casualties, and to kidnap several TCN drivers or U.S. Soldiers. The initial ambush disabled and set on fire the lead TCN vehicle, which effectively blocked the southbound lanes of ASR Detroit, stopping the convoy in the kill zone. The squad leader, Staff Sergeant Timothy Nein, directed the squad to move forward, traveling on the right shoulder and passing through the engagement area between the enemy and the convoy. Sergeant Hester directed her gunner to provide heavy volumes of MK 19 and M240B fires into the field where an overwhelming number of insurgents were executing a well coordinated ambush on the convoy. Raven 42 elements were outnumbered five to one. Staff Sergeant Nein ordered the squad to flank the insurgents on their right side. The squad continued to come under heavy machine gun fire and rocket propelled grenade fire when Sergeant Hester stopped her vehicle, the middle vehicle, at a flanking position enfilading the trench line and the orchard field where over a dozen insurgents were engaging the squad and convoy. She then directed her gunner to focus fires in the trench line and the orchard field. Sergeant Hester dismounted and moved to what was thought to be the non-contact side of the vehicle. She ordered her gunner to continue to fire on the orchard field as she and her driver engaged insurgents in the orchard field with small arms. Sergeant Hester began engaging the insurgents with her M203 in order to suppress the heavy AIF fire. Sergeant Hester followed Staff Sergeant Nein to the right side berm and threw two well placed fragmentation grenades into the trench eliminating the AIF threat. Sergeant Hester and Staff Sergeant Nein went over the berm into the trench and began clearing the trench with their M4s. Sergeant Hester engaged and eliminated three AIF to her front with her M4. They then made their way to the front trench and cleared that as well. After clearing the front trench cease fire was called and she began securing the ambush site. The final result of the ambush was 27 AIF KIA (killed in action), 6 AIF WIA (wounded in action), and one AIF captured. Action Date: 20-Mar-05

SOURCES

http://en.wikipedia.org/wiki/Leigh_Ann_Hester

http://www.washingtonpost.com/wp-dyn/content/article/2005/06/16/AR2005061601551.html

http://www.npr.org/2011/02/22/133847765/silver-star-recipient-a-reluctant-hero

http://www.defense.gov/News/NewsArticle.aspx?ID=16391

http://www.americanrifleman.org/article.php?id=13024&cat=3&sub=0

http://northshorejournal.org/sgt-leigh-ann-hester

LENNIE DARRELL HOLBROOK
Sergeant
54th Mechanized Infantry
509th Radio Research Headquarters and Service Support
224th Aviation headquarters

Darrell is a product of the mountains of eastern Kentucky. He was born in Holbrook Town on July 15, 1946. His parents were Arius and Blanch Bolling Holbrook. Arius was a World War II Veteran. He served in the European Theater as a combat engineer. Darrell has his father's canteen in which his father inscribed all the places where he fought while in WWII.

His siblings were Arius, Samuel Harold, Flara Jane, and Mitchell. Harold served in Vietnam during the time that Darrell was deployed. Samuel Harold was involved with transportation. He developed diabetes and was flown out of country.

Darrell attended a four room school in Sergeant. He recalled the pot-belly stove which was the only heat source. There was not air conditioning and education was holistic in nature. He went to Whitesburg High School and after graduation decided to get married. Darrell married his lifelong company, Ruth Elaine Gilliam, on September 14, 1965. They moved to Detroit, Michigan and Darrell got a job working at one of the Ford Motor Company facilities. In February of 1966, he was drafted. He was given a leave from his job with Ford Motor and went to serve his country.

Sergeant Holbrook served from January 1967-68 with honor. When he returned home he went back to Detroit and assumed working for the Ford Motor Company. He worked his way up to supervisor and served as a General Foreman for ten years. He was offered a job at Sun Steel Heat Treating and worked at that location for seven years. He returned home to his roots in 1982.

Darrell became very active in developing a first class Veterans Memorial in Whitesburg, Kentucky. He has become the voice of the Veteran during Memorial Day, and other occasions honoring those who served. When asked why he felt it important to remember and honor Veterans, his demeanor changed. He spoke with humility as he offered a heartfelt response. *"Any person who has donned the uniform, left his or her family to serve our country is a hero. Those men and women whose names are written in stone are the true heroes, as they gave their all for their love of this great nation. It would dishonest their memory if we did not pay tribute to their sacrifices."* This says a lot about the man.

Darrell Holbrook is the proud father of Kimberly Dawn, Lennie II, and Christopher Holbrook. Mr. Holbrook continues to serve our Veterans as well as our nation by being one of the spoke persons at the Military Museum.

SOURCES

Interview with Sergeant Holbrook

LEONARD FOSTER MASON
Private First Class
Automatic Rifleman,
2nd Battalion
3rd Marines
3rd Marine Division
U. S. Marine
February 22, 1920–July 22, 1944
Recipient of the
MEDAL OF HONOR

Imagine you enlisted into the Marines in April of 1943. Imagine being freshly trained and had earned a promotion in March of 1944. Imagine landing on Guam on July 22, 1944. Now imagine being twenty-four years of age and thrust into battle. This was the destiny of PFC Mason, a man of legend.

Leonard Foster Mason was Kentucky born. He was born in Middlesboro, Kentucky, on February 22, 1920. He later moved to Lima, Ohio, and joined the Marines. He was given his basic training at the marine Recruit Depot at Parris Island, South Carolina. He was assigned to the Pacific Theatre. One month after being assigned to the 3rd Marines he was involved in the Bougainville Campaign.

During the landing at Guam, PFC Mason and his fellow Marines encountered stiff resistance on the Asan-Adelup Beachhead (Marianas Islands). Ignoring any personal danger, PFC Mason climbed out of a gully and pressed the Japanese. He was critically wounded during that assault but he managed to clear the enemy from their vantage point. Mortally wounded, PFC Mason was sent to the hospital ship where he died.

In honor of his sacrifice and bravery under fire, a destroyer was named after him: The U.S.S. Leonard F. Mason (DD-852) was a Gearing-class destroyer in the United States Navy. It served during Korea and Vietnam. Note: Leonard F. Mason is listed on the "Wall of the Missing" at the National Memorial Cemetery of the Pacific, Honolulu.

The following MEDAL OF HONOR citation was given
to him posthumously
By President F.D. Roosevelt

CITATION

"For conspicuous gallantry and intrepidity at the risk of his life above and beyond the call of duty as an automatic rifleman serving with the 2d Battalion, 3d Marines, 3d Marine Division, in action against enemy Japanese forces on the Asan-Adelup Beachhead, Guam, Marianas Islands on 22 July 1944. Suddenly taken under fire by 2 enemy machineguns not more than 15 yards away while clearing out hostile positions holding up the advance of his platoon through a narrow gully, Pfc. Mason, alone and entirely on his own initiative, climbed out of the gully and moved parallel to it toward the rear of the enemy position. Although fired upon immediately by hostile riflemen from a higher position and wounded repeatedly in the arm and shoulder, Pfc. Mason grimly pressed forward and had just reached his objective when hit again by a burst of enemy machinegun fire, causing a critical wound to which he

later succumbed. With valiant disregard for his own peril, he persevered, clearing out the hostile position, killing 5 Japanese, wounding another and then rejoining his platoon to report the results of his action before consenting to be evacuated. His exceptionally heroic act in the face of almost certain death enabled his platoon to accomplish its mission and reflects the highest credit upon Pfc. Mason and the U.S. Naval Service. He gallantly gave his life for his country."

SOURCES

http://en.wikipedia.org/wiki/Leonard_F._Mason

http://www.history.navy.mil/photos/pers-us/uspers-m/l-mason.htm

http://www.kentuckymarines.org/index.cfm/legends/leonard-f-mason/

http://en.wikipedia.org/wiki/USS_Leonard_F._Mason_(DD-852)

http://records.ancestry.com/Leonard_Foster_Mason_records.ashx?pid=42889819

LEWIS STOVALL
(& Brothers)
Sergeant
Company E
43rd Georgia
CSA
January 5, 1828-June 18, 1863

There were five brothers who heard the beat of a different drummer. They all chose to fight for Georgia, their homeland. Each fought bravely. Each sacrificed and suffered for the cause. They are part of the unsung heroes in our American history.

On May 16, 1863, General Pemberton attempted to make a stand at Baker's Creek (Champion's Hill). The fighting was intense but due to superior forces the Confederates had to withdraw to Vicksburg. Lewis's youngest brother was killed and James was captured in that battle. The three other brothers were in the siege of Vicksburg.

Lewis was born in Forsyth County, Georgia. He was the oldest of William and Mary Burgess Stovall. Not much is known of the lives prior to the war. All five brothers joined the 43rd Georgia, on March 10, 1862. Lewis was thirty-two years old. A year later (June 18, 1863) Lewis would die of measles while defending the city of Vicksburg, Mississippi. He is buried in Cedar Hills, grave number fifty-nine, of the 52nd Georgia Volunteers. He was buried in the same coffin as was J. W. Martin (52nd Georgia).

Private John Martin Stovall was born in Forsyth County Georgia February 20, 1831. He was the second son of William and Mary Stovall. John was captured at Vicksburg, Mississippi July 4, 1863 and paroled two days later.

George Wilkes Stovall was born in Forsyth County Georgia March 19, 1838. He was the third son of William and Mary. George was captured at Baker's Creek, Mississippi May 16, 1863, and was taken POW. He was sent to Fort Delaware. Pension record's shows he was discharged from Fort Delaware July of 1864, and he was at home at close of the war.

(Private James P. Stovall)

Private James Pleasant Stovall was born 1840. He was the fourth son of William and Mary. James was also captured at Baker's Creek, Mississippi May 10, 1863. James and George were in the battle where their youngest brother, Patrick was killed in action.

Patrick M. Stovall was the fifth and youngest son. He was killed at the Battle of Baker's, Creek, Mississippi, on May 16, 1863. He is buried on that hallowed ground.

SOURCES

http://sharing.ancestry.com/3635344?h=16219d&fb_action_ids=10202042714364284&fb_action_types=og.likes&fb_source=aggregation&fb_aggregation_id=288381481237582

http://sharing.ancestry.com/3634797?h=0694fd

http://www.findagrave.com/cgi-bin/fg.cgi?page=gr&GRid=7355907

Fisher Funeral Home Burial Records, 1860-65, Page 57.

http://www.johnbgordon.com/Roll%20of%20Honour/ButchJones.htm

MABEL LEWIS MULLINS
Major
Army Nurse Corps
June 26, 1906-January 10, 2004

Here is a saga of mental fortitude and determination of a mountain girl who heard the call of her country and served with honor. She is an unsung hero.

Mabel Lewis Mullins was the daughter of David Crockett (D.C.) Mullins and Jane Lewis. She was the youngest of nine siblings. She was from the Partridge area of Letcher County, Kentucky. The farm is located along the Cumberland River. She loved to farm and after thirty years of a nursing career she returned home to enjoy tiling the soil and harvesting the fruit of her labor.

Miss Mabel went to Maggard School and Pine Mountain Settlement School. She then attended Berea College where she obtained her nursing license. Miss Mabel practiced in Maysville, Jenkins, and Ary, Perry County. All of these locations are in the state of Kentucky.

At the onset of the war, Miss Mabel joined the Nursing Corps. Her service number was N1942. She was first sent to Camp Stewart, Georgia. Her duties took her to the South Pacific in New Caledonia and New Hebrides. She served her fellowman for twenty-seven months.

Miss Mabel was humble about her service. In an interview she stated, "I saw little of actual war" she said. *"Once the New Caledonia area was attacked by Japanese planes, but all the bombs they dropped were duds. Still, I have never been so frightened in my life. Later in the Pacific Ocean our transport ship was attacked, and there was real danger, but I was not as scared as I was in New Caledonia. I guess the difference was the droning of the planes buzzing over the hospital there."*

Miss Mabel returned stateside for an overdue rest. She was then sent to England, France and finally Normandy (Camp Lucky Strike located near the coast). After the war ended, Major Mullins continued her nursing career until she retired on May 31, 1958.

After a long career as a nurse (thirty years) Miss Mabel retired to become a farmer. Miss Mabel returned home to her beloved home in the mountains. That was her passion and love.

Cecil Hensley Letcher County Soil Conservation District stated that Miss Mabel *"Farm work, from the lettuce bed to the 5,000 shortleaf pine trees in her reforestation project, is according to the most modern and most approved scientific methods."*

When asked if she practiced any medicine, her wit came through. "Very little," *she replied.* "I don't keep any livestock—not that well advanced as a farmer—so I don't even have a hog to which I could give a cholera shot."

Miss Mabel lived a productive life and was visited by her siblings. One of her sisters lived with her. Her name was Della Mullins. Miss Mabel's other brothers and sisters were Rhoda Smith (Oneca, Florida), Jim Mullins of Collier's Creek, Sally Romeo of Whitesburg, John Mullins Centreville, Indiana, Ida Martin, Corbin, Leila Martin lived in Cumberland, Kentucky and Nancy Owen lived in Tampa, Florida.

Major Mabel Lewis Mullins never married. She chose to live her life quietly on the farm of her mother and father that she loved. Mabel Lewis Mullins was ninety-seven years old when she departed this world.

SOURCES

http://www.fold3.com/image/312597545/

http://yeahpot.com/mullins/davidc.html
<u>Ex-Army Nurse Runs Model Farm; Letcher Woman Takes to Soil After 30 Years In Service</u>; Larry Caudill

https://www.facebook.com/photo.php?fbid=10151821181913296&set=gm.562898687087056&type=1&theater (Connie Bentley Adkins Beverly Walker, June 11, 2013, post on the web site

The Courier-Journal; Louisville, Kentucky; July 23, 1961
"<u>Coming Down Cumberland: A History of the Maggard Family of Eastern Kentucky</u>"; Bud Philips with collaboration by Mabel Lewis Mullins

http://www.fold3.com/image/312597545/

http://www.fold3.com/image/312128657/

http://www.fold3.com/image/312773686/

MICHAEL DWAYNE ACKLIN II
Sergeant
1st Battalion
320th Field Artillery
101st Airborne (Air Assault)
January 14, 1978-November 15, 2003

"He fought and died trusting in Jesus"

Michael was a young man from Louisville, Kentucky, which is located in Jefferson County. His friends called him Mikie. He was a devout Christian and had aspirations to become a minister. His friends and family recall his, "quiet peace". As most youthful soldiers, he joined the army to make a difference. He joined in 1998. He was assigned to the 1st Battalion, 320th Field Artillery of the 101st Airborne Division, based at Fort Campbell. He was sent to Iraq where, on November 15, 2003, two UH-60 Black Hawk helicopters collided. Sergeant Acklin was one of the seventeen soldiers killed during that collision. He was twenty-five years of age. The casualty city was Mosul, Iraq in geographic code IZ. The area is located in Northern Iraq. He was among many who died during Operation Iraqi Freedom. During the funeral, Acklin's parents were given the Purple Heart and Bronze Star their son was awarded posthumously. Michael was their only child.

According to the obituary and those who knew Mikie, he was a person of faith and wanted to make a difference. His grandmother remembered her husband telling Miki, *"You're not a man until you go in the service. The service will make a man out of you," "And when Michael entered and when he did come back home, we saw that change,"* His great-grandfather served in World War II and his grandfather in the Korean War. Mikie was proud to carry on the tradition of serving his country.

According to several who knew him, Michael will be remembered for his big heart" and for his strong character, devotion and loyalty. Retired Army Lt. Col. Charles Mitchell said that Acklin, his cousin, *"epitomized selfless service."* He said his cousin was a good soldier who also was part of *"God's army."*

Michael Dwayne Acklin's funeral was held at Christ Temple Apostolic Church. Mikie was buried in Zachary Taylor National Cemetery in Louisville with full military honors. The tributes under Fallen Heroes are a testament to his sterling character. Sergeant Sean Schmitt from, Scofield Barracks, Hawaii, stated the following: "SGT Michael Acklin was one of the kindest guys you'd ever meet in life. He always had a positive attitude and would give his buddies something to smile about. I wish he were still with us, but I know that he was a man of God and that he will live on in Heaven. God bless you, Michael."

"He fought the good fight of a soldier and he fought the good fight of faith."

SOURCES

http://projects.militarytimes.com/valor/army-sgt-michael-d-acklin-ii/256948

http://www.fold3.com/page/630022159_michael_dewayne_acklin/

ttp://www.legacy.com/obituaries/adn/obituary.aspx?n=michael-d-acklin&pid=3097429

http://www.fallenheroesmemorial.com/oif/profiles/acklinimichaeld.html

MICHAEL GERALD GIBBS
Navy Corpsman
Petty Officer HM Third Class
Company K
3rd Battalion
3rd Marines
June 23, 1945-April 25, 1967

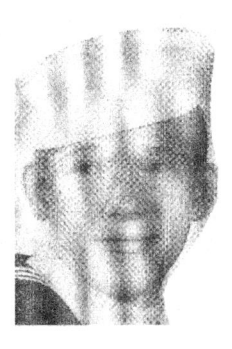

Michael was a boy from the little community of Del Rio, Tennessee. It is nestled in the foothills of the great Smokey Mountains towards Ashville, North Carolina. Michael Gerald was the son of Mr. and Mrs. Walter Gibbs. He had a sister by the name of Kaye Black. He was also survived by sisters Mrs. Tommy (Billy) Smith and Mrs. Charlie (Frances) Holt Junior.

Michael graduated from Cocke County High School In 1963. He was employed at Heywood Wakefield for awhile. He enlisted in the Navy and was trained at Great lakes, Illinois, and later at Quantico, Virginia. He became a Navy Corpsman. He was stationed at Camp Lejeune before shipping out with the Marines.

Being a Corpsman meant disregarding your own safety for the welfare of others. This was Michael's creed and calling. While stationed in the Quang Tri Province the following incident occurred, as recorded by Captain B. L Spivey JR's letter to Mr. and Mrs. Gibbs.

"Company K was given the mission of taking Hill 862 on April 25, (1967). This was a strategic hill controlling the avenue of approach to Khe Sahn, one of our vital bases in the northwestern corner of Vietnam. The hill turned out to be a heavily fortified bunker and trench complex manned by fresh, well-trained North Vietnamese forces of the 325C Division. Michael's platoon was in the midst of this attack, which began at noon on the 25th. By about 5 p.m. that afternoon the lead elements came under intense small arms and automatic weapons fire, suffering casualties in a short time. Immediately realizing that this was where he was needed most and not even awaiting a summons, Michael proceeded directly into the midst of the heavy fighting. Without regard for his own safety he moved about the battlefield treating wounds, and helping others back to positions of safety. He himself received two wounds which he largely ignored as he continued with his lifesaving work. He did this until killed instantly by an enemy mortar round falling near him." He died of multiple fragmentation wounds.

Jim Wodecki (from a Vietnam Vet) wrote the following entry: "On April 25th, K/3/3 found the enemy at Hill 861: 9 Marines Killed, 8 wounded, 4 MIA. On April 26th of 1967, the 9th and the 3rd on Hill 861 lost 22 men Killed, on the 27th one KIA, the 28th one KIA, and the 29th two KIA."

For his bravery, Michael was presented posthumously the Purple Heart, National Defense Service Medal, the Vietnam Service Medal, Republic of Vietnam Campaign Ribbon Bar and Purple Heart certificate. These were presented to his parents at their home in a ceremony including Denton Baptist Church Pastor Fred Burgin.

The Vietnam Wall has Michael listed as Protestant in faith Body was recovered. He is buried in Jones Cemetery. The pallbearers at the Fugate Church funeral were Ronnie Wilds, Jimmy Hance, Frankie, Turner, John Dale Ramsey and D.C. Ramsey.

He was twenty-one years of age when killed in action (KIA). Michael Gibbs is a true American hero and his unselfish sacrifice is worthy of a Silver Star, along with a nations gratitude for his ultimate forfeit. On April 25, 2010, forty-six years to the day, Michael G. Gibbs received the Silver Star posthumously, for gallantry during the Vietnam War. Note the discrepancies in the reports. One states Hill 861 and the other Hill862. Note there were two Hill 861s. One was called 861s and the other 861a. I tend to accept the Captain's descriptor since he was there. Also one reports his death on April 25, 1967 while the Silver Star certificate states April 26, 1967. In either event BOTH demonstrate this young man's bravery and devotion to his country. Michael Gibbs is one of the 692 Navy Corpsman listed on the Vietnam Memorial Wall. His name is on panel 18E, line 85.

SILVER STAR CITATION

"The President of the United States of America takes pride, in presenting, the Silver Star, (Posthumously) to Hospital, Corpsman, Third Class, Michael G. Gibbs, (NSN: 7959992) United States Navy, for conspicuous gallantry and intrepidity, in action, while serving, as a platoon, Corpsman, with Company K, Third, Battalion, Third, Marines, THIRD, Marine Division, in connection, with operations against, insurgent, communist forces, in the vicinity, of Khe Sanh, in the Republic, of Vietnam, on 25, April 1967. Hospitalman Gibbs, displayed exceptional valor, in the heroic performance, of his duties, while engaged in intense conflict, with a numerically stronger force, of North, Vietnamese, Army regulars. Hospitalman, Gibbs' platoon, was leading the company assault, upon the strongly fortified, heavily defended, Hill 861, a strategic area, commanding the approaches, to Khe

Sanh. As the assault, commenced and advanced toward the crest, of the hill, the lead platoon, became subjected, to intense, enemy fire, from small arms, automatic, weapons and grenades. In the initial contact, the platoon sustained heavy casualties, from the enemy's, surprise fire and became, temporarily halted. Heedless of his own personal, safety and dangerously exposing himself, to enemy fire, Hospitalman Gibbs, without hesitation, or summons, advanced, to the point of crisis, to administer medical assistance, to the wounded. While administering vitally needed aid, to his fallen, comrades and assisting them to areas, of safety, Hospitalman Gibbs sustained, a painful, back wound. In spite of his wound, he returned to the front, of his own accord and continued, to treat casualties. He then received, a more serious wound, which broke his leg. Physically unable to continue, Hospitalman Gibbs lay silent, until darkness came and he then allowed himself, to be removed, to the casualty, collection point. Despite his wounds, Hospitalman Gibbs maintained, an undaunted spirit and provided, vitally needed medical aid, to the critically, injured and was a source, of encouragement and inspiration, to all who, observed and served with him. On the morning, of the 26th, of April, while awaiting medical evacuation, Hospitalman Gibbs was mortally wounded, during an enemy, mortar attack. Hospitalman Gibbs' loyal devotion, to duty and uncommon valor, were an inspiration, to his comrades and upheld, the highest traditions, of the United States, Naval Service. He gallantly gave his life, in the service, of his country. Action Date: 25-Apr-67. Service: Navy, Rank: Hospital Corpsman, Third, Class, Company: Corpsman, (Attached) Company K, Battalion: 3d, Battalion, Regiment: 3d, Marines. Division: 3d, Marine Division. Apr 25, 2010."

In an article written by Rick Hooper (Newport Plain Talk), a war hero finally received a headstone worthy of his sacrifice. Norman Smith is a nephew of Gibbs and spearheaded the project. The Newport Plain Talk reported that Norman said, "I started on this about three months ago. At the time he died, his parents couldn't afford to buy a head stone. I started contacting people and family and friends all contributed to get one. Cocke County Monument also gave us a good deal." Gibbs only surviving sibling, Frances Holt, offered a fitting tribute when she said, "I'm sure he's looking down at us now and he's smiling."

SOURCES

Ultimate Sacrifice; The Newport Plain Talk; November 9-10, 2013; volume 114; Number 57

The Newport Plain Talk/www.cocke.xtn.net

Information submitted to the paper by Kaye black (sister) on April 25, 1967

http://thewall-usa.com/info.asp?recid=18410

http://thewall-usa.com/guest.asp?recid=18410

awards/recipient.php?recipientid=23498

http://vietnam-casualties.findthedata.org/l/52930/Michael-Gerald-Gibbs

http://www.usfallenwarriors.com/index.php?page=directory&rec=100654

http://www.1stcavmedic.com/Navy_Corpsman_Names.htm

http://www.vietvet.org/jwodecki.htm

NARCE WHITAKER
Major, U. S. Air Force
WWII
May 1914-November 1994

MAJ. NARCE WHITAKER WINS MORE MEDALS THAN ANY KENTUCKIAN

Article on Major Narce Whitaker courtesy of Mountain Eagle and permission
By Author Ben Gish

I don't think I ever met the man but I do vividly recall his family. We lived in Perkins Branch, just across the mountain from Mill's Branch. On occasion mother would take me across the mountain to visit her sister Goldie who lived in Big Branch. We crossed from Uncle Essie and Aunt Myrtle's farm through the big gate, past the grove of walnut trees into Mill's Branch. Close to the mouth of Mill's Branch, mother would stop and talk to an elderly lady by the name of Ida, who always gave us lemonade and cookies before we walked toward Tolson, Kentucky. Her husband was Squire Whitaker. These were the parents of an American hero.

As a boy of twelve or thirteen I remember hearing mother talk to the lady about her son who was a pilot. I recall Mrs. Whitaker saying something about him fighting in World War II and having won the Silver

Medal for heroism. But what really impressed me was she said whenever a jet went over she wondered was that her son flying by and tipping his wings at the family home. I thought that was simply amazing! She invited us in and showed us his pictures. It was then I knew I wanted to be a pilot. A dream unfulfilled due to my visual acuity.

Mother told me once we were distant kinfolk through the Caudill and the Whitaker lineage. I was always proud of that unproven fact. Narce was born to Esquire and Ida Hogg Whitaker. Squire's mother was Nancy Jane Caudill and his father was Moses Whitaker. *DPC*

When the March 4, 1943, edition of *The Mountain Eagle* hit the streets, many Letcher Countians began learning for the first time about the outstanding military career of then-U.S. Army Air Forces Major Narce Whitaker, a highly-decorated pilot in World War II.

Whitaker lived at Mill Branch at Roxana and attended the Stuart Robinson School at Blackey. He enlisted in the U.S. Army Air Corps as a flying cadet in June 1938.

The first notice of Whitaker's achievements appeared in that March 4 edition and was written by a "double first cousin" who wasn't identified. The account the cousin wrote was largely a combination of clips that had appeared in Louisville's morning paper, *The Courier-Journal*, and its afternoon counterpart, *The Louisville Times*.

The following are some of what the cousin wrote:

"The 'morgue,' or library, of the *Courier-Journal* and *Times* is accumulating quite a voluminous record of the achievements of Narce Whitaker, now a major in the Army Air Forces on active duty in the Solomon Islands.

"... The first clipping about Major Whitaker is dated January 30, 1939, and says the 'intricacies of the maze of instruments on the basic training airplanes at Randolph Field, the 'West Point of the Air,' are rapidly being mastered by Flying Cadet Narce Whitaker, Roxana.'

"An October 1942, clipping tells of the gathering of Japanese Naval forces in September for the first effort by the Japanese to recapture Guadalcanal from the U. S. Marines. Airmen in Flying Fortresses (Boeing B-17 bombers) sighted two Japanese fleets.

"Another dispatch dated last Whitaker, of Roxana, Letcher County, Ky., said the group he saw was headed into rough weather October 12 [1942] describes conditions under which Narce and his mates fought on Guadalcanal, a mountainous island where neighbor feasted on neighbor until modern blitz warfare drove the cannibals to the high hills. This clipping tells how another bomber pilot entered the mess tent, slapped Major Whitaker on the back and said: 'Hey, Whit, heard you smacked 13 Jap Zeros with two bombs at Buka today. How could you tell there were 13?'

"Whitaker swallowed a hunk of salmon and shot back: 'Counted the wheels and divided by two.'

"Apparently a large number of us mountaineers can proudly 'claim kin' with Maj. Whitaker. His father, Squire Whitaker, is the son of Moses Haydon 'Little Mose' and Nancy Jane Caudill Whitaker. Jane was the daughter of 'Stiller Bill' Caudill. {Stiller Bill was a Confederate Soldier. He was a 4th Sergeant in Company B. He was the son of William C. Caudill and Nancy Craft. His second wife was Nancy Dixon. Stiller Bill had sixteen children. He died on November 26, 1908, and is buried in the Caudill Cemetery (Lower Caudill's Branch, Old Dixon Road, Blackey, KY-taken from the Ben Caudill Muster Roll}

Receives most medals of any Kentuckian

Letcher Man Honored With Fourth Award, First In History Of Our Country

4th Silver Star Given Kentuckian

Stuart Robinson High School Graduate

Washington, May 26—Col.

ATTENTION TO HIGH SCHOOL BAND

All members of the W burg High School Band will meet at the g school auditorium Mo June 2 at 9:00 a. m. to pictures taken for the ier Journal. Those de individual pictures in uniforms may have made that afternoon.] urgent that all band appear and on time!

Six months after the March 1943, article appeared, the September 2, 1943, edition of *The Eagle* carried a report released by U.S. Army Headquarters in the South Pacific acknowledging Maj. Whitaker for becoming the most decorated Kentuckian who fought in the South Pacific in World War II.

Here is what that report said:

"A total of 56 awards had been given to 35 Kentuckians up to July 19, 1943, by Lt. Gen. Millard F. Harmon, commanding U.S. Army forces in the South Pacific.

"[The] most decorated Kentuckian is Major Narce Whitaker of Roxana, formerly a 13th Air Force bomber pilot, with seven awards. He won the Distinguished Flying Cross with an Oak Leaf Cluster in July after his return to the states. Previously Major Whitaker had been given the Silver Star, the Air Medal, and three Oak Leaf Clusters.

"This Kentucky pilot was one of the pioneer army aviators of the South Pacific. His awards cover his activities from February 13, 1942, to February 5, 1943.

"One of the Oak Leaf Clusters was for an attack on a Japanese naval force near Savo Island last November 13 when a number of damaging hits were scored on a battleship.

"Major Whitaker won the Silver Star when his Flying Fortress shot down several Zeros [Japanese military aircraft] on December 10, 1942. The Air Medal was given after he had been flight leader in a bombing raid on Buka airfield October 12."

First in Army Air Force to receive Four Silver Star medals

On May 29, 1947, *The Eagle* carried a Army report issued three days earlier announcing that Col. Whitaker, by now a senior pilot, became the first member of the Army Air Force to hold four Silver Star medals when he was presented the third Oak Leaf Cluster to his Silver Star by Lt. Gen. Ira Baker, deputy Army Air Force commander.

The Silver Star is the third-highest decoration for valor awarded to any person in any of the five military branches that make up the U.S. Armed Forces. The Army said the latest medal was for "gallantry in action over Midway Island from June 3 to 7, 1942." The citation said Col. Whitaker, then a captain, demonstrated outstanding courage and proficiency throughout a period of bitter aerial combat with the Japanese.

After receiving his fourth Silver Star, Colonel Whitaker, who also was awarded the Legion of Merit, was selected to attend the Air University at Maxwell Field, Alabama, after which he will attend the University of Denver to complete work for the degree of civil engineering. His hard work lead to job as commander.

On September 9, 1954, *The Eagle* carried a column from W.J. Cooper, superintendent of the Stuart Robinson School, in which Cooper tells of his appreciation for the hard work showed from an early age while attending school at Stuart Robinson. Cooper wrote the column after he read in the *Courier-Journal* that Col. Whitaker had assumed command at Wilkins Air Force Depot Station in northern Ohio in July 1954.

Wrote Supt. Cooper: "Narce graduated from Stuart Robinson at the age of 20 on May 8, 1934, in the upper half of his class, after four years of hard work in school and also hard work on the farm and campus of Stuart Robinson, which was the only means he had of paying his school expenses.

"He not only worked out his own expenses, but by putting in extra time and work after all others had left their jobs and during the summers, he earned a large part of the expenses of his two sisters, Mary Jane and Dana. To get to his work he walked daily between seven and eight miles up and down one of our steep Kentucky Mountains. He is undoubtedly one of the best workers and with the very best spirit of any that we have ever had.

"During his four years of stay at Stuart Robinson, never once did I hear him grumble or even hint anything in that direction. He was always so busy and so interested in what he himself was doing that he never had time to compare himself with others or to find fault with others.

"When the Japanese bombed our fleet in Pearl Harbor on December 7, 1941, he was called to that area as a leader of one of the Bomber Squadrons [the 72nd]. He had a fleet of air planes under his command. It has been said of him, he numbers among those daring and efficient pilots who kept the Japanese away from our western shores.

"... Needless to say we are proud of Narce, and no doubt those who read this story and who have had a part in contributing to our work scholarship fund will also feel a bit proud at having made it possible for him to go to school here."

"When I finished reading the [*Courier-Journal*] article, I immediately picked up my Kodak and asked Mr. (Jack) Burkich, our high school principal, to go with me on an important errand. We boarded our car and climbed several hundred feet and down several hundred feet, a distance of about six miles [from Blackey to Tolson], and then up a hollow [Mill Branch] on the roughest one-way road that I have ever travelled for another distance of about two miles.

Colonel Whitaker died in November 1994. His brother Neldon, who also served in the Army during World War II, died in February 2004 at age ninety-two (92). Whitaker had been returning to his family's home at Roxana.

On February 12, 1956, the Whitaker family suffered a tragedy when the younger brother of Narce and Neldon was killed in a car wreck on his way home to Letcher County from Dayton, Ohio.

Kelly Reed Whitaker, 23, died just a few hours after he finished his tour of duty with the Air Force. He had been stationed at Wright-Patterson Base at Dayton and was killed when his car plunged over a 25-foot embankment near Hazard.

The Mountain Eagle noted the following in their September 4, 2013, edition (courtesy of Ben Gish). "U.S. Army Air Corps Major Narce Whitaker of Roxana has been awarded more medals than any other Kentuckian by Lt. Gen. Millard F. Harmon, commander of U.S. Army forces in the South Pacific. Whitaker, formerly a 13th Air Force bomber pilot, was presented by Harmon with seven more awards recently, including the Distinguished Flying Cross and the Oak Leaf Cluster for the DFC. Whitaker had already been presented with the Silver Star, the Air Medal and three other Oak Leaf Clusters. The awards cover his activities in the South Pacific, where he was one of the pioneer Army aviators, from February 13, 1942 to February 5, 1943."

SOURCES

Mountain Eagle Editions
March 4, 1943
September 9, 1954
By permission of Ben Gish

http://www.afhra.af.mil/factsheets/factsheet_print.asp?fsID=10524

PATRICK DANIEL TILLMAN
75th Ranger Regiment
2nd Ranger Battalion
Army Ranger Corporal
November 6, 1976–April 22, 2004

Pat Tillman was a man of destiny. He chose the battlefield instead of the football grid. Few men in this day and age have given their all for their belief and love of country. He followed the ranks of those brave men of yesteryear who saw their duty to their country and did it, giving up riches and fame. He walks the halls with such great men of valor including James Stewart, Ernest Borgnine, Kirk Douglas, Dale Robinson, Lee Marvin, Forrest Tucker, Mickey Rooney, Charlton Heston, James Arness and Audie Murphy, to name a few.

Pat was born in San Jose (Fremont), California to Mary and Patrick Tillman. He was the first born. He had two brothers, Kevin and Richard. Pat was a family man and loved his friends. He was a natural athlete. He played football for Leland High School. His skills did not go unnoticed on the football field. He was drafted by the NFL and began playing professionally with the Arizona Cardinals after a very impressive college career as a linebacker for Arizona State University. As a prelude to the character of the man, he was offered nine million dollars to play for the St. Louis Rams but turned it down to stay with his beloved Arizona team. Imagine giving all this up for the sake of duty, honor and love of country. This fielder wonders how many would do the same if given the opportunity.

He won many awards including going to the Rose Bowl, voted PAC 10 Defensive Player of the year, Clyde B. Smith Academic Award for excellence and he was inducted into the College Football Hall of Fame in 2010. Jersey #40 was retired by the Arizona Cardinals. His college number (42) was also retired by ASU.

When he saw the high cost of freedom on September 11, 2001, he began questioning his choices. Within a few months he made a life changing decision. In June of 2002, he gave up a 3.6 million dollar contract to follow the calling of becoming an Army Ranger. Coach Dave McGinnis recalled his impression of Tillman visiting with his former teammates. *"When he walked in, there was just a tremendous amount of respect," McGinnis told TIME. "I can still see vividly in my mind each player shaking his hand, everyone saying thank you and touching his shoulder."* This shows the merits of a true unsung hero.

When duty called he enlisted. He married his high-school sweetheart, Marie Ugenti, just before he left to be deployed. His brother, Kevin Tillman, enlisted with him on May 31, 2002. Pat was twenty-five years of age. Brother Kevin gave up a chance to play for the Cleveland Indians. They finished basic training and then went on to the Ranger Assessment and Selection Program (RASP). He entered Ranger School (Fort Benning, GA) and graduated on November 28, 2003.

Ranger Tillman served a couple of tours of duty. On April 22, 2004, Ranger Tillman was killed while on active Duty in Sperah, Afghanistan. The cause of death was reported as KILLED IN ACTION but later was changed to FRIENDLY FIRE. According to documentation, the following was reported. *"On April 22, 2004, he was initially reported to have been killed by enemy combatants. An Afghan Militia Forces allied soldier was also killed in the action. Tillman's platoon leader first lieutenant David Uthlaut and his radio telephone operator (RTO), 19-year old Jade Lane, were wounded in the incident. The Army initially claimed that Tillman and his unit were attacked in an apparent ambush on a road outside of the village of Sperah about 25 miles (40 km) southwest of Khost, near the Pakistan border. It wasn't until after his burial that investigations by the Department of Defense and US Congress were launched, eventually ruling his death as 'friendly fire'. The Army Special Operations Command initially claimed that there was an exchange with hostile forces. After a lengthy investigation conducted by Brigadier General Gary M. Jones, the U.S. Department of Defense concluded that both the Afghan militia soldier's and Pat Tillman's deaths were due to friendly fire aggravated by the intensity of the firefight."*

Controversy still brews at the writing of this tribute to Ranger Tillman. Several, including his mother believe he was murdered and there was a cover up surrounding his death. Mary Tillman stated, *"By making up these false stories you're diminishing their true heroism. [The truth] may not be pretty but that's not what war is all about. It's ugly, it's bloody, it's painful. And to write these glorious tales is really a disservice to the nation."*

There were several discrepancies in the reports. One brave specialist testified to that fact. *"On April 24, 2007, Specialist Bryan O'Neal, the last soldier to see Pat Tillman alive, testified before the House Committee on Oversight and Government Reform that he was warned by superiors not to divulge information that a fellow soldier killed Tillman, especially to the Tillman family. Later, Pat Tillman's brother Kevin Tillman, who was also in the convoy traveling behind his brother at the time of the 2004 incident in Afghanistan but did not witness it, testified that the military tried to spin his brother's death to deflect attention from emerging failings in the Afghan war."*

The House Committee on Oversight and Government Reform made the following ruling: *"The pervasive lack of recollection and absence of specific information makes it impossible for the Committee to assign responsibility for the misinformation in Specialist Tillman's and Private Lynch's cases. It is clear, however, that the Defense Department did not meet its most basic obligations in sharing accurate information with the families and with the American public."* No matter the cause of death, this man of valor gave his full measure for what he believed. He served with distinction and honor, choosing the road less taken; that of self sacrifices and service to his country.

Ranger Tillman was awarded several medals including the Silver Star, Purple Heart, Meritorious Service Medal, Army Achievement Medal, National Defense Service Medal, Global War on Terrorism Expeditionary Medal, Global War on Terrorism Service Medal, Army Service Ribbon, Presidential Unit Citation and Joint Meritorious Unit Award. Several locations have been named in honor of this American hero and we, as Americans, can only continue to apply pressure to those powers that be in an effort to get the records released on this tragedy.

In honor of his supreme sacrifice, many scholarships, foundations and organization have been established in his name.

SOURCES

Where Men Win Glory, the Odyssey of Pat Tillman; Krakauer, Jon; Doubleday;

http://www.npr.org/templates/stor16210

http://en.wikipedia.org/wiki/Pat_Tillman

http://www.washingtonpost.com/wp-dyn/articles/A35717-2004Dec4.html

http://www.imdb.com/title334/

http://www.biography.com/people/pat-tillman-197041

http://projects.militarytimes.com/valor/army-cpl-patrick-d-tillman/263007

http://bleacherreport.com/articles/935500-veterans-day-remembering-pat-tillman

PERRY BENALLY
Navajo Warrior
Specialist 4th Class
Company C
1st Battalion
12th Cavalry Regiment
1st Cavalry Division
Recipient of
Two Purple Hearts
Silver Star

(Photo by Marley Shebala)
(Left to right-Lucindie Benally, Perry Benally, Vaughn Benally)

Many of our American heroes go unnoted in the annals of history. Some are remembered for their deeds but they soon fade with the rising of another generation. Then there are those rediscovered years later. This is the saga of one who was recognized and given a Silver Cross after forty-four years.

Perry Benally was born into the Navajo Tribe from the Tohatchi area. He is Ashiihi (Salt Clan), born for Kinlichii'nii (Red House Clan). In the tradition of the Native Americans, the Benally family has a proud history of service to their nation. According to the article written by Marley Shebala and documents found in Fold 3, Perry's father was Grant Benally Senior. He was a World War I veteran. Perry's brother Norman was a Korean veteran. Harry Kinsel was a World War II veteran. John Benally (paternal uncle) was a World War II veteran as well.

Upon entering the military and after being trained, Perry was assigned to Vietnam for his tour of duty. On his twenty-second birthday he found himself lying on a grave of a Vietnamese farmer fighting for his life during the Battle of Tam Quan. The battle lasted fifteen days. The Battle of Tam Quan involved elements of the 1st Cavalry, 50th Infantry pitted against the NVA (Yellow Star) Regiment of the Third. The battle occurred in the Central highlands coastal (Binh Din Province). It was part of Operation Pershing and was considered a victory for the U.S. forces). The casualties for the United States were fifty-eight. The engagement was fierce and considered to be one of the fifteen major battles of the war. Perry was there.

Perry's platoon was ambushed on day ten of the fight. Army Sgt. Doug Warden, then 21 years old, recounted in his book "Boy Sergeant, A Young Soldier's Story of Vietnam," that Benally and five other members of the 4th platoon, "Walked right into a major fortification of the NVA." The NVA didn't open fire until they were right on top of them, which resulted in several casualties. Perry was wounded during the exchange but kept on fighting. *"Enemy sniper rounds began to crack around them as they moved into the village,"* Hawkins reported. *"Fragments from an enemy rifle grenade tore into Benally's right leg."*

Perry found himself cut off from his platoon. Three gallant efforts were made to rescue him. Finally, Perry fired his weapon and made a dash from the grave surrounded by stones to reach the safety of his men. During his escape effort he lobbed a grenade in the vicinity of the NVA.

After the battle, Perry was taken to the 15th Evac Hospital at Bong Son. Benally heard an APC close to where he was and he waved. It was Warden who recognized him and assisted in his rescue. Specialist 4th Class Benally has undergone sixteen surgeries due to his injuries in Vietnam.

In an interview he stated that while on the battlefield he promised God, *"To work and help his people...if I made it out of there."* He kept his word. He returned to the reservation and began working on his BA. He then went on for a master in social work. He worked at the Las Vegas, N. M. Medical Center. He was employed for the Division of Social Services and finally the U. S. Veterans Affairs Center in Farmington, New Mexico. He retired in 1999.

Mr. Benally is a member of the Disabled American Veterans, Military Order of the Purple Heart, Vietnam Veterans of America, Veterans of Foreign Wars and the Tohatchi Veterans Organization. Mr. Benally is an avid supporter of programs to help his people, the Dinah. He supports teen suicide prevention, parental involvement with their children, scholarships and is involved in helping the youth have a better life through understanding their uniqueness.

On October 10, 2011, Specialist 4th Class Perry Benally was finally given his long overdue recognition for his bravery. He was awarded the Silver Star. Among those honoring him was four of his fellow Vietnam veterans who had been searching for him for over forty years. Sergeant Warden, the man who recognizes Benally on the battlefield and saved him from being a casualty of friendly fire. He helped rescue him and along with Charlie Church, was one of those brave men who traveled so far to honor their brother-in-arms.

CITATION

"The President of the United States of America, authorized by Act of Congress July 9, 1918 (amended by an act of July 25, 1963), takes pleasure in presenting the Silver Star to Specialist Fourth Class Perry V. Benally, United States Army, for gallantry in action from 15 December to 16 December 1967, while serving as a Rifleman in the weapons platoon of Company C, 1st Battalion, 12th Cavalry Regiment, 1st Cavalry Division, in support of operations in the Republic of Vietnam. Specialist Fourth Class Benally's platoon was engaged by a numerically superior force of North Vietnamese soldiers and sustained heavy casualties. Despite being wounded in the leg by fragments from an enemy grenade, he continued forward to assault the enemy with his unit. He was wounded in the right temple as his element continued to sustain heavy casualties. His platoon began rescuing the wounded Soldiers, when the rescuers were fired upon by the North Vietnamese. Specialist Fourth Class Benally successfully engaged and destroyed the enemy force firing upon the rescuers, enabling several wounded soldiers to be evacuated. However, other enemy forces increased their assault and Specialist Fourth Class Benally was separated from his unit. He continued fighting until running out of ammunition, at which point he decided to hold out until help could arrive. He retreated to a graveyard, where he encountered two enemy combatants, who he destroyed with his empty M-16 rifle. He spent the night at the graveyard, where he was rescued by his company the next morning. Specialist Fourth Class Benally's actions are in keeping with the finest traditions of military service and reflect great credit upon himself, the 1st Cavalry Division, and the United States Army."

SOURCES

http://navajotimes.com/news/2011/1011/101011silverstar.php#.UvogemJdUzI

http://books.google.com/books?id=AoTraFGlXFYC&pg=PA44&lpg=PA44&dq=perry+Benally,+navajo&source=bl&ots=9ctqzPW23S&sig=_VfWFs83HaMKjrF5bKEp19aeBpA&hl=en&sa=X&ei=UU_6Uvi3KcXn0wGyv4GYCA&ved=0CC4Q6AEwAQ#v=onepage&q=perry%20Benally%2C%20navajo&f=false

https://www.facebook.com/IndianArtsCulture/posts/222125654518202

Soldier finally receives Silver Star for service in Vietnam; Marley Shebalaf; Navajo Times; Window Rock, Arizona; October 10, 2011

http://www.ichiban1.org/html/news_pages/news_36.htm

http://projects.militarytimes.com/citations-medals-awards/recipient.php?recipientid=54119

http://www.charliecompanyvietnam.com/class_custom1.cfm

http://www.charliecompanyvietnam.com/000/2/6/6/22662/userfiles/file/Perry_Benally_Newspaper_Article.pdf

PEYTON REYNOLDS
71H30
Personnel Management Specialist

I have known Mr. Reynolds for years. He was my lawyer, my friend, and well known throughout the region. I interviewed at the Military Museum in Whitesburg after I spoke to Darrell Holbrook.

Peyton was born in Ermine, Kentucky, in the front room of a four room house. His parents were Jim and Chelsie Hogg Reynolds. His brother's name was Stuart and his sister was Eloise. They grew up in the communities of Mayking and Ermines.

He went to elementary/middle school at Whitesburg and attended three years of high school at Whitesburg High. He finished his high school at Oak Ridge, Tennessee.

While in law school Peyton received his draft notice on Friday the 13th June of 1969. There were ten others who received their calling along with him. Bobby George Fields was the only one of the eleven who was killed in action. According to Mr. Reynolds (and other eye witnesses), Bob was killed when the NVA fired upon a helicopter. The missile missed the helicopter but unfortunately hit where Sergeant Bobby G. Fields was located. He was killed instantly. Contrary to the report on cause of death (friendly fire), eye witnesses stated Bobby was killed by enemy fire and deserves recognition for his heroism.

Peyton went to Ft. Knox, Kentucky, for OJT (On the Job Training) and was assigned to personnel management, which was a very big operation. He was assigned to headquarters in Ben Lay, Vietnam. Every 10th of the month he was rotated to perimeter guard duty. He was part of the Cambodia invasion and was on line for days. He was selected for an interview and became a permanent fixture in management. During this time Peyton was assigned to helping with the 'pull out' of Vietnam. His duties entailed reassigning officers (from Lieutenant to Lt. Colonel) to other deployment. Some were stateside duty and others were in different countries.

Upon being released from the military, Peyton finished law school and served eastern Kentucky. In 1976, Peyton married Ann Whitaker. They have two children by the name of Bradley and Cyndee. Peyton retired from his law practice after thirty years.

One thing Mr. Reynolds recalled was that his parents didn't tell anyone where he was or had been. A neighbor once asked Peyton where he had been and his reply was, *"I've been here and there."* The war was that unpopular due to the image portrayed by the press. He felt he had to keep his service quiet.

When asked why he felt it important to honor our Veterans, Peyton stated, *"Theirs were the ultimate sacrifice. They were those people who laid down their lives. All gave some; some gave all."* He continued to say that, *"As we get older, our hearts grow tenderer when they die or get sick. Their stories sometimes die when they pass."*

SOURCES

Interview with Peyton Reynolds

PHILIP JOHNSTON
Staff Sergeant
U.S. Army 319th Engineers
USMCR
WWI & WWII
September 17, 1892-September 11, 1978

There are few in this land who has not heard of them. They saved our country during World War II. They were the Code Talkers! Several tribes sent their young men to serve in that capacity and use their unique language to baffle the enemy. These men are American heroes whose names should be household words. Such men of valor are these, the twenty-nine original Navajo Code Talkers: Charlie Begay, Roy Begay, Samuel Begay, John Ashi Benally, Wilsie Bitsie, Cosey Stanley Brown, John Brown, John Chee, Benjamin Cleveland, Eugene Roanhorse Crawford, David Curley, Lowell Smith Damon, George H. Dennison, James Dixon, Carl Nelson Gorman (the oldest of the code talkers and my friend), Oscar B. Iithma, Allen Dale June, Alfred Leonard, Johnny Manuelito, William McCabe, Chester Nex, Jack Nez, Lloyd Oliver, Joe Palmer (also known as Balmer Slowtalker), Frank Danny Pete, Nelson Thompson, Harry Tsosie (KIA), John W. Willie, and William Yazzie.

Yet how did their languages become known to our military? Who introduced this impenetrable code to them? The answer is a man by the name of Philip Johnston.

I first heard of his story when I worked in Window Rock, Arizona area and became familiar with the legendary Navajo Code Talkers (NCT). My mentor, Carl Gorman talked of him and shared his saga. I was mesmerized with admiration to the teller of the story and the person talked about.

Philip Johnston was born in Topeka, Kansas, to a family with vision. His father, William Johnston, wanted to bring the word of God to the Navajo people. On September 16, 1896, when Philip was only four years of age his father moved the family to Flagstaff, Arizona to build a missionary . During that time a clash between whites and Navajo was going on over livestock. It was called the Padre Canyon Incident. William was able to intervene. The chapters of the area led by the clan leaders, allowed the minister to build a mission near Leupp, Arizona. The Reverend Johnston continued to work on the behalf of the people.

Philip went to school with Navajo children and had to learn to speak the language since English was the secondary language. His skills were so good that in 1901, he was the interpreter for the Navajo people when they met with President Teddy Roosevelt regarding the expansion of the western portion of Navajo land. Philip was only nine at the time.

Philip attended Northern Arizona Normal School and in March of 1918, he enlisted into the army. According to the research, he enlisted, *"In the U.S. Army's 319th Engineers, where he received a reserve commission. Between March and September 1918, he trained in Camp Fremont at Menlo Park, California before being shipped to France as part of the AEF to participate in the Great War."* It has been suggested that it was during World War I that he heard of Native

Americans using their language to confuse the Germans.

Philip moved to California but kept close ties with the people on the reservation that he grew up with. He obtained an engineering degree and worked in the L.A. Water Department. Then the war came with the sneak attack on Pearl Harbor. Immediately Philip called upon four Navajo friends who worked in the shipyards. He called upon General Clayton Vogel to listen to the code. The general was immediately sold on the idea. The Code Talkers were born.

The original twenty-nine was expanded to over two hundred and other native languages were utilized. Several more volunteered and soon learned the encrypted code to dumbfound the enemy. The code was an impregnable wall to the Japanese. Staff Sergeant Johnston (USMCR) became a recruiter and administrator for the program.

Philip Johnston went back to California and continued his work as an engineer. He died on September 11, 1978, in San Diego, California, and is buried at Glendale, California. Through his vision and the gallantness of those Native Americans, we now can sit at our table as free men and women.

SOURCES

http://www.history.navy.mil/faqs/faq61-2.htm
http://en.wikipedia.org/wiki/Philip_Johnston_(code_talker)

http://library.thinkquest.org/J002073F/thinkquest/Philip.htm

Johnston, Bernice E. (1972). *Two Ways in the Desert: A Study of Modern Navajo-Anglo Relations*. Catalina Stations, California: Socio-Technical Publications.

McClain, Sally (2001). *Navajo Weapon: The Navajo Code Talkers*. Tucson, Arizona: Rio Nuevo Publishers. p. 300. ISBN 978-1-887896-32-0.

Rottman, Gordon L. (November 30, 2001). *U.S. Marine Corps World War II Order of Battle: Ground and Air Units in the Pacific War, 1939–1945*. Westport, Conn: Greenwood Press. p. 608. ISBN 978-0-313-31906-8.

P. K. 'KEN' KEEN,
Lieutenant General
Commander at 1st Battalion,
75th Ranger Regiment
505th Parachute Infantry Regiment
82nd Airborne Division
Chief at Office of the U.S. Defense Representative to Pakistan, U.S. Embassy, Islamabad
Military Deputy Commander at U.S. Southern Command
Commander, Joint Task Force-Haiti at U.S. Southern Command
J3 and Chief of Staff at European Command
Commanding General at United States Army South
Commander at United States Military Group, Bogota, Colombia

Eastern Kentucky is known for its brave people in time of adversity. The mountain region is known to produce leaders from the rank of private to general. One of those is a man from Hyden, Kentucky. Some tower above and demonstrate a higher calling to duty. Such is the saga of Lieutenant General Keen who has served with humility and humbleness in service.

Lieutenant General Keen is a native of Hyden, Kentucky. He knew his calling as a young man. He wanted to serve his country. He attended Eastern

Kentucky University and graduated in December of 1974. He commissioned as a 2nd LT in the Infantry. He was a distinguished military graduate from that institution. He continued his education, having attended the University of Florida, where he obtained a Masters in Latin American Studies. He attended Brazilian Command and General Staff College and U.S. Army War College. He was Associate Dean of Leadership Development at Emory's Goizueta Business School at Emory University. He was a Senior Fellow and Senior Mentor at National Defense University and Joint Staff J7 Member, Board of Directors at J/P Haitian Relief Organization.

General Keen served on three (Colombia, Haiti, and Pakistan) U.S. Embassy teams. When a crisis occurred, he was the leader of the military forces. While in Pakistan, he led the Office of Defense (annual 1.05 billion securities). As a humanitarian, General Keen was Commander of the Joint Task Force in Haita when the January 12, 2010, earthquake happened. He was in charge of twenty-two thousand men and women assisting the country during that disaster. He coordinated efforts with the U.N. and other governments in the relief effort.

Lieutenant General Keen served his country for over thirty-eight years. He retired from a distinguished career on March 1, 2013. His accomplishments were numerous. He was commander of a company and brigade while in the 82nd Airborne. He became a master parachutist. He was with the 1st Ranger Battalion and the 75th Ranger Regiment (Special Forces). He was with the military Group in Colombia and Office of Defense in Pakistan. He was commander of the United States Army Sough and Joint Task Force units participating in combat operations in Iraq and Panama.

There is so much more I could add but due to space I simply must say that General Keen continues to serve. He is the Associate Dean of Leadership Development for Emory University's Goizueta School of Business in Atlanta, Georgia.

He is the product of eastern Kentucky who has distinguished himself and makes us proud of who we are. We salute the good general for his service and his accomplishments. He is a green beret.

The following is a synopsis of Lieutenant Keen's brilliant career:

Member, Board of Directors
- J/P Haitian Relief Organization
- Nonprofit; 201-500 employees; Nonprofit Organization Management industry
- March 2013 – Present (1 year 2 months)

Chief
- Office of the U.S. Defense Representative to Pakistan, U.S. Embassy, Islamabad
- July 2011 – January 2013 (1 year 7 months) Islamabad, Pakistan

Military Deputy Commander
- U.S. Southern Command
- 2009 – 2011 (2 years)

Commander, Joint Task Force - Haiti
- U.S. Southern Command
- Government Agency; 501-1000 employees; Military industry
- January 2010 – April 2010 (4 months)
- U.S. Military's response following the 12 Jan 2010 earthquake in Haiti.
- J3 and Chief of Staff
- European Command
- Government Agency; 501-1000 employees; Military industry
- 2007 – 2009 (2 years) Stuttgart Area, Germany

Commanding General
- United States Army South
- Government Agency; 10,001+ employees; Military industry
- 2005 – 2007 (2 years) Fort Sam Houston, Texas

Commander
- United States Military Group, Bogota, Colombia
- Government Agency; 10,001+ employees; Military industry
- 2001 – 2003 (2 years) Bogota, Colombia

Commander
- 75th Ranger Regiment
- 1999 – 2001 (2 years) Ft. Benning, GA

Commander
- 1st Battalion, 75th Ranger Regiment
- 1995 – 1997 (2 years) Savannah, Georgia Area

Commander
- 1st Battalion, 505th Parachute Infantry Regiment, 82nd Airborne Division
- 1993 – 1995 (2 years) Ft. Bragg, North Carolina
- 82nd Airborne Division
- US Army
- Government Agency; 10,001+ employees; Military industry
- 1993 – 1995 (2 years)

MEDALS AND DECORATIONS

- Army Distinguished Service Medal
- Defense Superior Service Medal
- Legion of Merit, Special Forces Tab
- Ranger Tab
- Pathfinder Badge,
- Combat SCUBA Diver
- Combat Infantry Badge
- Expert Infantry Badge
- Master Parachutist Badge.

SOURCES

http://en.wikipedia.org/wiki/Ken_Keen

http://www.drlatulane.org/leadership-corner/interviews/ken-keen-interview

http://usacac.army.mil/cac2/AOKM/aokm2009/bio/Keen_PK_LTG_Bio.pdf

http://tarpley.net/2010/01/18/to-save-haiti-fire-gen-%E2%80%9Cbrownie%E2%80%9D-keen-start-air-drops-cancel-the-debt-and-kick-out-the-imf/

http://fortbragg.patch.com/groups/politics-and-elections/p/lt-gen-keen-former-special-operations-82nd-leader-to-retire

http://online.wsj.com/news/articles/SB10001424052748704281204575003173316615894

http://www.linkedin.com/pub/dir/Ken/Keen

RAY HARDLING HOGG
B-26 Marauder Bomber
WWII
"Mayking's Marauder Man"
September 10, 1920-December 31, 2010
First published in the July 3, 2013, edition of the Mountain Eagle.
Permission to use given by Ben Gish
Written by Victor Annas

Letcher County native Ray Harding Hogg piloted a B-26 Marauder bomber during World War II in Europe. In this photo, the Marauder is seen dropping 300-pound bombs to blast hangar buildings and dispersal areas of the Airdrome at Triqueville, France, on November 26, 1943, where the famed "Yellow-Nosed" German fighter squadron was based. Hogg was transferred to France less than 14 months after this photo was taken. (AP Photo)On September 10, 1920, Ray Harding Hogg was born in the community of Mayking, the fourth child of Charles and Lina Hogg. Quiet and unassuming, Ray would be anything but average. He attended school faithfully, and in 1939 graduated from Whitesburg High School. That fall, Ray enrolled at Eastern Kentucky State College to pursue a degree in education. By 1941, it was becoming clear that the United States would eventually be drawn into another world war. Seeing the news, Ray began to think about the options that he would have should he be called to duty.

Ray Harding Hogg (above) was a Flying Cadet at Dorr Field in Florida when this photo was taken in 1943. The Japanese attack on Pear Harbor in December 7, 1941; thrust the United States headlong into WWII. Like so many young men and women of that generation, Ray felt it was his "duty" to do his part in trying to defeat the Axis powers then determined to dominate the world.

Following tests and examinations, Ray was sworn into the United States Army Air Corps on February 26, 1943. When asked how he came to be selected by the Army Air Force, Ray said, "Well, the recruitment officers told me that they needed pilots. They thought I would probably do well as I had been to college. I told them that it sounded good. I had to wait for the Army Air Force to complete the required testing and exams, but the next thing I knew, I was on my way to basic training and primary flight school."

Streaking flames which nearly enveloped the next plane in formation, a Martin B-26 Marauder of the U.S. Army 8th Air Force was a victim of intense German anti-aircraft barrage encountered during a bombing in the Pas de Calais area on Feb. 24, 1944. (AP Photo/U.S. Air Force)Following basic training in Miami, the Army Air Corps sent Ray to Dorr Field near Arcadia, Florida for primary flight training. Ray completed this training flying the Stearman PT-17. From there, Ray was sent to Moody Field, Georgia for twin-engine flight training.

The training was intense. The warm mornings were filled with "PT" (Physical Training) followed by breakfast. The cadets would then go to classes filled with lectures, quizzes and examinations. Then came drill exercises and military detail. Daily inspection of their barracks was normal. Following dinner, the cadets would study training material in preparation for the next day.

An American B-26 Marauder medium-bomber of the U.S. Army 9th Air Force, based in England, lost a rain of 26 100-pound bombs during a raid on German installations somewhere in France on May 31, 1944. Mayking native Ray Hogg piloted a Marauder for the 9th Air Force. Hogg told his story to his great-nephew Victor Annas before Hogg died on December 31, 2010. (AP Photo) "There were days that we were all very tired." Ray said. "But that was just the way it was. We had a job to do and a duty to perform."

Ray's introduction to flying twin engine aircraft began in the Curtis Wright AT-9 "Jeep." The AT-9 gave flying cadets the knowledge to fly a larger more complex aircraft. It was here that he learned the details of navigation, fuel management, instrument flight, emergency procedures and high-speed landings.

A crew of a B-26 was interrogated after a mission was completed and they had returned to an airfield somewhere in England during WWII. Questionings of crews were always very thorough and detailed. (AP Photo) When asked how he came to fly the B-26 Marauder, Ray said "One day our cadet class had a visit from the wing commander's liaison. We were informed by the liaison officer that we would soon begin transition training in preparation to fly the Martin B-26 Marauder. That was a shock to us because we had heard stories that the B-26 was a tough plane to fly. The rumor was that it could be your coffin if not handled properly. Several cadets decided to quit when they heard that news. Most of us stayed in the program though."

The decision to stay with the medium bomber training program would prove fortuitous. Those who completed the rigorous training came to be known as "Marauder Men". The B-26 Marauder was a difficult aircraft to master. Many trainees simply could not handle the plane. Approximately 70% of the flying cadets were "washed out" by their instructors. Those who did master flying the Marauder were considered the best of the best.

Ray was then sent to Barksdale Field, Louisiana, for advanced training in the B-26. The cadets quickly realized that the Marauder was a very different plane from the trainers they had flown. Early in the war, crews had not been properly trained to fly the Martin Marauder. Many cadets were killed in training during the early months of WWII. Because of the high accident rate, the B-26 had been dubbed "The Widow Maker." Ray reflected on his first impressions of the sleek new aircraft.

"The first time I saw a B-26 it struck me as being the most advanced aircraft ever built," he said. "From the beginning, I knew I was flying something real different. Our instructors drilled into us that the Marauder had to be flown like a fighter rather than a bomber. It used the same engines that had been installed in the P-47 Thunderbolt. Those engines gave the B-26 plenty of power, but it was also a heavy plane. Even with low fuel and no bomb load, it was a hot ship. Our biggest fear was getting too slow and stalling the wing. If that happened, it was certain death. As long as we kept the airspeed up, it would fly just fine. I learned to bring it in over the runway threshold at 135 mph, flare and keep the power on until the wheels touched the ground. The B-26 was so heavy, it never bounced on landing."

On June 27, 1944, Ray graduated from flight training as a second lieutenant and was awarded his "Silver Wings." He was granted a 15-day leave and returned to Mayking before going overseas. He enjoyed the time with his family and friends in Letcher County during the brief visit. Following his leave, Ray was ordered to Hunter Field, Georgia in preparation to join the US Army Air Forces in Europe.

Orders were issued and on November 15, 1944, Ray boarded the HMS Aquitania bound for England. After nine days of "zigzagging" across the Atlantic Ocean to avoid German U-Boats, the Aquitania arrived in Stowe, England.

Ray recalled, "I stepped off the ship and the first thing that I saw was that cold dense fog that you always hear about when people speak of England. It was so thick, I could not see the end of the gangway. That fog hung around for three days before it finally lifted."

Orders were issued for Ray to transfer to Chilbolten, England, where he was assigned to the 9th Air Force's 397th Bombardment Group (Medium) 597th Bombardment Squadron. Remembering England, Ray said "Once they assigned us to the 9th Air Force, we went to Chilbolten and began what was called 'Theater Training'. We had to fly and assemble aircraft for mock bombing missions. We flew several of these theater training missions getting ready for operational missions in Europe. One thing about Chilbolten were those damp and dreary 'Nissin Huts' we stayed in. It seemed that even with a wood stove burning, they never really dried out."

Originally based at Rivenhall England, the 397th BG relocated to France shortly after D-Day to support Allied troop movements at the front. This kept the medium bombers within 30 minutes flying time of enemy positions. By January 10, 1945, Ray had joined the 397th BG now based in France at Peronne Airfield. Peronne is located in northern France near the French village of Bouvaincourt-sur-Bresle. The men of the 9th Air Force, along with so many other American servicemen, struggled against the northern European winter weather.

"It was bitter cold all the time," Ray said. "The runways were often covered with snow and ice. So we had to take off and land our planes on a snow packed runway. We had canvas tents to billet the crews in. Sometimes, the winds would blow in from the north and bring the temperature down to 5 degrees below zero. When we had to fly missions, they would wake us up at 4 a.m. for breakfast. Sometimes the food would be cold. We lived in our flight suits.

"The ground crews and maintenance personnel had to work on the planes out in the open because we had no hangers. They tried to park the planes near tree lines for windbreaks, but that didn't help much. I remember sitting in the tent talking and remembering how warm and nice it had been in Florida. We laughed about that. When we were cadets we thought we had it hard because of the heat in Florida, Georgia and Louisiana. We were freezing in northern France wishing we could go back to Florida. We never really warmed up while flying either. It was extremely cold at altitude. We just endured it. Of course, we had it better than the men at the front. So many of them had no shelter at all. Those fellows just had to deal with the weather as it came."

As tactical bombers, the B-26 Marauder and B-25 Mitchell flew a different mission than the B-17 and B-24 strategic bombers of WWII. The typical B-17 or B-24 bomb group would fly one mission per day to a target within occupied Europe and return to their base in England. The B-26 and B-25 bomb groups would fly between 2 and 5 missions per day.

Another aspect of the medium bomber mission was their operational altitude. B-17's and B-24's would typically fly at 30,000 feet. They were susceptible to the German 88mm FLAK and Luftwaffe fighters. Because the medium bombers were providing tactical support, they operated from altitudes of 10,000 to 12,000 ft. This made them vulnerable to 88mm, 37mm and 20mm anti aircraft fire as well as fighters. These missions were extremely stressful as the crews would face the enemy not once, but twice and in some instances up to 5 times per day. This was the life of the Marauder men.

When asked about flying the B-26 in combat Ray, with a stern look on his face, said, "Well, we mainly flew against enemy communication targets: bridges, railroad yards, fuel storage facilities and ammunition dumps. It was our job to deny the enemy of his supplies. We would also be called in to support troop movements in heavily defended areas. We would fly in first and 'soften up' a target area prior to the army beginning an offensive. Occasionally, we would be given a NOBALL target. At the time, we didn't know what NOBALL targets were. At least not officially. We figured it out as we went along though."

NOBALL missions were undertaken against the German V1 and V2 rocket sites. The B-26 Marauder groups were selected to attack them because of their reputation for accurate bombing against difficult targets.

"We had been told that the Germans were killing more civilians in England than they were Allied soldiers in the field with those V1 and V2 rockets. They had to be stopped," Ray said. "The Marauder could handle the mission's requirements very well. I remember taking off from our field at Peronne in the early morning just before sunrise to attack a NOBALL target. We got to 11,000 ft. and formed up in a tight [combat] box. As we approached the IP (Initial Point), we turned with the lead aircraft heading toward the AP (Aiming Point). I looked out the window and all I could see was a thick solid wall of dense black cloud in front of us. At first, it looked like a storm cloud, but I could see red flashes inside the cloud. That's when I realized it was FLAK. The Germans had acquired our altitude and were shooting everything they could at us. We were too close to the target to take evasive action, so we flew straight into that mess. I could hear chunks of metal hitting the airframe and striking the propeller blades. We could hear and feel explosions under the airplane and we saw red flashes several times. I still don't know how we managed to make it through that stuff. It really was so thick that you thought you could step outside and walk on it. The Norden bomb site was like an auto-pilot and it was in total control of the airplane from the AP (Aiming Point) on. With the bomb sight controlling the aircraft, it was straight and level flying during the bomb run. My co-pilot and I could only talk about our strategy for exiting the area once the bombs were dropped. A typical bomb run lasted about three or four minutes, but it felt like time was standing still. Once the bombs were dropped, we banked hard left with the rest of the group and tightened up the formation to maintain the defensive firepower of the [combat] box. When we got back to base, our plane was riddled with holes and pock marks from all the FLAK we had flown through."

When asked if he had flown the B-25 Mitchell bomber Ray said, "Well, yeah I flew the B-25 several times. It was a good flying airplane, but I sure am glad I didn't have to fly it in combat." Ray then continued with a smile, "The B-26 was a tough old bird. That thing was tougher than 10 acres of garlic. We took so many hits in those planes. Sometimes, it was unbelievable. There were times that we wondered how it kept flying. I remember once, a plane in our [combat] box took a hit directly under the right wing. It was an 88mm FLAK battery. That German 88 blew a hole completely through the wing and ripped most of the aluminum sheeting off the top surface. The aileron was just barely hanging on. We thought he would go down, but he didn't. He stayed right there and made it back to base."

On April 19, 1945, Ray flew his 25th and final mission from Peronne, France. The 397th BG was sent in to Germany to bomb a railroad bridge that prevented the Nazis from resupplying troops near the French boarder. After that mission, he was given a 30-day R&R leave and traveled to Paris, France. While returning to duty from his R&R leave, Germany surrendered to the Allies, bringing an end to the bitter war in Europe.

During the summer of 1945, Ray remained in France as part of the American occupation forces. The 397th BG was relocated to Mons-En-Chausse, France and later to Clastres, France before being formally disbanded.

By the end of WWII, the reputation of the Martin B-26 Marauder, known as "The Widow Maker," had been completely transformed. Thanks to the efforts of flight training, ground school instructors, support personnel and flight crews, the Marauder achieved the record of incurring the least losses of any Allied bomber. In fact, the B-26 lost less than 1% of the crews that flew them. Yet, the end of hostilities brought a sad fate to the surviving Martin B-26 Marauders. The aircraft that had so faithfully served its crews during the war were scrapped in Europe. The metal was given to Germany to help rebuild its crushed economy. Only a few Marauders survive today as a memorial to those who flew them.

On December 1, 1945, Ray boarded the USS Argentina to return to the United States. By December 12, he arrived at Fort Knox, Kentucky, and was given leave to return to his family in Letcher County for the Christmas holiday.

In the years to come, Ray would earn a bachelor of science and master's degrees in agriculture from the University of Kentucky. He worked and served the Commonwealth of Kentucky as an educator in Falmouth, Kentucky. Ray continued to serve as a reserve officer in the United States Air Force. For eighteen years, Ray served as the liaison officer for Kentucky to the United States Air Force Academy. He retired in 1982 as a Lieutenant Colonel.

On December 31, 2010, Ray Harding Hogg died at the Thomas Hood Veterans Center in Wilmore, Kentucky.

In a private ceremony, he was buried at the Hogg family cemetery in Mayking.

Quiet and unassuming, Ray Hogg was a true American hero. He would be remembered by most for his lifetime accomplishments. For our family, however, Ray will always be Mayking's Marauder Man. *Victor Annas is a greatnephew of Ray Hogg.*

RAYMOND SMITH
Staff Sergeant
82nd Airborne Division
101st Airborne (Screaming Eagles)
April 3, 1924- December 31, 1997

Purple Heart and Bronze Star Recipient

Raymond Smith was a child of Appalachia. In this depressed region of our nation times were hard. Families struggled just to put food on the table. Each family member had to pull his or her weight in order to survive.

Raymond was born in Seco, Kentucky. He later moved to Mayking and finally to Thornton. Seco (South East Coal Company) was a mining town in eastern Kentucky. There was not much to offer a young man in terms of employment but due to the hard times Raymond was forced to work at any odd jobs that were available. His educational opportunities were also limited. At the youthful age of sixteen, Raymond Smith joined the army. The date was June 6, 1940. Ironically four years from his enlistment would be a historical milestone.

Raymond Smith trained as one of the original parachute paratroopers. His training was intense and very important; for he was one of the men selected to parachute behind enemy lines and make a trail for the invading U.S. forces to follow. They were specially trained to operate navigation aids to guide the main body on where to make their drop.

The Pathfinder teams were comprised of a group of eight to twelve men and a group of six bodyguards whose job was to defend the Pathfinders while they set up their equipment. The Pathfinders were dropped approximately thirty minutes before the main body. This enabled them to locate designated drop zones, provide radio data, and offer visual guides for the main force. After the main body landed, the Pathfinders would join up with their original units.

On a sidebar note, Raymond had an opportunity to be in a motion picture. Before being sent for deployment Raymond had an opportunity to be in a movie entitled 'Parachute Battalion'. It was a prelude to their heroic deeds.

He was assigned to a base near Nottingham, England. He was part of a secret plan known as Operation Overload. It was directly under General Dwight D. Eisenhower's control. The forthcoming evasion would be the largest in history and Ray would be the first Kentuckian to land on occupied French soil.

World War II was rampant and a Letcher County native was right in the heat of the battle. Raymond was one of approximately two hundred Pathfinders of the 101st Airborne.

Staff Sergeant Smith's platoon circled the English coast in an aircraft. They wished to confuse the enemy as to their destination. Just before dawn the Pathfinders parachuted near the town of St. Germain de Filliers, France. They were brave souls who parachuted into France on that early morning of June 6, 1944.

They landed behind German lines on that predawn D-Day morning. Unfortunately Smith landed in an apple tree and broke his foot when he hit the ground. He did not falter in his mission. Ignoring the pain of a broken foot he reported gun emplacements and set up panels to assist incoming planes. The mission of the Pathfinders was a complete success. On his twentieth birthday, Sgt Smith witnessed the beginning of the end for the German war machine.

In September of 1944, Staff Sergeant Smith was part of the invasion force to free Holland. The 101st had the directive of keeping the roads open along Purple Heart Lane (so named due to the casualties). The mission took seventy-two days and the price in American wounded and dead was high.

At the age of twenty-one Staff Sergent Smith fought the Battle of Bastogne, Belgium. The winter was merciless and caused Smith to have frostbite. His friend from Letcher County, Elmon Potter, also suffered through the cold nights and frigid winter weather alongside of Smith.

When the weather broke, Sgt Smith became part of the Alsace-Lorraine offensive. He was stationed there when word came of the end of hostilities. He was assigned to guard the area around the Eagle's Nest, Hitler's secondary command post. It was located in Berchtesgaden, Germany. From there he was stationed in Marseilles, France. He was discharged from military duty on September 23, 1945. He was twenty-five years old. Upon his return to Letcher County, he married his childhood girlfriend (he carried her picture all through the war). Her name was Irene Bates. They were married on December 8, 1945, four years and a day after the attack on Pearl Harbor, December 7, 1941. Their marriage produced one daughter.

Raymond and his father-in-law, Hennie Bates, went into the coal mining business in 1946. They called it the Irene Coal Company. This was but was one of his business adventures. He ran a glass company at Pine Mountain Junction, Whitesburg, Kentucky. He worked for the South East Coal Company. During this time he became friends with Cornelius Ryan. Ryan was a British author and after several conversations with Raymond, wrote a book entitled, The Longest Day. It later became a movie. Raymond kept in contact with several of his comrades and on occasion attended reunions of the Screaming Eagles.

Raymond Smith, the first Kentuckian to touch occupied soil in the D Day Invasion, passed away on December 31, 1997. He was seventy-three years of age. He was buried in Arlington, Virginia, with full military honors.

SOURCES

"Paratrooper Raymond Smith was First Kentuckian to Land in France on D-Day," William T. Cornett; (The Mountain Eagle, November 9, 1988.)

Kentucky Explorer Magazine, January 1995 Issue; Pages 11 – 14.

http://en.wikipedia.org/wiki/Pathfinders_%28military%29

http://www.benning.army.mil/infantry/rtb/1-507th/pathfinder/content/pdf/pathfinder%20history.pdf

http://www.benning.army.mil/infantry/rtb/1-507th/pathfinder/content/pdf/pathfinder%20history.pdf

RICKY S. WARF
First Sergeant
Charlie Company
3rd Battalion
325th Infantry Regiment
82nd Airborne Division
November 26, 1964-Present

There are times when our unsung heroes come home and simply fade into the woodwork. We don't realize the significance of their service. We see them and think they were in the military at one time. They don't brag or pound their chest. They usually end up serving the community as proud Veterans. Such is the case of Rick Warf.

Rick was born on Thanksgiving Day in 1964, at Whitesburg Appalachian Regional Hospital. He is the son of Samuel Lee and the late Eunice Phil Warf. His childhood was typical of a child raised in the foothills and mountains of eastern Kentucky. He attended Martha Jane Potter during his grade school years. He went to Whitesburg High School and then attended Mayking Christian Academy. Upon graduation he enrolled into Alice Lloyd College.

At the age of twenty Rick was on active duty. He received his basic training at Fort Benning, Georgia. His specialty was 11C-Indirect Fire Infantryman. Upon completion of his OSUT training, he completed airborne school and was assigned to Charlie Company, 3rd Battalion, 325th Airborne Infantry Regiment, 82nd Airborne Division at Fort Bragg, North Carolina, for the next fourteen months.

The 325th Airborne Infantry Regiment is a unit of the 82nd Airborne Division. They can deploy anywhere within eighteen hours and are known as elite parachutists. The 82nd Airborne Division has been in existence since August 5, 1917. The 82nd Airborne Division is based out of Fort Bragg, North Carolina. They have gallantly served virtually in every war up to current day Afghanistan. Note that PFC Charles N. DeGlopper of the 82nd was awarded the Medal of Honor for his ultimate sacrifice during World War II in 1946. Such is the bravery of the Americans who wears the 82nd patch.

While serving at Fort Bragg, Rick completed the Jungle Expert Training Course at Fort Sherman, Panama. After his time at Fort Bragg, North Carolina, he rotated to Italy as part of the 3rd Battalion, 325th Airborne Battalion Combat Team (ABCT). While there he participated in numerous NATO exercises in Germany, Spain, and Turkey, completed Cold Weather Survival Training in the Alps, and Urban Warfare Training in Berlin, Germany. Rick trained with the German paratroopers at Mertzig, Germany, and received his German Jump wings in 1986. He was discharged from active duty after obtaining the rank of Sergeant.

Upon his return to stateside he joined the United States Army Reserve and was assigned to B Troop, 3rd Squadron, 397th Calvary at Whitesburg, Kentucky, and completed 19D Calvary Scout reclassification training. While in the reserves he began a trucking business for a couple of years. He then transferred to the 80th Training Division out of Bristol, Virginia.

Ricky attended Drill Sergeant School and began training soldiers at Ft. Jackson, South Carolina, Ft. Knox, Kentucky, and Ft. Lewis, Washington. During this time, Rick also obtained his Bachelors and Masters Degree in teaching. He was chosen as his brigade's Drill Sergeant of the Year in 1997, and was also appointed as the first Commandant of the newly formed 1st Brigade, 100th Division Drill Sergeant Prep Unit.

In 2000, he was promoted to First Sergeant and served in that capacity in Alpha Troop based out of Corbin, Kentucky, for four years. During that time, he was NCOIC (Non-Commissioned Officer in Charge) of numerous training missions at Fort Knox, Kentucky and Fort Lewis, Washington. He also continued teaching, but in 2005 he felt a calling to serve his country once again. He volunteered for a tour in Iraq and was assigned to a MITT team with the Iraqi Assistance Group. Rick served as the Brigade NCOIC during training at Fort Carson, Colorado, Kuwait, and Iraq.

Upon arrival in Taji, Iraq, Rick was appointed as the Senior Brigade Operations Advisor/NCOIC where he was in charge of the brigade tactical operations center (TOC) and assisted his Iraqi counterparts in planning and conducting numerous combat operations. He received the Meritorious Service Medal and the Bronze Star Medal for his service in Iraq.

He rotated back home after his nine month tour expired and was selected to attend the United States Army

Sergeants Major Academy in 2006. At that juncture, First Sergeant Warf (P) felt the field of education calling him, so he went back to school and obtained a second masters in school administration. In 2008, before being assigned to the position of Command Sergeant Major, Rick instead decided to retire and pursue a position as a school administrator. Soon thereafter, he became a principal and served at Beckham Bates Elementary and when the school closed, he became principal at Letcher Middle School.

During the interview principal Warf stated that upon reflection, he felt he made the right choice in working with children instead of going on and serving in the rank of Command Sergeant Major. He believes that education of the rising generation is the key to keeping America strong.

Ricky lives in Letcher County with his wife Wendy and two children, Sierra and Tanner. His service is an indication of his character; then it is painted in sterling gold.

AWARDS

- Bronze Star Medal
- Meritorious Service Medal
- Army Commendation Medal
- Army Achievement Medal (6)
- Good Conduct Medal
- Army Reserve Components Achievement Medal (4)
- National Defense Service Medal
- Iraq Campaign Medal
- Global War on Terrorism Service Medal
- Armed Forces Reserve Medal with, M Device
- NCOES Development Ribbon
- Army Service Ribbon
- Overseas Service Ribbon
- Parachutist's Badge

SOURCES

Interview with Mr. Warf

http://en.wikipedia.org/wiki/325th_Infantry_Regiment_(United_States)

http://www.history.army.mil/html/forcestruc/lineages/branches/inf/0325in.htm

http://www.history.army.mil/documents/WWII/LaFiere/325-LaF.htm

http://www.bragg.army.mil/82nd/2bct/Pages/default.aspx

http://www.bragg.army.mil/82nd/2bct/Pages/history.aspx

http://en.wikipedia.org/wiki/82nd_Airborne_Division

ROBERT ADRIAN MARKS
Lieutenant
U.S. Navy Pilot
WWII
1917?-March 7, 1998

(Photo-National Archives)

There are heroes and then there are those who were part of greatness. There are those men and women who looked into the eyes of death and said, 'Not today'. Such was the caliber of Lieutenant R. Adrian Marks.

R. Adrian Marks was born in Ladoga, Indiana. His father was a lawyer and young Adrian followed his footsteps. He graduated for Northwestern University and then attended the University Law School. He was at Pearl Harbor on that infamous day of December 7, 1941. He became a pilot and also trained potential pilots for the Navy.

On August 2, 1945, another forgotten hero by the name of Lt Wilber C. Guinn (U.S. Navy Pilot) was on a routine submarine patrol in his Ventura Bomber. He spotted men in the water and radioed it to headquarters. They were the men of the U.S.S. Indianapolis. Lieutenant Marks heard the report and flew in that direction from the island of Peleliu. He notified the USS Cecil Doyle of the report of men in the water.

The USS Indianapolis was on its way back to the Philippine port after delivering parts for the first atomic bomb. Note that it was unescorted and was not taking evasive zigzag movements as were ordered. A Japanese submarine found it and fired. Two torpedoes found their mark and the ship sank in a little over ten minutes. Of the twelve hundred (1,196) crew members, approximately nine hundred escaped into the darkness of the water. The distress signal was not heard and the men bobbed up and down in the sea surrounded by sharks for four days before being rescued.

Upon arrival of the scene Lieutenant Marks saw hundreds of men in the water. To his horror he also saw the sharks and the attacks. He later recalled in a speech given to the survivors that it was a, 'Sun-swept afternoon of horror.' He knew he had to do something quickly. He talked to his crew and they were of the same mind that they had to land on the sea. They dropped three rafts but one did not stay afloat. He then proceeded to attempt a landing in the twelve feet swells with his Dumbo (PBY5A Catalina). The plane was tossed into the air several times but made a landing. Disregarding order to never land in the Philippine Sea, he proceeded to land. His crew of eight men began loading survivors. They selected men most vulnerable to a shark attack. He and his crew rescued fifty-six sailors on that day.

The manner in which he rescued the men is astounding. The plane was not to ever land except in calm water. The sea was not calm and he had specific order not to land under any circumstances.

His conscience overruled the order. The crew threw life rings to men who were alone and targets for a shark attack. He shut off the engines and put additional survivors on the wings. He placed them in all compartments, and tied some down with parachute material. He refused to allow those men he could save to perish. Yet he always said he wished he could have done more to save the men.

That night as the plane bobbed up and down in the sea, Lt. Marks recalled, *"Even though we were near the equator, the wind whipped up. We had long since dispensed the last drop of water, and scores of badly injured men were softly crying with thirst and with pain. And then, far out on the horizon, there was a light."* That light was the destroyer christened the Cecil Doyle. The captain disregarded the destroyer's safety and sent a beacon skyward for other rescue vessels to find the location and assist in the rescue. The rescue began including Lt. Marks and his crew. The Dumbo was too badly damaged to take off again. Later the destroyer sank the brave little plane. Twelve days later World War II was over in the Pacific.

Of the approximately nine hundred men who entered the water, only three hundred seventeen survived. I cannot imagine the depravation the survivors endured. The longing for water, hunger, exposure to the water and possible wounds took a heavy toll on the men. Then there were those dreaded shark attacks. Each and every man on the USS Indianapolis is true heroes.

For his heroic actions Lt. R. Adrian Marks was given the Air Medal by Admiral Chester Nimitz, commander in chief of the Pacific Fleet. All his life he was haunted by what he saw and not being able to rescue more men.

R. Adrian Marks, died on March 7, 1998, in Clinton County. He had come full circle and was at his hometown of Frankfort, Indiana. He was eighty-one years of age. He is survived by his wife, Elta; a son, Robert, of Bellevue, Washington; three daughters, Pamela Levine of Lakeville, Mass., Alexis Shuman of Enumclaw, Wash., and Lynn Larson of Olympia,

Wash; a foster son, John Barlas of Mercer Island, Wash., and ten grandchildren.

SOURCES

http://www.nytimes.com/1998/03/15/us/adrian-marks-81-war-pilot-who-led-rescue-of-56-is-dead.html

http://www.ussindianapolis.org/story.htm
http://srv1.geetel.net/~cchsm/lt_cmdr_adrian_marks.htm

http://indymaru.tripod.com/indymaru6.htm
http://www.youtube.com/watch?v=aXeeoBeNtqY
http://www.humanities360.com/index.php/uss-indianapolis-tragedy-13252/

http://www.ussindianapolis.org

http://www.history.navy.mil/faqs/faq30-1.htm
http://indymaru.tripod.com

http://www.ussindianapolis.org/intro.htm

ROBERT QUEATEN KELLY
Captain
United States Air Force
Fighter Pilot
WWII

This is what I have learned to date about this unsung hero. Robert was a resident of Blackey, Kentucky. He attended school at Stuart Robinson. He became a fighter pilot and was in the first wave of the invasion of North Africa. I would love to learn more of this man.

"Robert Queaten Kelly, 22, formerly of Blackey, Ky. Capt. Kelly, a fighter pilot in the air force, took part in the first invasion of North Africa, and is now in Sicily (Italy). Capt. Kelly attended school, at Stuart Robinson School at Blackey. We feel proud of men like young Kelly and all who are doing their bit for their country. Let's back them up by doing without something and buying bonds."

SOURCES

Courtesy of Ben Gish and the Mountain Eagle

ROGER DALE CAUDILL
Private First Class
C Company
1st Battalion
26th Infantry
1st Infantry Division
May 06, 1947-April 29, 1967

I do not remember Roger. His picture looks familiar though. I am sure we were related. I have Caudill heritage flowing in my veins from the Revolutionary soldier, James Caudill. Roger was from Whitesburg, Kentucky. As of the writing of this tribute I do not have much information about Roger. Some of his friends have painted a picture of this young man from the mountains though. I offer their words as posted on the web.

Roger's MOS was 11C10 (Indirect Fire Infantryman). His ID number was 51643383. He was killed in 1967, having been in country for only three months. The official report states that he was in Bien Hoa Province, and was killed by multiple fragmentation wounds. He is listed as a ground casualty. His body was recovered and was buried in the Sandlick Cemetery with full military honors. Roger Dale Caudill was nineteen years of age when he was killed. He is on the Vietnam Memorial Wall: Panel 18E-Row 113.

On August 22, 1999, Mitchell Hyden (cousin) posted the following on the wall: *"Roger was, very well liked, by everyone, he was living, in Illinois, at the time of his call, to duty. He was happy, all the time and very funny. When I was, in the service, in Oklahoma, he would write my wife, to be and me, telling us, what a horrible place, Vietnam was and how he knew, that it wasn't, right for us, to be over, there. All the letters, that we received, all he would say, was he knew, he would not, be coming home, alive. Roger Dale lived, with his Grandparents, from the day he was born, until coming, to Illinois, to visit us. They were, his only parents, according to him. Roger also arranged, for me and my wife, to go out, on our first date, together. Very unselfish person. We have, missed him, a great deal and still, have the letters that he, wrote to us. Roger would, be very proud, that VVMF., was established, to remember all, of the brave people, who served, their country, even though, they did not agree, with the reason, or virtual outcome. My wife and I contribute, to the fund and the wall, when we can and all, of it is a tribute, to my cousin and very good friend, ROGER DALE CAUDILL, HE WILL, NEVER BE FORGOTTEN.*

On August 11, 2010, Roger Tyree posted the following on the wall about his childhood friend: *"Roger was a good child hood friend of mine. I remember him as an always smiling young man. He graduated from Whitesburg High School in 1965, I in 1963.The last time I saw Roger Dale we were both getting ready to go to Vietnam. May he live forever in our hearts I visited his resting place in Sandlick Cemetery also The Vietnam Wall several times. May Roger Dale and all the others that gave the ultimate sacrifice be in our prayers and thoughts .Roger Dale may we meet again. Sorry old friend that it took so long."* Roger you are remembered! DPC

SOURCES

http://www.virtualwall.org/dc/CaudillRD01a.htm

http://army.togetherweserved.com/army/servlet/tws.webapp.WebApp?cmd=ShadowBoxProfile&type=Person&ID=43215

http://thewall-usa.com/info.asp?recid=8472

http://www.vvmf.org/Wall-of-Faces/8488/ROGER-D-CAUDILL

RONNIE JORDAN CAMPBELL
Petty Officer 2nd Class
CT2
U.S.S. Liberty
Navy
November 4, 1942-June 8, 1967
Recipient of the Purple Heart

In the peaceful rolling hills of Arlington National Cemetery rest the mortal remains of Navy Seaman Ronnie Jordan Campbell. He died honorably in service to his country on the 8th of June, 1967. He was only twenty-four years old at the time of his death.

The story of his short life began some five hundred miles to the south in the shadows of the Great Smoky Mountains of east Tennessee. Ronnie was born in the autumn of 1942, in his Grandfather and Grandmother Franklin's log cabin located in the sleepy little community of Pigeon Forge.

Ronnie spent his early years working hard on the farm alongside his parents Raymond Charles and Iva Ellen Campbell, as well as his two brothers and one sister. He grew up hearing stories about his father Raymond Charles' time spent as a Navy medic during the turbulent years of World War II. The Campbell family were proud of the part their family had played in helping to defend the sacred freedoms of the United States and this no doubt played a role in Ronnie's fateful decision to join the navy after he graduated from high school. He enlisted in 1961.

Upon completion of basic training, he was eventually stationed in Scotland where he sent for his bride to be. They were married shortly afterwards and in 1964, their first son, Ricky, was born. Ronnie continued his career in the navy and achieved the rank of CT2 and was considered by his commanding officers to be a very skillful Cryptologic Technician.

Seaman Campbell would later be assigned to the USS Liberty, an electronic intelligence ship; the most advanced of its time. There was only one other ship in the world like the Liberty and it was her sister ship, the Belmont. Using her advanced equipment, the Liberty could transmit information from any location in the world back to the United States using the moon as a relay satellite.

During the summer of 1967, the Liberty was patrolling International waters when the war between Israel and the Arab nations of the Middle East began in a violent firestorm. The United States military ordered the Liberty to move to the Mediterranean Sea and position itself off the coast of Gaza, near the Sinai Peninsula, twenty-five and a half miles from the Egyptian city of El Arish. The ship was positioned approximately fifteen miles off the coast in neutral waters keeping a close watch on the progress of the fighting.

On the morning of June 8, 1967, the trouble began. From daylight to just past noon, Israeli war planes buzzed the USS Liberty. Over the next six and a half hours, eight fly-overs were conducted by the Israeli Air Force. The planes flew as low as mast-height with the

American sailors on deck clearly able to see the Israeli pilots, evening exchanging waves with one another.

At 2 P.M., the Israelis suddenly launched an unprovoked attack upon the USS Liberty. Three Mirage jets opened up with deadly cannon and rocket fire. The first pass partially disabled what little armament the Liberty possessed, four fifty caliber deck machine guns. Eight U.S. servicemen were killed with over seventy-five wounded from the strafing. The Mirage jest fired until they ran out of ammunition and then two Dassault Mysteres fighter planes swooped down, dropped napalm and phosphorous bombs onto the deck of the Liberty. The superstructure was set ablaze as drums of fuel exploded from the heat. The attacking planes continued to strafe the ship and proceeded to knock out the entire communication antenna. Also the ship's Stars and Stripes flag, which had been flying all morning, was riddled and shot down in the barrage of cannon fire. The entire time that the attack was taking place, the Israelis jammed the ship's radio frequencies in an attempt to isolate the Liberty.

Finally crew members jerry-rigged a transmitter to a small antenna sending out an urgent call for help to the Sixth Fleet, which was stationed some four hundred miles to the north. The message was received and relayed back to the Defense Department in Washington, while U. S. planes were launched in an attempt to come to the rescue of the Liberty. However, before the American fighter jets could reach the embattled ship, they were suddenly called back by Defense Secretary Robert McNamara who took his orders straight from the White House.

The attack on the USS Liberty continued on for some time with a total of a dozen aircraft bearing down on the damaged ship. In addition, three Israeli torpedo boats joined in on the one-sided fight. These small, fast running attack boats fired five torpedoes at the Liberty.

One struck the ship on the starboard side blasting a forty by twenty-nine foot hole and killing twenty-five more men. The other four torpedoes missed, but the attack boats continued circling the now helpless Liberty for approximately forty minutes more, pumping hundreds of rounds of 50 caliber machine gun fire at the crew members of the Liberty who were trying to put out the raging fires. Even the wounded men lying topside were fired upon. When the Liberty began to list in the water, with the real possibility that she might sin, the life boats were ordered over the side. Survivors of the attack would later testify that the Israelis deliberately took aim and riddled the small boats with the machine gun fire destroying them all but one.

When the attack finally ended after an hour and fifteen minutes, thirty-four Americans had been killed, including naval officers, seamen, two Marines and one civilian. Every one of them paid the ultimate price for their unselfish duty to their country.

Ronnie Jordan Campbell was one of those who died. He was seated in the Communications room at his desk at the time of the surprise attack and was killed while writing a letter home to his dear wife, who was then pregnant with their second child. The Liberty had a full crew of two hundred ninety-three men on board. Of this number two hundred five Purple Hearts were earned and awarded.

Even though this calculated and vicious attack on America occurred almost half a century ago, the controversy that it created still lives on today. It is considered by many historians and military scholars to be one of the greatest cover-ups in our nation's military history.

The Israeli government never admitted to its true reason for attack a clearly marked American naval vessel. Their claim has always been that it was a case of mistaken identity, even though at the time two intercept stations overheard Israeli pilots clearly identify the ship as American. In recent years, one of the Israeli pilots who flew on the mission has come forward and revealed that he personally radioed back to the Israeli command headquarters that the ship was an ally from the United States. He stated that he was ordered to attack anyway, but he refused to do so. He was later arrested upon his landing.

The Israelis further claim they believed the USS Liberty was an Egyptian ship by the name of El Quseir, even though it was only forty percent the size of the Liberty and was a rusted out horse transport ship. The Liberty looked like no other ship in the world at the time. It was equipped with the first microwave dish with forty-five communication antenna projecting upward from the deck. The USS Liberty also had ten foot high hull numbers painted on the sides that indicated that it was a non-combatant ship and the word "Liberty" was clearly visible on the stern. In addition, the survivors of the attack confirmed that the ship was flying a large American flag under clear weather conditions.

Roger Kelly interviewed a close relative of Ronnie Campbell. Her name was Ersa Ray Noland Smith. She attended his military funeral services at Arlington National Cemetery (Section 13, Site 11445-C). At the internment, Mrs. Smith reported that she was quietly spoken with her Cousin Ronnie's best friend, who was also on board the Liberty at the time of the attack, and he confirmed to her that the ship was indeed flying the American flag in plain view. He also stated that all of the ships survivors had been warned not to say anything about the entire incident.

Many sources believe that the Israeli attack was initiated to prevent the United Stated from finding out vital information about the forthcoming Jewish attacks on the Golan Heights that were scheduled for the next day, June 9, 1967. It is believed by some that the Israeli military wanted to gain control of the Syrian held heights before a cease fire could be brokered and therefore wanted nothing to interfere with their plans.

In addition there's also some reported evidence that the Israeli military forces were so overwhelmed by the number of enemy combatants being captured during the fighting they may have simply resorted to killing some of the prisoners for lack of facilities and men to guard them. If that were true then the USS Liberty was possibly attacked because they had discovered this egregious violation of the Geneva Convention.

The Lyndon Johnson Administration quickly accepted the apologies of the Israeli government, publicly saying that it was all an unfortunate accident. Those men in high political positions at the time refused to be forthcoming and open about the entire incident of the cold-blooded murder of American servicemen.

Joint Chief of Staff Admiral Thomas Moorer would be quoted as saying, "I can never accept the claim that this was a mistaken attack. Those men were betrayed and left to die by our own government."

Over the years survivors of the USS Liberty have presented voluminous evidence to the United States Congress of Israeli guilt and have repeatedly requested an investigation into the matter, but without success. It remains to this day a shameful and unresolved page in the long history of our nation.

Without the full cooperation of both the Israeli and American governments, the question of why the attack occurred on the USS Liberty will likely never be answered fully. Whatever the reasons for this well-guarded and covertly hushed military disaster, loyal Americans like Ronnie Jordan Campbell died and their sacrifice should never be forgotten.

Post Script: After reading the story of Ronnie Campbell my heart went out to his family and to the families of the other men whose families were forever changed by this deliberate attack on an American ship. I began reading and doing research as well. I was appalled at what I found. I was also stirred by what the daughter of Petty Officer Campbell wrote regarding her loss.

On January 21, 2004, Deborah (Campbell) Casswell wrote the following moving tribute about her father, Petty Officer Campbell: *"Who was Ronnie Campbell has always been a mystery to me. I never had the opportunity to know this man, never gazed up into his kind loving eyes, never heard the gentleness of his voice as he told me he loved me, and never felt the warmth of his arms as he held me. Sometimes we are dealt a hand of cards that we will never understand. I was born 5 1/2 months after my father was killed on the USS Liberty. I am now 36 years old and just beginning to find out what happened on that day in June of 1967. I am very saddened and disturbed by what I've read so far. Instead of bringing answers for me, my search has only brought more questions. I've only heard bits and pieces about my father throughout my life. I've heard he was a very gentle and caring man--one that would open his home to anyone who needed a warm place to stay. I've heard he loved God and lived his life in a way that showed that. He had a great imagination, and as he was growing up my Granny (his mom) would see him outside, by himself, for hours on end, playing cowboys and indians, having a grand ol time. I've met some of those who knew him growing up, and to this day they are still overtaken by sorrow as they try to talk to me about him. He was a good-looking man, and from what I've heard had no problems in the dating department during his school days. I don't know how he and my mom met--she doesn't talk much about him. I imagine it brings up a lot of pain for her. But, from what I understand, they were very much in love. My brother was born in Scotland in 1964. He is the spittin' image of my father! He doesn't remember much, if anything, about him either, as he was just short of 3 when Ronnie was killed. I can't imagine the grief, fear and anger my mom must have had as a young widowed mother with a baby on the way in 1967. So many lives were turned upside down that day. Thirty-four families ripped apart and countless others shaken to their core. One day, when my life on this earth is done, I will meet this man who has been such a mystery to me. I have so much to tell him about my life. So much he missed out on. So much we missed out on."* Deborah, Ricky, and Eileen are entitled to the truth. Americans, do not the families of these brave men deserve an answer? The people must demand to know what really happened!

By reading the statements of those in the know and you will realize there is something terribly wrong with this picture. Was it a conspiracy? All pertinent data point in that direction. Captain Ward Boston stated, *"The evidence was clear. Both Adm. Kidd and I believed with certainty that this attack...was a deliberate effort to sink an American ship and murder its entire crew. It was our shared belief that the attack could not possibly have been an accident. I am certain that the Israeli pilots [and] their superiors were well aware that the ship was American."*

Chairman of the Joint Chiefs of Staff Adm. Thomas Moorer also made the following statement: *"Congress has never investigated the recall by the White House of U.S. Navy aircraft sent to rescue the Liberty while the ship was still under attack. The White House cancellation of the Navy's attempt to rescue the Liberty is the most disgraceful thing I have witnessed in my entire military career."*

There is even a statement by some high ranking officers alleging that President Johnson ordered McNamara to have the U.S. planes going to the aide of the U.S. Liberty to return to base. Why? Was it an effort not to embarrass an ally or was it a cover-up of a plan which went afoul? Those brave men put up a fierce defense of their ship and the Liberty refused to sink. As an American I am angered by such antics and realize they continue to this day. I spurn the concept of Politics taking precedent over the People. Those broken families will never be the same. My prayers go out to all and I pray that we as Americans continue to call for answers in this and other unanswered questions regarding our unsung heroes.

Below is a list of the dead from the Israeli sneak attack on the U.S.S. Liberty on June 8, 1967.

LEST WE FORGET!

- LCDR Philip McCutcheon Armstrong, Jr. Navy Cross
- LT James Cecil Pierce
- LT Stephen Spencer Toth, Silver Star
- CT3 William Bernard Allenbaugh
- SN Gary Ray Blanchard
- CT2 Allen Merle Blue
- QM3 Francis Brown
- CT2 Ronnie Jordan Campbell
- CT2 Jerry Leroy Converse

- CT2 Robert Burton Eisenberg
- CT2 Jerry Lee Gross
- CT1 Curtis Alan Graves
- CTSN Lawrence Pasul Hayden
- CT1 Warren Edward Hersey
- CT3 Alan (NMN) Higgins
- SN Carl Lewis Hoar
- CT2 Richard Walter Keene, Jr.
- CTSN James Lee Lenau
- CTC Raymond Eugene Linn
- CT1 James Mahlon Lupton
- CT3 Duane Rowe Marggraf
- CTSN David Walter Marlborough
- CT2 Anthony Peter Mendle
- CTSN Carl Christian Nygren
- SGT Jack Lewis Raper, USMC
- CPL Edward Emory Rehmeyer, III, USMC
- IFCN David (NMN) Skolak
- CT1 John Caleb Smith, Jr.
- CTC Melvin Douglas Smith
- PC2 John Clarence Spicher
- GMG3 Alexander Neil Thompson, Jr.
- CT3 Thomas Ray Thornton
- CT3 Philippe Charles Tiedke
- CT1 Frederick James Walton

SOURCES

http://www.findagrave.com/cgi-bin/fg.cgi?page=gr&GSvcid=149900&GRid=32121520
&

http://www.findagrave.com/cgi-bin/fg.cgi?page=vcsr&GSvcid=149900

http://www.uss-liberty.com/2009/10/14/the-cover-up-of-israel%E2%80%99s-crime-against-the-uss-liberty-crewmen-continues/

http://my.firedoglake.com/edwardteller/2010/06/08/in-memoriam-june-8th-1967-june-8th-2010/

http://en.metapedia.org/wiki/USS_Liberty_attack

http://www.examiner.com/article/the-war-crime-you-have-never-heard-of-attack-on-the-uss-liberty

http://www.fold3.com/page/636352158_ronnie_jordon%20campbell/details/

Interview with Family (Ezra Rhea Smith)

(Ronnie, Ricky and Eileen)

ROY G. SEALS
Private First Class
1st Marine Division
7th Marine Regiment
Rifleman/Flamethrower
(1925-1983)
&
MARTIN J. LICHENTENBERG
Command Sergeant-Major
Division's S-3 (Plans & Operations).
1st Marine Division
1901-1978
Story compiled by Randy Seals, Nephews & Great Nephews
(Paul Dalton & David Collins)

Photo Courtesy of
(Roy Seals children, Great Nephews & Niece Randy, Phillip
Seals & daughter, Deborah Seals Davidson)

Many veterans deal with the unimaginable things they see and have to deal with in combat. Roy G. Seals never talked about his experiences as a Marine Rifleman in the Pacific during World War II. Most of this information was from short answers to direct questions when he was willing to talk about his experiences, letters and newspaper accounts.

Roy grew up in the hills of West Virginia and Southwest Virginia. Growing up Roy didn't have contact with his mother's family. His maternal grandparents and most of his aunts & uncles live in Koblenz, Germany. One of his mother's brothers, Martin J. Lichtenberg, came to the United States in the 1930. He joined the United States Marine Corp to establish permanent residence. Martin excelled in the Marine Corp raising the rank of Command Sergeant-Major. Roy never met his uncle until he arrived at Parris Island for his Marine Corp basic training, Martin was the Sergeant-Major of Roy's unit. Martin kept his distance from Roy during training so he wouldn't be treated any differently than the other trainees. Martin did keep an eye on Roy during training and report to sister on how well Roy was progressing in his training. Martin was proud that his nephew followed him into the Marine Corp.

Both Martin and Roy left Parris Island for the 1st Marine Division and the invasion of Peleliu. Roy was a rifleman (he also operated a flamethrower) assigned to the 7th Marine Regiment and Martin was assigned to the Division's S-3 (Plans & Operations). Martin was the S-3 NCO and was the chief draftsman for the invasion. Roy's unit landed on Peleliu where his unit was involved in some hardest fighting of the war. Because of the difference between their ranks and their jobs there wasn't an opportunity for Martin to check on Roy.

After Peleliu the Division went to the island of Pavuvu to rest, resupply and refit. Martin transferred to the 1st Marine Regiment as the Regiment's Command Sergeant-Major. The next stop for the division was the Invasion of Okinawa.

The division landed and faced light resistance for the first few days. The division swung north after dividing the island in half, resistance stiffened and was overcome quickly. In the south troops faced a tougher strongpoint. The division shifted to the south with two regiments on the battle line and with one in reserve. (5th & 7th on battle line with 1st in the rear). A reporter wrote an article that appeared in his hometown newspaper that was titled "Seals Gets Cave Full of Japs". He engulfed them in the fire from his flamethrower. When the reporter asked him how many he had killed Roy quietly replied, *"I don't know, I didn't stop to count."*

It was during the fight for Shuri Castle that the 5th & 7th were on battle line when Martin went forward to see Roy. Roy's company commander wouldn't let Martin go to the front but told him he would send for Roy. While Martin waited for Roy, a Marine came in and told the CO there was a wounded Marine in need of a stretcher. Martin said the Commanding Officer pointed to four Marines, told them to grab a stretcher and go bring back the wounded. As soldiers do, they grumbled and left. Roy made his way to the rear sometimes under enemy fire (In the picture with this article you can see a hole on the right side of his helmet. A Japanese sniper shot and killed the four stretcher bearers and shot Roy in the helmet. The snipers bullet hit Roy's helmet on the left side was deflected by his helmet liner circled around and came out on the right side, Roy got the sniper.

When Roy finally made it to the company's command post he went straight to his Company Commander and reported, *"Sir, you know those men you just sent out? They're dead."* Then he saw his Uncle Martin and the two battle tested Marines shared hugs. Roy said the first thing his Uncle Martin said to him was, *"Marine, you need a haircut"* and they both had a good laugh. The two share letters and talked of family things. Both enjoyed their brief break from combat and the time together. Later during the fight for Shuri Castle, Roy was wounded for the second time by shrapnel. He was sent to a hospital ship and then onto a state side hospital. The shrapnel was never removed because it was to near his heart. Doctors told him the shrapnel could walk on him and if it moved closer to his heart it could pierce the heart or sever an artery. The shrapnel did move, missing his heart and end up on the opposite side of his body. He lived the rest of his life in pain from that reminder of his time in the Marine Corp. After Okinawa, the 1st Division went to China Martin's job there was to interrogated Japanese prisoners of war. Martin retired from the Marine Corp and worked for the Department of the Army doing many of the same jobs as a civilian, as he did in the Marine Corp. Roy returned home to Southwest Virginia where he married the love of his life and raised three remarkable children.

SOURCES

Reflections by the Seals, Collins, & Dalton Family

http://search.ancestry.com/cgi-bin/sse.dll?gl=ROOT_CATEGORY&rank=1&new=1&so=3&MSAV=1&msT=1&gss=ms_r_f-2_s&gsfn=Roy&gsln=Seals&msbdy=&msbpn__ftp=&msddy=&msdpn__ftp=&cpxt=0&catBucket=p&uidh=000&cp=0

RUBEN WATTS
168th Field Artillery Battalion; Battery B
Asiatic Pacific Theater
March 5, 1943, to January 11, 1946
WWII
Recipient of
Two Bronze Stars
Philippine Liberation Ribbon
Two Purple Hearts
World War II Victory Medal
Good Conduct Medal
September 7, 1923-February 15, 2011

Ruben Watts was born on September 7, 1923, to Gobel and Georgeann Watts. They lived on a working farm in Hallie, Kentucky. He had seven siblings by the name of Curt, Shelby Gene, Bernard, Frank, May, Mary, and Loraine.

Ruben was a man of the mountains and a family man. He worked beside his father and brothers in the fields when he wasn't attending school. Upon the onset of the war, Ruben went to fight for his country. The date was March 5, 1943. He was trained in the field of artillery and saw action in the Asiatic Pacific Theater where he was wounded on two occasions. His gallantry under fire was duly noted and he became the beneficiary of two bronze stars.

After World War II ended Ruben came home. He decided to further his education and received a degree in history from Morehead State University. He began teaching in Letcher County, became a principal, and served as an assistant school superintendent. He decided to further his education and went to the University of Tennessee where he pursued a degree in law. He returned to the county and ran for sheriff. He held that position for three years (1974-1977). He then acquired a job for the Kentucky Department of Labor and worked in that post until 1982. At that juncture he ran and won the position of Letcher County Judge Executive. He served in that capacity for twelve years. During his tenure as judge he created a senior citizens facility along with meeting places for them to meet, built a library in Blackey, Kentucky, created the Mountain Heritage Festival, worked with the March of Dimes, volunteered with the American Red Cross and continued contributing to the well being of Letcher county.

Surviving are his wife, Betty Jo Collins Watts, Blackey; a son, Michael Ruben Watts and wife Donna, Roxana; three daughters, Claudia Kyle Godbey and husband Michael, Nicholasville, Nola Yvonne Caudill and husband Jerome, Blackey, and Gwenda Sue Day and husband Tommy, Fredonia; three brothers, Franklin Watts, Alexandria, Curtis Watts, Hallie, and Bernard Watts, Blackey; three sisters, Loraine Caudill, Georgetown, Artha Mae Williams, Blackey, and Mary Blair, Dayton, Ohio; five grandchildren, and two step-grandchildren. He was eighty-seven at his passing.

The Following is a joint resolution designating KY Route 7 as the 'Ruben Watts Highway.'

A JOINT RESOLUTION designating Kentucky Route 7 in Letcher County from the Perry County line to its intersection with Kentucky Route 15 at the western limits of Isom, as the "Ruben Watts Highway" in honor of former Letcher County Judge/Executive Ruben Watts.

WHEREAS, Ruben Watts was born September 7, 1923, in Letcher County; and

WHEREAS, Ruben Watts courageously defended his country by fighting in World War II from March 5, 1943, to January 11, 1946, with the Battery B 168th Field Artillery Battalion; and

WHEREAS, while in the Asiatic Pacific Theater, Ruben Watts received 2 Bronze Stars, a Philippine Liberation Ribbon with 1 Bronze Star, 2 Purple Hearts, the World War II Victory Medal, and a Good Conduct Medal; and

WHEREAS, when Ruben Watts returned from World War II, he attended Morehead State University and received a degree in history; and

WHEREAS, Ruben Watts went on to teach high school for several years in Letcher County and eventually became Letcher County's assistant school superintendant; and

WHEREAS, seeking to continue his education, Ruben Watts attended law school at the University of Tennessee; and

WHEREAS, after his return to Letcher County, Ruben Watts decided to run for the position of Letcher County Sheriff, a position he won and served in from 1974 to 1977; and

WHEREAS, when his career as sheriff ended, Ruben Watts went on to work for the Kentucky Department of Labor; and

WHEREAS, he could not ignore his political calling, and in 1982 Ruben Watts became Letcher County Judge/Executive, a position he held until 1993; and

WHEREAS, during his time as Letcher County Judge/Executive, Ruben Watts played an integral part in many projects that benefitted the citizens of Letcher County, including the creation of the Mountain Heritage Festival and the Blackey Public Library; and

WHEREAS, Ruben Watts' dedication to public service reached beyond his position as Letcher County Judge/Executive. For several years he volunteered for the American Red Cross and the March of Dimes; and

WHEREAS, Ruben Watts is a loving husband to his wife Betty, a loving father to is children: Yvonne Caudill, Gwenda Day, Mike Watts, and Kyle Watts, as well as a proud grandfather to his grandchildren: Micca Watts-Gordon, Michael Ruben Watts, Laura Caudill, Jaime Day, and Elliott Day;

NOW, THEREFORE,

Be it resolved by the General Assembly of the Commonwealth of Kentucky:

Section 4. The Transportation Cabinet shall honor the achievements and public service of Ruben Watts by designating Kentucky Route 7 in Letcher County, from the Perry County line at mile point 0 to its intersection with Kentucky Route 15 at the western limits of Isom at mile point 13.497 as the "Ruben Watts Highway" and shall erect signs denoting this designation.

SOURCES

http://www.themountaineagle.com/news/2011-02-23/Obituaries/Former_judge_sheriff_Ruben_Watts_dies_at_87.html

Interview with Michael Ruben Watts, son of Ruben Watts

RUDOLPH VALINTINO SHORT
Airman 1st Class
Stewart AFB
August 18, 1930-March 30, 1954

Every time I go up to the family cemetery, I go past his grave. I pause for a moment and say thank you. Cousin Rudolph is buried in the same row as my uncles, grandmother, grandfather, brother and mother. The grave was always well kept and had a flagpole above his grave. There was a picture of him enshrined in the stone as well.

I think of him along with my mother's Uncle Lester and Aunt Una B. Short. I remember when mother got the news of his death. We were living in Red Oak, Michigan, and she received a letter. She cried and told me that his plane had crashed. I was seven at the time. I do remember mother stating he was so young to die. He was twenty-three years of age at the time of the crash.

Rudolph Valintino Short was born at home in Jeremiah, Kentucky. The family lived just across the railroad crossing in a lovely brick home approximately three miles from Isom (119) on Route 7. The inside of the home was knotty pine and as a child I remembered how spotless it was.

Until I read the report out of Ft. Bragg, North Carolina, I did not realize that another Letcher County soldier was there as well. His name was PFC William Cook and he was from Whitesburg. According to the official reports, he was in the mess hall at the time of the crash. I also did not recall Rudolph's being declared as missing.

The following is the story as posted by the sources listed:

Ft. Bragg, N.C., March 30 (UP) -- SEVEN KILLED AT FORT BRAGG WHEN BURNING C119 FLYING BOXCAR SMASHES MESS HALL

A crippled C119 Flying Boxcar, its pilot fighting to make an emergency landing on a narrow parade field, crashed into a mess hall here today, killing seven men and injuring 10 others. The bodies of five servicemen were recovered. The heroic pilot, 1st Lt. ALBERT W. PARKS of Cannelton, Ind., died later in the hospital. The body of another soldier aboard the plane was still missing in the ruins. Ten others, including four from the plane, somehow managed to escape with their lives and were rushed to the hospital with injuries.

Officials here said that of the four crew members of the plane, the pilot was killed, two others were injured and one was missing. Three of the five Army passengers were killed and the other two injured. Of the seven men known to be in the mess hall, two were killed and five were injured. The 10th injured man was a rescue worker sprayed with flame when a gas tank exploded.

Eyewitnesses said the huge troop-carrier, listing badly from a burning engine, came roaring over the crowded "Smoke Bomb Hill" troop area at 10 a.m. (EST), struck the top of an officer's barracks and skidded across the parade grounds into the mess hall. The plane exploded into flames and it was nearly two hours before firemen could bring under control the blaze that swept the building.

Airman 1C EUGENE R. SNYDER, 23, of Donelson, Tenn., the flight engineer and the only crew member to walk away from the plane, said PARKS gave orders for the men to prepare to jump as the plane lost altitude.

"The pilot told me to go back and tell the men to get ready to jump. When I got out of my seat, I noticed we were very low. I asked if we were too low. About that time something hit. I looked out the window and saw a telephone pole go by and hit the left wing. Then I ducked down behind the pilot's seat, put my head down and just rode it out."

One officer who saw the crash said the pilot was trying to pull back on the controls as the plane roared down on the barracks area.

"He was trying to avoid hitting the barracks and get in at the best angle for a landing on the parade ground," the officer said.

When the plane struck the roof of the bachelor's officer's quarters, its tail section was torn loose. The plane glided part of the way across the 150-yard wide parade field and then skidded about 100 feet into the mess hall. Soldiers rushed into the flaming mess hall moments after the crash and pulled three men from the rear section of the wrecked plane. However, it was nearly two hours before rescue workers could again get to the plane, which was buried under the charred timbers of the mess hall.

Lt. Col. B. A. KATZ, another eyewitness to the crash, said it "appeared unbelievable that anyone could have survived, either in the plane or in the mess hall. The pilot did a heroic thing trying to avoid hitting a barracks and in attempting to land in the open parade ground, thus saving as many lives as possible," KATZ said.

One officer said that if the plane had crashed two hours later, about 200 men would have been eating lunch in the mess hall.

Official List of the Dead, Missing and Injured

Fort Bragg, N.C., March 30 (UP) -- The official list of dead, missing and injured in today's crash of a C119

Flying Boxcar into a mess hall in the "Smoke Bomb Hill" troop are listed here:

AIR FORCE

- 1st Lt. Albert W. Parks, 25, son of Albert W. B. Parks, Rt. 1, Channelton, Ind., pilot.

ARMY

- Cpl. Osman S. Palmer, 23, Locke Mills, Me.

- Cpl. Robert Dervan, 21, 1014 Whitney Ave., Albany, Ga.

- Pvt. Albert G. Marin JR., 20, Wampole, Mass. -- all attached to the 82nd Airborne Division Quartermaster Co., Ft. Bragg, N.C.

- Cpl. Donald f. Greenlee, 22, Albion, Pa., attached to the Psychological Warfare Center, Ft. Bragg.

- Pvt. 1st C James A. Macre, 22, of Bonnie Doon, N.C., and Creekside, Pa., attached to Psychological Warfare Center, Ft. Bragg.

MISSING

- Airman 1st Class Rudolph V. Short (my cousin) , Stewart AFB, Smyrna, TN
CRITICALLY INJURED

- Pvt. R. E. Salisbury, 18, Columbus, O.

- Chief Warrant Officer William Angeloff, 39, both passengers on the plane.

- Sgt. Henry C. Clay, Cullman, Ala., in the mess hall at the time of the accident

IN LESS SERIOUS CONDITION

- Co-pilot 1st Lt. Raymond Fitzsimmons.

- AFC Eugene r. Snyder, of the plane's crew.

THREE MEN INJURED IN THE MESS HALL

- Edward A. Ross, Darlington, S.C.

- Pfc. Edward Ellison, Chicago, ILL

- Pfc. William Cook, Whitesburg, KY

*Capt. Charles L. Shirley, who rushed to the crash scene, was burned about the hands and arms aiding in rescue efforts.

SOURCES

http://www3.gendisasters.com/north-carolina/11900/ft-bragg-nc-transport-crashes-hall-mar-1954

Ft. Bragg, NC Transport Crashes into Hall, Mar 1954

North Carolina, Death Certificates, 1909-1975

RUSSELL BLAIR
Specialist Five
United States Army
February 1969-December 1970
Army Security Agency Top Secret
Cryptographic Security Clearance
224th Aviation Battalion (RR) Cover name for 224th Army Security Agency Battalion (Aviation) Republic of Vietnam
December 31, 1948-Present

Russell Blair was born on December 31, 1948, to Arlie and Mollie Gay Whitaker Blair. His brother is Arlin James Blair. Arlin is a fellow Vietnam Veteran. His sisters were Deanna Blair Back and Janet Blair Nichols. They are my first cousins. Russell married his childhood sweetheart, Connie Adams Blair. They have one child by the name of Chris Blair.

I first became acquainted with Russell on a visit to Detroit with my mother when I was but a child. We stayed at Aunt Gay's home. I recall seeing the children dressed in cowboy outfits and I thought if I could have something that shiny, I would be a cowboy too.

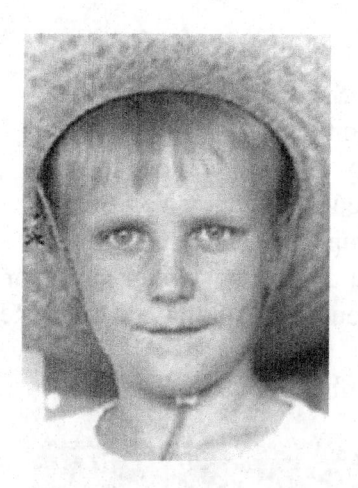

We played, talked and laughed. I became very close to them on that visit. Later mother purchased Uncle Arlie and Aunt Gay's old home place on the left hand fork (Known as Deer Fork). Russell's family moved to Kentucky as well and we became inseparable. We were boys of the mountain and enjoyed the usual rhetoric of youth. Aunt Gay lived on Route 7 just across the railroad bridge. I lived in the first holler as you traveled down the old river road known as Route 7. It was about a mile in distance at the most. The times we spent as youth playing, attending school and dreaming was priceless.

Russell went into military service in 1969, at the height of the Vietnam War. Following Basic Training at Fort Knox, Kentucky, he was assigned to the Army Security Agency, at Vint Hill Farm Station, Warrenton, Virginia. From there he went to Vietnam, where he served in the 224th Aviation Battalion (Radio Research), at Long Thanh North Army Airfield.

The 224th Aviation Battalion (Radio Research) was activated in Saigon, Vietnam, on June 1, 1966. Four companies with a total of six aircraft and one hundred fifty-nine personnel initially comprised the battalion, but it quickly expanded in size. By July 1967, the battalion had reached its highest strength of one thousand sixty-six personnel. Within two years thirty aircraft had been assigned to the unit. On December 1, 1968, it was re-designated Headquarters and Headquarters Company, 224th Aviation Battalion.

During his tenure as a soldier in Vietnam, several operations transpired. Included in them were Operation Menu (a covert bombing campaign conducted in Cambodia), Battle of Hamburger Hill made famous by the Clint Eastwood movie, Apache Snow (A Shau Valley), and Operation Hammer. All operations had to have intelligence and surveillance from above. These men who did so are unsung heroes.

On May 19, 1971, the battalion was re-designated the 224th Army Security Agency Aviation Battalion. The battalion participated in fifteen campaigns and received three awards of the Meritorious Unit Commendation, along with the Vietnamese Cross of Gallantry with Palm during its service in the Vietnam Conflict.

Upon discharge, Russell followed his passion of serving his country and became a celebrated United States Marshal. He retired from the U.S. Marshals Service in 2001, and resides in Jeremiah, Kentucky. He lives only a few hundred yards from his Kentucky childhood home. I admire his achievements and am proud to have him as a 1st cousin.

SOURCES

Interview with Russell Blair

ttp://www.nasaa-home.org/history/lineage/224.htm

wikipedia.org/wiki/1969_in_the_Vietnam_War

http://en.wikipedia.org/wiki/United_States_Army_Intelligence_and_Security_Command

http://www.inscom.army.mil/Contact.aspx?text=off&size=12pt

http://www.airspacemag.com/military-aviation/mohawk.html

RUSTY HUNTER CHRISTIAN
Staff Sergeant
Company C
2nd Battalion
1st Special Forces Group Airborne
Green Beret
November 15, 1985-January 28, 2010

Staff Sergeant Christian was a young man from Greenville, Tennessee. He was well liked by all who met him. He loved his family, life and his country. He was to become a man of destiny. He was a Green Beret. This is his story.

Rusty was born to Donna Morelock Ball (remarried). His stepfather is James 'Jim' Ball of Kingsport, Tennessee. Michael Christian (biological father) lives in Laurel Bloomery, Tennessee. Rusty has one brother, Aaron Christian, who resides in Kingsport. Rusty attended school in Greenville and graduated from Greenville High School. While at Greenville High School he played football until a knee injury curtailed his playing. He was a drummer and played in a band called Bell Tower Band.

Rusty Hunter Christian enlisted in the U.S. Army on February 4, 2004. He completed basic training and advanced individual training (AIT). He was assigned to the 3rd Brigade, 2nd Infantry at Joint Base Lewis-McChord, Washington. He was deployed to Afghanistan. Upon his return he decided he wanted to do even more for his country so he applied and was accepted in several different trainings.

He went to different schools and attended the following: U.S. Army Airborne School, Advanced Leaders Course, Warrior Leaders Course, Combat Life Savers Course, Survival, Evasion, Resistance and Escape Course, Defense Language Institute Indonesian Course and the Special Forces Qualification Course.

In 2008, Christian volunteered and was accepted into the Special Forces. He qualified in August of 2009, and was bestowed the coveted Green Beret. He became one of the elite. His assignment was to the 2nd Battalion, 1st Special Forces as an engineer sergeant.

On January 28, 2010, while on patrol in Oruzgan Province, Afghanistan, Staff Sergeant Rusty Hunter Christian was Killed In Action (KIA) by an Improvised Explosive Device (IED). He was stationed in Camp Cobra. This was his second deployment. Sgt Christian was buried in Arlington Cemetery with full military honors worthy of his sacrifice. His mortal remains rest in section 60, site 9050. He was twenty-four years old.

Staff Sergeant Christian is a true unsung American hero and continues to wear his green beret with pride. Christian is survived by his wife, Amber Christian and their children, Taylor and Gavin Christian of Orting, Washington, along with his parents.

MEDALS AND AWARDS

Two Army Commendation Medals, Army Achievement Medal, Army Good Conduct Medal, National Defense Service Medal, Iraq Campaign Medal with one campaign star, Global War on Terrorism

Service Medal, Non-commissioned Officer Professional Development Ribbon with numeral 2 device, Army Service Ribbon, the Overseas Service Ribbon, Army Valorous Unit Award and the Meritorious Unit Citation, Parachutist Badge, Combat Infantryman Badge, Expert Infantryman Badge and the Special Forces tab. He was posthumously awarded the Bronze Star Medal, Purple Heart, Afghanistan Campaign Medal with one campaign star and the Meritorious Service Medal.

SOURCES

http://greenberetfoundation.org/index.html

http://arlingtoncemetery.net/rusty-christian.htm

http://projects.militarytimes.com/valor/army-staff-sgt-rusty-h-christian/4494728

http://freedomremembered.com/index.php/staff-sgt-rusty-h-christian/

http://genforum.genealogy.com/morelock/messages/537.html

http://army.togetherweserved.com/army/servlet/tws.webapp.WebApp?cmd=ShadowBoxProfile&type=Person&ID=277407

http://www.linkedin.com/groups/Today-we-remember-SSG-Rusty-3921872.S.208626830

http://arlingtoncemetery.net/enduring-freedom.htm

SERGEANT DRISCOLL
69th New York Volunteers
Irish Brigade
Federal Army of the Potomac
Malvern Hill, Virginia
July 1, 1862

From the annuals of history comes a gripping saga of war. It is a tragic incident that was not unique during the War Between the States. This incident took place in Virginia, when fellow Americans clashed in an epic battle for freedom.

During the Seven Day's Campaign around Richmond, Virginia, General Robert E. Lee had a string of victories in which he pushed the Federal forces from the doorsteps of Richmond back towards Washington City. The cost would be over thirty thousand casualties lost from both armies. Each battle was intense and the final assault at Malvern Hill proved to be just as deadly. From June 25 through July 1, 1862, America was torn asunder by the drums of war. This is just one of the thousands of stories left upon the battlefield.

His name was Sergeant Driscoll. He enlisted into the Union army based on his beliefs and was considered to be one of the best shots in the Brigade. His son had chosen to join the Confederate army and, due to his tenacity of spirit and audaciousness, was promoted to an officer. Both served their hearts' calling. Both loved their country. Both loved their family yet each heard a different drum.

On July 1, 1862, a fierce battle raged at Malvern Hill, in Henrico County, Virginia. The Federal forces found themselves being hammered by a company of Confederates within the tree line. Every time the boys in blue tried to advance, they were greeted by a hail of bullets which were singing and stinging like hornets. They were in dire straits.

Captain D.P. Conyngham, of the famed Irish Brigade, noted that the well trained rebel soldiers within the clump of trees were commanded by a bold and daring officer. The junior officer was seen dashing around fortifying his position and directing the volley with precision. He knew if he was to advance, he would have to take out the leadership. He called upon his sergeant to do just that. Sergeant Driscoll took careful aim and waited until the Confederate officer stepped out from behind the tree line. He did not have long to wait. As predicted, the officer showed himself and Sergeant Driscoll's bullet immediately found its mark. The Confederate officer was cut down in his tracks and his company began to dissolve.

The company under Captain David Power Conyngham rallied and moved towards their objective. Upon reaching the body of the brave Confederate officer, the captain told Sergeant Driscoll to insure that the officer was dead. The words of Captain Conyngham captured the moment.

"I stood looking on, Driscoll turned him over on his back. He opened his eyes for a moment and faintly murmured 'Father' and closed them forever.

"I will forever recollect the frantic grief of Driscoll; it was harrowing to witness. The dead soldier was his son who had gone South before the war."

Sergeant Driscoll stood there in shock and the look upon his face cannot be expressed by words. The company was ordered to charge but the Sergeant remained glued to the scene. The men in blue pressed on and soon were in the heat of the battle. Suddenly the men noticed Sergeant Driscoll charge past them. He had taken off his coat and probably laid it over his son as tribute to him. He charged them without thought of himself, calling out to all to follow him. A bullet hit its mark and he fell but immediately was up charging those men who had followed his son in battle. Suddenly another volley hit him and he fell to the ground to move no more. He answered the call of his son and went home to once again become the boy's father.

I cannot fathom the father's anguish, as he gazed down upon his son knowing that he had killed him. It reminds me of yet another story. This is a story of hope. This is a story of altruistic love, as described in John 3: 16: *"For God so loved the world that He gave His only begotten son, that whosoever shall believe in Him shall not perish but have everlasting life."* Can you imagine the anguish in God's heart as He offered His only begotten son to die for all of humanity? Can you grasp the significance of that moment when God looked away so that His son could die in order for us to live?

God's innocent lamb was tortured for six hours and died upon a cross in the most agonizing manner, yet He suffered with dignity for humanity. No wonder the centurion cried out that *'surely this was the son of God'*. How could God watch His only begotten son beaten, battered, and bruised for the sins of others, since God is separated from sin like the east is from the west? The answer is that God could not watch. Upon Jesus' death, the veil was torn and the earth trembled. The door to heaven was opened for mankind. Grateful for my heavenly father who loved m enough to offer His son.

SOURCES

http://www.eyewitnesstohistory.com/malvern.htm

The Irish Brigade and Its Campaigns, Conyngham, D.P., With Some Accounts of the Corcoran Legion, and Sketches of the Principal Officers, (1867) (reprinted in Botkin, B.A., A Civil War Treasury of Tales, Legends and Folklore, 1960);

Battle Cry of Freedom: The Civil War Era, McPherson, James P, (1988)

http://www.bencaudill.com/chaplain/lesson269_10.html
http://news.google.com/newspapers?nid=950&dat=19790525&id=f1tQAAAAIBAJ&sjid=21gDAAAAIBAJ&pg=4954,2409361

https://archive.org/details/irishbrigadeand00adgoog

http://en.wikipedia.org/wiki/69th_Infantry_Regiment_(New_York)

SHELBA JEAN PROFFITT

Doctor Shelba Proffitt was born on Little Colley Creek, in Letcher County, Kentucky, which is located in the mountains of southeastern part of the state. Her parents were Stanley and Frankie Proffitt, both descending from the early pioneers in the mountains of southeastern Kentucky and southwestern Virginia. Shelba also had a brother, Wallace, who is now deceased. Growing up, she was an avid sportswoman and hunter, being a very good shot with a rifle. After attending one of the small elementary schools in the county, she graduated in 1954 from Whitesburg High School.

Upon graduation, she was faced with either continuing her education or becoming a book keeper for her father's coal mining company. Her desire for a better education won out and she attended Centre College in Danville, Kentucky, where she obtained a Bachelors degree in chemistry and physics. Upon graduation, Shelba attended the University of Alabama in Huntsville, where she received her Masters. Then she obtained her Doctorate in technology management from the Southeastern Institute of Technology in Hunstville.

She began her federal government career with the Wernher von Braun's space team in Huntsville. She later joined the U.S. Army Missile Command, where she spent thirteen years developing advanced tactical weapons. It was during this time period in 1973, she obtained one of her dreams, becoming a licensed pilot. Also during this time period, Shelba developed liquid crystals, that when applied to wings and fins of rockets or missiles, would show structural flaws. She was also instrumental in developing a thermometer using liquid crystals to monitor a human's temperature, especially helpful for infants.

In 1980, she moved to the U.S. Army Space and Missile Defense Command (USASMDC). Her research in this area helped establish her as an expert on battle management; command, control and communications; and space surveillance technologies as well as national and international threats. Dr. Proffitt acquired an in-depth knowledge of strategic and tactical defense architectures and each weapon system concept required to support both the national defense missile and the theater and tactical missile defense missions. This staggering defense job was handled perfectly by a young woman from the mountains of Kentucky.

In 1990, Dr. Shelba Jean Proffitt became the first female member of the Senior Executive Service of the USASMDC. As director of Advanced Technology Directorate and later director of Sensors Directorate, she managed programs to assess and resolve technology issues for both tactical and strategic missile defense.

In 1995, Shelba received the prestigious Meritorious Executive Presidential Rank Award for exceptional service. The presentation of the award was performed at the Pentagon by the Secretary of the Army, Togo West Jr. Nationally and internationally recognized as an expert in leading edge strategic and tactical defense technologies, Dr. Proffitt was responsible for executive management of the Army's Surveillance, Acquisition, Tracking and Kill assessment program under the Ballistic Missile Defense Organization. Her responsibilities ranged from establishing requirements through design and development of future defense sensors, as well as directing system definition, development and test demonstrations for the ground-based elements of the NMD System, including the interceptor, radar and associated battle management. She was also responsible for maintaining and managing the Missile Defense Data Center. As a result of her success in research and development, the doctor has served as an adviser to the North Atlantic Treaty Organization (NATO), the directors of the DBMO, Army Science Boards, the Army Space Council and numerous other organizations. This special lady continued to make the people of the mountains of southeastern Kentucky proud of her.

In 2000, Dr. Proffitt became deputy program executive officer of the Air and Missile Defense. Some of her responsibilities were to develop, acquire and field air and missile defense weapons systems and sensors, such as the much acclaimed advanced Patriot Missile. In 2001, she was appointed the acting Program Executive Officer. Through 2005, Dr. Proffitt interfaced with the Secretary of Defense Department of the Army, the Missile Defense Agency, State and National legislators and local community officials. In this position, she secured and executed an annual budget of over two billion dollars. Currently the doctor is a consultant on Air, Space and Missile Defense. She recently loaned a piece of the first Scud Missile to be shot down by a Patriot Missile to the Letcher County Military Museum, which is located in her home town of Whitesburg, Kentucky. The piece of missile was presented to her on behalf of a grateful nation. Many more of Dr. Proffitt's achievements and awards are displayed in the Whitesburg Museum as well.

Dr. Proffitt currently resides in Huntsville, Alabama, and remains active in not only consulting work, but in local, as well as national, private organizations. Not to be lessened in nature, but Shelba also helped transfer Department of Defense technology to private industry, including several medical applications. An example was using unique laser beams to determine the reproduction of cancer cells. Another example was using liquid crystals as thermal sensors for cancer detection and mapping. In the regular industry, current applications that use liquid crystals for television and digital readouts are based on her early research into liquid crystals for defense applications.

As if all of her research and work was not a full time schedule, Shelba has also published over twenty-five technical papers and holds two patents. The woman who became the U.S. Army Space and Strategic Defense Command's first female member of the Senior Executive Service received the prestigious Meritorious Executive Service Presidential Rank Award. She has also received second place for Outstanding Woman in the Department of the Army, Women in Science and Engineering Lifetime Achievement Award, the 1999 Von Braun National Space Club's Engineer of the Year Award, and the Kentucky's Outstanding Young Woman of America. In 2004, she was inducted into Kentucky's Aviation Hall of Fame, and in 2005, inducted into the Air, Space and Missile Defense Hall of Fame.

After having worked over forty years in managing space and missile research, as well as in the fields of development, demonstration, acquisition and fielding, this hard-working lady now finds herself consulting in these areas. She has also been recognized for her efforts in helping and encouraging other women to pursue their dreams, especially in the fields of science and engineering. When asked what she considered to be one of her best accomplishments, the doctor replied that overseeing the fruition of a defense system for incoming, long-range missiles had been, and still is, her biggest goal. This woman from the mountains has proven that regardless of your gender or where you are from, one can still become a benefit to your country's call, and an exceptional one at that. Dr. Proffitt has shown this by her unapproachable contributions to a grateful nation. Though having slowed down in her work, this remarkable lady explained her not stopping completely when she said *"Success is a journey, not an event"*. Submitted by Richard G. Brown

SHELBY WAYNE NEASE
Battery D
4th Missile Battery
59th Artillery
February 6, 1943-July 18, 1989

I have the honor of having dear friends whom I have grown quite attached. The family has always been receptive to me and I have found them to be fun loving and full of life. As I became more acquainted I learned of the husband and father. I remembered him as a police officer and a Letcher County native. His story and that of the family is a vivid example of a true unsung hero.

Shelby Wayne Nease was born on February 6, 1943 in the hills of Appalachia. He was reared in the Colson area of Letcher County, Kentucky. His parents were Bradley and Verna Nease. His brother Roger still lives in Colson and he has three sisters by the name of Judy Wilson of Amelia Island, FL, Carol Ann Nease of Lexington (she is a dear friend of mine from the Calvary College days!) , and Freida Townsend of Atlanta, Georgia. He also had half brothers and sisters.

Shelby loved the mountains and made friends easily. He graduated in 1961 from Whitesburg High School.

In October of 1961, he joined the United States Army and was sent to Fort Knox, Kentucky. He graduated on January 12, 1962. At that juncture he was with Company C, 15th Battalion, of the 5th Regiment. In 1962, he was assigned to Fort Story, Virginia.

According to the source listed below, *'Fort Story is the Army's only training facility for logistics-over-the-shore operations to train troops on amphibious equipment and to practice the transfer of military cargo from ship to shore.'* It is located on the beautiful Chesapeake Bay within the city of Virginia Beach, Virginia. His wife Brenda recalled visiting the area on vacation with their two children, April and Rachel.

Shelby was discharged from the military on September 30, 1967. He decided to return to school. He attended Lee's Junior College in Jackson. He then applied and was accepted as a candidate with the Kentucky State Police. He successfully completed the KSP Academy on May 27, 1966, and began his career as a Kentucky State Trooper. He served the following areas: Morehead Post, Pikeville Post, Hazard Post and Richmond Post.

On March 1, 1971, he resigned his position to become a Railroad Police Officer (Special Agent) with the L and N Railroad. His area was much of Eastern Kentucky and parts of Virginia. His job was to investigate crimes against the railroad. One month later Shelby married Brenda Brashear who was from Fusonia, Kentucky. They built a home in the Viper community. They have two daughters by the name of April Michelle and Rachel Beth. According to Mrs. Nease, *"He was a woodworker as he made dulcimers as well as pieces of furniture from walnut wood; he was a bee keeper who loved to share sashes of honey with friends, family, and neighbors. He enjoyed landscaping and reading. He had a special love of history and particularly enjoyed traveling to Civil War sites."*

On July 18, 1989, Shelby was senselessly murdered in Harlan County, Kentucky, while he was investigating a copper wire theft which belonged to CSX Railroad. Shelby had been working in Virginia during the summer of 1989, due to strike issues. He was to return to Virginia, but switched because of the amount of copper wire thefts occurring in Harlan County, Kentucky. Reportedly Shelby attempted to overtake men fleeing the scene. The four men involved in the theft overpowered him. Shelby was a strong athletic man and it had to take all four to subdue him. Shelby was brutally beaten to death while serving as a Special Agent of the railroad. He had been employed as a Special Agent for the railroad of eighteen years and died in the line of duty serving the people and property he was sworn to protect.

Brenda Nease, his widow stated, *"He was a well-respected community man who shared his laughter, humor and good nature with so many. He was so proud of his daughters as he encouraged them to appreciate the love of the outdoors, the importance of learning and assuming duties around the home, as well as being responsible for their own actions. As I am always mindful of the loss of my husband, I embrace his memory and treasure the devoted love we shared. How can I forget carrying limbs from trees Shelby cut as we cleared the land where we would build our home, sitting up together with our children when they were sick, or looking forward to his kiss on the check when we would leave and return from work each day, and that last kiss as he drove off to work on July 18, 1989."*

Mrs. Debbie Fugate (sister to Brenda Nease) shared with me the following information. *"There were mines in Harlan County, Kentucky, that was having a strike in 1979, and Shelby was having to spend a week on and a week off over there where they would have to drive the trains across the picket line and then let the union rail workers take it from there. While in Harlan County, Kentucky, someone blew up the track and wrecked the engine he was riding. We were all very worried about him doing that work and were relieved when he returned home."*

One of the many tributes to Shelby was from a mother who lost her son to such a dastardly deed. Her reflections are: *"Your heroism and service is honored today, the twenty-first anniversary of your death. Your memory lives and you continue to inspire. Thank you for your service. My cherished son Larry Lasater was a fellow police officer who was murdered in the line of duty on April 24, 2005, while serving as a Pittsburg, CA police officer. Time never diminishes respect. Your memory will always be honored and revered. Rest In Peace. I pray for solace for all those who love and miss you for I know both the pain and pride are forever. Phyllis Loya, mother of fallen officer Larry Lasater; dated July 18, 2010".*

Shelby's legacy lives on through his family members, widow and girls. All have been productive and work for the betterment of our region. They say a good person touches seven generations and a great person touches eternity. Shelby Wayne Nease touched the hearts of many and will be remembered by countless generations.

SOURCES

Interview with Mrs. Brenda Nease

Mrs. Brenda Nease personal reflections and writings

Interview with Mrs. Debbie Fugate (sister-in-law)

http://www.military.com/base-guide/fort-story

http://usmilitary.about.com/od/armybaseprofiles/ss/story.htm

http://www.odmp.org/officer/reflections/9873-special-agent-shelby-wayne-nease

http://www.themountaineagle.com/news/2010-10-20/Obituaries/Services_are_held_for_Verna_Nease.html

Email data from Rachel Nease Lingenfelter

STEVIE RAY GIBSON
Private First Class
A Company
2nd Battalion
7th CAVALRY
1st Cavalry Division
April 23, 1948-March 15, 1967

I remember Stevie. I was in a band called The Penny Royals and we used to play at the community center in Blackey. Roaxana is only about five miles from that location. Stevie would be in the crowd either dancing or talking to our friends. At breaks the band members got to know him and others, as the area is rural.

Stevie was born on April 23, 1948. He was from Roxana, Kentucky. Roxana is a little villa surrounded by mountains and winding roads. Stevie was in the army and trained as an 11 B (bush) 20: infantryman. His Id number was 13870240. He arrived in Vietnam on February 27, 1967. Less than a month later he was killed in the Binh Thuan Province. He was eighteen years of age. His body was recovered and returned home for a military funeral. His name is listed on the Vietnam Memorial; Panel 16E, Line 84.

On homestead one of his brothers-in-arms wrote the following: *"Stevie Ray Gibson was a 17 year old kid from Kentucky when he joined the Army and was assigned to A/2/12 for Basic Training along with the original group in December, 1965. He remained with* us through our training and was on our roster as late as July 31st, 1966. At first I thought that Stevie did not deploy with us because he was only 17, but after some research, I found out that he had turned 18 years old on April 23rd, 1966. It may be one of those mysteries we'll never unravel. Stevie eventually arrived in Vietnam on February 27th, 1967 as a replacement troop for the 1st Cavalry Division in II Corps area. He survived 16 days in country. We will honor him as a Brother as long as one member of the Association is around to carry on the proud tradition. The last time I went to the Wall I took a photo of panel 16, showing Thomas Nickerson and Clint Smith's inscription. Little did I know at the time that I also recorded most of Stevie Ray's inscription."

SOURCES

URL: www.VirtualWall.org/dg/GibsonSR01a.htm

http://army.togetherweserved.com/army/servlet/tws.webapp.WebApp?cmd=ShadowBoxProfile&type=Person&ID=49781

http://www.memorialbracelets.com/details.php?nameID=72585&eventID=26&catID=1&pid=67&subID=32&pagenum=18&letter=G

http://alphaassociation.homestead.com/files/gibsontribute.htm

TED COOK
Supply Sergeant
19th Ordinance/17th Ordinance
Survivor of the Bataan Death March
WWII
August 25, 1919-March 28, 2013

(Patsy and Ted Cook-2011)

Few can fathom the suffering some men endured for their country. Few have witnessed such destruction and death. Four Letcher County men were there during the death march of Bantaan. This is one of their stories. May we all realize the price of freedom is paid with the blood of martyrs.

Ted Cook was born on August 25, 1919. He was born in a little place named Democrat, Letcher County, Kentucky. He grew up in typical mountain fashion, enjoying the games of the hills and hollows. He was a typical young man who loved sports. Little did he realize the significance of his life and the example he placed on the altar of freedom for us all. Ted went to Whitesburg High School where he played basketball and football. He graduated in 1938, and was recognized for his sports skills by receiving a trophy from Mayor Bill Collins. He was named to the All county Basketball team.

On June 17, 1940, approximately two years after he graduated from high school, Ted volunteered for military service. He enlisted and was sent to Fort Knox. He became a supply sergeant for the 19th Ordinance Company. The 19th was later renamed as the 17th Ordinance and trained with the 192nd Tank Battalion. Sgt Cook's position was maintenance on tanks.

On a summer day in 1941, Ted was sent overseas. His company left from Angel Island (San Francisco) on their way to the Philippine Islands. The 17th Ordinance was accompanied by the 194th to an uncertain destiny. They arrived in the Philippines on September 26, 1941.

In the latter part of the month of November, 1941, the 192nd joined with the 17th and the 194th Tank Battalion. They formed the 1st Provisional Tank Group. Sgt Cook's job was to keep the one hundred four tanks in working order.

Upon the sneak attack on Pearl Harbor the battalions were ordered to guard the Clark Airfield. On December 8, 1941, Ted was eating his lunch when he heard the sound of planes. He stated he was about three miles from the airfield. He watched as Japanese Zeros bombed the airfield. One can only imagine the feeling of those men seeing aircraft scarp the land.

On December 22, 1941, a platoon of B Company, 192nd Tanks engaged Japanese tanks near Lingayen Gulf. Four tanks were lost, and the tank crew of the lead tank was captured. One of the worst experiences Sgt Cook had to do was to remove the body of Private First Class (PFC) Henry Deckert. He was a machine gunner on the surviving tank. During the engagement with the Japanese, a shell hit the bow gun port. The concussion from the shell entered the tank blowing off Deckert's head. Ted remembered that the surviving tank crew members and the floor of the tank were covered in blood.

As the Allied forces of Filipinos and Americans withdrew into the Bataan peninsula, Sgt Cook reflected upon blowing up fifty-five gallon drums of gasoline so they wouldn't fall into enemy hands. Sgt Cook recalled that they were harassed all the way during the withdrawal.

The fighting was fierce but on April 9, 1942, Sgt Cook and his company became Prisoners of War (POW). A Letcher County Native would take part in the Bataan Death March from Mariveles to San Fernando. One incident he remembered was when the death march took them by Cabcaben. The POWS were ordered to sit in front of the artillery. The Corregidor fired back and as the shells landed they attempted to find any cover available. Apparently the POWS were being used as human shields.

When interviewed by Military.com Sgt. Cook described the deprivation he felt: "There were times when I was so thirsty, I could see water when it wasn't even there. I could see the little creek that used to run by my family's home very often."

Sgt Cook stated that at San Fernando, they were packed into boxcars used to haul sugarcane. They were one hundred men per car. Several men died in route. The men were forced to march from Capas to Camp O'Donnell.

At Camp O'Donnell conditions were harsh. The base was unfinished and there was one water faucet for the base. Cook became a victim of malaria. He stated that if it wasn't for Sgt Albert Onacki, he would have died. The sergeant gave money so a Filipino could get him quinine, thus saving his life.

In early June 1942, Cook was transferred to Cabanatuan when the new camp opened. He remained in the camp until he went out on a work detail to Clark Field to build runways. In the summer of 1944, American planes began to appear in the sky. Cook and the other Americans knew that U. S. troops were getting nearer to the Philippines. Knowing that it was just a matter of time before the Americans would invade the Philippines, the Japanese began to ship large numbers of POWs to Japan or other occupied countries.

On August 25, 1944, on his 25th birthday, Sgt Cook was sent to Bilibid Prison. Two days later, he was among one thousand thirty-five prisoners placed on the "hell ship" Noto Maru which sailed for Japan. The ship stopped at Takao (Kaohsiung) and Keelung, Formosa (Taiwan). The ship docked at Moji in southern Japan where the POWs were split up and sent to several camps. Sgt Cook sent to Nagoya #6B. Mr. Cook's wife, Patsy, said that he told her the eleven day journey on the hell ship was "the worst part of the imprisonment."

The prisoners in the camp worked smelting manganese, in a machine shop, and in a quarry. Cook remained in this camp until he was liberated in 1945. He returned to the U.S. in October of 1945, aboard a ship that landed in San Francisco, California.

After the war, Mr. Cook returned to Whitesburg and married Lettie June Craft on August 30, 1948, at Thornton. Mr. Cook enrolled at Eastern Kentucky State Teachers College in Richmond where in 1953; he was honored for his "superior record." He was hired to teach and coach at Lebanon High School in Marion County. He also taught at Lafayette High School and Bryan Station High School in Lexington.

In September 1960, Lettie Cook died (39 years old) in Cincinnati, Ohio. Ted Cook went back to Letcher

County and was hired as supervisor of instruction. In 1961, he became an assistant principal and athletic director at Whitesburg High School and was in charge of the Whitesburg city swimming pool that summer. He also married Patsy Back Cook that year. In 1963, Cook left Letcher County to accept a job as Director of Adult Education with the Kentucky Department of Education, a position he held for 16 years.

Patsy Cook said her husband rarely talked about his war experiences until the 1980s, when they took a trip to the Philippines with other survivors of Bataan. "That seemed to just start to open things up," she said. "He started remembering more detail." He became an active member of The Defenders of Bataan and Corregidor.

He also was a member of Beaumont Presbyterian Church and because of his faith in God, he forgave those who did him harm while he was a POW. He enjoyed playing golf and watching sports, especially the University of Kentucky Wildcats.

Ted Cook, 93, of Lexington, died Thursday, March 28, 2013, at Thomson-Hood Veterans Center in Wilmore. He is survived by his wife of 52 years, Patsy Back Cook, and three children, Richard Cook and his wife Patricia, Jackie Merrifield and her husband Ron, and Libby Leedy and her husband Steve, all of Lexington.

The following was provided by permission of
Mountain Eagle and
Author Ben Gish
Published in April 10, 2013

It was a Saturday night in April and members of a Whitesburg High School organization known as the Girl Reserves were busy with a banquet they sponsored yearly to honor the school's football and basketball players. As the girls and their guests sat in the basement of the Whitesburg Presbyterian Church for a dinner of meatloaf, potatoes, hot biscuits and coleslaw, Reserves President Judy Craft asked the attendees to remember WHS graduate Ted Cook.

Cook, a 22-year-old supply sergeant in the U.S. Army, hadn't been heard from since he was transferred to the Philippines late the previous November, about two weeks before the United States officially entered World War II.

Miss Craft's words, spoken on April 4, 1942, were "so well chosen and sincere they brought tears to the eyes of everyone," The Mountain Eagle reported six days later. "She told the audience that as she sat there she had been looking at the trophy which was won by the football team of 1938, and she recalled that this handsome trophy was received by Sgt. Ted Cook. After a minute of silence the entire assembly burst into resounding applause."

Nearly a year after the banquet, Cook's possible whereabouts became known when his parents, Floyd and Ella Richardson Cook, received a telegram from the Army Adjutant General's office informing them their son may have been taken prisoner by the Imperial Japanese government. The message was dated March 25, 1943.

What no one would know for certain until after World War II formally ended was that Cook had indeed been captured on April 9, 1942, just five days after his service was honored at the WHS banquet. He was taken prisoner with about 63,000 Filipino soldiers and 12,000 American soldiers after they were forced to surrender after three months of fighting on the Bataan Peninsula to keep the Japanese from capturing the Philippines.

The story of Sgt. Cook, a native of the community of Democrat in Letcher County, is being revisited in the wake of his death about two weeks ago in a veteran's center in the central Kentucky town of Wilmore. Cook was 93 when he died on March 28, and had been one of the few remaining survivors of the World War II atrocity that became known as the Bataan Death March.

The six-day, 78.9-mile "death march" from the southern tip of Bataan to POW camps to the north began on the same day Cook and the other troops — including at least three other soldiers from Letcher County — surrendered. Japanese soldiers forced the prisoners to walk through extreme tropical heat with little food or water. Many of the prisoners were already severely malnourished before their capture because Japanese blockades and a Navy decimated by the bombing of Pearl Harbor had prevented the U.S. from getting food and supplies to the Philippines.

The Army says that as many as 50,000 Filipino prisoners and 8,000 American soldiers died as prisoners from the Battle of Bataan. Many died en route to POW camps after being denied food and water. Some were run over by trucks after they fell from being too weak to walk. Others were beheaded, shot, or bayoneted.

Even after the prisoners reached the POW camps, as many as 400 of them continued dying each day, some from torture and malnutrition, others from malaria, dysentery, beriberi and other tropical diseases.

"In Bataan we had eaten, among other things, lizards and monkeys and horse meat," Pvt. Clarence J. Daniels of McRoberts wrote in a letter to The Eagle in January 1946. "At Cabanatuan [a POW camp] we ate, if we could get them, dogs, cats, snakes, and water buffalo. Our main diet usually consisted of rice and thin watery soup. Lugaw, by the way, is boiled watery rice, and there were plenty of worms and weevils in what we got."

The first soldier from Letcher County to be released from a Japanese prison camp associated with the Battle of Bataan was Army Air Corps Sgt. James Monroe Combs, whose story was told in the April 12, 1945, edition of The Eagle.

Sgt. Combs, a 1938 graduate of Whitesburg High School, was rescued from Bilibid Prison by American forces on February 4, 1945. While visiting the newspaper's offices after returning to Letcher County about two months after he was freed, Combs said of his Japanese captors: "None of them treated the Americans like humans. [They] were to a man cruel and brutal."

"Sgt. Combs said that at one time he got down to weighing only 110 pounds, whereas he normally weighs anywhere from 190 to 195 pounds," the front-page story said. "When he was liberated he weighed 134 pounds, and since February 4 he has gained 50 pounds."

(Combs was a son of a former Letcher County sheriff, Jim Combs, who had been killed in an auto accident at Rockhouse a few years earlier.)

Sgt. Cook, also a 1938, graduate of WHS, joined the Army in 1940, and went to the Philippines after being assigned to a tank maintenance unit there before Japan bombed Pearl Harbor. The first written evidence that his family members and friends were concerned about his safety appeared on the front page of the March 12, 1942, edition of The Eagle. The story mentioned that Cook had last been heard from on November 24, 1941. Aside from Cook's being mentioned at the WHS banquet that following April, it was nearly another full year before his name would appear in print again. This time a headline on the front page of the April 1, 1943, edition of The Eagle announced "Telegram Brings Sad News" and told of Cook's parents being notified by telegram of his apparent POW status.

The fourth Letcher County soldier known to have survived captivity after being taken prisoner after the Battle of Bataan was Sgt. Daniel O. Webb of Mayking. Just four months after the Allies surrendered, Webb was among the first group of prisoners crowded into cargo holds of "hell ships" and transported from the Philippines to Japan, where they were forced into slave labor.

The hell ship on which Webb was placed, the Tottori Maru, left the Philippines on October 8, 1942. On August 25, 1944, Sgt. Cook and Pvt. Daniels were among 1,035 prisoners placed on the hell ship Noto Maru. Once in Japan, all three men were forced to work under grueling conditions in an enemy steel mill until August 14, 1945, when they were liberated after the Japanese agreed to surrender.

On Sept. 20, 1945, The Eagle reported that Cook's parents "received word this week that their son, who has been a prisoner of the Japs for more than three years had been liberated and was OK. Whitesburg people were all rejoicing along with the family, as Ted was one of the best loved boys in town. He is a graduate of WHS and was captain of the football team while in school. He also has another brother, Amos Cook, somewhere in the European theatre."

Cook, Daniels and Webb were finally returned to the U.S. in October 1945 aboard a ship that landed in San Francisco.

The October 14, 1947, edition of The Eagle carried the news that both Sgt. Cook and Sgt. Webb were among the surviving war prisoners cited in formal charges against Captain Keigi Nagahara, who was convicted of war crimes for his treatment of the Bataan prisoners after they arrived in Japan.

Known as the "One Armed Bandit" because he only had one arm, Nagahara was convicted of charges related to forcing sick prisoners to work and with misappropriating Red Cross supplies. The charges also said Nagahara forced Cook, Webb and others to be held without blankets in freezing-cold cells that were too small to permit them "to lie down, stand up or sit down."

"The walls had barbed wire around them so that the imprisoned could not even lean against them," the complaint against Hagahara said.

"All prisoners in the camp were utilized by the Japanese as laborers in two steel plants where the heat from the blast furnaces was unbearable," the complaint added. "As a punishment for prisoners, guards are said to have forced the men to stand a few feet away from the furnaces facing the intense heat and looking into the blinding light."

"Beatings usually accompanied this treatment while prisoners were allegedly forced to hold 50-pound wrenches over their heads while facing the furnaces," the complaint continued. "Severe burns and blisters always resulted from the treatment. One prisoner was rendered blind by the intense light."

After leaving the Army in 1947, Ted Cook returned to Letcher County and was married at Thornton to Lettie June Craft on August 30, 1948.

After a wedding trip to Canada, Cook enrolled at Eastern Kentucky State Teachers College in Richmond, where in 1953, he was honored for his "superior record." He was hired later that same year to teach and coach at Lebanon High School.

After Lettie Cook died at age 39 in Cincinnati in September of 1960, Ted Cook was hired as supervisor of instruction in the Letcher County School System. In 1961, he became an assistant principal and athletics director at Whitesburg High School and was in charge of Whites-burg city swimming pool that summer.

While here, Cook served on a committee that adopted a new "student report card" that would remain in use for many years to come in Letcher County. In addition to changing the card's release date from every month to every six weeks, the new card replaced the grade letter "F" with "E" and adopted the word "citizenship" instead of "conduct."

In 1963, Cook left Letcher County to accept a job as director of adult education with the Kentucky Department of Education, a position he held for 16 years.

Early editions of The Eagle also show that:

On September 16, 1937, Cook was vying for one of two starting end positions on the Whitesburg High School football team, as the Yellow Jackets prepared for their season opener against the Van Lear Bank Mules. He won the right end position and helped the Jackets to a 32-0 win over Van Lear in that first game.

On March 10, 1938, Cook was presented a trophy by Whitesburg Mayor Bill Collins for being named to the All-County basketball team after Whitesburg beat Fleming, 38-23, for the 56th District Championship.

Cook was later married for 52 years to Patsy Back Cook, who survives him. He is also survived by three children, Richard Cook, Jackie Merrifield, and Libby Leedy, all of Lexington.

SOURCES

Special thanks to Ben Gish of the Mountain Eagle for graciously allowing me to use his excellent article

http://www.proviso.k12.il.us/bataan%20Web/Cook_T.htm

"Cook Was Among 4 Here Who Came Back: Battle of Bataan," Ben Gish, The Mountain Eagle, April 10, 2013 issue, Pages A5 & A12

"World War II Vet Survives Bataan Death March," Karla Ward; the Lexington Herald Leader, March 31, 2013, Page B3.

TOM CHASE McKENNEY
Lieutenant Colonel

I first met Colonel McKenney at the Relic Show held in Military Pigeon Forge, Tennessee, held at the Smoky Mountains Convention Center. He was promoting his book, <u>Jack Hinson's, One-man War</u>, and I was at a table next to him promoting mine. I was very impressed when he stated he had researched for over fifteen years on Jack Hinson's story. But what impressed me most was his humble yet military nature. After talking for a few minutes I soon realized I was in the presence of an American hero who did not self promote but simply served. We talked of his writings but not of the wars in which he had served. I left very impressed with his patriotism and his pride in being a Marine. Such men and women are the very fiber of this country.

Lieutenant Colonel McKenney has an impressive resume. He is a graduate of the University of Kentucky, having earned a Bachelor's Degree at that institution. He also attended and graduated from the University of North Carolina, located at Chapel Hill. He has served tours of duty in Korea and Vietnam. He was retired in 1971, by the military. In an interview he stated, *"I was retired for disability incurred in Vietnam. I am a writer, specializing in Christian, historical and military subjects. For the past 22 years, I have directed an international Bible teaching ministry, Words for Living, inc., with headquarters in Marion, Kentucky".*

He is a proud Veteran and very involved with our American Prisoners of War. He is an advocate for the Veteran and one of the voices for those unaccounted souls. He has appeared on Fox News, The Today Show, CBS Morning News, and the 700 Club. He is a military historian as well as a well known author. He has published articles in The American Legion, Guideposts, Journal of Naval History, Military and Leatherneck magazines. He has spoken on numerous radio shows as well. He is the author of several books and is published through Pelican. The rights to his life's story have been purchased by Columbia Pictures. The colonel's personal reflections of war have been featured in a book entitled, The Last Secret of the War in Vietnam. One of his works involved investigating the Clinton administration. He has taught in biological sciences at Paducah Community College and the University of South Carolina. He lives on a farm near Marion, Kentucky, with his wife, Marty. He also has lived in Long Beach, Mississippi. He is a devout Christian.

SOURCES

http://www.goodreads.com/author/show/661817.Tom_C_McKenney

http://www.pelicanpub.com/products.php?cat=389

http://www.idfiles.com/mckenney-affidavit.htm

http://www.zoominfo.com/p/Tom-McKenney/21839370

http://breadoflifegreenville.com/tagged/bookstore/page/2

Informal interview with Colonel McKenney

VICTOR GAYLE ALEXANDER
Army Air Corps pilot

As I read an article by Jim Warren, I was captivated by the ninety-two year old interviewee. What a story to share with others! I felt compelled to offer this unsung heroes story.

Victor Gayle Alexander was born in Versailles but later moved to Lexington, Kentucky. He always was in love with flying. From the days of his youth in Lexington, Kentucky, he dreamt of those moments of flight. At the youthful age of fifteen he obtained his pilot's license. In the interview he stated, *"If you have the talent, I guess it comes naturally,"* he said. *"I remember that back then I could ride my bike out to the Cool Meadow field on Newtown Pike, rent a Piper Cub for $3 and spend an hour just flying around the area."*

The day that changed his life was on a Sunday. Pearl Harbor was bombed on that fateful December 7, 1941. He felt called to duty and was accepted as an Air Corps Pilot. His first mission was training other pilots because of his skills but Gayle was not content with that. He wanted to fight for his country. Two years later he was given that opportunity and fight he did. He became a World War II pilot flying B-24 and B-17. Never losing his sense of humor he called his plane the 'Kentucky Kloudhopper'. He also had a hillbilly painted on the nose!

Alexander flew what is known as a 'Mikey ship'. The B-17s were equipped with radar from M.I.T. The radar could see through clouds and would be the lead planes for other bombers. When it was first seen it reminded pilots of Mickey Mouse's ears. The name stuck. H2X operators were called, 'Mickey Operators'.

Gayle Alexander flew on eighteen missions. On one mission he returned with two engines out, a portion of the tail missing and three hundred eight holes in the fuselage. On his nineteenth mission twelve hundred bombers attacked Merseburg, Germany. The date was November 2, 1944.

On his nineteenth mission, Alexander led one of the war's biggest raids: twelve hundred bombers attacking a synthetic oil plant at Merseburg, Germany. The date was November 2, 1944. His plane was hit and exploded, killing all but seven of the crew. Alexander parachuted out and was captured by the Germans upon landing. He stated he lost his shoes when he was ejected from the plane. He spent the next seven months as a POW and somehow lived through the harsh conditions. He stated as they marched he ate potatoes that were tossed to the hogs by local farmers. He weighed only one hundred nineteen pounds upon being liberated. Mr. Alexander stated in the interview that he saw General Patton proudly standing in his jeep on the day the prisoners was rescued.

Alexander returned home to Lexington, Kentucky, after spending time on a hospital ship. He decided to become a veterinarian. He did so until he retired. He now lives in his home quietly enjoying the fruit of being an unsung hero.

SOURCES

http://digital.olivesoftware.com/Olive/ODE/Lexington HeraldLeader/LandingPage/LandingPage.aspx?href=T EhMLzIwMTQvMDQvMjE.&pageno=MQ..&entity=Q XIwMDEwMw..&view=ZW50aXR5

http://www.anti-semitism.net/tag/victor-gayle

http://www.kentucky.com/2014/04/20/3204783/lexingt on-wwii-veteran-shares.html?sp=/99/322/&ihp=1

http://www.482nd.org/h2x-mickey

(From Mr. Alexander's collection)

WEARY CLYBURN
Private
Company E
12th South Carolina Volunteers
Black Confederate

(Weary with Confederate uniform)

Some historians don't recognize their existence much less their significance during the War Between the States. Nevertheless many existed. Many blacks chose to fight beside their white counterparts because of the love they had for the South. Yes, some were slaves. Yes, some were free Persons of Color. Yes, some of them fought beside their master. But all, YES all, were brave men who must be remembered in the annuals of history and heritage. We cannot separate the significance of service by the 'US Colored Troops' and the 'Colored Confederates'. All were brave men worthy of recognition.

Weary Clyburn was born sometime in 1841, Lancaster County, South Carolina. He listed his father as Phillip Blair (Union County) on his marriage license dated

December 1857. He was born a slave but died a free man. Weary married Viney Moore (daughter of Edman Horne) on December 21, 1867. He later married Eliza Brown. He was known for his fiddle playing and jovial nature. According to his daughter, Mattie Clyburn Rice, her father, "went to war willingly, though his story is complicated. He ran away with his best friend, who was white and the son of his master. Rice says no matter how historians view that narrative, she's glad she proved her father contributed to the Confederate cause." "I wanted the world to know what he did," she stated to the interviewer.

Additional information from the documents reviewed more details. Weary, "volunteered for the Confederacy with Capt. Frank Clyburn, who was the son of the man who owned Wary Clyburn According to the pension documents, "Wary Clyburn served as the bodyguard for Frank Clyburn in Company E of the 12th Regiment. Wary carried Frank on his shoulders to rescue him during intense fighting. Wary also served as a special aid to Gen. Robert E. Lee." (Note: The documents spelled his first name several ways: Werry, Weary and Wary. His daughter says the correct spelling is Wary)."

In yet another segment listed under sources, the following details were reported. "When Frank joined the Confederate Army, he was sent to Columbia, South Carolina, for training. A short time later, Weary shows up in Columbia telling Captain Clyburn that he wishes to join him. He joined his friend out of a sense of loyalty and friendship. Through the years of the war, Weary served alongside Frank in Co. E, 12th South Carolina Infantry. Weary was reported to have carried the wounded Frank Clyburn off the battlefield, on two different occasions saving his life. According to Ms. Mattie Clyburn Rice, a living daughter of Weary Clyburn, he also served General Robert E. Lee towards the end of the war. Like many men during the war Weary, a slave, chose to be part of the Confederate

Army. Weary lived out the later parts of his life and raising a family in Union County, North Carolina."

These records were accepted by the United States as authentic after careful scrutiny. To this fielder that is enough to declare Private Clyburn an unsung hero, as well as his daughter, Mattie Clyburn Rice.

(Mrs. Mattie Clyburn Rice with picture of her father)

Mattie Clyburn Rice is the second Black Real Daughter to be recognized by the United Daughters of the Confederacy. At the time of the sources listed there were twenty-three real daughters who were still living. Mrs. Rice has spent years researching her father. She has several documents inclusive of the Confederate pension filed in 1926. Weary was eighty-eight when he filed. She was a mere four years old at that time.

Ms Mattie stated that no one believed her stories about her father's military service to the Confederacy, not even her family. Yet she persisted and insisted on sharing them. How many more blacks go unrecognized for their service?

According to Mrs. Rice, the North Carolina pension application provides documentation of his service. "At Hilton Head while under fire of the enemy, he carried his master out of the field of fire on his shoulder, that he performed personal service for Robert E. Lee." Weary was a childhood friend (according to Ms Rice- best friend) to Frank Clyburn. They grew up together; they played together, they fished, swam and hunted together. No doubt they broke bread together. When Frank joined the Confederacy, his friend volunteered to go with him. Friendship knows no color.

Weary died on March 30, 1930, in Union County North Carolina. He was buried in his gray uniform. He is buried in Hillcrest Cemetery, Stafford Street, Monroe County, North Carolina.

Weary Clyburn and his descendants were honored by two special ceremonies by the Sons of confederate Veterans. One was held during a convention and the other at the newly erected gravestone in Hillcrest Cemetery. The mayor of the City of Monroe offered a proclamation declaring that day 'Weary Clyburn Day'. Earl James and Nelson Winnbush were the featured speakers.

SOURCES

http://www.npr.org/2011/08/07/138587202/after-years-of-research-confederate-daughter-arises

http://cwmemory.com/2010/02/13/mr-ijames-was-weary-clyburn-a-soldier-or-a-slave/

http://www.findagrave.com/cgi-bin/fg.cgi?page=gr&GRid=60770561

http://www.southernheritage411.com/bc.php?nw=061

http://www.cwreenactors.com/forum/showthread.php?9600-Black-Confederate-Weary-Clyburn-to-be-honored

WILFRED DURDE COYER
Sergeant
B-25C Mitchell 41-12485
Gunner
WWII
Article by Ben Gish-Mountain Eagle
(Permission given to reprint in book)

As was the case with many of the one hundred forty-nine (149) soldiers from Letcher County who were killed in World War II, little information was released about Sergeant Wilfred Durde Coyer after the B-25C bomber on which he was a crew member went missing soon after taking off from an airstrip on the island of New Guinea early in 1943.

"Friends in Jenkins are again deeply grieved to hear of the missing in action of some of their boys," Mrs. O.O. Parks wrote at the end of her Jenkins News column in the February 11, 1943, edition of *The Mountain Eagle*. "News [was] received this week of Durde Coyer missing in New Guinea."

On the morning of January 18, 1943, just four days after Sgt. Coyer's twenty-second birthday, Coyer and six other crew members stationed at an airstrip near the south coast of New Guinea boarded an aircraft officially known as "B-25C Mitchell 41-12485," but nicknamed the "Algernon IV."

Sergeant Coyer was one of three gunners on the plane, and was charged with manning either a single .30-caliber machine gun in the nose turret or one of two .50-caliber machine guns in dorsal turrets atop the B-25C's fuselage, between the wings and twin tail. The two other gunners on board that morning were Sgt. Herman H. Elsner of Hemlock, Mich., and Staff Sergeant Michael Ewas of Detroit, Michigan, Corporal LaVerne D. Van Dyke of Zeeland, Michigan, was the flight engineer, and Lieutenant Colonel Dan Searcy of Lewisville, Ark., was the observer. The co-pilot was Major Donn Young of Dillonvale, Ohio, and the pilot was Major William G. Benn of Washington, Pa.

According to information gathered by PacificWrecks.com, a website dedicated to documenting World War II plane crashes in the Southwest Pacific Theatre, the Algernon IV took off from 7-Mile Drome at 9:45 a.m. New Guinea Time (15 hours ahead of Eastern Standard Time) on that Monday. Its mission was to fly to the north coast of New Guinea to conduct aerial reconnaissance of Japanese forces. After no reports were received from the crew at any time after take-off, the plane was presumed crashed and all on board were declared missing in action (MIA). Two days later, on January 20, 1943, a search of the east-west Mountains that make up the New Guinea Highlands region where officials believed the plane had gone down ended without success.

Sgt. Coyer's career with the U.S. Army Air Forces began in late 1941. According to a front-page article in the June 18, 1942 edition of *The Eagle*, then-Pvt. Coyer, 21, was undergoing training at the U.S. Army Air Corps Gunnery School in Las Vegas, Nevada. The article said Coyer, son of Mr. and Mrs. Fred H. Coyer of Jenkins, had attended Jenkins High School, where he played football. He was single and had worked as a shuttle car driver in an underground coal mine before joining the Army on December 18, 1941, the report said.

After successfully completing gunnery school, Coyer was promoted and assigned to the 5th Air Force, 3rd Bombardment Group, 13th Bombardment Squadron and stationed at 7-Mile Drome airstrip near the city of Port Moresby on New Guinea's south coast.

The world's second largest island, New Guinea is located north of Australia. U.S. soldiers and other

Allied Forces were sent there after Japanese forces landed there in 1942. The Allies feared the Japanese would be able to take Australia if they weren't stopped in New Guinea.

Ironically, it was the Algernon IV's newest pilot, Major William C. Benn, who had been credited with helping a U.S. Army Air Forces left nearly in shambles after the bombing of Pearl Harbor regroup in the ensuing months to slow further Japanese advancements to New Guinea and elsewhere in the Southwest Pacific.

Maj. Benn is known as the pilot who perfected "skip bombing," a low-level bombing technique developed by the British Royal Air Force but abandoned as being too dangerous.

According to Benn's great-nephew Alfred Hagan, who was the subject of a History Channel documentary on attempts to recover the Algernon IV from the New Guinea mountains, Benn wiped out more than 100,000 tons of Japanese war ships and cargo ships one night in October 1942, by putting a B-25 bomber "into a dive, achieving a high level of speed, then leveling out at a low altitude" before sending bombs into the sides of Japanese ships. The bomber was flying only 60 feet above water in darkness.

General George C. Kenney, who commanded the Allied Air Forces in the Southwest Pacific Area, said no pilot made a greater contribution toward helping defeat the Japanese than Maj. Benn and his use of skip bombing. General Douglas MacArthur awarded Benn the Distinguished Service Cross, the second-highest military award that could be given to a member of the U.S. Army Air Forces.

On December 20, 1945, Sgt. Coyer, Maj. Benn and the five other crewmembers of the Algernon IV were listed "presumed dead" by the Office of the Secretary of War.

In August 1956, more than thirteen (13) years after the Algernon IV disappeared; the crash site was discovered in a jungle in the Mount Strong area of the New Guinea Highlands by a Kiap (patrol officer) from Tapini, New Guinea. Remains of at least one crewmember were believed recovered by the Kiap.

Five months later, in late January 1957, a Royal Australian Air Force team charged with searching for missing aircraft returned to the site and recovered six sets of remains and five identification tags. RAAF Searcher Team investigated the wreckage and determined the crash, which occurred in bad weather, resulted from the plane losing an engine after taking enemy gunfire. The team's findings were reported to U.S. Air Force officials on February 13, 1957.

(Picture courtesy of the History Channel documentary)

On March 9, 1957, the Army reopened its World War II casualty books to change the status of Sgt. Coyer and the others from presumed dead to "Killed In Action." Coyer's remains were returned to Kentucky, and he is buried with the other crewmembers in the Zachary Taylor National Cemetery near Louisville.

According to news reports on March 11, 1957, the Army had no immediate explanation for RAAF Searcher Team's not finding the remains of one crew member or the identification tags of two, later identified as the co-pilot, Maj. Donn C. Young, and the flight engineer, Cpl. LaVerne D. Van Dyke.

Forty years later, sometime in 1997, Van Dyke's dog tags were found by natives of the New Guinea Highlands and turned over to a French priest. This finding inspired a search team funded and directed by Philadelphia businessman Alfred Hagen, the aforementioned great-nephew of Maj. Benn, to return to the jungle of steep Highlands for the fourth time in four years to look for the wreckage of Algernon IV.

In November 1998, Hagen's team, with the help of local natives, finally found the wreckage and in the process recovered Maj. Young's dog tags. The Hagen team had been unsuccessful the previous three tries because the cause of the crash site had been located on the opposite side of Mt. Strong than the RAAF Searcher Team had indicated some 50 years before.

Hagen's three unsuccessful trips to New Guinea and the successful fourth trip was the subject of a History Channel documentary, "B-25 Down: Hunt for a Hero." The documentary was released on DVD in July 2008, and is available at Amazon.com. The documentary can also be accessed on YouTube.

The B-25C bomber was nicknamed the Algernon IV by its first pilot, Captain Ronald D. Hubbard, in honor of a soup-ed up car Hubbard owned as a teenager. Hubbard was promoted after flying the plane in the summer and fall of 1942. Hubbard was later presented with the

Distinguished Service Cross for heroism he showed participating in bombing missions against Japanese targets while suffering from dengue fever.

SOURCES

Courtesy of the Mountain Eagle & writer Ben Gish
June 18, 1942
February 11, 1943

http://www.themountaineagle.com/news/2013-02-13/Features/Jenkins_soldier_on_bomber_that_went_missing_in_WW_.html

PacificWrecks.com

History Channel documentary,
"B-25 Down: Hunt for a Hero."

WILLIAM J. CAUDILL
Private
KIA
WWII

Unfortunately I do not know much about this unsung American hero. I have visited his grave in the Dixon Cemetery and am a distant relative. Several of my relatives are buried close to his grave. To my shame, I do not have enough knowledge of him or his sacrifice. The following information was obtained by permission of Ben Gish.

"The remains of Pvt. William J. Caudill arrived home Tuesday, June 22nd accompanied by Escort: T. Sgt. William Darifield of the Columbus General Distributing Depot, Columbus, Ohio. He was killed in action, at Manila, Philippine Islands, after two years of service, on February 23, 1945. He was the son of Mr. and Mrs. Solomon Caudill of Ulvah, he was a fine young Christian boy, loved by all' who knew him.

'Funeral services were held at the home Tuesday evening and Wednesday morning, by Elders, Buddy Caudill, Becha Fields, James Fields, Wesley Caudill, Hendricks Caudill, Roy Whitaker, Wesley Caudill, Alva Caudill and Jim Pratt, which was attended by several hundred friends and relatives. William is survived by his parents, four brothers James A. Lester and Harvie of Ulvah, and Little Caudill of Milwaukee, Wisconsin. Three Sisters: Mrs. Andy Fields, Kingdom Come; Mrs. Raymond Fields, Premium, and Sylvania Fields, Ulvah.

Burial was in the Dixon Cemetery by members of the Johnson Funeral Home.

SOURCE

Mountain Eagle; June28-July 3, 1948 edition

WILLIAM KYLE CARPENTER
Lance Corporal
Rifleman
Company F
2nd Battalion
9th Marines
Regimental Combat Team 1
1st Marine Division
I Marine Expeditionary Force
October 17, 1989-Present

What would you do for a friend? What would you do for a comrade? What are you willing to give for your country? The Bible says in John 15:13, *"Greater love has no man than this, that a man lay down his life for his friends."* William Kyle Carpenter lives by those words.

On November 21, 2010, while deployed in the vicinity of villages nicknamed Shady and Shadiest, (Marjah, Helmand Province) Afghanistan, Lance Corporal Carpenter was fighting a Taliban attack with his fellow Marine. Insurgents threw three hand grenades on top of a building into the middle of his fellow Marines. Without thought of his own life, Lance Corporal Carpenter shielded Lance Corporal Nick Eufrazio (from Plymouth, Mass) from the blast by throwing himself onto the grenade. Kyle's wounds were catastrophic.

In fact he was labeled as being dead. It took two and one half years of surgery for him to get back on his feet. He lost an eye, most of his teeth, collapsed his right lung, depressed skull, fractured some of his fingers, and had major trauma breaks to his right arm. He has scars on his face and lost one third of his jaw. Carpenter endured over thirty surgeries while at Walter Reed National Military Medical Center located in Bethesda, Maryland.

Lance Corporal Carpenter stated: *"My last few seconds before I lost consciousness, I had accepted the fact that ... I was not going to survive and make it off that rooftop."* *"There are guys who I was with who didn't come back, so it's hard for me to wear this and have the spotlight on me the rest of my life when they lost their life on a hot, dusty field in Afghanistan and most people don't even know their names,"* Carpenter said. *"Even at Walter Reed, I recovered with quadruple-amputees. How am I supposed to wear this knowing and seeing all the hardships that are much worse than mine that guys have gone through without any recognition?"* In a statement Lance Corporal Carpenter recalls that he *"got right with God"* as he was enveloped by the sensation of *warm water pouring all over him (It was his own blood)*. Such is the heart of a humble warrior.

William Kyle Carpenter was born in Flowood (Jackson), Mississippi, and spent much of his childhood in Brandon. He enlisted in the Marine Corps on a delayed entry program in February 2009. He completed Recruit Training in July 2009, at Paris Island, South Carolina. He was sent to Camp Geiger, North Carolina, and there he was assigned to Fox Company, 2nd Battalion, 9th Marines, 6th Marine Regiment as a gunner (Squad Automatic Weapon (SAW).

Kyle is currently a student at the University of South Carolina. On June 19, 2014, Sergeant William Kyle Carpenter was bestowed America's highest award for bravery: The Congressional Medal of Honor. He is the eighth living recipient of such an honor for actions in Iraq or Afghanistan and the second Marine.

I find his words in an interview to best demonstrate his Christian character and humble nature. *"Please take it from me ... enjoy every day to the fullest, don't take life too seriously, always try to make it count, appreciate the small and simple things, be kind and help others, let the ones you love always know you love them and when things get hard, trust there is a bigger plan and that you will be stronger for it."*

SOURCES

http://en.wikipedia.org/wiki/Kyle_Carpenter

http://www.washingtonpost.com/world/national-security/veteran-long-celebrated-by-marines-to-be-awarded-medal-of-honor/2014/05/19/2fc52ade-df5b-11e3-9743-bb9b59cde7b9_story.html

http://www.theguardian.com/world/2014/may/20/us-marine-medal-of-honor-grenade-afghanistan

http://thisainthell.us/blog/?p=48008&cpage=1

http://www.marinecorpstimes.com/article/20140519/NEWS/305190040/It-s-official-Medal-Honor-Marine-Kyle-Carpenter

http://www.stripes.com/news/marine-corps/former-marine-cpl-kyle-carpenter-to-be-awarded-the-medal-of-honor-1.283944

http://www.huffingtonpost.com/2012/12/08/lance-cpls-kyle-carpenter_n_2138958.html

http://www.cnn.com/2014/05/20/us/medal-of-honor-carpenter/

http://www.nbcnews.com/news/us-news/obama-award-medal-honor-hero-who-blocked-live-grenade-n109561

http://www.google.com/#q=william+kyle+carpenter&safe=active&tbm=nws

http://www.stripes.com/news/report-afghanistan-veteran-william-kyle-carpenter-to-receive-medal-of-honor-1.271296

http://www.theblaze.com/stories/2012/01/28/fellow-marines-call-on-kyle-carpenter-to-receive-the-medal-of-honor-for-using-his-body-to-shield-others-from-grenade-blast/

WILLIAM LLOYD BROWN
Seaman First Class
U.S.S. Mississippi
WORLD WAR II
By Richard G. Brown

The recent dedication of the World War II monument in Washington, D.C. has increased interest in the time period that is now known as "The Greatest Generation." What American would argue that this was not an appropriate name? Hundreds of thousands of American boys died defending not only their country's freedom, but that of the world as well. Many more would be wounded, thousands crippled before they were even old enough to vote. The mountains of eastern Kentucky sent more than her share to defend the concept of liberty and pursuit of happiness. Some of these boys were drafted while others volunteered, but all did their duty. This story is about one of these unsung heroes, Seaman First Class William Lloyd Brown.

William was born September 9, 1924, at Crown, a small community on Dry Fork in Letcher County. His father was William Henry Brown and his mother Florence Richmond Brown, both descendents of the original pioneers that settled in the rugged mountains of Kentucky. He was the oldest of five children, having three brothers, (Glenn, Earl and Roy) and one sister (Lillian). Two of his brothers would later follow in his footsteps into the military, Glenn in the Occupation of Germany and Earl in Korea. As several William Browns lived in the area, William was known locally by his middle name, Lloyd, the name that he still uses.

Lloyd's father was a firm believer in education and wanted the best that he could afford for his children. Having been born on the head of Linefork which was located on the Harlan and Letcher County line, William Henry Brown knew of the boarding school in Harlan County known as Pine Mountain Settlement School. Lloyd was enrolled there to attend high school. His teachers were impressed with his swiftness at acquiring knowledge and talent in wood working. They sent an example of his work to an advanced school in St. Louis, Missouri, to review which resulted in the offer of a full scholarship. However this offer would go unfulfilled for the young man with all of that talent was notified during his senior year that he had been drafted to serve in the U.S. Navy in the ongoing war. Devastated that their young son had to go to war, his parents asked for and received a deferment allowing Lloyd to finish high school before reporting for duty.

Upon completion of his senior year, Lloyd reported for duty on July 7, 1943, at Huntington, West Virginia. From there he was transferred to the Naval Training Station at Great Lakes, Illinois, arriving there on July 16th. Upon completion of six weeks of boot camp, his company was awarded the honor of being best in the class. At this time his company was informed that they would be stationed aboard the battleship U.S.S. Mississippi whose crew had been depleted due to several of them being killed and wounded in combat.

The young boy from the mountains of Kentucky whom had never seen anything bigger than the Kentucky River was heading for action on the Pacific Ocean!

On October 7, 1943, Lloyd and his company boarded the mighty battleship at a dock named Bethlehem Steel in San Francisco, California. Seeing the name of the dock gave Lloyd a twinge of homesickness as Bethlehem Steel operated several mines back home in Letcher County. The next month would be spent training the new sailors for their assignments during battle. Lloyd was trained for at least two duties, one as a loader on the No. 3 Turret (fourteen inch guns) and the other as a 20 mm antiaircraft gunner. The big guns of the ship would be used for sea engagements and bombardments and was located on the main deck. The 20 mm guns were located on the boat deck, a floor above the main deck and would be used for defense against air attacks.

On November 10, 1943, the Mississippi left the port at San Francisco and began to sail for the Gilbert Islands in the South Pacific. Lloyd had gone from seeing nothing but green mountains to nothing but blue water. On November 20, the Mississippi began bombarding Makin Island in preparation for the assault and capture of one of the Japanese strongholds. It was at this time that Lloyd would see the first of many casualties of the war. The No. 2 Turret had what the sailors called a flare back which ignited the powder in the magazine of the big gun, resulting in an explosion. This tragedy killed 41 men and wounded several others. The well trained fire and emergency crews immediately began to fight the fires while the remaining guns continued to fire. At the end of the battle, the Mississippi and her crew received a commendation for her refusal to quit fighting though badly wounded.

When the firing ceased, the Mississippi had time to bury her fallen sailors. As the mournful sound of Taps echoed across the ocean, Lloyd noted that even the hardened veterans had tears in their eyes when the canvas bags weighted down with a 5" shell slid off the platform and into a watery grave. Unfortunately, the sad scene of burial at sea would repeat itself throughout the war, a scene that Lloyd can still see in his mind even to this day. It is little wonder that he and other veterans still cannot bring themselves to buy vehicles made in Japan. He can forgive but not forget.

With the battle for Makin Island now over, the Mississippi was ordered to sail to Pearl Harbor to be repaired. With all of her structural damage, it was feared that she would be vulnerable if engaged with the Japanese fleet. During the two month stay at Pearl Harbor, Lloyd visited the island and obtained one of his tattoos, a custom of naval men. This custom would be repeated in ports all over the Pacific as this teenager from the mountains had definitely become a man.

Late in January of 1944, the Mississippi, having been repaired, got her orders to sail for the Marshall Islands. Upon arriving at the Marshall Islands, she immediately was instructed to bombard the Island of Kwajalein, one of the first steps in retaking the islands from the

Japanese. Completely demolishing the island's coastal defenses with her big guns, the assault on the island by the Marines were a huge success. To show their appreciation to the battleship, the officers assigned to the land assault named the beach that they landed on Mississippi Beach. Continuing the stepping stone method of retaking the Marshall Islands, the Mississippi bombarded the Island of Taroa on February 20th and the Island of Wotje the next day. Both bombardments were considered beneficial in the success of retaking the islands.

With the Marshall Islands now controlled by the Americans, the Mississippi was now ordered to sail for New Ireland. Arriving there in the middle of March, they immediately began to shell Kavieng. What started out as a diversion soon became a major engagement as the Japanese returned fire with everything they had in their arsenal. The duel ended with the complete destruction of Kavieng's defenses. The battleship's big guns had hurled tons of munitions once more, resulting in another step toward victory.

During this last bombardment it was noticed that the big guns accuracy had fallen off dramatically. Upon inspection, it was discovered that the rifling had been shot out of the guns. The tremendous amount of shots fired had taken their toll on the big guns. The Mississippi was ordered to return to Bremerton Navy Yard in Washington to be re-gunned and refitted. On April 24, the battle weary ship and crew arrived back in the United States. Hoping to show their support to the crew, the citizens of Seattle requested that the Navy allow these brave sailors to march through their streets. Honoring this request, Lloyd and his fellow sailors donned their best uniform and marched through the streets of Seattle to the cheers of thousands of their fellow countrymen.

We paraded in Seattle

Knowing the Navy desperately needed her battleship back, the workmen at the navy yard worked around the clock, seven days a week for almost three months. During this time they installed the latest equipment available and upgraded the big guns. While training on the new and improved systems of the big guns, Lloyd had a finger horribly crushed. Within a week Lloyd was back at his post, ignoring the pain from the useless finger. Ready to fight once more, the Mississippi sailed into Pearl Harbor in August.

Stopping only long enough to pick up some of her crew that had been left there, the battleship sailed to Purvis Bay on Florida Island in the Solomons, arriving there in late August. This was the staging area for the much anticipated Western Caroline Islands Operation. From here the Mississippi sailed to Pelelieu Island, a part of the Palau Islands. On September 12, the big guns of the battleship began to pound the Japanese defenses. After a week of bombarding the island with over 6,000 rounds, the Mississippi was ordered to cease fire and sail to Manus Island to prepare for the Philippine Operations.

On October 12, the battleship left Manus Island and sailed for Leyte Gulf in the middle of the Philippines. Three days later a terrible typhoon hit the Seventh

Fleet, sinking some of the smaller warships. Nature had almost done what the Japanese Navy could not; destroy the Seventh Fleet. On October 18, the Mississippi began to bombard Leyte Island in preparation for the upcoming invasion. The operation was going so well that a major part of the fleet was ordered to go north in search of the Japanese navy. Rear Admiral J. B. Oldendorf was left in command of the naval forces with the Mississippi being used as the flagship. On October 24, Oldendorf received disturbing news; the main Japanese fleet was converging on Leyte Gulf. The American naval fleet was badly outnumbered and had a huge decision to make. If they retreated, the Marines on Leyte Island would probably be annihilated, if the fleet stayed to fight, it was likely they would be destroyed. Oldendorf and his staff decided that they could not abandon the Marines and would stay and fight. The Battle of Surigao Strait was about to begin.

Calculating the speed of the approaching Japanese fleet, Admiral Oldendorf realized that they would arrive at Leyte Gulf in the darkness of early morning. He lined every ship that was available in an ambush that hardly ever was given the opportunity to be used, the "crossing of the T". Expecting to surprise the Americans, the Japanese fleet sailed right into the ambush and at 3: 00 A.M. on the morning of October 25, the order to fire was given. Every gun of the American fleet including the battleships, cruisers, destroyers and the little pesky torpedo boats opened up. The Japanese attempted to fight back but the ferociousness of the American attack confused the Japanese commander. He had been told that less than half of the Seventh Fleet would be there and expected to easily destroy them. Believing that he had been misinformed and that the whole American fleet was attacking his fleet, he ordered a full scale retreat. The courage and the tenacity of the men of the depleted Seventh Fleet had resulted in full victory against overwhelming odds. So many of the Japanese warships had been destroyed or damaged that the Japanese navy was rendered ineffective for the remainder of the war. Lloyd had now been a part of one of the largest American naval victories of all time.

Having lost most of their navy, the Japanese commanders turned to one of the most dreaded weapons of the war, the Kamikaze. This Japanese word meant "divine wind" and referred to the Japanese pilots that would use their planes loaded with explosives in a suicidal attempt to sink the American ships. For thirty six of the next thirty eight days these suicide planes attacked the Americans. On one occasion, a destroyer that was badly damaged attempted to save itself by jettisoning the torpedoes aboard ship. One of these torpedoes locked upon the Mississippi and only the quick thinking of the Captain saved her from being hit by friendly fire, ordering her to be turned sharply at the last minute. With the fall of the Japanese defenders on Leyte Island, the kamikaze attacks ended in this area.

For more than a month Lloyd had seen constant combat, when he wasn't helping fire the big guns in Turret No. 3, he was firing the 20 mm antiaircraft gun. The remainder of 1944 was spent supporting the Mindoro Operation which the Japanese did not contest as heavily, giving Lloyd and the rest of the crew a greatly needed respite. On January 2, 1945, the Mississippi was ordered to sail to the China Sea to be part of the Lingayen Attack Force. With most of her navy annihilated, the Japanese again turned to the Kamikazes as their first line of defense. On January 4, they sunk the escort carrier, Ommaney Bay. The Mississippi picked up 158 of the surviving crewmen from the sea. Two days later, the bombardment of Luzon began, stirring up a hornet's nest of Kamikazes. Wave after wave of the suicide planes hit the American fleet. Lloyd and the other men of the antiaircraft crews could not leave their post even to eat. During the hectic firing, some of the Mississippi's crew were killed and wounded by friendly fire from antiaircraft crews from other ships, another tragedy of war. On this same day, the USS Louisville was heavily damaged from the suicide planes.

The Japanese learned one lesson during this time and it would later come back to haunt the Mississippi. They had discovered that the best two times of the day to attack with their suicide planes was at dusk and dawn which put the sun in the American defender's eyes. By January 9, the beach defenses of Luzon had been totally destroyed by the navy's big guns, creating a false sense of peace. That evening Lloyd was sitting on the boat deck at his 20mm gun while his assistant on the gun was standing by it. At this time tragedy struck when a kamikaze came out of the sun at incredible speed. By the time that a general quarter was sounded, the plane had already brushed the bridge, hit the boat deck and fell to the main deck. Having set down to rest had saved Lloyd's life as the plane killed his fellow sailor that was standing at the 20mm gun, the wing cutting him in half. The explosion of the bomb aboard the plane wounded Lloyd, knocking him unconscious.

Lloyd's 20mm gun

The emergency crews fought and contained the fires that resulted from the 250 pound bomb and airplane.

They mistakenly thought that Lloyd was dead and continued to step over him, dragging their water hoses over his still body. During a lull in the fighting, one of the firefighters noticed Lloyd move and immediately evacuated him to the infirmary. The attack had killed 26 men and wounded 63 more, some seriously. It also had caused serious structural damage. The blisters (side of the ship) had a large hole blown in it, allowing sea water to enter the ship. A coffer dam was constructed and lowered by the center gun of the No. 4 turret into place which allowed the crew to temporary repair the blisters. Though severely damaged, the Mississippi would not leave her post for 34 more days.

At this time a typical error that occurs during hectic times of war happened. Confusing Lloyd with another sailor that had been killed, the navy informed his father and mother by telegram that he had been killed in action. For almost three days his family grieved for the lost son until the navy informed them of their mistake. In typical government fashion however, the Mississippi's war book still list William Lloyd Brown as killed in action. One can only imagine the relief and joy that his family experienced upon learning that their son had once more been added to the list of the living.

Though severely damaged the old battleship could not leave combat for badly needed repairs. With Luzon now occupied by American forces, she was ordered to participate in the Iwo Jima Operation. The Japanese air force had started running out of planes which resulted in fewer kamikaze attacks which delighted the battleship's crew. As soon as the Iwo Jima Operation was declared a success, the Mississippi was ordered to return to Pearl Harbor for repairs. While there, Lloyd got the last of his tattoos, a list of the battles that he had participated in. On April 9, Lloyd was transferred to a Naval Hospital at Farragut, Idaho and on June 18, 1945, discharged from the Navy.

Arriving back home to his beloved mountains of south east Kentucky, he soon married a local girl, Grace Tyree, that had also attended Pine Mountain Settlement School. They were blessed with four children, Elizabeth, Don, Wade, and Nancy whom all have been successful. Lloyd operated several underground coal mines until he built a small market at Dry Fork in 1970. He appropriately named the store Dry Fork Market and advertised it as the biggest little market in the country. Due to his honesty and friendliness, the store was a huge success. Recently his son, Don, took over the family ran store, retaining the name. In 1980, he decided to enter politics and ran for magistrate in District One of Letcher County. Though this district was considered a Democrat stronghold, he won the election as a Republican, a testament to his standing in the community. In 1992, after serving three terms as magistrate, Lloyd officially retired from politics. Unofficially, people still stop by the store to ask his opinion on some issue or to ask for his help in an election.

World War II was one of our nation's most defining events when Kentuckians of all ages and gender volunteered and sacrificed for the cause of freedom. Lloyd was one of many teenage mountain boys that had to become a man too early. Thankfully he survived the war as many young men gave the ultimate sacrifice. Today Lloyd and Grace enjoy riding around the country and spending time with their grandchildren and great grandchildren. Lloyd also is helping with the formation of a war museum that is dedicated to Letcher County veterans. The driving force behind this unique museum is another highly decorated Letcher County veteran, SGT Major Ben Buster Taylor.

No. 3 Turret Crew

WILLIAM T. JENT
Staff Sergeant
Air Force

At a morning dress parade, Staff Sergeant William T. Jent of Jeremiah, now of the Moses Lake Army Air Base in the state of Washington, was decorated with the Distinguished Flying Cross, which was awarded to him "in recognition of extraordinary achievement while participating in aerial flights, having participated in 200 hours of operational flight against the enemy in the Middle East theatre."

SOURCE

Staff Sergeant William T. Jent; The Way We Were; The Mountain Eagle; September 29, 1943

WILLIAM HORSFALL
Drummer
Company G
1ˢᵗ Kentucky Infantry
March 3, 1847–October 22, 1922

William was a Kentucky boy living close to the Ohio River in Newport, Campbell County. He was a typical lad doing what young men do to entertain themselves. When the war broke out, young William and three of his friends decided to join the cause of the north. William was fourteen years of age. He stood four feet three inches in height. His eyes were blue, sandy hair and light skin.

The boys decided to sneak on board a steamship headed for a Federal encampment. At the last moment the three friends 'chickened out' and left William on the ship heading out of Cincinnati, Ohio. Horsfall found himself alone headed to an unknown location. Later (as recorded in the Campbell County Historical Society archives) he wrote that he, *"Left home without money or a warning to his parents and stealthily boarded the stearmer, Annie Laurie, moored at the Cincinnati*

Wharf at Newport on the 20th of December 1861." There he stayed hidden, "Until the boat was well under way." Upon being discovered he lied and said he was an orphan.

Two weeks later (January 1, 1862) William was enlisted into Company G, 1st Regiment Kentucky Volunteers. He was assigned as a drummer in Camp Cox, Virginia. That area is now known as Charleston, West Virginia, having seceded from Virginia during the War Between the States. His unofficial occupation was listed as 'schoolboy.'

After basic training and learning to play the drums, William found himself traveling to Corinth, Mississippi. There, upon the sacred battlefield, William saved a wounded officer's life by risking his own during the Siege of Corinth.

The following account is from his writings: On May 21, 1862, during the Siege of Corinth Horsfall, who then described himself as "an independent sharpshooter," recounted how a Union captain was wounded in "a desperate charge across (a) ravine," and was caught between the lines. "*Lt. Hocke* ... said, '*Horsfall, Captain Williamson is in a serious predicament. Rescue him, if possible.*' "*So I placed my gun against a tree and, in a stooping run, gained his side and dragged him to the stretcher bearers, who took him to the rear.*" This act of heroism would earn him our country's highest medal.

William's drum could be heard throughout the campaigns of 1862. At Stones River (Murfreesboro, TN) he became surrounded by rebels. When they saw the small adolescent, they "*took pity on his youth*" and allowed him "*to run for his life.*"

Sometime later, the little drummer boy became ill and was hospitalized in Nashville. Upon recovery he served and reenlisted twice. On March 20, 1865, he was mustered into Company K, 4th Regiment of the US Veteran Volunteers at Todd Barracks in Cincinnati. He had grown to a height of five foot two inches during that period of time of his enlistment. He remained a small man in stature throughout his life but the heart of a lion beat within his chest. He remained at Camp Stoneman, Maryland, until his discharge in 1866.

After his service he looked for gainful employment but his age was a factor. Later in life his rheumatism and heart disease was at the point of where he had to have someone providing care for him. He was forty-six. He wore and published several poems and songs. He also commanded the William Nelson GAR Post in Newport, Kentucky.

On August 17, 1895, William Horsfall became one of the youngest recipients of the Medal of Honor. William, the heroic drummer boy, died at the age of seventy- five. A historical marker is located near the Evergreen Cemetery in Southgate.

OBITUARY

Kentucky Times-Star, Wednesday, October 25, 1922

Funeral of W H Horsfall, Civil War Hero
Was Commander of William Nelson Post GAR

The funeral of William H Horsfall, 75, civil war veteran, was held Wednesday at 2 pm with services at his home 218 West Third Street, Newport. Burial was in the Evergreen Cemetery.

Horsfall joined the union forces as a drummer boy and later took part in many engagements. He was the author of a number of war poems. He took an active part in the GAR.

Horsfall was commander of William Nelson Post GAR of Newport. The body will be interred in the organization's lot at Evergreen. He is survived by his widow Mrs. Lucretia Horsfall, one son, Carl Horsfall and three daughters, Mrs. George Bogart, Mrs. Charles Schweikert Newport and Mrs. Olive Guy of the state of Washington.

Members of Garfield Council No 34, Jr. O U A M of which Horsfall was a member, met at Third and York streets, Newport, Tuesday evening at 7 o'clock and held services at the late home.

SOURCES

http://cincinnati.com/blogs/ourhistory/2011/05/09/drummer-boy-among-civil-war-heroes/

http://en.wikipedia.org/wiki/William_H._Horsfall

http://www.thekentuckycivilwarbugle.com/2012-1Qpages/horsfall.html

http://www.rootsweb.ancestry.com/~kycampbe/horsfallobit.htm

http://www.rootsweb.ancestry.com/~kycampbe/horsfallcareer.htm

http://www.rootsweb.ancestry.com/~kycampbe/horsfallobit.htm

WILLIE DEAN SMITH

My friend, Ben Gish submitted this information regarding Willie Dean Smith. I was friends with Willie' brothers and grew up around them. They lived in the Sycamore loop where my Aunt Renae May and Uncle Arnold resided. I have paid my respects at his grave and often wondered what happened. The information below answers several questions about Willie Dean.

Letcher County Soldier Dies in N. Carolina

"Funeral services were held at Jeremiah Tuesday for T. Sgt. Willie Dean Smith, twenty-six year-old Letcher County soldier who died at Fort Bragg, North Carolina Thursday of injuries suffered in an automobile accident. Facial injuries were given as the cause of death.

"Born at Jeremiah, November 18, 1945, Sgt. Smith was the son of Madison Smith of Jeremiah. His mother precedes him in death by seven years. He had been in the army twelve years and was a veteran of World War II.

"Besides his father, he is survived by his wife, four brothers, Henry, LeRoy, Home and Jake, and three sisters, Imogene, Christine and Florence.

'Burial was in the Dixon Cemetery, Craft Funeral Home in charge. Military honors were accorded at the funeral by a detachment from Fort Knox, Kentucky." After reading and retyping the article, I realized the dates did not match.

SOURCES

The Mountain Eagle, October 23, 1952 edition

WILLIE SANDLIN
SERGEANT
MEDAL OF HONOR RECIPIENT
World War I
132nd Infantry
33rd Division
January 1, 1890-May 29, 1949

Stories abound of the heroism of a man by the name of Alvin York and rightly so. He was a true American hero, who remained loyal to his belief and his heritage. There was a Kentuckian who also followed his heart and remained loyal to the mountain life of eastern Kentucky. His name was Willie Sandlin. He was the only Kentuckian to win the Medal of Honor in World War I. The only person to receive more decorations from World War I was Alvin York.

Willie was a boy of the mountains. Willie loved roaming the hills and soon learned the ways of the mountains. He loved eastern Kentucky and like most young men of that era was powerful. It is said he possessed coal black eyes, black hair and of sturdy stock. His father's name was John Sandlin (March 17, 1867-February 3, 1947). He was married three times. His first wife and mother of Willie was Lucinda Abner Sandlin. She died when Willie was but a lad.

In researching Sergeant Sandlin, I found a conflict in the date he was born. Most stated he was born on January 1, 1890, while one source stated he was born on January 1, 1891. Again said source listed, argued that he was not born near Buckhorn, in Perry County but rather was most likely born in Owsley County because of his family ties. Another stated he was born in Jackson, Kentucky. From the research it appears that he most likely was born near Buckhorn and his tombstone is engraved with the date of January 1, 1890, as his birth date. No matter the date or place of birth, his legacy is what lives on in American history.

In 1914, at the age of twenty-four, Willie left home and joined the Army. He saw duty on the Mexican border and in 1917, he found himself on the front lines in France. Willie's skills soon yielded him sergeant stripes. On September 26, 1918, while at a place called Bois de Forges, Sgt. Sandlin single-handedly destroyed three German machine gun emplacements and killed twenty-four of the enemy. Sandlin's line was ordered to advance but was receiving blistering machine gun fire. He noted a narrow lane between the 'swing' of the machine gun nest. Securing several hand grenades, Sgt Sandlin charged. It was reported that he was responsible for destroying eight Germans in one nest. For such bravery under fire and thinking only of his men, Willie Sandlin received the highest medal a soldier can obtain: The Congressional Medal of Honor. Sergeant Sandlin served faithfully until the war's end.

Willie returned to his beloved eastern Kentucky, where he purchased a farm near Hyden (Owls Nest Creek). His wife, Belvia Roberts Sandlin, was active in the Frontier Nursing Service and soon Willie became involved. Willie remained true to his roots and enjoyed the simply things in life, like raising a garden, family and enjoying friends. The marriage between Willie and Bevia yielded four daughters and one son.

On May 29, 1949, after a long battle with lung disease due to poison gas from the Battle of the Argonne, he succumbed to death. He was fifty-nine years of age. He was buried near Hyden in the Hurricane Cemetery but in 1990, he was reinterred in the Zachary Taylor National Cemetery (Section E, grave 10A), located in Louisville, Kentucky. Bevia lived to be ninety-six years old. Willie Sandlin's Congressional Medal of Honor was donated to the Kentucky Military Museum in Frankfort, Kentucky.

General Pershing's Recommendation
U. S. Official Bulletin, Feb. 13, 1919 pg. 9

"Sergt. Willie Sandlin, Company A, 132nd Infantry (A.S. No. 278103.) For conspicuous gallantry and intrepidity above and beyond the call of duty with the enemy at Bois de Forges, France, September 26, 1918. Sergt. Sandlin showed conspicuous gallantry in action at Bois de Forges, France, on September 26, by advancing alone directly on a machine gun nest which was holding up the line with fire. He killed the crew with a grenade and enabled the line to advance. Later in the day Sergt. Sandlin attacked and put out of action two other machine gun nests, setting a splendid example of bravery and coolness to his men."

War Department, General Orders No. 16
January 22, 1919

"The President of the United States of America, in the name of Congress, takes pleasure in presenting the Medal of Honor to Sergeant Willie Sandlin (ASN: 2078103), United States Army, for extraordinary heroism on 26 September 1918, while serving with Company A, 132d Infantry, 33d Division, in action at Bois-de-Forges, France. Sergeant Sandlin showed conspicuous gallantry in action by advancing alone directly on a machinegun nest which was holding up the line with its fire. He killed the crew with a grenade and enabled the line to advance. Later in the day he attacked alone and put out of action two other machinegun nests, setting a splendid example of bravery and coolness to his men."

CITATION

"He showed conspicuous gallantry in action by advancing alone directly on a machinegun nest which was holding up the line with its fire. He killed the crew with a grenade and enabled the line to advance. Later in the day he attacked alone and put out of action 2 other machinegun nests, setting a splendid example of bravery and coolness to his men."

SOURCES

http://hazardkentucky.com/more/sandlin.htm
"SANDLIN, WILLIE" Army of Medal of Honor website. 2009-08-03

http://www.jkhg.org/willie_sandlin.htm
http://projects.militarytimes.com/citations-medals-awards/recipient.php?recipientid=3398

http://www.owsleykyhist.net/modules.php?name=News&file=article&sid=613

PICTURES OF THE PAST
World War I

World War II

80th Division with captured Nazi flag

318th Inf., 2nd Bat. France 1944

Photo # USMC 127-MN-57875 Toledo Cousins, Navajo Indian Code Talkers, July 1943

(Carl N. Gorman)

Captured German Tiger Tank (80th in Sept 1944)

Korean War

Vietnam War

(Dog Patch below Freedom Hill '327' Da Nang)

1971

U.S. 1st Cavalry Infantrymen huddle a group of frightened South Vietnamese children into a ditch to protect them from enemy sniper fire. The battle scene is 10 miles South of Da Nang.

Iraqi War

Afghanistan War

WAR DOG
SERGEANT STUBBY
102nd Infantry
26th Yankee Division
WORLD WAR I
1916/17-April 4, 1926

Sometimes we forget the service provided by loyal animals and the love they have towards their owners. In the case of Stubby, his war record is amazing. This is the saga of the most decorated dog of World War I and the first dog to be officially promoted to the rank of sergeant.

He was a stray on Yale Campus when discovered. He was considered to be a pit bull. Due to his short tail he was called Stubby. Robert Conroy, one of the soldiers in training hid Stubby aboard a troop ship when it was time to be deployed. Legend has it that Stubby was trained to salute and when discovered he saluted the commanding officer who was impressed with the dog's soldier abilities. Stubby became the official mascot of the 102nd Infantry even though animals were prohibited to be with the soldiers.

Stubby's service began in World War I on February 5, 1918. He was in the trenches in France. During the battle at Chemin des Dames (north of Soissons) he was constantly under fire for over a month. He was wounded in April 1918, from shrapnel in the foreleg while fighting in Scheiprey. He was gassed and from that experience he learned to warn others of such future attacks. He would run through the trenches barking and biting at the sleeping soldiers in an effort to warn them of the gas.

He was noted for finding wounded soldiers. He did this by recognizing English versus the German language. When Corporal Conroy was wounded, his loyal companion stayed by his side and had to be taken to the Red Cross Hospital with Conroy. He returned to duty only when Conroy did.

He also recognized incoming artillery and warned his unit whenever he heard them. He learned bugle calls and alerted the men whenever they did not hear it over the sounds of battle. Another one of his escapades was capturing a German spy. He served gallantly for eighteen months, fought in seventeen battles and returned home with Corporal Robert Conroy. Sergeant Stubby received over twelve medals for his service to his unit. One medal was presented by General Pershing. He was so well thought of that he was given membership in the American Legion and YMCA.

After the war he was a popular attraction and even had the privilege of meeting presidents (Wilson, Coolidge and Harding). He participated in parades and was a 'spokes dog' for the Red Cross. He was always by the side of his master and even attended college with Conroy. He became the team mascot for Georgetown Hoyas.

Stubby died on April 3, 1928. The New York Times offered a three column obituary which reads in part,

"On Feb. 5, 1918, he entered the front lines of the Chemin des Dames sector, north of Soissons, where he was under fire night and day for more than a month. The noise and strain that shattered the nerves of many of his comrades did not impair Stubby's spirits. Not because he was unconscious of danger. His angry howl while a battle raged and his mad canter from one part of the lines to another indicated realization. But he seemed to know that the greatest service he could render was comfort and cheerfulness."

SOURCES

http://en.wikipedia.org/wiki/Sergeant_Stubby

http://amhistory.si.edu/militaryhistory/collection/object.asp?ID=15

http://www.ct.gov/mil/cwp/view.asp?a=1351&q=257892

http://www.cesarsway.com/node/1905

http://www.historylearningsite.co.uk/sergeant_stubby.htm

THE SEARCH CONTINUES

Special Thanks to Ben Gish for his wonderful efforts in recognizing unsung Heroes in his column in the Mountain Eagle entitled,

THE WAY WE WERE

We have not even scratched the surface of our service men and women who are unsung heroes. May each of us who has a story put it to pen so that the rising generation will have a better understanding of the high cost of freedom. May we never forget...

Two brothers, including one from Letcher County, were reunited for the first time since infancy this week after meeting at Keesler Army Airfield in Mississippi. Pvt. Dan Napier, 20, of Leslie County, and Pvt. Charlie Napier of Letcher County were separated when Charlie was 10 months old. Dan grew up on his father's farm at Hyden. Charlie lived with his mother at Cromona.

Lt. Taylor W. Dixon, son of Mr. and Mrs. T.A. Dixon of Blackey, has been returned to limited duty after twice being wounded in action with enemy bayonets during the North African invasion.

SP4 Donnie Wayne Caudill, 21, was killed in Vietnam on March 13th.

Word has arrived in Letcher County for the first time since the fall of Corregidor Island that Capt. W.W. Buckhold is being held prisoner in the Philippines, making him the only known Kentucky physician in the hands of the Japanese. Captain and Mrs. Buckhold have a daughter, Mrs. I.D. Caudill.

Major Marcus W. Adams, of Whitesburg, was a recent visitor to the 79th Station Hospital in North Africa, which is under the command of his brother, Lt. Col. Edward Adams. The two brothers, sons of Mr. and Mrs. J. Wash Adams of Whitesburg, hadn't seen each other in more than two years, when Major Adams was attached to the Cavalry unit as a first lieutenant. The 79th Station Hospital was organized and trained by Edward Adams more than a year ago in New Orleans. Lt. Col. Adams and the organization left New Orleans for North Africa, in April 1943. The Adams family is well represented in the service with 10 members now serving in various branches of the Armed Forces."

WORLD WAR I

The following are Letcher County men who gave their lives for our freedom.

- Adams, John
- Adams, Ralph
- Anderson, Clell
- Brown, David N
- Brown, George
- Brown, Sylvan
- Bukhart, Bradley
- Cornett, Curtis
- Day, Douglas
- Dixon, Elijah B
- Dixon, William
- Ford, Charlie J
- Hall, Patrick H
- Hardy, Joe
- Hubbard, Henderson M
- Igo, Emery
- Johnson, Tom
- Maggard, Henry
- McKnight, George W
- Scruggs, Frank W
- Sexton, Joseph

(Courtesy of the Whitesburg Military Museum Monuments)

WORLD WAR II

The following Letcher County men gave their lives for our country.

- Adams, Claude
- Adams, Eugene A.
- Amburgey, Lawrence L.
- Anderson, Lloyd R.
- Anderson, Mander Jr.
- Arthur, Fred L Jr.
- Back, Edgar
- Back, Freelin
- Back, Thurman
- Bailey, Paul D.
- Bailey, Silas S.
- Baker, Ewing
- Baker, Herbert
- Baker, Ivory C.
- Baker, James R.
- Baker, Roy
- Banks, Dishman E.
- Barney, Pete Jr.
- Bates, Lee C
- Bates, Lenville
- Bates, Pony W.
- Bell, William F.
- Benge, Jack
- Bentley, Ballard J.
- Bentley, Clifford
- Bentley, Hayes
- Berry, Edward H.
- Blair, Charles O.
- Blair, Elihu
- Blanton, George
- Boggs, Harold P.
- Bostain, Luther D.

- Brashears, Estill
- Brewer, James O.
- Buckhold, Wilbert W.
- Burns, Daniel B.
- Calton, Melvin
- Cashman, Junious M.
- Caudill, Cecil
- Caudill, Clyde
- Caudill, Darwin
- Caudill, William Jr.
- Centers, Chris
- Chandler, Paul B.
- Childers, Mack T.
- Collins, Glenn
- Combs, Billy F.
- Combs, Bradley
- Combs, Gerny
- Combs, William F.
- Cook, Arnold
- Cook, Hansford
- Cornett, Chester Jr.
- Cornett, Eldred L.
- Cornett, Haywood
- Coyer, Wilfred D.
- Craft, Bill
- Crase, Hubert
- Davidson, Larry
- Davis, Jack
- DePriest, William R.
- Dills, Ernest Jr.
- Dingus, Teddy M.
- Dixon, James E
- Dixon, Kirby
- Duncan, William M.
- Eldridge, Delza
- Ellish, Lewis
- Fields, Arlie
- Fields, Dixon

- Fletcher, Jesse L.
- Flint, Chester
- Fouts, Murray
- Frazier, James M.
- Fugate, Lewis
- Gilliam, Jesse J.
- Green, James H.
- Griffith, Hargis R.
- Grigsby, Cecil K.
- Halcomb, Gatthel
- Hall, Hershel W.
- Hall, Ralph
- Hall, Rush
- Hall, Wade
- Hammonds, William C.
- Hampton, Jerry P.
- Harris, Winzer
- Hart, Hugh J.
- Hatton, David Sr.
- Hendrix, Arthur R.
- Hoffman, Gatewood
- Holbrook, Chester F.
- Holbrook, Dolphia
- Holbrook, Wesley
- Holland, John R.
- Hopkins, Raymond V.
- Howard, Earnest
- Howington, Orville J.
- Hudgins, Hershel
- Hughes, Worley C.
- Hyatt, Willard D.
- Ison, Bill
- Ison, Earl
- Ison, James
- Ison, Roland
- Jenkins, Harold S.
- Jones, Gilbert O.
- Jones, Walter H.

- King, Sterling
- Kissinger, Clayton
- Lee, Fritz Jr.
- Lewis, John S.
- Logan, Fulton
- Logsdon, David E.
- Looney, Clyde
- Lucas, Eli
- Lucas, Luther J.
- McCarty, Cecil
- McRoberts, Billy
- McRoberts, Ruben S.
- Marshall, R.B.
- Martin, James V.
- Monhollen, Willie D.
- Morris, Doyle
- Mullins, Earnest
- Mullins, Gilmer
- Mullins, Glen
- Mullins, Henry
- Mullins, Lester B.
- Newsome, Marvin
- Nicholson, Harold T.
- Norton, Edward
- Pece, James T.
- Pennington, Hershel
- Permestta, Marvin
- Pigman, Sidney
- Polly, Eugene
- Polly, Willard
- Potter, A.C.
- Potter, Edward
- Profitt, Fernoy
- Ramey, Benjamin F.
- Reed, Emmett J.
- Reynolds, Virgil
- Roberts, Virgil E.
- Rudd, Carl

- Salyer, Braton
- Salyer, William B.
- Sanders, James R.
- Sanders, William F.
- Settles, Orville E
- Sexton, Ora J. Jr.
- Sexton, Vernon
- Smith, Edgar
- Smith, George D.
- Stamper, James W.
- Stamper, Paul E.
- Stidham, Robert L.
- Strange, Ellis E.
- Sturgill, William K.
- Thompson, John W Jr.
- Thornton, Harold B.
- Tolson, Clyde
- Tubbs, Roy W.
- Vance, Lindsay
- Vinson, Charles W.
- Wassum Joseph C.
- Watts, Lawton
- Watts, Vinson
- Webb, Bruce
- Whitaker, Gale
- Whitaker, James R.
- Whitaker, Ottis
- Wilder, Glenn E.
- Wilder, Henry O.
- Wolfe, Malcolm B.
- Wright, Comey
- Wright, James H.
- Young, Guy L Jr.

SOURCES

http://genealogytrails.com/ken/letcher/wwii_casualties.html

http://www.accessgenealogy.com/worldwar/kentucky/index.htm

(Courtesy of the Whitesburg Military Museum Monuments)

http://media.nara.gov/media/images/28/30/28-2948a.gif

KOREAN WAR

The following forty-five Letcher County men gave their lives so we would be free.

- Adams, Troulius
- Anderson, A.C.
- Bentley, Elwood
- Blevins, Billy J
- Breeding, Herman Jr.
- Brown, Ray
- Caudill, Charles L
- Cline, George H
- Collins, James E
- Combs, Bobby V
- Cornett, Crowden
- Craft, Richard Jr.
- Elswick, Erwin C
- Griffie, Leslie
- Griffith, James A
- Hampton, Carmel
- Huges, Jack W
- Isaac, Willie D
- Ison, Earl
- King, Denver
- McFall, Billie E
- Meeks, Charles E
- Menken, Donald L
- Miles, David
- Moncrief, Douglas
- Mullins, Elmer
- Mullins, James C
- Pridemore, Don K
- Putman, Donald C
- Riley, George
- Roark, William J
- Roberts, James W
- Sanders, Thomas

- Saulsberry, Robert
- Scott, Thomas
- Smallwood, Herbert H
- Smith, Willie D
- Tackett, Donald F
- Terry, Simon
- Trent, Ira V
- Tyree, James A
- Watts, Edward
- Webb, James
- White, James H

(Courtesy of the Whitesburg Military Museum Monuments)

VIETNAM WAR

The following twenty-two Letcher County men gave their lives for our country.

- Anderson, Douglas R
- Adams, Emmit C
- Ashbrook, Delmar V
- Caudill, Roger D
- Charles, Earl E
- Collins, Lee
- Culp, Everitt T
- Duty, Anthony
- Fields, George B
- Gibson, Stevie R
- Hall, Brownie
- Hampton, John E
- Holbrook, Jerry R
- Maggard, Larry D
- Pace, Gary
- Sexton, Andrew B
- Spangler, James N
- Sumpter, Bobby R
- Sumpter, Joseph B
- Tackett, Ruben N
- Tolliver, Jimmy E
- Watts, Aster

(Courtesy of the Whitesburg Military Museum Monuments)

LETCHER COUNTY VETS ON VIETNAM MEMORIAL WALL

Army PFC Emmitt Colon Adams; Isom

Army PFC Roger Dale Caudill; Whitesburg

Army SP4 Anthony Duty; Neon

Army SSGT Bobby George Fields; Blackey

Army SSGT Brownie Hall; Deane

Army PFC John Edison Hampton; Whitesburg

Army SGT Larry Dwight Maggard; Isom

Army SP4 Ruben Noah Tackett; McRoberts

Air Force 1LT James Nelson Spangler; Mayking

Marine PFC Joseph Boyd Sumpter; McRoberts

Marine SSGT Jimmy Ellison Tolliver, Cromona

IRAQ and AFGHANISTAN

The following men gave their lives for our American way of life.

- Chadwick Gilliam
- James T. Hoffman

SAYINGS

"Only the dead have seen the end of war."
Plato

"The willingness with which our young people are likely to serve in any war, no matter how justified, shall be directly proportional as to how they perceive the veterans of earlier wars were treated and appreciated by their nation."
George Washington

"I must study politics and war that my sons may have liberty to study mathematics and philosophy."
John Adams

"I love peace, and am anxious that we should give the world still another useful lesson, by showing to them other modes of punishing injuries than by war, which is as much a punishment to the punisher as to the sufferer."
Thomas Jefferson

"The patriot volunteer, fighting for country and his rights, makes the most reliable soldier on earth."
Stonewall Jackson

"It is well that war is so terrible, lest we should grow too fond of it.'
Robert E. Lee

"Freedom makes a huge requirement of every human being. With freedom comes responsibility. For the person who is unwilling to grow up, the person who does not want to carry is own weight, this is a frightening prospect."
Eleanor Roosevelt

"The soldier above all others prays for peace, for it is the soldier who must suffer and bear the deepest wounds and scars of war."
Douglas MacArthur

"I hate war as only a soldier who has lived it can, only as one who has seen its brutality, its futility, its stupidity."
Dwight D. Eisenhower

"You've never lived until you've almost died. For those who fought for it, life has a flavor the protected will never know."
Unknown Soldier from Viet Nam (1968)

"Freedom is never more than one generation away from extinction. We didn't pass it to our children in the bloodstream. It must be fought for, protected, and handed on for them to do the same."
Ronald Reagan

"Whether we bring our enemies to justice or bring justice to our enemies, justice will be done."
President George W. Bush
September 20, 2001

IT IS THE VETERAN

It is God who gives us the Veteran.

It is the Veteran, not the preacher, who has given us freedom of religion.

It is the Veteran, not the reporter, who has given us freedom of the press.

It is the Veteran, not the poet, who has given us freedom of speech.

It is the Veteran, not the campus organizer, who has given us freedom to assemble.

It is the Veteran, not the lawyer, who has given us the right to a fair trial.

It is the Veteran, not the politician, who has given us the right to vote.

It is the Veteran, who salutes the Flag,

It is the Veteran, who serves under the Flag,
To be buried by the flag,
So the protester can burn the flag.
(Author Unknown)

NOTE: This is only the beginning. They are still thousands upon thousands out there waiting. They wish to have their stories told but for many the grave has silenced their voice. We, the current generation, have upon our shoulders the honor of remembering and documenting their deeds. Let us rise to the occasion and continue Freedom's voice through these unsung heroes…DPC

CPSIA information can be obtained at www.ICGtesting.com
Printed in the USA
LVOW04s2119100215

426473LV00030B/1218/P